More Praise for *Fearless Feeding*

"Fear not! This rational, practical, and joyful book gives parents the knowledge and tools to feed their families confidently and fearlessly."
—Michelle May, MD, author, *Eat What You Love, Love What You Eat*

"So many experts, books, magazines, and busybodies seem determined to convince parents that they can't do anything right. Here's a book that silences the din of 'You're doing it wrong!' and makes raising healthy eaters easy."
—Lenore Skenazy, author, *Free-Range Kids*

"In this book on infant and child nutrition, two well-trained, experienced nutritionists bring an evidence-based approach to the WHAT, HOW, and WHY of feeding to make infant and child nutrition an enjoyable pastime for parents who are concerned about their child's diet and their overall health. *Fearless Feeding* is an excellent guide for parents concerned about an appropriate approach to feeding their children."
—Allan Walker, MD, director, Division of Nutrition, Harvard Medical School

"At last! A book that offers parents a clear road map to what should be a natural and instinctive endeavor: feeding one's child. It will be a pleasure to recommend this book as a solid resource for helping children build a healthy, long-standing, and perhaps lifesaving relationship with food."
—Nancy Beveridge, MD, pediatrician, Nashville, Tennessee

"You no longer can use the excuse 'My child didn't come with an owner's manual' when it comes to finicky eaters. Castle and Jacobsen have created the quintessential one just for you and your child."
—David Grotto, RD, LDN, author, *The Best Things You Can Eat: For Everything from Aches to Zzzz, the Definitive Guide to the Nutrition-Packed Foods that Energize, Heal, and Help You Look Great*

"This sanity-saving resource will help parents gain confidence in the kitchen and at the dinner table and even help them face the biggest challenges like coping with picky eaters, weight problems, and food allergies. Every parent should have a copy of this book in their kitchen!"
—Aviva Goldfarb, cookbook author and founder of the family-dinner planning service, The Six O'Clock Scramble

"In today's frenzied food world, families want wise counsel—not just on WHAT to feed their children, but HOW to feed them as well. *Fearless Feeding* accomplishes both with reassuring, practical, easy-to-digest advice for children of all ages."
—Dayle Hayes, MS, RD, president, Nutrition for the Future

"*Fearless Feeding* takes a relaxed and reassuring approach to the often difficult task of nourishing children. As the mother of three, I appreciate how the authors blend their professional know-how and parental wisdom to provide parents with a valuable resource for guilt-free feeding."
—Elizabeth M. Ward, MS, RD, author, *MyPlate for Moms, How to Feed Yourself & Your Family Better*

"Jill Castle and Maryann Jacobsen leave no stone unturned as they expertly guide families toward better eating. This dynamic duo of family nutrition has written the go-to book for parents eager to understand the science behind good nutrition. For parents of toddlers, teens, and all ages between, mealtimes just got a whole lot easier!"
—Liz Weiss, MS, RD, coauthor, *No Whine with Dinner*, and cofounder, MealMakeoverMoms.com

"*Fearless Feeding* is not only a must-read for parents but also for pediatric health providers. The WHAT, WHY, and HOW approach allows providers to assess each area and helps parents address nutrition concerns and problems. Most books on feeding do not address adolescents; however, *Fearless Feeding* does an excellent job in providing ways to improve adolescent eating habits."
—Bonnie A. Spear, PhD, RD, professor, pediatrics, University of Alabama at Birmingham

Fearless Feeding

How to Raise Healthy Eaters from High Chair to High School

Jill Castle • Maryann Jacobsen

Be fearless!

Jill Castle

JB JOSSEY-BASS™
A Wiley Brand

Published by Jossey-Bass
A Wiley Brand
One Montgomery Street, Suite 1200, San Francisco, CA 94104-4594—www.josseybass.com

Jossey-Bass books and products are available through most bookstores. To contact Jossey-Bass directly call our Customer Care Department within the U.S. at 800-956-7739, outside the U.S. at 317-572-3986, or fax 317-572-4002.

Wiley publishes in a variety of print and electronic formats and by print-on-demand. Some material included with standard print versions of this book may not be included in e-books or in print-on-demand. If this book refers to media such as a CD or DVD that is not included in the version you purchased, you may download this material at http://booksupport.wiley.com. For more information about Wiley products, visit www.wiley.com.

Library of Congress Cataloging-in-Publication Data has been applied for and is on file with the Library of Congress.
ISBN 978-1-118-30859-2 (paper); ISBN 978-1-118-41995-3 (ebk.); ISBN 978-1-118-42155-0 (ebk.);
ISBN 978-1-118-60299-7 (ebk.)

Printed in the United States of America
FIRST EDITION
PB Printing   10 9 8 7 6 5 4 3 2

CONTENTS

FOREWORD

All parents know the anxiety of coming home with their first baby and panicking as the baby loses half a pound in the first day. Our anxiety about feeding our children starts the day they're born, and leads us to feel like superstars if we can get them to eat and get their weight up. I don't think this early feeling of "the more food, the better" ever quite leaves us until it's too late.

Fearless Feeding: How to Raise Healthy Eaters from High Chair to High School is an invaluable book for the parent who has a breastfeeding newborn or the parent who has a finicky teenager. Besides nailing the core nutrition concepts, it shows how we can nudge all children to become healthier eaters. Using a triad approach (WHAT to feed, HOW to do it, and WHY kids behave the way they do) called the Fearless Feeding Strategy, Jill Castle and Maryann Jacobsen remind us it's never too late to turn a problem eater into a model eater.

At one time or another, most parents believe there's little to nothing they can do to influence what their kids eat. That's not true. In my book *Mindless Eating*, I showed that the parent who purchases and prepares most of the food in the household—the nutritional gatekeeper—influences about 72 percent of all of the food the family eats. The problem is that this influence, either knowingly or unknowingly, is either for the better or for the worse. It's for the better if the nutritional gatekeeper has a fruit bowl on the counter, but for the worse if there's a cookie dish.

Fearless Feeding shows how we can make the most of that 72 percent of what we can influence. Some of that has to do with adjusting the foods we feed our

children, but much of it has to do with how we feed them. A core value of
Fearless Feeding is using positive feeding strategies to raise children who *want* to
eat healthy. Not only do the authors provide anticipatory guidance for each stage
of childhood but also they take it to the next level—offering practical examples,
stories, and vignettes to make solutions come alive.

As a father of three high-energy daughters under the age of seven, I
particularly like the tone in which the authors offer their advice—the book is
evidence based but practical. It deals with the reality of parenting and not the
theory of parenting—the reality of coming home listless and a tad cranky and
wondering whether you should just order pizza or whether there's another, better
option that isn't as hard as you think. It delivers great insights that are rooted in
evidence, but it does so using "parent speak," making the information come alive
in a way that we can use tonight—instead of ordering pizza.

Brian Wansink, PhD
Author of *Mindless Eating* and *Slim by Design*
Director of the Cornell Food and Brand Lab

ACKNOWLEDGMENTS

This book would not be possible without the following extraordinary professionals and dedicated parents. Thanks to Karen McGrail, Jamie Stang, Sharon Collier, Aida Miles, Angela Lemond, Leah McGrath, Eileen Myers, and Adrienne Forman for reviewing chapters. More thanks to Aviva Goldfarb, Liz Weiss, Janice Bissex, Sally Kuzemchak, and Estela Schnelle for donating tasty and nutritious recipes. We learned so much from Connie Evers, Dayle Hayes, Diane Neumark-Sztainer, Beth Hirsch, Michelle May, Michelle Segar, Nancy Mohrbacher, Ian Paul, Kristen Hurley, Joyce Nettleton, Kay Toomey, Linda Piette, Melanie Potock, Scott Sicherer, Lucky Cooke, Ekhard Ziegler, Elizabeth Ward, and Lisa Raum, who provided expert advice. We are also grateful to Lisa Gross for her attention to detail in the appendices, and to Ellyn Satter for paving the way. Last but not least, a big thank you to all the parents who contributed stories and quotes—you continue to be our inspiration!

Fearless
Feeding

Introduction

If you picked up this book, it's very likely that you are up to your eyeballs in one of the most challenging aspects of parenthood: feeding kids. Feeding—and the planning and preparation and worrying that go along with it—will consume more of your time than any other family activity. In fact, it is estimated that you will feed your child a total of twenty-eight thousand times by the time he is ready for college!

But don't worry. You can feed your child without fear or guilt. As registered dietitians who work closely with families, we believe all parents want to raise healthy children, even when their actions seem to tell a different tale. Take Lauren, mom of eight-year-old Jeff. When Lauren was pregnant, she swore her child would never eat any of the typical kid foods other children eat. They got off to a great start, but when Jeff turned picky (as so many kids do) at the age of two, things gradually went downhill. The food battles started, and Jeff's will was stronger than his mom's fortitude. Somewhere along the line Lauren's goal of feeding her child healthy food was replaced with the goal of getting him to eat *anything*. Now he only eats foods like macaroni and cheese, chicken nuggets, and waffles. And Lauren lives with intense guilt every time she feeds her son.

What Lauren doesn't know is this: picky eating is very normal during toddlerhood, when growth slows and kids strive for independence. She needs to be prepared, have meals and structure in place, provide accepted foods along with new foods, and above all keep her poker face on—no battles necessary.

There are hundreds (thousands? millions? probably!) of stories like Lauren's in which feeding has gone off track. Our experience tells us that parents aren't getting the support and preparation they need to be great feeders and raise healthy children. Parents' intentions are often in the right place, but they don't always get the right information at the right time. And although there is an overemphasis on "getting kids to eat healthy," the essential tools, strategies, and knowledge parents need to make it happen are missing. That's why we came together to write *Fearless Feeding*.

What makes us qualified to write such a book? A book that will change the current fear-based model of feeding to one filled with joy and confidence? Well, in addition to being registered dietitians, we are also moms who understand the challenges of feeding kids in the twenty-first century. Everything we've done up to this point, both personally and professionally, has prepared us to write this book. You could say it has been thirty-five years in the making. Allow us to introduce ourselves.

Meet Jill Castle

When I was growing up, my mother shopped every week, set the menu and the budget, and prepared our meals like clockwork. She never had to tell us when it was time to be home—we knew that dinner was served promptly at 6:00 p.m. Mealtime was secure and predictable, and almost always delicious and nourishing, and we were regularly introduced to new menu items, as my mother was an adventurous (and good!) cook. Looking back, I am forever thankful to my parents for not making nutrition an issue, a prominent subject, or a struggle in our home.

Fast-forward thirty years. After studying nutrition in my college days at Indiana University and even practicing in the specialized area of pediatric nutrition, here I was, faced with my own first child. And I thought I was a pro! I entered motherhood confident, secure in my extensive pediatric nutrition knowledge, and ready to raise a healthy eater. Breastfeeding was mildly difficult in the beginning, and ultimately rewarding, but the transition to solid food was challenging. I allowed my daughter to take the lead in eating, responding appropriately. But when we went for our twelve-month checkup, she wasn't gaining the expected weight that the pediatrician had hoped for. He said, "Make sure she finishes her meals." That advice shook my fundamental beliefs about feeding children, so I silently resisted. I continued to follow her cues and not make an issue out of how much she ate. She continued to gain weight slowly and remained proportionate for her length (height), but at our eighteen-month checkup, she was diagnosed with anemia. I felt upset, knowing that I had failed at the job in which I considered myself an expert. I had made two mistakes: I was too focused on the HOW of feeding my daughter, allowing her to take the lead with types of food and when to eat, and I had failed to fill in the nutritional gaps with appropriate food items (the WHAT). As a result, she slowly replaced her solid foods with milk. I learned an important lesson—success with feeding comes from an equal *and* balanced focus on the WHAT, HOW, and WHY of feeding. And my feeding tenets have forever been changed.

I semiretired from working when my oldest daughter turned two and our family continued to grow. I became a mother of four, all under the age of five! I got caught up in what most stay-at-home mothers spend a majority of their time doing—feeding the kids. When I counted the amount of time I spent preparing meals, feeding, and cleaning up—can you believe it was six to seven hours a day?!—it was nearly a full-time job.

Despite my early mistakes, my knowledge of pediatric nutrition was an immense resource for me. I credit my four healthy children to the fact that I had a rich knowledge of nutrition from the start. I not only knew WHAT to feed them but also had a deeper understanding of HOW to do it and WHY they behaved like they did.

Through those years and my friendships with other mothers, I learned that feeding is one of parents' most important concerns. I was answering questions daily (once I let people know I was a pediatric nutritionist). So when my youngest child entered kindergarten, I went back to work with the mind-set of helping other families with their nutrition problems. My long-term goal then, and now, is to help American families see that feeding is one of the most important jobs of parenthood, and create a resource that makes it simple, practical, and successful.

Meet Maryann Jacobsen

One of the best decisions I ever made was to join a gym after high school. This led to a love of high-impact aerobics, healthier eating, and a major in nutrition. Even though this change in diet changed my life for the better, I still struggled with eating sweets in moderation and maintaining my weight. During my ten-month dietetic internship in New Orleans, where the beignets flowed like water, I discovered that I could eat indulgent foods without going hog wild or sacrificing healthy eating. I started listening to my body and stopped eating when I was comfortably full. This more balanced, intuitive approach led to a stable weight for the next ten years (until I became pregnant), and it liberated me from my food struggle.

In my early years as a dietitian, I was intrigued by how this simple change in mind-set could revamp my entire relationship with food. I kept coming back to one question: *How did I develop an unhealthy relationship with food in the first place?* I realized that at least part of it had to do with HOW I was fed as a child. I came from a big family with four other siblings, and we fought over food. When sweets were in the house, I had to act fast or they would be gone. I carried this "need to eat as many sweets as possible" thinking into adulthood. I also realized that the dieting culture—one that taught me to distrust myself with eating—influenced me as well. Making these connections empowered me because I finally had the WHY behind my previous eating habits.

As the years went by, I researched the effect of feeding styles and food attitudes on eating habits and found there was indeed a link. This motivated me to ask my clients how they were fed as kids. Many with weight problems said they were forced to clean their plate. Others remembered how palatable food was used to reward good behavior or withheld as a form of punishment. And I'll never forget the man who was so picky and thin as a child that his parents shuttled him back and forth to doctors, gave him a slew of vitamins, and begged him to eat. He finally got the message, gained too much weight as an adult, and needed weight loss surgery.

After my first child was born in 2006, I focused on both the WHAT and the HOW of feeding so my daughter could be healthy *and* develop a healthy relationship with food. I was disappointed to find the most popular feeding book hadn't been updated in eight years! I gathered information on starting solids by evaluating research studies, using books and various Internet searches. I kept thinking: *Why isn't there one updated resource for feeding kids?* When my daughter transitioned to finger foods I had a moment of panic. She was only eleven months old, and I couldn't believe I'd be doing this for *seventeen more years*. Why didn't anyone tell me how much time and effort feeding would take? I never really learned how to cook either—and failed at my goal of finding a husband who knew his way around the kitchen. This whole feeding gig was a lot harder than I ever imagined.

Around the birth of my second child I created my blog (*Raise Healthy Eaters*) to share what I had learned about feeding children. Many parents thanked me for making nutrition less confusing. Other parents realized they didn't want to repeat the same, undesirable feeding cycle that came from their own upbringing. But most important, I got a front-seat view of the real struggles parents face, which weren't all that different from my own. I also had the chance to interview leading child nutrition experts, including Jill Castle. In the back of my mind, I was hoping eventually to write a feeding book with one of these experts. When I met Jill, the seed for a book was planted. And you know what? It grew pretty darn fast.

How Fear Brought Us Together

We met when Maryann interviewed Jill for a nutrition series on her blog. We joked about writing "the bible" for child nutrition together, and said we should continue talking. And that's exactly what we did.

One thing was certain: feeding was a passion for both of us. As we started creating a vision for a nutrition and feeding book, we discussed the current environment and myriad obstacles parents face. Parents today, we concluded, have it much harder than those of previous generations. Things are so radically different: there is less time and support for making balanced meals, more confusion about nutrition, and endless choices concerning what could go into those meals.

You might be thinking, *There's a supermarket on every corner, Whole Foods and other natural food stores in many areas, and grocery delivery services like Fresh*

Direct or Peapod in most towns. Buying healthy food is easy. But is it really? Here's what modern parents are up against every day—obstacles that their own parents or grandparents never even considered:

- **Information saturation.** The Internet has forever changed the way people receive information on food and nutrition. There are millions of blogs, news stories, and websites offering nutrition news and advice. Some of it is credible, but a lot of it is not. Although some of the right nutrition information can be useful, too much of it can confuse, contradict, overwhelm, and lead to unintended feeding mistakes.

- **Endless choices.** Feeding is no longer about shopping at one store and getting a balanced meal on the table. Parents today have to choose whether or not to buy organic, whether or not to make baby food, and where to shop from among a plethora of options. Since 1994, food labels and health claims on products have exploded, and so has the list of undesirable ingredients, such as high-fructose corn syrup and various preservatives and food dyes. Although choice is a good thing, too much can overwhelm, leaving parents unmotivated.

- **Overwhelming pressure.** Almost every nutrition-related disease in children is on the rise: obesity, eating disorders, food allergies, behavioral conditions, heart disease, and diabetes. At the same time that nutrition-poor food is highly available, the desire to be thin is highly prevalent. Today's parents have much more pressure to get feeding right, bringing even more complexities and worries to the table.

- **Inadequate cooking and feeding skills.** Unlike in years past when women learned how to cook for their family, today many adults jump into parenthood unprepared for feeding a family. Even if grandma is living nearby, her recipes may not work for modern-day lifestyles. Not to mention that few parents have positive role models, as family meals went out of style when most of us were children. Bottom line: there's little support and virtually no real-life training for feeding a family.

- **A knowledge deficit.** We are out of balance when it comes to feeding knowledge. There is endless information about WHAT to feed kids, but very little information about WHY kids eat the way they do and HOW to feed them. Understanding how childhood development relates to food, nutrition, and feeding, and how each feeding stage builds on the next, is vital to getting feeding right. Just as important is understanding how parents' attitudes and actions around meals have a profound effect on kids.

- **A food-centric environment.** Food is everywhere—at playgroups, at sporting events, and even in retail stores. There are more opportunities to eat mindlessly than ever before, making it difficult for parents to do their job of feeding. There are also more packaged and processed options that children easily accept—a great temptation for parents.
- **Insufficient time.** Parents have less time than ever before. The number of married mothers who work more than quadrupled from 1948 to the mid-1990s, leaving less time to prepare and plan meals.[1] Even mothers or fathers who stay at home may need more time and more support, making meal planning and preparation challenging.

The biggest hindrance, we believe, is what these barriers have created: *fear.* Parents have so much on their plate when it comes to feeding that fear, stress, and worry have taken over the kitchen table. Instead of being sources of pleasure, feeding (and, by default, eating) have become chores that are riddled with feelings of self-doubt and guilt.

This was our big "aha" moment. All of this fear surrounding feeding was making matters worse—and we knew it had to stop. Let's face it—good decisions can't be made in the face of too much fear. So we wrote this book to take your fear away, one chapter at a time.

Fearless Feeding as the Solution

So how exactly do you take the fear out of feeding? First, the solution must address each of the modern-day obstacles that contribute to the problem. Too much information focuses on the WHAT of feeding—and promises that getting the right food into kids is all that matters. But we know that even parents who have all their nutrition ducks in a row are still fearful and struggling.

Take Jody, mom of five-year-old Ryan. She and her husband were healthy eaters and started their son on healthy fare from day one (breastfeeding and homemade baby food). As Ryan got older, they noticed he went crazy around sweets at parties and outings. They didn't provide him with any sugar-filled foods at home. They got even stricter with Ryan after they saw how obsessed he got—and the problem got worse. They went as far as calling their friends and family ahead of time to make sure there was nothing sweet that Ryan could binge on.

What parents like Jody need to become Fearless Feeders are the missing pieces to the feeding puzzle, including the important HOW and WHY. Seldom will you hear about these aspects of feeding—not from your mother, your doctor, or your neighbor. This is what makes our book so useful and practical. It outlines a comprehensive approach to feeding, including the three Fearless Feeding Fundamentals: WHAT, HOW, and WHY. Each is equally important, and when used synergistically they are a powerful force in feeding.

Jody didn't understand that all children are drawn to energy-dense foods— this is normal because of their rapid growth and these foods' natural taste appeal. This is an example of the WHY—understanding your child's development and why your child eats the way he does. Jody also needed coaching on how to teach her son to eat sweets in moderation by including them periodically and having a neutral attitude about whether he eats them or not. This is the HOW of feeding, which is vital in shaping your child's relationship with food.

With a closer look, we found that Jody didn't quite have the WHAT of feeding down either—although she thought she did. She was feeding her son what was healthy for adults, not children, focusing almost solely on fruits and vegetables. Her son was getting too little dietary fat, thus fueling his desire for energy-dense foods. Jody just didn't realize how important fat still was after the age of two, and that her son's obsession was in part his body's way of filling in what it needed.

And last but not least, Jody didn't understand the real motivation behind keeping sweets away from her child. The truth? She didn't trust herself around those foods and had battled her own weight since she was a child. She remembered how her mom let her eat whenever and whatever she wanted. Jody was a victim of the parent trap (see Chapter Six), and was practicing *reactive feeding*, doing the complete opposite of what her parents did.

Once Jody was able to see the big picture of why she fed the way she did, and learned the Fearless Feeding Strategy, she became much more confident with feeding. She no longer worried about every decision she made. And guess what? Her son stopped obsessing about sweets, and Jody finally came to peace with food herself. Her whole family enjoyed eating and mealtime—guilt-free!

This modern approach to feeding enables you to raise not just healthy eaters but also fearless ones. What is a Fearless Eater? Someone who consumes balanced meals, eats the right amount of food for her body type, enjoys healthy foods, and doesn't feel guilty for eating Fun Foods in moderation. Most important, Fearless Eaters grow into adults who make feeding themselves and their family a priority. If, as a parent, you aren't already a Fearless Eater, we believe learning how to feed your child can transform your own eating for good (for examples of fearless and fearful feeding, see Table I.1).

Table I.1 Fearful and Fearless Feeding		
Stage	**Fearful Feeding**	**Fearless Feeding**
Infancy	Parents constantly question each feeding step—when to upgrade texture, try the sippy cup, or introduce finger foods—and wonder how much to feed their child. As a result, the child is under- or overfed. Both parent and child are anxious at mealtime.	Parents understand when and how to introduce certain foods, check for allergies, and up the food texture. They are able to read feeding cues of hunger and fullness, and are in sync with their child. Confidence with feeding allows parents to focus on developing the important bond between parent and child.
Toddlerhood	Parents live in constant fear that their child is not getting enough to eat. They often cater to their child, hiding veggies in food or coercing the child to eat more. Mealtimes are tense, or in some cases outright battles.	Parents understand that growth slows and kids' eating is erratic. They feed the child a variety of food five to six times a day, letting her eat until full. They do not make a big deal about what the child eats or label her as "picky." Mealtimes are pleasant for both parent and child.

Table I.1 *(continued)*		
Stage	**Fearful Feeding**	**Fearless Feeding**
School age	Parents are afraid of the types and amounts of food their child is eating. They overcontrol food and exposure to outside influences, such as parties, school lunch, and media. They label food as "good" or "bad," and they feel conflicted and guilty about their child's increasing independence with food and eating. They may give up leadership when it comes to meals and food.	Parents offer well-balanced meals regularly and value the family meal table. They expect independence around food choices and allow experimentation. They are relaxed around outside influences, making sure to strike a healthy balance in the home. Parents include their child in meal planning and food preparation, encouraging open dialogue about food.
Teenage years	Parents feel a lack of connection around the meal table. There are minimal opportunities to eat with their teen. They are afraid to talk about nutrition with her, and they allow her to be in charge of most meals and eating. They are out of touch with their teen's eating practices, and feel guilty that she doesn't eat healthy food.	Parents value the family meal table and encourage gathered meals several times per week. They offer well-balanced meals that are pleasing to the family. They have open communication about food and nutrition with their teen, encouraging their teen to take responsibility for her health. They offer the teen opportunities to plan, shop for, and cook meals for the family.
Adulthood	The adult does not always make feeding herself a priority, so skipping meals and eating out are common. The adult sees food as good or bad, and her motivation to eat nutritious foods is low unless she is following a new diet or trying to lose weight. She often undereats or overeats, with poor overall food regulation. Eating and food preparation are a struggle, especially at times of stress or change. The adult experiences feelings of guilt and regret about what is eaten or should have been eaten.	The adult makes feeding herself (and her family, if applicable) a priority, and she does it in a positive manner. She plans regular meals and snacks that are satisfying while applying basic nutrition concepts. She is able to regulate intake well, enjoys meals, and maintains weight. She may be challenged at times of stress, but she has confidence in her ability to eat well under a variety of circumstances. She rarely associates guilt with eating.

Most of the feeding resources on the market focus on babies and toddlers, leaving parents of older kids out in the cold. As kids get older, feeding is just as important, but the dynamic changes. For example, instead of teaching kids about food, you have to educate them about nutrition. Instead of spending all the time in the kitchen yourself, you need to invite your child in to learn about meal preparation. And as your child's body changes and grows, you need to help her develop a positive body image. Family meals become even more important—and difficult to plan—as kids get older. Above all, this book helps you see that the different feeding stages are connected.

Fearless Feeding is not based on our opinions and biases. Rather, it is based on the latest science and research. We do the work of gathering, reading, and analyzing the latest studies for you, so all you have to do is decide what is right for your family. This is much better than making decisions based on a trend, someone's opinion, or a Google search that brings you to a questionable website. And most of the challenges we sprinkle throughout this book are not ones we made up, but are drawn from stories of real parents like you.

Fearless Feeding is your comprehensive and credible road map to conquering all of the modern-day nutrition and feeding obstacles. This book is filled with positive strategies for raising healthy kids. Make these components part of how you feed your child, and you will have a much easier time navigating nutrition. And, best of all, your fear, worry, and guilt will melt away.

How to Use This Book

You'll want to start by digging into Chapter One, The Fearless Feeding Strategy, which lays the foundation for the Fearless Feeding Fundamentals. This is the modern feeding approach used for each of the age-based chapters: exploring the WHAT, HOW, and WHY. Next, you'll want to head over to the chapter of the book that correlates to your child's age and stage: Chapter Two on infants and young toddlers, Chapter Three on toddlers and preschoolers, Chapter Four on school-age children, or Chapter Five on teenagers.

To make the book easy for you to navigate, each stage of development has the same corresponding sections, including Nutrition in Practice; Feeding with Confidence; Real Life Challenges; and Real, Easy Recipes. Nutrition in Practice provides guidance about WHAT foods to offer your child in a very simple, straightforward way. You'll find the WHY behind nutritional needs and growth, the age-specific Fearless Food Guide (in Chapters Three through Five), and the Fearless Five Nutrients. Feeding with Confidence will help you with the HOW of feeding by explaining the WHY behind food-related behaviors, feeding strategies that work, and ways to educate your child about nutrition. Real Life Challenges puts it all together by showcasing real-world case studies. Each age-based chapter ends with Real, Easy Recipes, providing you with tips and meal ideas targeted to the specific age group.

Chapter Six, The Parent Trap, will show you how to evaluate, and change, your attitudes and actions around food to help you to become a Fearless Eater yourself, which will in turn make it easier for you to raise a Fearless Eater. Chapter Seven, Childhood Nutrition Problems, provides you with guidance on food allergies, extreme picky eating, weight problems, eating disorders, and behavioral challenges. Chapter Eight, Getting Meals on the Table, teaches you how to plan meals, shop, and get started cooking for your family.

Throughout the book you'll find Fearless Facts, useful details about children and food, as well as Fearless Tips, quick ideas on what to do in a variety of different feeding situations. We will also direct you from time to time to the appendices, which include fruit and vegetable lists, nutrient lists and food sources, answers to your beyond-basic nutrition questions, and other helpful resources. You can always check our website (www.fearlessfeeding.com) too, which is home to more resources and important emerging research. As modern-day parents, we know your time is precious, so our goal is to make this book as easy to read and use as possible. Let's get started!

CHAPTER 1

The Fearless Feeding Strategy

Every night millions of families gather to have dinner together. To make sure their kids eat well, some parents don't allow more bread or pasta until their children eat more veggies or meat. If dessert is on the menu, many kids will need to demonstrate eating a good portion of what is on their plate if they want to participate in the fun. And some kids are asked to take a certain number of bites before they can leave the dinner table, whereas others are only offered foods they will eat in the first place.

The problem with these strategies is not only that research shows they are ineffective but also that most parents don't always think them through or even realize why they feed in this way. They really have no plan or preparation when it comes to feeding—*no real feeding strategy*. They are simply struggling to get healthy foods into their kids, day in and day out.

Why is this? Our culture of feeding is very short-term focused and quick to offer advice on WHAT to feed, rather than on HOW or WHY. Take the baby food–making craze as an example. Most babies only accept pureed foods for a few months until they transition to table foods, yet the focus is on buying equipment and spending hours making baby food. Although we acknowledge the importance of feeding babies whole food ingredients (WHAT), we also encourage parents to introduce as many flavors as possible, because it's the rare time children will accept and try almost any food (WHY). We also ask parents to bond with their children through feeding and invite their little ones to join the family table early (HOW) to help prevent feeding problems later on.

Fearless Fact

Babies are more accepting of new flavors if they've been exposed to a wide variety of flavors early on.[1] You can take advantage of this during the honeymoon stage of feeding, something discussed in more detail in Chapter Two.

Megan was shocked when she heard her one-year-old could join her and her husband at the dinner table. "My daughter, thirteen months, was eating completely separate meals, very bland, and usually pureed," she says. "When I used your suggestion and gave her a chopped version of our adult food, she ate every single bite and loved it! Now we eat the same food every night, from curry to tilapia to tacos. Who knows how long our daughter would have kept eating baby food unnecessarily!"

Our culture's short-term view of feeding and tendency to look for a "quick fix" keep you from understanding that every feeding stage is connected. It's vital to be prepared for (and possibly prevent) the challenges that await, something health professionals call "anticipatory guidance." After all, how you feed your baby will affect how he will eat as a toddler. How you feed your toddler affects how she will eat as a school-age child. And just when you think you have everything figured out, your child becomes a teenager who worries about body shape and size, experiments with dieting, and starts eating what his friends are eating.

You don't have to be a registered dietitian to master the fundamentals of feeding your child—you just need an effective feeding strategy.

Take the Long-Term View

Feeding, carried out thousands of times in the course of childhood, is often laden with emotions and failures, and few home runs. But there is a way to make feeding easier, more rewarding, and effective—and it all starts with having a long-term view, which we outline in Table 1.1.

Table 1.1	Short-Term Versus Long-Term Feeding Strategies	
	Short-Term View (No Real Strategy)	**Long-Term View (Fearless Feeding Strategy)**
Focus	WHAT to feed	WHAT, HOW, and WHY
Goal	Getting kids to eat healthy today	Teaching kids how to eat healthy for a lifetime
Parents . . .	Are frustrated. They either give up or push kids too hard. There is tension at the table.	Are fearless. They are able to weather the storms and maintain a positive eating atmosphere.
Children . . .	See food as good or bad. They may not regulate intake well (eating too much or too little). They associate food and eating with negative feelings or rewards.	See almost all food as enjoyable. They regulate intake well (eating the right amount for their body type). They enjoy eating and coming to the table most of the time.

We have this "big picture" perspective with other aspects of our kids' learning. We understand that it takes kids years to master reading and writing, and that all children learn at different rates. Even when our kids may be slower learners, we still feel confident that they'll eventually get it. We need to have this same attitude about eating—all kids can learn how to eat well, but it takes time, patience, and courage to let each child learn at his own pace.

When you keep your focus on the long-term goal of raising a Fearless Eater, you will be less tempted to take part in the daily food drama—and this takes the pressure off everyone. You will begin to see the power your attitudes and actions have and how they shape your child's emerging relationship with food.

Fundamental 1: WHAT to Feed Your Child

Simply put, the WHAT of feeding is all about *food* and *nutrition*. Although food is the aspect of feeding that is most talked about, it is also filled with its share of confusion and misinformation. One mom tells you that juice is bad, while another says it's the only way she can get fruit into her child. One thing is for sure—food fads are not for children who rely on nutritious food to grow and develop. You need to know WHAT to feed your child at each stage so you can match her nutritional needs.

When you have a basic understanding of your child's nutritional needs—and how to meet them using food or supplements—it gives you peace of mind. After all, your child is undergoing a dynamic process called growth, and will therefore have different nutrient requirements throughout the stages of childhood. If you don't understand this, as many parents don't, you will be more fearful and likely to make mistakes in the name of nutrition.

Joy was so worried that her preschooler, Emily, was missing key nutrients by not eating vegetables (except corn and carrots) that she bribed her with dessert and hid greens in mixed dishes. One night Emily was so upset to see small pieces of broccoli in her favorite lasagna that she refused to eat dinner from then on. When Joy learned that her daughter didn't have to eat a lot of vegetables to meet her needs, she couldn't believe it. A variety of fruits along with Emily's favorite vegetables were enough until her taste buds grew up and she could learn to appreciate the taste and texture of vegetables. It took Joy a little while to rebuild trust with Emily, but now Emily is eating dinners again—and even trying some vegetables on her own!

Understanding your child's nutritional needs is vital, but so is navigating the not-so-good stuff children are naturally drawn to. Many kids are overexposed to foods that have little nutritional value and lots of calories—at sporting events, in schools, on advertisements, and in homes.[2] Many parents don't realize that early and frequent exposure can generate a preference for these foods in many kids, perpetuating their consumption in a child's diet.[1,3,4]

> **Fearless Fact**
>
> More than one-third of children have a diet that consists of energy-dense, nutrient-poor foods, such as soda; fruit drinks; grain-based desserts like cookies, cakes, and pastries; dairy desserts; and pizza.[2] Even our youngest toddlers have an unprecedented exposure to these foods, which is showing up in their weight as preschoolers and in their pickiness at the dinner table.[4]

These factors make it important for you to shift the balance of WHAT your child eats to healthier options and more food variety, while keeping nutrition-poor foods in check. WHAT your child eats affects not only his overall health and wellness but also his lifelong food preferences.

Fearless Food Guide

The answer to fearless feeding is not to eliminate the foods that are everywhere but to learn—and teach kids—the art of balance. We believe all foods are "legal" and can fit into a healthy diet.

Children of all ages need an assortment of foods from the different food groups to meet their nutritional needs. We give you the specific recommendations for serving sizes and optimal daily amounts from food groups in the Nutrition in Practice sections throughout the age-based chapters.

The foods you provide most frequently will be nutrient-dense, what we call Nourishing Foods, and will be drawn from the major food groups: fruits, vegetables, dairy and nondairy, grains, meat and nonmeat sources, and fats. What we call Half-and-Half Foods are those that aren't as nutrient-dense but still supply important nutrients. These will be offered less often.

The Fun Food category includes the foods that offer little nutrition but big taste, such as sweets and fried foods. We generally follow the 90:10 Rule by striving for a diet that contains about 90 percent Nourishing and Half-and-Half Foods, with the remaining 10 percent made up of Fun Foods, as detailed in Table 1.2. On some days, kids will eat more, and on others less, from each food category, but the goal is an overall diet that is balanced to be mostly nutritious while leaving room for enjoyable treats.

> **Fearless Tip**
>
> Rotate different fruits, vegetables, grains, dairy products, and protein sources frequently in your child's diet. The more variety your child eats from within the Nourishing Food category, the better her chances are of meeting specific nutrient requirements. Remember not to get hung up on how your child eats on *one* day; instead, consider her intake *over the course of the week*.

Table 1.2	Food Balance	
	Frequency	**Food Items**
Nourishing Foods	Offered daily, and frequently throughout the day	Fruits; vegetables; whole grains; lean protein sources (lean meats, poultry, fish, and beans); healthy fats; and low-fat dairy
Half-and-Half Foods	Offered daily or weekly—less frequently than Nourishing Foods	Fruit and vegetable juices, refined grains, full-fat dairy, high-fat meats, and animal fats
Fun Foods	Offered least frequently—making up about 10 percent of the diet	Cake, cookies, candy, ice cream, chips, and fries

Fine-Tuning Nutrients and Portions

Although our specific food guides will help you decide WHAT types of food to offer and how often, children won't always eat in a balanced manner. That's why we highlight the Fearless Five Nutrients in each Nutrition in Practice section. These will help you identify the typically low nutrients for each age group and fill in with alternative nutrient-rich foods to match your child's nutritional needs.

Portion size is another factor to consider. We believe that children should eat until they're satisfied, which sometimes translates into having seconds or even thirds (usually during growth spurts). We also live in a portion-distorted nation, where portions are larger than life. Instead of *portion control,*

Fearless Fact

During the past forty years, portion sizes have increased substantially in stores, in restaurants, and at home.[5] For example, twenty years ago a blueberry muffin was about 1.5 ounces and 210 calories, whereas today the typical muffin is 5 ounces and contains 500 calories!

we like to think of it in terms of *portion awareness,* especially as children get older, eat out more often, and become influenced by their environment. Knowing what a normal portion looks like for your child at each stage will help you teach your child portion awareness as he progresses through childhood.

You also have endless decisions to make in terms of meal preparation and food choice. In our Real, Easy Recipes sections, and in Chapter Eight, Getting Meals on the Table, we help you get started. All of our recipes are intended for the busy parent—requiring simple ingredients and little preparation time. And we help you interpret food labels so you can make the best choices for your family.

Our goal is to take the confusion and guesswork out of food and nutrition—simplifying and streamlining feeding. Obviously, understanding the WHAT is very important, but knowing WHAT to feed isn't the whole enchilada. Read on for more about the fascinating and underrepresented HOW of feeding.

Fundamental 2: HOW to Feed Your Child

Have you ever *really* thought about your approach to feeding? Is it nurturing, demanding, or controlling? Are mealtimes pleasant or a chore or something in between?

HOW you feed your child is extremely powerful. Your attitudes, your actions, and the structure you set at mealtimes are the basis for the parent-child relationship, which can be positive or negative, potentially coloring how your child views the world of food, eating, and his own self.[6] Mastering this aspect of feeding has the potential to transform the mealtime dynamic—something food could never do alone.

HOW you feed is a key to preventing many childhood eating problems, including obesity, picky eating, dysfunctional attitudes about food, and eating disorders.

Meal Structure: A Parent's Secret Weapon

Shari had never heard about the HOW of feeding—in fact, she was very proud of her nutrition knowledge and the emphasis she placed on healthy food in her home. She spent a lot of time making sure that meals were organic, fresh, preservative- and additive-free, home cooked, and heavy on fiber. Despite the quality and health of the meals, her five-year-old, Will, wasn't eating well. In fact, he was outright refusing most of what was offered him. Worried about Will's weight, Shari began to offer him his few favorite healthy foods at any time of the day. Feeding Will became a chore and a worry for everyone. And Will was in the trap of eating the same foods every day.

Like many American mothers, Shari was sold on the promise that getting food "right" would naturally lead to a healthy child. But it didn't. In fact, it led to a child who was small for his age; who was eating less than he should and at erratic times; and who was in control of his mother, the food, and the family meal.

The first thing we did when working with Shari was address the *structure and timing* of her son's meals and snacks. We asked her to use a feeding structure that provided meals and snacks at three- to four-hour intervals, and to stick to a set location where eating happens, preferably the kitchen table. We assigned times for breakfast, lunch, and dinner and a midmorning, afternoon, and before-bedtime snack. We emphasized that the responsibility of determining the feeding structure lay with the parents, not their son.

Adding structure accomplished two important things: it provided several opportunities for Will to get adequate nutrition throughout the day, and it prevented major swings in appetite (feeling too hungry or too full). It also allowed Will to eat for the perfect reason—hunger—and to refuse to eat if he was not hungry, putting the control over his internal appetite regulation in his hands. We discuss further the benefits of structure when you need it the most—the toddler years (see Chapter Three).

> **Fearless Fact**
>
> Kids are more secure around food, and less focused on it, when a predictable and reliable feeding structure is used.[7,8] Kids with structured feeding times also tend to eat amounts of food that are right for them and choose healthier options.[9]

Structure + Fearless Feeding Style = Success!

Although structure is important, so is your feeding style—the basic approach you use or your manner when you interact with your child around food and eating.

This attitude and your actions during mealtime have a profound effect on how your child eats.

Research defines four common feeding styles: authoritarian, permissive, neglectful, and authoritative.[10,11] Parents generally use all four styles in day-to-day feeding, but one style usually dominates. Knowing your own tendencies in regard to your approach to feeding, and its consequences, is an important connection to make as you become a Fearless Feeder.

> **Fearless Fact**
>
> *Transgenerational feeding* connects how you feed your child today to the way your own parents and grandparents fed their children. Simply put, many parents either "inherit" their feeding style from their own parents, or may reject their parents' style and feed in an opposite way (more on this in Chapter Six).

Authoritarian Feeding Style

A common approach to feeding is "Just do as I say," whereby the parent sets and enforces rules around food and eating, with minimal regard for the child's food preferences or hunger and fullness signals. The parent has high expectations and strict rules around eating performance.

Elizabeth experienced this feeding style as a child. She described being forced to "eat what she was served" and "clean her plate" before she could leave the dinner table at night. There were nights as a young child when she sat at the table until nine or ten o'clock at night because she wouldn't eat her green beans.

According to research, children raised with this approach lose sight of their own hunger and fullness

> **Fearless Fact**
>
> Daily feeding practices aligned with an authoritarian feeding style include rewarding, restricting, and pressuring or prompting. *Rewarding* is used to get children to eat better or to eat certain foods (like vegetables). *Restricting* can take the form of limiting access to certain foods or controlling the amounts children eat. And putting on the *pressure* or *prompting* is another way parents try to get their kids to eat certain foods, or eat more, at mealtime.

signals—they don't know when to stop eating and may ignore body signals telling them it is time to eat.[11,12,13] As a result, children may overeat, leading to weight problems. Also, children eat fewer fruits and vegetables with this approach compared to other feeding styles.[10,12,13,14]

Permissive Feeding Style

This feeding style is characterized by parents' oversensitivity to the hunger and fullness cues of their child, while having low expectations around eating behaviors and meal structure. The parent who uses this style may be referred to as a "yes" parent who maintains few boundaries around food and eating and is prone to allowing the child to consume anything he wants.

Elizabeth is a classic example of a parent who rejected the feeding style that was used during her own childhood. Because she was raised with an authoritarian feeding style, she adopted an opposite feeding style with her own children—the permissive style. Elizabeth often allowed her kids to eat anything they wanted, or to eat anytime they indicated they were hungry—even shortly after a meal. Many activities were centered around food, and the meal structure was very loose.

Kids raised with the permissive feeding style eat more sweets and high-fat foods than children raised with any other approach to feeding.[14,15,16] Children may gain too much weight, and in the long run may be out of touch with knowing how much food—or which types of food—to eat. You can see how this can be a recipe for lifelong eating struggles and weight problems.

That's why Elizabeth sought help. She was dealing with an overweight five-year-old and a very picky eight-year-old. The mealtime environment was so problematic, it was affecting everyone in the family—nobody was happy at meals,

> **Fearless Fact**
>
> Daily feeding practices aligned with a permissive feeding style include constant feeding (letting children graze on food all day), short-order cooking, and allowing children to make most of the food choices during mealtime. Children who graze all day from constant feeding usually eat too much or too little, and children who know an alternate meal is waiting for them are less likely to expand their food repertoire.

and the physical health of both of her boys was taking a hit. Elizabeth realized that her upbringing dictated HOW she fed, and it was having a negative impact on her own children.

Neglectful Feeding Style

This feeding style is characterized by low sensitivity to a child's needs around food and eating, and few expectations concerning mealtime and eating behavior. Parents may fail to stock and shop for ingredients or to plan and prepare meals in a regular and timely manner, and they may "fly by the seat of their pants" when it comes to meal structure and content.

Grace Anne's mother was not intentionally neglecting to feed her daughter, she was just very busy. Working out of her home and managing a packed work travel schedule, in addition to raising a child, was difficult. When deadlines were pressing, shopping and cooking fell to the bottom of the list. Meanwhile, Grace Anne compensated for this chaotic and unpredictable food environment by ensuring that she would never go hungry, hiding food in her closet and keeping chocolate under lock and key in her trinket box.

In the case of a neglectful feeding style, food may be a low priority for the parent, but it becomes a high priority for the child. Children raised with this feeding style tend to be insecure about food, overly focusing on food and perhaps asking many food questions ("When are we eating?" "What are we eating?" "Will there be enough?").[13,17] Because children are fixated on and insecure around food, they may overeat or undereat, and they may have difficulty trusting their caregiver when it comes to food.

Many of the daily feeding practices associated with common feeding styles have a "reverse effect," resulting in the opposite outcome of what is intended. When parents reward their child for eating vegetables with dessert, for example, the child places a higher value on the dessert (reward food). And when parents restrict their child's access to sweets to help her eat less, the child values and wants those restricted foods even more and is more likely to eat them, even when not hungry. Pressuring children to eat also results in poor eating. In fact, pressuring kids may lead them to experience early fullness, a worsening in their picky eating, and poor weight gain.[18]

According to a 2007 study published in *Appetite,* 85 percent of parents try to get their children to eat more at meals using reasoning, praise, and food rewards.[19] Because these feeding practices are so ineffective and tiring, we often see parents give up entirely or go back and forth between an authoritarian (controlling) and a more permissive (no boundaries) feeding style. Yet research shows there is a better and much more effective way of feeding.

Authoritative Feeding Style (a.k.a. the Fearless Feeding Style!)

The most effective and positive approach to feeding children is an authoritative feeding style, characterized by responsiveness to the child, structure and boundaries around mealtime, and respect for the child's food choices. The parent takes care to ensure that meals and food are served on time, responds to the child's hunger and fullness, allows reasonable choice around food, and lets the child regulate his own eating (deciding how much and which foods to eat).

Julie didn't appreciate her parents' feeding style until she went away to college. She noticed her friends went crazy with their newfound freedom around food, while her interest in nutrition grew. Her parents were authoritative feeders, providing reliable, healthy meals while never pressuring her to eat more or less. They were relaxed about Fun Foods but offered them less often—and didn't make a big deal about healthy eating, even when she went through stages of trading lunches and ordering onion rings at restaurants.

Children raised with this feeding style tend to have a healthy weight, be good at self-regulating their own eating, eat healthier types of food (vegetables, fruit, and dairy products), and be more physically active.[9] The key to this feeding style's success is the warmth and

---

Fearless Fact

The feeding practice aligned with an authoritative feeding style is Ellyn Satter's Division of Responsibility in feeding, whereby parents determine the *what, when,* and *where* of feeding, and children decide the *whether* and *how much* of eating.[3,8] It's based on *trust* and *choice*: the child trusts that the parent will come through with reliable meals, the parent trusts that the child knows how much to eat—and the kid ultimately understands that he has the choice to eat or not.

Table 1.3	Parent Feeding Styles	
Feeding Style	**Example**	**Effects**
Authoritarian (controlling)	*Kid:* "I'm done." *Parent:* "You're not done yet, four more bites or else no dessert for you."	The child may have a loss of appetite regulation and be less likely to eat fruits and veggies. This feeding style is correlated with overweight and obesity.
Permissive (no or few boundaries)	*Kid:* "Can I have a cookie, Mom? Please!" *Parent:* "I guess so . . . you really shouldn't since you have been snacking all day. But okay."	The child is likely to eat more sweets and high-fat foods, gain weight, and have a reduced ability to self-regulate eating.
Neglectful (not a priority)	*Kid:* "What's for dinner, Mom? Do we have any food?" *Parent:* "We'll figure out something dear, give me a minute."	The child is worried and anxious about food, and overeats or undereats. The child may develop trust issues with the caregiver and with food.
Authoritative (leadership and autonomy)	*Kid:* "Can I have a free cookie from the store bakery? Please!" *Parent:* "Dinner is only an hour from now, and I don't want you to spoil your appetite. The next time we shop during snack time you can have one."	The child self-regulates eating and is aware of appetite cues. The child eats more fruit, vegetables, and dairy products, and is more physically active than children raised with the other feeding styles.

responsiveness of parents along with high expectations and consistency around food and eating.[8,17]

Table 1.3 sums up the differences between the four feeding styles. Being responsible for your child's feeding is like being a boss. If you've ever had a boss who tightly regulated every move you made, you know how it degrades self-confidence and makes work drudgery. The walk-all-over-me manager lacks the leadership needed to be effective and gain respect. And the boss who never seems to be around or give you any support makes you worry about how you are going to get your work done properly. It's the boss who provides leadership, compliments you effectively, trusts you, and finds a balance of freedom and support who inspires you and makes you *want* to work hard.

We hope you now understand that HOW you feed—the structure, feeding style, and practices—is vital in shaping your child's relationship with food. Now that we have introduced the WHAT and HOW, there's one more component to the Fearless Feeding Strategy that takes this entire approach to a new level.

Fundamental 3: WHY Your Child Behaves That Way

Children weave through expected and typical aspects of child development and relate to their environment based on their own temperament. Although it can drive parents crazy, most kids aren't behaving like this intentionally.

Knowing what to expect and WHY your child behaves the way he does with food gives you peace of mind. From expecting that your toddler will be picky to understanding why your teen eats out more often than not, knowing your child's developmental stage and temperament helps you anticipate, understand, and react appropriately to his behavior.

Child Development Is Predictable

Child development occurs on a continuum, with predictable characteristics that can influence eating.[17] During infancy, babies are a blank slate, and everything they do (and you do) is an imprint on their memory. Their main job is to form an attachment to their caregiver. They are learning how to trust you, that you are dependable and that the world is a good place to be.[20] Feeding your baby provides an opportunity to develop this attachment. Toddlers spend their time separating from you and exploring the world around them— and that includes the world of food. Getting messy with food can be frustrating for parents, but it is developmentally productive for the toddler. Besides, at what other time

Fearless Fact

Many of the things that frustrate you about your child—picky eating, an erratic appetite, and being highly influenced by friends' eating—are a normal part of development.

in life do you get to lather yourself in yogurt? By school age, kids are more skill oriented and influenced by a growing body of friends, community members, and neighbors. The world is creeping in, and your kid is soaking it up, because that's what children do at this age—they learn and develop skills. When they learn new skills and become "good" at them, their self-esteem starts to blossom. Just as those skills and new confidence accumulate, the grade-schoolers turn into teenagers, ready to experiment, make decisions for themselves, and be independent. Once again, the normal process of separating from you occurs for the last time as your teen prepares for adulthood.

All Children Have Their Own Food Personality

Not only do you need to anticipate your child's development but also you want to be mindful of her temperament. Is she demanding? High maintenance? Easygoing? Difficult? Or is she sometimes one and sometimes the other? Your child's temperament can influence how wells she reacts to, accepts, and eats foods on any given day. For example, positive encouragement to eat can be met with rebellion or complete refusal with the stubborn child, whereas little pushes with an easygoing child may work like a charm. Oftentimes you don't know until you try (and get instant feedback), but appreciating your child's temperament can help you tailor your interactions so that they are most effective and positive for all.

"My daughter, Kendall, is four and a very picky eater," says Nicole. "I often say her eating habits are payback for all the times I smugly thought that my son's eating habits, who has always been easy to feed, had something to do with my parenting." Each child experiences his own taste and texture world. Some are more sensitive to the bitter taste of vegetables, whereas others are not. The same family may have one child who is a sensory seeker, enjoying different textures and spicy foods, and another child who is more sensitive, needing increased time and patience. Our experience has taught us that each child accepts food in her own unique way, with the following tendencies:

- **Eager eater:** Otherwise referred to as an "adventurous eater," this eater will try and accept new foods easily, and learns to like a variety of foods sooner than most children. These eaters often have big appetites.

- **Somewhere-in-between eater:** Most children fall into this category. This eater is cautious with new foods, but over time and with exposure he gradually adds a variety of foods to his repertoire.
- **Cautious eater:** Some children are extremely timid with food—slow to try new foods and careful, typically revealing this eating style when solid foods are started. Some children may even be "supertasters," with a heightened sense of taste (which may or may not make some foods taste offensive), or may be more sensitive to all of the sensory components of food (taste, smell, texture, and appearance).

> **Fearless Tip**
>
> Don't judge your success as a feeder by your child's fruit and vegetable intake or the number of foods she will eat. Children go through different stages, learning to eat a variety of healthy foods at different paces. We believe all children can grow up to be Fearless Eaters. You're doing a good job if your child enjoys eating and is being exposed to a variety of foods.

The fundamental WHY gives you an understanding of who your child is, where he is in his developmental stage, and what is normal behavior for him—priceless information for successful feeding.

Putting It All Together

Many parents have one or maybe two of the Fearless Feeding Strategy components up their sleeve, but few have all three. The WHAT, HOW, and WHY are extremely powerful when used together.

Now that you are familiar with the Fearless Feeding Strategy, you can begin to see how dependent each component is on the others. When just one of these elements is missing, feeding can go awry and become challenging. Always return to each of the fundamentals when you or your child begins to struggle with nutrition, at any time. Check your WHAT, HOW, and WHY, as outlined in Table 1.4, so that you can pinpoint where feeding has gone haywire—something we help more with in the Real Life Challenges sections.

This is the beginning of a transformation that has the power to change your whole family's eating habits and relationship with food. With this complete

Table 1.4 Fearless Feeding Fundamentals	
WHAT: Food and Nutrition	• Understanding nutrient needs • Improving food quality and incorporating variety • Balancing Nourishing, Half-and-Half, and Fun Foods • Paying attention to portion awareness
HOW: Attitudes and Actions with Feeding	• Using structure with feeding • Adopting an authoritative feeding style • Avoiding negative feeding practices • Seizing opportunities for nutrition education • Role modeling
WHY: Behavior with Food and Eating	• Appreciating the stages of child development • Understanding your child's unique food personality • Acknowledging child temperament

knowledge of feeding, and a long-term view, you will feel more confident with the decisions you make. This allows you to take control of what you can and let go of the rest. Congratulations, you are on your way to becoming a Fearless Feeder!

CHAPTER 2

Fearless Feeding for Your Infant and Young Toddler (Six to Twenty-Four Months)

Babies have a steep learning curve when it comes to eating. In this chapter, we help you make spot-on transitions during the first two years while meeting your child's unique nutritional needs. Yet WHAT to feed is only part of the story; fearless feeding is also about forming an attachment with your child through feeding; being responsive to her; and introducing variety, variety, variety. It's a tall order, but we know you can do it!

Nutrition in Practice: The Nutrient-Rich Diet

A couple of months after her baby was born, Allison had gotten into a good routine with feeding her daughter. As the time to start solids approached, she could feel her anxiety level rise. She heard a lot of conflicting advice. "The hardest part for me was knowing *when* to start and *what* to start with," she says. "Advice from friends, the pediatrician, and books all had varying suggestions, and as a first-time parent, I just wanted one answer."

One of the biggest challenges of feeding during this stage is sifting through all the information and figuring out what to do. Luckily, we do that for you, providing a clear, research-based guide for feeding babies and young toddlers. Although this section focuses on WHAT to feed your baby and young toddler, it starts when solids are introduced, not at the beginning of feeding. We won't be talking about the benefits of breastfeeding over formula—although we will point out specific feeding considerations for children who are breastfed and those who are formula-fed. Here, we focus on best practices for transitioning baby from a liquid diet to food the whole family eats.

What to Expect

The first year of life showcases rapid growth. In fact, the growth that happens now is unmatched by any other growth stage in childhood. Most infants will double their birth weight by five months, and triple it by one year. The brain experiences tremendous growth as well, doubling in weight by the child's first birthday. An infant's head is much bigger relative to the size of the rest of the body, taking up 25 percent of the body's real estate, twice that of adults. The average baby gains fifteen pounds and grows nine inches during the first year. Infants also have a unique body shape, which includes a rounded stomach, short bowed legs, and more fat tissue that increases from four to six months.

Growth slows down during the second year of life, with the average child gaining about 5.5 pounds and growing 4.7 inches, only half the growth of the first year. During this time, you will watch your child transform from baby into toddler: walking, talking, and feeding himself. Your child's tiny limbs begin to lengthen, and his body becomes more active—walking and eventually running. As a result of this growth and activity, body proportions change, with some thinning out and a loss of that "baby look."

We often get questions about the rounded "potbelly" babies and young toddlers have. "My thirteen-month-old's belly sticks way out, and it looks really funny," says Kay. "Is this normal?" The answer is yes. Having a thicker middle and a big,

> ### Fearless Fact
>
> High growth means high appetite. Weight increases in the first year by 200 percent, body length by 55 percent, and head circumference by 40 percent, changes that are reflected in a hearty appetite for most babies. Although birth weight triples during the first year, it doesn't quadruple until age two, so you can expect growth and appetite to decrease in the second year.

round belly is typical at this stage, with most kids outgrowing this shape by school age.[1]

The Hallmark of Health: Steady Growth

During the first year, growth is assessed at least every three months at doctor visits and is a vital tool for tracking health status in infants and young toddlers. For kids under the age of two, the focus is on steady growth in length, weight, and head circumference. The World Health Organization (WHO) growth charts are recommended for evaluating growth for children ages zero to twenty-four months (see www.cdc.gov/growthcharts/who _charts.htm).[2]

Your child's pediatrician should alert you if your baby is showing signs of faltering growth. Failure to thrive (FTT) occurs in 5 to 10 percent of U.S. children and usually presents before eighteen months of age.[4] FTT is referred to as either organic (due to medical problems) or inorganic (due to social and environmental factors). Yet most cases are multifactorial, without a medical diagnosis at all. In other instances, accelerated growth may be of concern. Although research shows that children who are larger and experience rapid weight gain during the first two years of life may be at increased risk for excess weight in the future,[5,6] this does not mean that every big baby will become obese (most will not!). As we mention throughout this book, and showcase in the Real Life Challenges section in this chapter, you are looking for steady growth over time, and not big jumps in either direction. We believe that when you feed appropriately, children grow the way nature intended, meaning some children will be smaller or bigger, and others will be in between.

> **Fearless Fact**
>
> According to one study, parents of smaller babies were more concerned about their child's weight than parents of bigger babies.[3] There seems to be a bias that a large baby signals good health. Yet size does not determine the health of a baby—steady growth does.

Opportunity Knocks: Are You Ready?

The first two years are thought to be a critical window of opportunity when it comes to nutrition, as children are developing food preferences and learning to eat. Nutritional status, the state of one's health as related to the adequacy of nutrients and energy, is of particular concern because if a certain nutrient is not available during a critical period of development, there can be negative effects that may become irreversible. Certain factors will increase the risk of nutrient deficiencies in children during infancy, such being born to a mom with an iron deficiency (anemia), low–vitamin D status, hypertension, or uncontrolled diabetes. Because the last trimester of pregnancy is when most of baby's iron stores accrue and docosahexaenoic acid (DHA) accumulates in the brain and retina (eye), preterm infants (less than thirty-seven weeks of gestation) and those with low birth weight are also at increased risk for these nutrient deficiencies.[7,8]

Fearless Fact

Research shows that iron deficiency during the first two-year "brain growth spurt" can cause permanent changes to the structure and function of the brain if left untreated or treated too late.[9] "Babies with the lowest iron endowment at birth are at the highest risk for iron deficiency," says Ekhard Ziegler, professor of pediatrics at University of Iowa Children's Hospital. Although the at-risk populations are more vulnerable, his studies show iron status at birth can be highly variable and may even be genetically linked. This is why prevention of and screening for iron deficiency are so important, especially in babies fed breast milk, which is low in iron even when mom's diet is adequate.

By four to six months of life, a baby's gastrointestinal tract becomes mature enough to handle solids, and breast milk is no longer enough to cover his complete nutritional needs. (Although formula will cover nutritional needs, solids are needed for development and satiety.) Iron stores, which the baby accumulated in the last trimester of pregnancy, begin to run low, so other sources of iron are needed.

Fat is another nutrient that is important during the first two years of life. Babies need energy, not just for maintenance but also for growth—and this is a time when growth is at its highest. Fat should make up about 50 percent of an infant's diet in the first six months (the amount in breast milk and formula), and should gradually decline after the introduction of solids to a range of 30 to 45 percent of calories. Diets with less than 25 percent of calories from fat do not support adequate growth (fat has twice as many calories as protein or carbohydrate). Moreover, fat and cholesterol are "building blocks" for structural elements of cellular membranes—including those in the growing brain. Two fatty acids that are of particular importance to infants are DHA and arachdonic acid (AA). DHA makes up half of the total fatty acids in the retina and is a critical component of brain tissue.[8] AA has various roles pertaining to the structure and function of the developing brain as well.

Food Acceptance and Learning to Eat

The first few years of life are also critical for the development of patterns of food acceptance. Exposure to flavors first occurred when your baby was in the womb and swallowed amniotic fluid. Then he tasted the liquid diet of breast milk, formula, or a combination of the two at birth and throughout the first months of life. The introduction of solids is another key time when you can expose your infant to different tastes and textures, including those fruits and veggies you'll want him to eat later.

"In hindsight, the main problem I had with my son was that I worried too much about how much solid food he ate," says Emma. "This resulted in me falling back to foods and textures (purees) that I knew he liked, instead of using that time to get him used to different tastes and textures." This is the time to introduce various foods because babies are more accepting: research shows it takes very few exposures for a six-month-old to accept a new food, whereas it can take between ten and twenty exposures for preschoolers.[10]

Babies also need to physically *learn* to eat solid foods, and there are critical developmental windows of opportunity during which to maximize learning.[11,12] Readiness for solids becomes apparent between four to six months of age, and is determined by a combination of gross motor skills (large muscles); fine motor skills (small muscles); and oral motor skills (mouth, tongue, swallowing). First signs of readiness include head control; an ability to sit with support; the loss of tongue thrust (pushing food out with the tongue); and a desire to control eating demonstrated by leaning forward and opening the mouth, or rejecting foods to show fullness. Until infants can display these basic cues, feeding may be a forced act, and overfeeding can result. Every child is different, and we've seen infants ready at four, five, and six months—and some even later than that.

Refer to Table 2.1 to see how baby's motor skills translate to eating skills. For example, between five and nine months of age, most babies are able to control the food in their mouth; can sit unsupported; and begin to master fine motor skills, such as the pincer grasp, making this the time to expose them to lumpier textures and finger foods. Once babies accept finger foods, they can eat much of what the family is eating and can practice using a spoon. Between one and two years, babies eat mostly chopped food and develop fine motor skills that allow them to dip into and scoop food and bring a spoon to their mouth without much spilling. Although you never want to force your child to advance to the next stage, you do want to give her the opportunity to transition at developmentally appropriate times.

> **Fearless Tip**
>
> Don't wait too long to upgrade textures. According to one study, children introduced to lumpy solids after nine months of age had more feeding problems at seven years than the children introduced to lumpy textures between six and nine months.[13]

In summary, your baby is growing at the fastest rate of his life, and complementary foods play an important role. Nutrients, food exposure, and feeding development are vital components to include during the first two years. It's not that your baby has to do everything on a certain timeline, but you'll want to make sure he gets the nutrition he needs and is challenged with textures—and that variety keeps coming. But before we move on to the actual feeding of your baby, we've got some important "food for thought" for you.

Food for Thought

Should you buy organic food? Do you really need to make your own baby food? Is rice cereal even needed? In the following paragraphs, we provide you with the information you need to make good decisions and start off feeling confident about feeding.

Table 2.1 Developmental Skills for Eating

Age Range	Gross Motor Skills	Fine Motor Skills	Oral Motor Skills	Translation to Eating Skills
Birth to five months	• *Newborn:* Has poor head control • *Three to five months:* Has emerging head control	• Brings toy to mouth	• Coordinates sucking, swallowing, and breathing	• Bottle-feeds, breastfeeds, or both
Four to seven months	• Has good head control • Sits with support	• Uses whole hand to grab objects	• Moves pureed food to back of mouth with tongue to swallow • Opens mouth to spoon	• Swallows pureed food in addition to liquids
Five to nine months	• Sits without support • Begins crawling	• Begins to use pincer grasp to pick up food	• Gains better mouth control • Achieves lip closure around spoon • Positions food between jaws for chewing	• Eats pureed, lumpy, and mashed foods • Begins to self-feed with hands • Drinks from cup with help
Eight to eleven months	• Easily sits alone • Transfers objects from hand to mouth	• Masters pincer grasp • Begins to hold cup and spoon	• Uses tongue to move food from side to side • Swallows with mouth closed	• Drinks from sippy cup • Can eat small pieces of food with fingers • Plays with spoon

Table 2.1 (continued)

Age Range	Gross Motor Skills	Fine Motor Skills	Oral Motor Skills	Translation to Eating Skills
Ten to twelve months	• Pulls self up to stand • May begin first steps	• Holds sippy cup well • Begins to put spoon in mouth	• Practices rotary chewing (jaw moves diagonally to move food to side or center of mouth) • Drinks from straw • Chews more skillfully	• Begins self-spoon-feeding • Eats pieces of chopped cooked food • Bites through different textures • Begins to drink from open cups
Twelve to twenty-four months	• Walks well • Runs	• Masters fine motor skills to scoop and dip into food • Spoon-feeds	• Makes smooth transfer of food to back of mouth using tongue • Cuts more teeth	• Uses two hands to hold open cup; swallows • Learns to use fork and gets better with spoon (may still prefer hands) • Can chew firmer foods with more skill

Source: Adapted from Normal nutrition for infants. (2012). In *Academy of Nutrition and Dietetics pediatric nutrition care manual.* Available from www.peds.nutritioncaremanual.org; U.S. Department of Agriculture, Food and Nutrition Service. (2002, July). Feeding infants. In *Feeding infants: A guide for use in the child nutrition programs* (Chapter 2). Retrieved from http://teamnutrition.usda.gov/Resources/feeding_infants.html.

Organic Versus Conventional Food

One of the first questions moms ask is whether or not they should buy organic food, especially fruits and vegetables. A 2012 review found no major differences in nutritional attributes and health-related outcomes from consuming either organic or conventional foods, but it did find evidence of reduced pesticide residues in the urine of children on an organic diet.[14] Although negative effects of high-level exposure to pesticides on neurodevelopment have been shown, adverse effects of lower-level exposure are still unproven.[15] Children are considered to be at the greatest risk from pesticide exposure because their brain is still developing and they ingest more, pound for pound, than adults do. To make things easy, we recommend buying organic produce for items that contain higher levels of pesticide residues, as recommended by the Environmental Working Group, and listed in the following box.[16] However, the health benefits of produce consumption in general outweigh any potential risks from pesticide exposure.

Best to buy conventional: Onions, sweet corn, pineapple, avocado, asparagus, sweet peas, mango, eggplant, cantaloupe (domestic), kiwi, cabbage, watermelon, sweet potato, mushrooms, and grapefruit.

Best to buy organic: Apples, celery, strawberries, peaches, spinach, nectarines (imported), grapes, sweet bell peppers, potatoes, blueberries (domestic), lettuce, kale, green beans, and cucumbers.

Homemade Baby Food Versus Commercial Baby Food

A 2011 survey found that 70 percent of moms who had been pregnant in the last three years made homemade baby food.[17] Even though this trend is hot, you may be feeling unsure. Remember, using jarred items doesn't preclude you from also feeding fresh, considering that much food can be made on the spot. And most babies are not on purees for long—two to four months, tops! Nutritionally, both types of baby food are similar, but using fresh food has the advantage of taste and enables you to add flavor, which can positively affect baby's food preferences later on. We have found that a combination of making your own food and buying

Table 2.2 Pros and Cons of Making Your Own Baby Food

Pros	Cons
• Baby experiences the taste of real, fresh food. • You control the ingredients. • You can puree food you are already making for the family. • There is a cost savings.	• Making your own food is not as convenient as using jars. • It can take more time (depending on your approach). • Homemade food is not tested for nitrates.[a]

[a] Commercial baby food is tested for nitrates that can cause methemoglobinemia (a rare type of anemia) in babies three months or younger.

regular jarred baby food products provides flexibility along with taste benefits. In Table 2.2 we summarize the pros and cons of making baby food.

When to Start Solids: Four Months Versus Six Months

There has been much debate on whether to start solid foods at four months or six months. Health experts agree that starting before four months is not beneficial and can raise the risk of infection, food allergies, and obesity. Yet despite this advice, almost 20 percent of moms start earlier than four months.[18] According to a 2012 American Academy of Pediatrics (AAP) policy report, babies exclusively breastfed for six months are at lower risk for ear infections, gastrointestinal diseases, respiratory illnesses, and atopic disease.[19] The report also states that the risk of developing celiac disease, which is triggered by the consumption of gluten (a protein found in wheat), is reduced (by as much as 50 percent!) in infants who are breastfed at the time of gluten exposure. The AAP, WHO, and Institute of Medicine recommend exclusive breastfeeding for six months.[19,20,21]

We believe it is safe to start solids anywhere from four to six months, taking into account developmental readiness. Those who have children at high risk for food allergies (having a parent or sibling with food allergies) or celiac disease may want to work with their pediatrician on the best time to introduce solids, as the research regarding best practices continues to evolve. The same goes for premature infants, who may have delays in development and special feeding needs.

Feeding Myths

Everyone you come in contact with will be dishing out advice about what and how to feed your baby. We help separate fact from fiction in the following paragraphs.

It's Better to Introduce Veggies Before Fruit

There is no evidence that introducing veggies before fruit makes any difference in the child's preference. Also, there is scant research about what to introduce, and when, as most sequences are based on common sense and nutritional needs.

The Introduction of Certain Foods Should Be Delayed

In 2008 the AAP retracted its previous policy statement recommending that families at risk for allergies hold off on introducing highly allergenic foods (milk, eggs, peanuts, tree nuts, soy, wheat, fish, and crustacean shellfish).[22] "Solids can be started without specific concerns for allergy or type of food," says Scott Sicherer professor of pediatrics at the Jaffe Food Allergy Institute of Mount Sinai School of Medicine. "Although the 2008 policy rescinded its previous recommendations, it did not say you had to feed allergens early. Adding foods that are developmentally edible (not a peanut or a walnut, for example) makes the most sense."

Starting Solids Early Helps Baby Sleep Through the Night

There are no data linking early introduction of solids to better sleep in infants—and adding cereal to a bottle of formula or breast milk is not recommended, as it can lead to excessive weight gain.

Infant Cereal Is Not a Good First Food for Baby

Rice cereal has traditionally been recommended as a first food due to its texture, digestibility, and low allergenic content. Most important, it provides a source of iron needed for the breastfed baby. Studies show iron-fortified cereals are effective in helping prevent iron deficiency.[23] We believe any single-grain, iron-fortified cereal makes a good first food—and whole grain options are also available. Due to concerns about arsenic levels in rice, provide a variety of grains (not just rice), and check our website, www.fearlessfeeding.com, for the updated recommendations.

Baby-Led Weaning (BLW) Is the Preferred Feeding Method
BLW is the process of skipping purees and allowing baby to take the lead, feeding herself whole food items starting around six months. Although BLW may work well for some babies, we don't feel comfortable recommending it for the general population because there is little research showing its effectiveness and safety. If you decide to follow BLW and are breastfeeding, make sure baby is meeting his needs for the Fearless Five Nutrients, discussed later in the chapter. If your baby is late to self-feed or gags frequently, you may want to reconsider.

Caution! Take Choking Risks Seriously

Choking is the leading cause of death in children under three years old. High-risk foods include those that are round, hard, and the same size as a child's airway: hot dogs, hard candy, peanuts, tree nuts, seeds, whole grapes, raw carrots, apples, popcorn, chunks of peanut butter, chunks of cheese, marshmallows, chewing gum, sausages, and raisins.[24]

Five Tips for Choking Prevention
1. Always supervise baby at mealtimes.
2. Cut food up into half-inch pieces.
3. Avoid round, firm food unless it is chopped completely, and be sure to cut round foods, like cheese sticks, lengthwise.
4. Have baby avoid eating while walking, talking, or laughing.
5. Make sure caregivers are certified in CPR.

Feeding Considerations

Now that we've covered common feeding myths, let's focus on what you *really* need to know before starting your baby on solid food.

Foods to Avoid the First Year
Honey or corn syrup should not be given in the first year due to the risk of botulism spores. Hold off on cow's milk as a beverage until one year of age, as early introduction increases the risk of iron deficiency and may cause intestinal bleeding if given before nine months.

Introducing Cups and Straws

At around seven to eight months you can introduce "sips" of water and diluted juice in a sippy cup while keeping breast milk or formula the primary fluid source. Once babies drink from the sippy cup (usually by nine months), transition to a straw cup, and have them practice on open cups.

Monitoring for Food Allergies

Introduce a new food every two to five days, and watch for such reactions as hives or rashes; red, puffy eyes; nasal congestion and sneezing; coughing; wheezing; swelling of the lips and tongue; nausea; vomiting; and dizziness or fainting (see Chapter Seven for a full list). Linda Piette, registered dietitian and author of *Just Two More Bites,* recommends children at high risk for allergies see a pediatrician who is a board-certified allergist and follows national guidelines. If a child is at low risk for food allergies, a shorter wait time between foods may be more appropriate (two to three days). "Parents don't need to get too caught up in long wait times," she says. "Babies are open to a variety of flavors, and waiting too long can hinder food acceptance."

> **Fearless Tip**
>
> Drinking from a straw strengthens oral (and speech) development! Melanie Potock, certified speech language pathologist specializing in feeding disorders, says, "After one year of age, kids who continually thrust their tongue forward to swallow, which happens with prolonged sippy cup usage, have difficulty acquiring speech sounds along with chewing and swallowing a variety of food textures. But drinking from a straw, specifically a very short straw, allows the tongue tip to rise up and press on the alveolar ridge (the bumpy ridge high above your front teeth) for developing proper swallowing patterns. Open cups are important too, but a straw builds oral motor strength and stability for talking and chewing more advanced foods, such as a chewy bagel or meat."

Food Supplements

The following supplements may be needed depending on your child's individual circumstances:

- The AAP recommends four hundred international units (IU) of vitamin D for breastfed or partially breastfed babies (receiving less than one liter of formula per day), starting from the first few days of life.[25] You can buy vitamin D drops over the counter to drop on your nipple right before baby feeds, or on his pacifier.
- The AAP recommends one milligram of iron per kilogram of body weight at four months for breastfed babies, until solids are started.[7] Check with your pediatrician on the specifics, as iron may not be appropriate for all babies.
- Fluoride supplementation is not recommended during the first six months of life, but after that time infants living in nonfluoridated communities may need fluoride supplementation, which is available through prescription only. Consult with your doctor or pediatric dentist and check your water supply for fluoride (http://apps.nccd.cdc.gov/MWF/Index.asp).
- International guidelines recommend at least two hundred milligrams of DHA for women during lactation, to keep levels in breast milk adequate.[8]

Infant and Young Toddler Feeding Guide

You'll want to keep an eye on the Fearless Five Nutrients to make sure your child's needs are being met. Because roughly half of babies either are exclusively breastfed or are being fed both formula and human milk at six months, we focus on key nutrients needed from outside sources.[18]

Table 2.3 shows you how to make sure your baby is getting enough of these five key nutrients.

Fearless Fact

Babies on iron-fortified formula (at least one liter per day) don't have to worry about iron, zinc, and vitamin D during the first year. However, once they transition to whole milk or take in less formula, these nutrients become important.

Table 2.3 Fearless Five Nutrients for Infants and Young Toddlers

Nutrient	Function	Recommended Daily Allowance (RDA)	Sources[a]	Comments
Iron	Iron carries oxygen and stores it in cells, a process that is accelerated in times of rapid growth. Fourteen percent of children under two are deficient.[26]	*Six to twelve months:* 11 milligrams *Twelve to twenty-four months:* 7 milligrams	*Heme:*[b] Chicken, strained (1 milligram); beef, strained (.7 milligrams); turkey, strained (.5 milligrams) *Nonheme:* 1 tablespoon infant cereal (1.1 to 1.8 milligrams); 3.4-ounce jar peas (.9 milligrams); 4-ounce jar green beans (.8 milligrams); 6-ounce jar sweet potatoes (.7 milligrams)	Provide two servings of iron-rich items per day. For example, 4 tablespoons of iron-fortified oatmeal mixed with egg yolk (7 milligrams), meat puree with green beans (3 milligrams), and 2 tablespoons of hummus and bread (1 milligram), for a total of 11 milligrams. For twelve- to twenty-four-month-olds, provide one to two servings per day. Animal sources of iron (heme) are better absorbed than plant sources (nonheme).
Zinc	Zinc supports normal growth and immune development. Humans need constant zinc intake, as storage ability is limited. Six percent of older infants are not meeting their zinc requirements.[27]	*Six months to three years:* 3 milligrams	Beef (2.3 milligrams); beans (.5 to 1.5 milligrams); dark meat chicken (.8 milligrams); whole milk yogurt (.7 milligrams); whole milk (.5 milligrams); zinc-fortified cereals (varies)	Provide single-meat dishes rather than mixed-meal dishes to maximize zinc.[c] For example, ¼ cup cheerios (1 milligram), 1 ounce meat (1.7 milligrams), ¼ cup beans (.5 milligrams), and ½ cup yogurt (.7 milligrams), for a total of 3.9 milligrams.

Table 2.3 *(continued)*

Nutrient	Function	Recommended Daily Allowance (RDA)	Sources[a]	Comments
Vitamin D	Vitamin D aids in the absorption of calcium for bone mineralization, and plays a role in the prevention of chronic disease. From 10 to 78 percent of unsupplemented breastfed infants may be deficient depending on the time of year.[28]	*Six to twelve months:* 400 IU *Twelve to twenty-four months:* 600 IU	Salmon (264 IU); canned light tuna in oil (76 IU); whole milk (64 IU); flatfish, such as flounder or sole (33 IU); fortified cereals (varies); sunlight	Supplementation is recommended for breastfed infants. Sunlight is not a reliable source of vitamin D due to sunscreen use, excessive time indoors, pollution, exposure to sun at nonpeak times of day, higher altitudes, winter months, dark-colored skin, and excess weight.
Total fat	Fat is an important source of energy. It is best to obtain fat from a variety of sources.	*Six to twelve months:* 30 grams *Twelve to twenty-four months:* 30 to 40 percent of total calories	Breast milk, formula, full-fat yogurt, whole milk, cheese, butter, avocado, nut butters, vegetable oils	No need to count fat grams! Provide breast milk or formula, whole milk, full-fat yogurt, and cheeses, along with plant sources of fat. Cook with fat and avoid a very low-fat diet.
DHA[29]	DHA plays a critical role in retinal and brain development during the first twenty-four months of life.	*Six to twenty-four months:* 10 to 12 milligrams per kilogram of body weight • 10 pounds: 45 to 55 milligrams • 20 pounds: 90 to 110 milligrams • 30 pounds: 135 to 160 milligrams	Salmon (412 milligrams); fortified eggs (50 to 300 milligrams); canned light tuna in water (63 milligrams); fortified milk (16 milligrams)	Breast milk or formula provides adequate DHA. Gradually add such sources as fish at nine months. After one year, provide one to two servings of low-mercury sources of fish per week, or consider supplementation if your toddler won't eat fish.

[a] Unless otherwise specified, servings sizes are 1 ounce for meat or fish, ¼ cup for beans, and ½ cup for milk and yogurt. For more extensive food lists and references, see Appendix B. Source for baby food iron: U.S. Department of Agriculture, Agricultural Research Service. (2012). USDA National Nutrient Database for Standard Reference, release 25. Retrieved from www.ars.usda.gov/ba/bhnrc/ndl.

[b] The serving size for meat is a 2.5-ounce jar.

[c] Single servings of meat (pureed chicken or beef) provide more iron and zinc than mixed-meal baby food (pasta, vegetables, and meat).

Quick Facts About Nutrients for Baby

- **Iron and zinc:** Breast milk contains approximately .35 milligrams of iron per liter (there are four cups in one liter). Recommendations jump from .27 milligrams to 11 milligrams starting at six months.[7] Zinc, closely tied to growth and a strong immune system, steadily decreases in breast milk over the first six months.[30] By nine months, breastfed infants need to get 90 percent of their iron and zinc from complementary foods to meet their nutrient needs.[31] We agree with the AAP, and recommend meat as one of baby's first foods. Not only has it been shown to be tolerated in babies but also it provides iron and zinc, being a good, absorbable source of the two minerals.[32] Other first foods we recommend include iron-fortified cereals and various fruits and veggies.
- **Vitamin D:** For decades, cod liver oil (one teaspoon = four hundred IU) was widely used to prevent rickets, a severe bone disease, in babies and young children. This, along with the fortification of milk and formula with vitamin D, made rickets a forgotten disease. When breastfeeding made a comeback in the 1970s, rickets began to be reported in the United States and around the world.[33] We now know vitamin D plays a larger role in health than just preventing rickets. Low vitamin D levels can increase the risk of osteoporosis and fractures in adulthood; compromise immunity; and elevate the risk of autoimmune diseases, including type 1 diabetes and multiple sclerosis. Exclusively breastfed infants, especially those with darker pigmentation, are at highest risk for deficiency, as breast milk contains low levels of vitamin D (about twenty-five IU per liter).[25]
- **Fat (total and type):** In addition to the energy-rich diet needed by babies, fat is important for satiety and the absorption of fat-soluble vitamins. The best way to achieve appropriate levels of total fat is to keep children on breast milk or formula until one year, switch to whole milk after age one, and introduce full-fat yogurt and cheeses. There are no restrictions set on cholesterol and saturated fat during the first two years of life. Between nine and twelve months, and especially after one year, when liquid intake decreases, ensuring baby gets the right types of fats, especially DHA, is important.

Now that you have a good handle on the Fearless Five Nutrients, let's get into the nuts and bolts of feeding infants with our monthly feeding guide.

Fearless Tip

Babies don't need teeth to chew! Most can gum food if it is soft enough and dissolvable. Babies learn to chew long before they get most of their teeth.

Fearless Tip

The AAP recommends breastfeeding for at least one year, and the WHO recommends two. When you decide to wean, Nancy Mohrbacher, coauthor of *Breastfeeding Made Simple: Seven Natural Laws for Nursing Mothers,* recommends a gradual approach. Substitute one bottle or cup in place of a breastfeeding session, wait two to three days, replace another session, and repeat until you are done. If your breasts feel uncomfortable, pump to achieve comfort, and make the morning and night feeds the last ones to go. This same strategy can work in weaning baby off the bottle. Start with one feeding a day and gradually decrease until baby has transitioned to the cup.

Month-by-Month Summary

- **Four to six months:** Make sure baby is ready for that first meal! Start with a texture that is almost watery—maybe a little thicker than breast milk or formula—and transition to a pureed, smooth texture. Feed baby when she is not too hungry or tired. Expect baby to push out with her tongue (extrusion reflex) initially. If it's clear baby is not ready—if she seems distressed, cries, or turns her head away—stop the feeding and try again in a few days. Never force!

- **Six to eight months:** Transition your baby to pureed and mashed and lumpy food while giving her the opportunity to self-feed with soft finger foods that are easy to pick up. Introduce a sippy cup filled with breast milk or water, and allow her to hold it (and probably throw for a while!). Always follow your child's appetite and desire for more or less food.

- **Eight to ten months:** Food independence blossoms during this period. Transition baby from mashed and lumpy pureed food to ground, finely chopped foods or pieces of soft foods. Let baby go wild with the spoon, even though she will prefer to eat with her hands.

- **Ten to twelve months:** Babies are able to eat chopped food pieces (table food) with the family and can use a spoon with quite a bit of mess. Give baby many opportunities to self-feed. Transition to a straw cup and use open cups (filled with an inch of liquid).

- **Twelve to twenty-four months:** Because children are still in the rapid phase of growth, we suggest keeping them on a mostly nutrient-dense diet until the age of two. The AAP recommends discontinuing the bottle between twelve and fifteen months of age while encouraging the use of open cups. This stage is all about rapid changes in eating patterns that can be tough to keep up with! Table 2.4 provides you with all the juicy details about how to progress with feeding, and Table 2.5 helps you put it all together in a sample day.

> ### Fearless Fact
>
> By fifteen months, 30 percent of toddlers are consuming sugar-sweetened beverages daily, and by eighteen months, more than 70 percent are having something sweet every day![34] Sugar-sweetened beverages and the regular offering of sweets and other Fun Foods are not recommended for children under two. Other "no-no's" include switching to low-fat dairy before the age of two, not providing enough iron-rich foods, and serving more than twenty-four ounces of milk daily.

Feeding with Confidence: The Honeymoon Period

When it came time to start solids with her third child, Lisa knew exactly how to do it. "I am doing much better as far as introducing more variety, getting away from prepared baby foods sooner, and being more adventurous with Emily's food," she says. "I am giving her just about everything I can, even if I have to throw it in my blender for a few seconds to chop it finely!"

New parents may not realize that they are in the honeymoon stage of feeding. That's right, feeding is the easiest during this time because a majority of babies and young toddlers (but not all) actually eat what you give them. As we discussed in the last section, deciding WHAT to feed can be challenging, but once

Table 2.4 Infant and Young Toddler Step-by-Step Guide

	Four to Six Months	Six to Eight Months	Eight to Ten Months	Ten to Twelve Months	Twelve to Twenty-Four Months
Texture	Transition from watery to pureed foods.	Transition from pureed to lumpy foods.	Transition from lumpy to chopped foods.	Serve chopped finger foods.	Serve chopped foods. Baby can take small bites and eat firmer foods.
Breast Milk or Formula	Breast milk and formula are still priority nutrition. Breastfeed on demand and provide up to 32 ounces of formula per day. Slight decreases may be seen in the amounts taken.		Breastfeed on demand and continue to feed formula three to five times a day (6 to 8 ounces each time) between six and eight months and three to four times a day between nine and twelve months. Some babies will take more, some less.		Offer breast milk or whole milk.
Foods to Introduce					**Daily Goals[a]**
Beverages	None except breast milk or formula	Sips of water and no more than 4 ounces of juice per day, keeping breast milk and formula as priority fluids			Whole milk, breast milk, and water, no more than 4 to 6 ounces of juice
Fruits	Cooked and strained apples and pears, raw bananas and avocado	Mild, raw fruits, such as mangos,[b,c] pears, honeydew,[b] nectarines,[b] peaches,[b] cantaloupe,[b,c] papaya,[b,c] and 100 percent fruit juice	Grated apple (without skin), chopped strawberries[b] and blueberries, kiwi[b]	Quartered grapes (½ inch), chopped citrus fruits[b]	1 cup of all kinds of fruit (with baby taking bites from whole fruits with supervision)

Veggies	Sweet potatoes,[b,c] peas, green beans	Broccoli,[b,c] carrots,[c] cauliflower,[b] winter squash,[c] potatoes[b]	Beets, spinach,[c] kale,[b,c] summer squash	Tomatoes,[b] finely chopped lettuce, all other veggies	¾ cup of veggies, including blanched and thinly sliced veggies for dipping
Grains	Single-grain, iron-fortified whole grain cereal, such as rice, barley, oats, and wheat	Mixed-grain cereal; crackers; soft, dissolvable finger foods to try	Unsweetened cold cereal (Cheerios), small pieces of bread and pasta, other soft grains	All grains	Two 1-ounce servings: iron-fortified cereal served daily, small bites from sandwiches allowed, with the use of a fork or spoon for grains
Meat, Fish, and Poultry	Chicken, turkey, beef	Fish	Mixed meals	All kinds	1.5 ounces
Nonmeat Alternatives		Egg yolk; tofu; beans (black, kidney, garbanzo, and so on); lentils	No-salt-added cottage cheese	Whole eggs, thinly spread peanut or other nut butters on toast	Can be used to replace animal sources of protein
Dairy or Nondairy Alternatives		Full-fat yogurt or soy yogurt	Natural cheeses or soy cheeses		2 to 3 cups of milk (½- to ¾-cup serving size)

a   Listed are minimums to meet needs and for starter portions—always feed per your child's appetite, which varies.

b   This item is rich in vitamin C.

c   This item is rich in vitamin A (provide one of each daily).

Table 2.5 Putting It All Together[a]

	Four to Six Months	Six to Eight Months	Eight to Ten Months	Ten to Twelve Months	Twelve to Twenty-Four Months
Morning	Breast milk or formula	Breast milk or formula	Breast milk or formula	Breast milk or formula	Whole milk (transition to milk with breakfast)
Breakfast	1 to 2 tablespoons iron-fortified cereal mixed with breast milk or formula 1 to 2 tablespoons fruit[b] or veggie (1 cube[c])	2 to 4 tablespoons iron-fortified cereal mixed with breast milk or formula 2 to 3 tablespoons fruit[b] or veggie (1.5 cubes) 1 egg yolk mashed with milk	4 to 6 tablespoons iron-fortified cereal mixed with breast milk or formula 2 to 4 tablespoons fruit[b] or veggie (1 to 2 cubes or chopped) 1 egg yolk mashed with milk	Iron-fortified cereal 1 well-cooked scrambled egg Chopped soft cantaloupe[b,d]	1 egg cooked with chopped veggies (frittata) Iron-fortified oatmeal ¼ cup chopped strawberries[b] ½ cup milk
Midmorning	Breast milk or formula	Breast milk or formula	Breast milk or formula	½ cup yogurt with cut-up bananas	½ cup yogurt with cut-up bananas
Lunch	Breast milk or formula	Breast milk or formula	Breast milk or formula 2 to 4 tablespoons meat or meat alternative Serving of grain (2 crackers, ½ slice bread, or 3 to 4 tablespoons pasta) 2 to 4 tablespoons fruit or veggie (1 to 2 cubes or chopped)	Breast milk or formula ½ tuna melt, chopped up ¼ cup carrot slices[d]	4 ounces 100 percent fruit juice 1 ounce chopped chicken with mashed potatoes ¼ cup blanched, thinly sliced carrots[d] dipped in hummus

Late Afternoon	Breast milk or formula	1 to 4 tablespoons iron-fortified cereal mixed with breast milk or formula 2 to 3 tablespoons fruit or veggie[d] (1.5 cubes) ½ cup yogurt	2 to 4 tablespoons fruit (1 to 2 cubes or chopped) ½ cup yogurt	Breast milk or formula Grated apple (without the skin) ½ string cheese, quartered or stringed	½ cup milk 1 slice whole wheat toast with thinly spread peanut butter ½ cup grated apple
Dinner	Breast milk or formula 1 to 2 tablespoons cereal or meat 1 to 2 tablespoons fruit or veggie[d] (1 cube)	Breast milk or formula 2 to 3 tablespoons meat or nonmeat alternative Serving of grain (2 crackers or ½ slice bread) 2 to three 3 tablespoons fruit or veggie[d] (1.5 cubes)	Breast milk or formula 2 to 4 tablespoons meat or nonmeat alternative Serving of grain (2 crackers, ½ slice bread, or 3 to 4 tablespoons pasta) 2 to 4 tablespoons veggie[d] (1 to 3 cubes or chopped)	1 ounce chopped chicken with mashed sweet potato 3 tablespoons chopped green beans and chopped pear Water	1 cup milk (some saved for before bed) ½ cup black beans and rice topped with avocado ¼ cup green beans
Before Bed	Breast milk or formula	Breast milk or formula	Breast milk or formula	Breast milk or formula	Leftover whole milk from dinner if desired

a   Listed are minimums to meet needs and for starter portions—always feed per your child's appetite, which varies.

b   This item is rich in vitamin C.

c   For making baby food: 1 ice cube (in a tray) is equivalent to 2 tablespoons.

d   This item is rich in vitamin A (provide one of each daily).

babies are on finger foods, you can pretty much chop most foods and watch them go at it. For most kids, this "eating anything" stage will not last, so it's important to make sure you do as much as possible to prevent undesirable eating habits.

Researchers have begun examining the first two years of eating more closely for clues on how it translates to future eating habits. We know that HOW parents and caregivers feed little ones is vital. From reading hunger and fullness cues to offering a variety of food the whole family eats and keeping meals pleasant, what you do in this two-year period sets the stage for future feeding and eating.

Yet feeding is not just a means of transporting nutrients into little mouths; it is an act of love and a way to connect. In our fast-paced, gotta-get-them-to-eat environment, this important connection is often overlooked. International feeding expert Ellyn Satter defines the Feeding Relationship as "the complex of interactions that take place between parent and child as they engage in food selection, ingestion, and regulation of behaviors."[35] When you lay the foundation for a positive Feeding Relationship early, feeding is bound to be a rewarding experience for years to come.

What to Expect

More than at any other time in their lives, babies and young toddlers rely on parents to meet their basic needs. During the first year, babies develop an attachment to those who care for them, which is a desire to maintain closeness. By seven months, babies develop clear-cut attachments with their primary caregivers. The most important type of attachment is secure attachment, whereby little ones look to their caregiver as a comforting, secure base and often feel distressed when that caregiver is not there.[36]

What matters most in the development of attachment is a caregiver's *sensitive responsiveness* to the infant. This includes being able to read signals from the infant and then respond appropriately. Caregiver and baby become *in sync* with each other, and behaviors occur responsively, producing mutual satisfaction. Erik Erikson's theory of psychosocial development for the first year of life describes how babies learn to either *trust* or *mistrust* depending on their experiences.[37] Securely attached infants trust that their caregivers will provide consistent care and meet their needs. Caregivers who are less sensitive, or those who fail to respond accurately to baby's needs on a consistent basis, may have babies who are less attached and who learn to mistrust, increasing the risk of anxious responses.

Jane knew her baby, Lilly, didn't eat as much as other babies, plus she was on the lower end of weight percentiles. Jane started pushing food on Lilly at every feeding, and the dynamic became negative, with Lilly eventually refusing to eat. The vicious cycle continued, and Jane kept forcing until a diagnosis of failure to thrive was made. Jane wasn't responding appropriately to Lilly, so Lilly pushed back, eating suffered, and feelings of mistrust and anxiety developed around food and feeding.

Although there are a variety of ways caregivers meet basic needs, feeding is the most consistent and frequent interaction between baby and parent. When infants' needs aren't being met, they put all their energy into trying to get those needs satisfied, either by refusing to eat or by screaming for more food. This stress negatively affects food learning and exploration.

Whether you realize it or not, you are developing a Feeding Relationship with your child. Keeping feeding positive and reciprocal not only fosters attachment but also has been linked to better cognitive and social competence in babies.[38,39] In addition, your child's plastic brain, which we talk about next, can learn that eating is a fulfilling act or one that is riddled with frustration and unmet needs.

The Plastic Brain

During the first few years of life, baby's brain is experiencing dramatic growth and development. In fact, it is the only time the brain is considered "plastic," meaning it can develop and change in response to its environment.[40] This is powerful stuff!

Babies are born with hundreds of billions of nerve cells (neurons) at birth. But these neurons need to become organized for children to learn how to perceive, talk, think, and remember. As neurons respond to stimuli, they build connections in the brain called synapses. During the first few years, new synapses are being formed at the highest rate in a child's life. This is thought to be a "use it or lose it" proposition because, over time, the synapses used most often will stay, and the ones that aren't used will go. This normal organizing process, referred to as "pruning," helps the brain work more efficiently. After the pruning occurs in certain areas of the brain, the brain becomes less plastic, making those first few years essential in brain development.

How Your Baby Thinks

Some of the most important work on infants' cognitive development was done by learning theorist Jean Piaget. He pointed out how babies solve problems differently than older children. This two-year period beginning at birth, during which dramatic changes occur, is termed the sensorimotor stage. Piaget gave the stage its name based on how babies get to know the world by using their senses.[41]

There are six different substages in the sensorimotor stage, which are reviewed in Table 2.6. When babies begin solids they are in substage 3 (four to eight months), exploring objects and discovering more about their qualities. They might drop the sippy cup on the floor, for example, to learn more about the cup by watching it fall and hearing the sound it makes. During substage 4 (eight to

Table 2.6 Cognitive Development for Zero- to Twenty-Four-Month-Olds

Sensorimotor Stage	Feeding and Food-Related Behaviors
Substage 1: Reflexive behaviors (zero to one months)	Sucking
Substage 2: Purposeful behaviors; discovering body (one to four months)	Thumb sucking; placing hand in mouth
Substage 3: Discovering qualities of objects (four to eight months)	Touching and exploring food to discover texture and temperature Throwing cup and food
Substage 4: Developing object permanence (eight to twelve months)	Looking under plate or high chair for food Throwing food under table
Substage 5: Creative problem solving (twelve to eighteen months)	More food and cup throwing and stuffing food in mouth to discover what happens
Substage 6: Using symbols (eighteen to twenty-four months)	Using sign language, pointing for food, or saying "more," "no," or "all done"

twelve months), babies engage in active problem solving, realizing objects exist even when they are out of sight (for example, they might look for the lost ball under the couch). By the last substage, from eighteen to twenty-four months, toddlers no longer need to act out sequences to figure out the outcome (thank goodness!) as they start using symbols to represent objects.

When Challenges Arise

Although most babies will advance textures by the book, eat appropriate portions, and have steady weight gain, others may take longer to feed, have difficulty advancing textures, and gain weight more slowly. It's important to recognize and listen to what your child is telling you. Early treatment for potential problems is key, because stressful feeding can hurt the child's psychological and mental development, bonding with caregivers, and future relationship with food. As upsetting as feeding difficulties can be, avoid pushing, forcing, and creating stressful feeding conditions, as they make matters worse. The following list contains red flags for children ages six to twenty-four months that signal they need professional help:[42]

- Chewing or swallowing problems
- Gagging or vomiting frequently
- Not eating table foods by the first birthday, or still not eating pureed food at ten months
- Not drinking from cups by sixteen months
- Rejecting specific food groups (all having the same flavor and texture)
- Exhibiting consistently difficult behavior at meals; acting fussy

Also see Chapter Seven for more on feeding challenges.

Remember that individual texture preferences do not always indicate a problem. It's not uncommon for some babies to want to skip pureed food, only to do well on table foods. Other infants may want to stay on purees a bit longer. "With my daughter (she's now four), I fed her solids at six months, primarily my own purees," says Elana. "My son (nearly eight months) started solids the day he turned four months and spit out my purees. Both kids are growing steadily and so far are terrific eaters. Bottom line: be tuned in to your kids!"

The Ultimate Food Regulators

Early in the twentieth century babies were fed in a very prescriptive manner, meaning caregivers determined *how much* and *what* their infants ate. During this time, anorexia (the term used at the time to describe infant food refusal) became commonplace.[43] In 1939 pediatrician Clara Davis conducted one of the most ambitious and detailed food experiments to date.[44] She fed infants a varied diet of whole, unprocessed foods and allowed *them* to self-select the food they wanted by pointing, opening their mouth, or self-feeding, something unheard of at the time.

None of the infants in the study experienced anorexia. They all had a good appetite, weren't constipated, ate a variety of food, and thrived, with the average daily calories close to recommendations. This classic study helped change the approach to infant feeding from one of control to one of trust. It is now well accepted that parents should be in charge of providing babies with nutrient-dense food, and children should decide *what* and *how much* to eat. So if your child is developing normally and doesn't have any apparent feeding or growth problems, you can rest assured that he knows how to get enough food without your interference.

> **Fearless Fact**
>
> Distrust in a child's appetite can lead to ineffective feeding. According to one study, mothers who thought their child couldn't recognize appropriate cues of hunger and fullness were more likely to use restrictive feeding practices and fear their child would be overweight in the future. Further, mothers who used more pressure at feeding were more likely to see their child's appetite as smaller than that of other babies, and fear their child would be underweight in the future.[45]

"For the first many months of feeding solids, I limited my daughter to 'normal-size' servings and watched her become obsessed with food over time," says Megan. "It's been a long and challenging process, but we now have a toddler who eats calmly because she determines how much to eat."

Ian Paul, professor of pediatrics at Penn State College of Medicine, conducts research on infant feeding, and says subtle overfeeding practices are common. These include pushing baby to finish all the contents of the bottle or food, and paying more attention to how much she eats rather than hunger and fullness signals. Parents may feed baby at the first sign of crying, without trying other things, such as soothing or changing a diaper, which one study showed occurred more frequently for children with negative temperaments.[46] Finally, Paul says parents often feed to distract children or keep them entertained, which could lead to poor food regulation over time.

Remember, there is no time in a person's life, other than infancy, when he is able to regulate his food intake with such precision.[47] Preserving this tendency toward food regulation relies on cue recognition from parents and appropriate feeding practices.

Why the Honeymoon?

Although babies prefer sweet tastes and tend to reject bitter and sour, most have an open palate. Flavor learning research shows that frequent exposure to fruits and vegetables during infancy increases acceptance and liking.[48] And other studies reveal that children exposed to more fruits and vegetables at weaning are more likely to eat them when they are older.[49,50] Instead of focusing on facial expressions or how much a child eats of a new food, parents should focus on a child's *willingness* to eat an item. Yes, many children will make funny faces when a new food is initially given to them, but they will often open up their mouth to eat more, or try the food again at a later date. As discussed in Chapter Three, when food neophobia (fear of new foods) kicks in at around age two, toddlers become very reluctant to even try a food, much less keep eating it. Getting in as much variety as possible now, when children are more accepting, is important.

To sum up, letting children explore food and developing trust and attachment are of the utmost importance at this time. Accepting your own child's eating capabilities and appetite—and getting help if needed—will make feeding a positive experience, now and in the years to come.

Feeding That Works

Here we outline four key areas on which to focus when feeding your baby and young toddler, including connection, responsive feeding, the family table, and the when and where of meals. With each example we provide tips on what works and what doesn't.

Connection Versus Disconnection

We are taught so much about getting the right nutrition into baby that we often overlook an important element: *connection.* In our fast-paced world, we can feed on autopilot in the rush to get everything done. Some examples of this phenomenon include using hands-free feeders for bottles while strolling with baby, serving squeezable baby food in the car, and sitting children alone to eat while doing the laundry or dishes and rushing back to provide more food. We have unintentionally moved to a "disconnected" feeding style that robs parents of the joy of connected interactions with their children. Disconnection in feeding has a negative impact on the Feeding Relationship.

> **Fearless Tip**
>
> Watch your expectations! The Feeding Relationship suffers when there is a mismatch between parental expectations and a child's eating capabilities. If you can accept your child—and her eating personality—it will enhance every feeding interaction, and she will do better with eating.

Responsive Versus Unresponsive Feeding

During their first year together, parents and babies learn to read each other's nonverbal and verbal cues, and this reciprocal process helps form attachment and bonding. Responsive feeding is grounded in responsive parenting, which is timely, supportive, and contingent on a child's communication skills.[51] Here are three basic tenets of responsive feeding:

- Make the feeding location pleasant and free of distractions, with the child sitting comfortably facing others. Offer developmentally appropriate food as part of a predictable routine that is organized around times the child should be hungry.
- Encourage and attend to the child's signals of hunger and satiety.
- Attend to the child promptly in an emotionally supportive way.

Responsive feeding is an *active process,* as babies are more interested in eating when caregivers engage them by talking, looking them in the eye, and assisting them with feeding as needed. Among the most important aspects of responsive feeding are responding to hunger and fullness cues as well as giving children the opportunity to progress to self-feeding.

"I was always really bad at judging when to stop spoon-feeding a big eater at mealtime," says Megan. "I could never tell if my baby was just eating because I was putting the spoon in front of her, or because she was still hungry." For some kids the signs are very apparent, like turning away when being fed. For others, slowing the pace of eating or becoming easily distracted are key indicators. Table 2.7 summarizes the signs to look for when your baby has had enough or wants more.[52] Young toddlers can often say or gesture when they are done eating.

Table 2.7	Hunger and Fullness Cues: Four to Twenty-Four Months	
Age	**Hunger Cues**	**Fullness Cues**
Four to six months	• Fusses and cries • Smiles, gazes, and coos at caregiver during feeding to show she wants to continue • Actively moves head toward the spoon or attempts to swipe food toward mouth	• Decreases rate of sucking, or stops altogether • Spits out nipple • Is easily distracted; pays attention to surroundings more than food • Moves head away from spoon
Five to nine months	• Reaches for or points to food	• Slows pace of eating • Bats at spoon or turns head
Eight to eleven months	• Reaches for or points to food • Shows excitement when food is offered	• Slows down eating • Pushes food away or clenches mouth
Ten to twelve months	• Uses words and sounds to indicate hunger and wanting food	• Shakes head to say no • Plays with or throws food
Twelve to twenty-four months	• Uses more words or signs to communicate hunger, such as "more"	• Plays with or throws food • Says "all done," or can sign when finished

Source: Adapted from U.S. Department of Agriculture. (2007). Development of infant feeding skills. In *Infant feeding guide* (Chapter 2). Retrieved from http://wicworks.nal.usda.gov/infants/infant-feeding-guide.

Nonresponsive feeding lacks reciprocity between parent and child because the parent is too domineering, lets the child control feeding situations, or is uninvolved and neglectful during feeding. The result is over- or underfeeding and a strained Feeding Relationship. Instead of happening in a distraction-free environment, for example, nonresponsive feeding might occur in the car, on the run, or simply in a rushed format. Instead of responding to signals of hunger and fullness, a nonresponsive feeder pushes food or takes it away too soon despite obvious signals. And instead of promptly responding to children in supportive ways, a nonresponsive feeder either ignores, dominates, or gives in to the child instead of guiding him.

> **Fearless Tip**
>
> Work to maintain a calm, supportive, and interactive feeding environment. Stressed children may shut down or act out.

"Parents often overthink feeding," says Kristen Hurley, assistant professor of pediatrics at the University of Maryland School of Medicine. "This anxiety often leads them down the wrong path, but once they learn about responsive feeding they get it."

Joining the Family Table

Megan's second daughter, Charlotte, was still rejecting food six weeks after starting solids. Then, one day, Megan ate yogurt while feeding Charlotte, and her baby opened her mouth wide to imitate her. From that moment on, Charlotte ate most of what Megan offered. "It's funny because I know it's important to all eat together," she says. "But it never occurred to me that a seven-month-old would benefit from family meals too!"

> **Fearless Tip**
>
> Rotate different fruits, veggies, soft meats, beans, fish, and grains. As baby gets better at biting and chewing around age one, try different sandwiches.

In addition to providing a setting for learning by watching, family meals expose the child to the same foods, variety, and textures you'll want her to eat later on. Bringing baby to the table also teaches her that eating is a social act and not all about her. Pulling the high chair up to the table, allowing her to pick foods (as able), and putting her on your lap to investigate your plate encourages her to be part of the family's eating. And even though nightly family dinners may not be possible due to early bedtimes, make a point to eat with your child as often as you can (breakfast, lunch, and snacks, too).

The When and Where of Feeding

Although you want to stay responsive to your child's hunger and fullness cues at meals, it's important to structure eating times instead of feeding food on demand. Even young children benefit from predictable feeding routines as they learn that eating occurs at certain times and places. In the Infant and Young Toddler Feeding Guide presented earlier, we map out what a typical day of meals looks like as your child develops and grows. After your child makes the transition to solids at one year, offer him food every two to three hours, spacing feedings so your child is hungry, not famished. You also want most meals to happen in a designated area—for example, in the high chair at home, or when stopping to have a snack at a picnic table in the park.

> **Fearless Tip**
>
> While establishing your routine of eating, remember that hunger is still unpredictable, so have some healthy emergency food on hand just in case!

Teaching Your Child About Food

During the first two years, you are introducing your child to the world of food. You can maximize learning with everyday dialogue, encouraging exploration and teaching your baby the names of food items.

Everyday teaching happens whether you realize it or not. In Table 2.8, we outline the subtle influences you have on your child's learning about food and nutrition.

Getting Messy with It

Sensory integration is how the senses "come together" to make discoveries, including seeing, smelling, and touching. According to Melanie Potock, who was introduced earlier in this chapter, trying to keep kids clean by constantly wiping

Table 2.8 Everyday Teaching During the First Two Years		
Key Feeding Area	**Daily Dialogue**	**What It Teaches**
Connection	*"Let's see what we have for breakfast today—eggs, oatmeal, and fruit"* (while talking, make eye contact and respond lovingly).	Eating is social and a time to connect.
Responsive feeding	*"You are telling me your tummy is full and you are done. Let's stop eating now."*	Fullness is the reason to stop eating.
The family table	*"I know you want X, but we don't eat the same things every day. We'll have that again soon."*	Variety is the way we eat around here, and you are an important part of this family.
The when and where of feeding	*"Let's sit down to eat this snack so we can really enjoy it—and then go play."*	Eating is important and deserves focus and attention.

their mouth or not allowing them to play with and touch their food is a big mistake. She says, "Kids need to experience food with their entire sensory system; this is how they learn about all varieties of taste, temperature, texture, and more!"

We suggest getting ready for the mess by placing a big towel or mat under the high chair and stripping kids down to their diaper while they eat. When children refuse to eat a food, encourage them to touch, smell, and even play with it (you can get creative here!). Using the developmental milestone chart in Table 2.1, give babies finger foods, the spoon, and other utensils, and watch them gain the skills they will use for a lifetime.

The World of Food

Children's language skills tend to take off around the age of two, and for some kids earlier. Even when babies aren't talking, they are learning the names of different items. They may be saying words like "ball," "cat," and "dog," but they will also start to say the names of foods. Here we list convenient opportunities to teach your child about food, from daily meal interactions to shopping at the grocery store.

- At every meal, name the items on baby's plate and continue to say the names during the meal: "This is chicken, green beans, and sweet potatoes."
- When picking food at a grocery store or farmers' market, say the names and allow the child to help (if able).
- Young toddlers may be able to help with very simple tasks in the kitchen.
- Get a play kitchen with food, and go over the names.
- Use measuring cups, plasticware, plates, and food containers as toys and in the bathtub.

Remember, most of what babies and young toddlers learn comes from the daily interactions with and exploration of food. Keep it positive, fun, and simple, and they are likely to respond favorably.

Real Life Challenges for Infants and Young Toddlers

Should poo really turn colors? Is spitting up common after six months? Is it normal that my son only wants finger foods—and not the wonderful pureed food I make for him? Why is Susie's daughter using a spoon when mine just throws hers? Now that your baby is eating solid food, you're probably wondering if what you are experiencing is normal—or not! Here we cover several topics by showcasing real life challenges.

My Baby Is Constipated

Challenge: Jackie's eleven-month-old girl, Emily, was constipated. It was difficult to watch Emily strain and grunt, only to find a little pebble there. Emily had a milk-heavy diet, more than thirty-two ounces per day, along with other dairy products. Most of her fruit and veggies came from cooked, pureed items, and she was just learning to crawl, so she didn't move much during the day.

Diagnosis: The reason behind Emily's constipation has mostly to do with the WHAT of feeding: too little fiber and water along with little activity is a recipe for constipation.

Intervention: Jackie was instructed to reduce the amount of milk to twenty-four ounces and to increase water between meals. She added two to four ounces of fruit nectar daily to Emily's diet, which helps soften stools. She also offered

Emily chopped-up fresh fruits, cooked veggies, chopped raisins, dates, and whole wheat bread, and she swapped plain rice cereal for whole grain oatmeal. And she gave Emily plenty of opportunity to move.

Outcome: In about one week, Emily was having softer stools that were easier to pass.

What's normal: Stool frequency can range from three times daily to three times weekly, and the stool can vary from formed to semiformed.[53] The color often reflects what baby ate (for example, red for beets). Hard stools occurring for less than two weeks are not uncommon.

What's not: Signs for concern are loose or watery stools accompanied by fever; decreased eating and drinking; or signs of dehydration, such as fewer wet diapers, less play, sunken eyes, a sunken fontanelle, loss of skin turgor, and dry mucous membranes.[53,54] Also problematic are hard stools for more than two weeks that are causing distress.[55] Further, watch out for blood or mucous in the stool or frothy, foamy, oily, white stools. Call the doctor if any of these occur.

Fearless Tip

Try resolving constipation at home first by feeding two additional ounces of water each day and two ounces of pear or prune nectar, or apple juice. See Appendix B for a list of fiber-rich foods to add to baby's diet. For short-term diarrhea, give plenty of fluids (no juice) and provide a regular diet that includes such high-carbohydrate foods as bananas, rice, potatoes, and bread.

My Baby Is Vomiting After Meals

Challenge: Joan's sixteen-month-old daughter, Jane, was experiencing poor growth due to vomiting after meals. Her mom was giving her three large meals a day consisting of more than two cups of food (mostly pureed) and one cup of milk. After meals, with just a little movement, Jane would throw up her meal. Joan was spoon-feeding and pushing Jane to finish her meals, giving the remainder as a snack. She didn't incorporate regular snacks, only offering them as a backup after vomiting or when Jane was not eating what Joan thought was "enough."

Diagnosis: Joan was still serving pureed food instead of finger foods (WHAT). She wasn't practicing responsive feeding (HOW), and was pushing Jane to finish her meals, causing her to eat too much and vomit. In addition, Joan didn't provide the frequent, smaller meals kids at this age need.

Intervention: Instead of serving Jane three big meals, Joan needed to spread meals over six eating occasions throughout the day and before bed to avoid inducing reflux and vomiting. She needed to keep the baby upright during feeding and encourage self-feeding by giving Jane a variety of finger foods and allowing independence at meals. Joan was encouraged to practice responsive feeding by watching her baby's hunger and satiety cues, smiling, talking, and connecting at meals to make feeding more pleasant.

Outcome: After just a few days the vomiting stopped, adequate weight gain followed, and Jane and Joan started to enjoy mealtime.

What's normal: The "happy spitter" has frequent regurgitation (two or more times per day) but grows and eats well and shows no other signs of distress.

What's not: Regurgitation that gets worse with time or is accompanied by eczema; poor growth; breathing problems (gagging, choking, coughing, or wheezing); swallowing issues; or food refusal is not normal. Baby also should not be vomiting large amounts or contents that are green or yellow or look like coffee grounds or blood.[56]

> **Fearless Fact**
>
> Gastroesophageal reflux (GER), also called spitting up, occurs when items from the stomach *reflux* back into the esophagus, a phenomenon that decreases in babies over time. For example, more than half of infants under six months experience GER, compared to only 5 percent at twelve months.[53] Gastroesophageal reflux disease (GERD) is GER coupled with the problems discussed here, and needs a doctor's attention.

My Baby Won't Eat Pureed Food

Challenge: Alyssa was excited to start her six-month-old baby, Sheila, on solids, and began with homemade brown rice cereal, mixed with breast milk. Sheila turned her head and pushed any little bit out. Alyssa and her husband kept trying twice a day and continued to get the same response from Sheila: arching her back, avoiding eye contact, and crying when food touched her tongue.

Diagnosis: The reasons for this issue are not so straightforward. Sheila didn't seem ready for pureed food or like its texture much (WHY). Even though Alyssa and her husband tried to be positive, they were pushing (HOW) when Sheila was showing signs of disinterest. Also, some babies do not respond to being fed with the spoon or like the texture of purees, so offering finger foods can be beneficial (WHAT). Other reasons could be a medical problem like GERD or underlying food allergies.

Intervention: Alyssa was told to give Sheila a break from solid food for a week, and then to start back up and eat together as a family. Alyssa offered different appropriate foods, such as a soft banana, avocado slices, or soft pieces of meat, and periodically attempted spoon-feeding as well. She tried to keep meals pleasant by offering finger foods without pressure. If Sheila still wasn't taking solids by eight months, Alyssa would take her to see the doctor.

Outcome: After about three weeks, Sheila was eating avocado, carrots, zucchini, green beans, sweet potatoes, grated cheese, apples, whole wheat pasta, yogurt chips, and puffs. "She has a totally different attitude," says Alyssa. "She laughs and chats it up with us for about twenty minutes while we all eat together."

My Baby Has Been on Pureed Food Too Long!

Challenge: Jake, a fourteen-month-old boy, was served mainly pureed food because that was the only way his mom, Janet, could get fiber into him (he suffered from constipation). He didn't like pureed food and held out for the few table foods he got: fruit and peanut butter on bread. Meals dragged on for over forty-five minutes, and there was plenty of tension at the table. Jake was a heavy milk drinker, the foods he was offered had little added fat or salt, and his weight took a nosedive.

Diagnosis: Janet wasn't offering enough energy-rich, tasty foods (WHAT), and was refusing to allow Jake to feed himself because she wanted the control of feeding (HOW).

Intervention: Janet needed to offer Jake more table foods, such as pancakes or waffles with butter, soft meats or beans, cut-up fruit and veggies sautéed with olive oil, and other tasty and nutritious items. She also needed to foster independence and bonding, not only by offering Jake table foods but also by giving Jake the spoon to practice. Jake should eat with the rest of the family and have fun at meals. To address Jake's constipation, Janet added apple juice or nectar, kept milk consumption to no more than twenty-four ounces daily, and provided fruits and veggies at meals.

Outcome: Jake enjoyed meals and feeding himself, and in no time his constipation and weight problems were resolved. Mom and son became closer and more in sync.

What's normal: There is a wide range of normal when it comes to feeding progression. According to a 2004 study, by six months 68 percent of babies are grasping food with their hands, and this number jumps to 98 percent by eleven months.[57] Whereas only 29 percent can self-feed with a spoon by fourteen months, 88 percent are successful at twenty-four months. Most can drink from a sippy cup by one year of age.

What's not: Not taking solids, such as pureed food, by ten months and not eating table foods by one year are potential problems. Constant gagging, choking, and distress with eating are also red flags that signal the need for an evaluation.

> **Fearless Tip**
>
> Check the developmental milestone chart in Table 2.1, and give your baby the opportunity to feed himself when the time is right.

My Baby Drinks Milk All Day Long

Challenge: Rachel's twenty-month-old son, Eli, drank milk with meals and throughout the day with a sippy cup. He had a low appetite and didn't eat well. Rachel liked that he got milk, as she knew it had protein and other important nutrients. When Eli seemed to be becoming more tired and less energetic, Rachel took him to the doctor. He was diagnosed with anemia, and Rachel was stunned: "I thought milk was good for him, how could this happen?"

Diagnosis: Rachel provided too much milk (WHAT) and allowed Eli to drink it whenever he wanted (HOW).

Intervention: Rachel was told to decrease Eli's milk consumption by keeping it to sixteen ounces, using a regular cup (not the sippy cup) and providing it at the end of the meal, serving only water between meals. She added iron-rich foods, such as soft cooked meats, iron-fortified cereals softened with milk, and chopped raisins, along with vitamin C–rich sources, in addition to the iron supplement the doctor ordered. Finally, she provided three meals and two to three snacks timed well (every two to three hours).

Outcome: Although Eli complained at first, his eating drastically improved, and his iron deficiency were resolved within a few months.

What's normal: After one year, baby should transition to an open cup, and should be drinking no more than twenty-four ounces of milk and four to six ounces of juice per day with meals or as part of a snack.

What's not: Consuming too much milk (more than twenty-four ounces) and juice (more than four to six ounces) per day leads these liquids to crowd out other nutrient-dense foods, resulting in an imbalance of nutrients, such as iron.

> **Fearless Fact**
>
> Young toddlers have small stomachs, about the size of their fist, and can easily fill up on liquids. Although some will eat less due to filling up, others may not adjust their eating to compensate for the additional calories, resulting in excessive energy intake.

My Baby Isn't Drinking Enough Milk

Challenge: Thirteen-month-old Laynee transitioned to whole milk in a bottle and was refusing milk from a cup. Her mom, Amanda, was trying to get rid of the bottle, but when she gave milk in the cup, Laynee wouldn't take it. Amanda asked: "What is the minimum amount of whole milk a thirteen-month-old needs?"

Diagnosis: Although some children transition to the cup easily, Laynee preferred the bottle over the cup and was fighting the transition (WHY).

Intervention: Amanda was advised to slowly phase out the bottle by fifteen months (eighteen months at the latest), giving Laynee time to accept drinking from a cup. Although the recommended daily amount of milk for this age is about two cups to match calcium requirements, she was informed that children can drink less than that as long as they get other sources of calcium. For example, to meet the recommended daily allowance of seven hundred milligrams for this age group, an infant could consume an ounce of cheese or a half cup of yogurt (two hundred to three hundred milligrams) plus a cup and half of milk. The AAP also recommends a vitamin D supplement of four hundred IU for children who are not getting enough of this vitamin from their diet.

Outcome: One month later, Amanda says, "Things are actually going great! She is drinking ten to twelve ounces of milk a day, along with yogurt and cheese, and she is getting her calcium!"

My Baby Isn't Gaining and Growing Well

Challenge: Mary was ten months old, and her parents, Sue and Jon, piled on the homemade pureed fruits and vegetables. They took pride in the wide variety and amounts of food Mary would eat at meals, and were stunned when their daughter was diagnosed with inorganic failure to thrive.

Diagnosis: Mary was still breastfeeding but wasn't getting as much milk as they thought. And although the fruits and veggies Sue and Jon provided were healthy, they were ultimately deficient in the calories, fat, and other important nutrients (like iron and zinc) their child needed to grow (WHAT).

Intervention: Mary's parents were instructed to include foods with fat, protein, and starch—such as eggs, butter on toast, whole grain cereals, soft meats, full-fat dairy, and avocado—in her diet. They were to scale back fruits and veggies, but were still to include them as part of meals.

Outcome: After a change in diet, Mary started to gain weight and show steady growth.

> **Fearless Fact**
>
> Potential causes of FTT include insufficient breast milk or formula, difficulty transitioning to solid food, excessive juice consumption, a low-fat and low-calorie diet, and poor parent-child bonding.

My Baby Wants to Eat All the Time!

Challenge: Jackie was about one year old and at the 85th percentile in terms of weight for length. She loved to eat large amounts, and seemed to want food all the time. Jackie's mom, Beth, tried to keep her to normal portion sizes, but her daughter never seemed satisfied and was becoming obsessed with food.

Diagnosis: Jackie had a bigger-than-average appetite (and size!), which wasn't being satisfied with the normal-size portions her mother was giving her, fueling her desire to eat. Beth was already providing Jackie with a wholesome variety of foods, and with structure, so that was not an issue.

Intervention: Instead of watching portions, Beth was taught to be more responsive to Jackie's hunger and fullness, allowing her to eat until she signaled she was done. Although Jackie's weight was above average, it tracked on a steady curve, meaning there were no big jumps up, and did not appear to be an issue.

Outcome: Once Jackie was in charge of how much she was eating, she became much calmer at meals. Rather than going up like her mom feared, Jackie's weight stayed consistent, and she no longer obsessed about food.

What's normal: You should look for steady growth, even at higher or lower percentiles, without major fluctuations over time.

> **Fearless Fact**
>
> Causes of excess growth acceleration may include overfeeding, low responsiveness to hunger and fullness cues, early introduction of solid foods (at under four months of age), and providing excessive amounts of energy-dense food and drinks.

What's not: Red flags pertaining to weight include sudden increases or decreases (that is, crossing two percentile lines on growth charts in either direction), and weight for length values above the 95th or below the 5th percentile. Remember that red flags do not always indicate a problem! Yet parents can get peace of mind—and find resolution when needed—by checking the WHAT, HOW, and WHY of feeding.

We hope these examples help you find easy solutions to any problems you might encounter with your constantly changing baby. Up next are tips for making baby food along with our real, easy recipes.

Real, Easy Recipes for Infants and Young Toddlers

Here we cover what you'll need to get started, with tips for the easy preparation of baby food and guidelines for stepping up purees and finger foods. We also cover more advanced finger foods in the next chapter, so jump over there for more ideas.

What You'll Need

- *High chair or strap-in chair:* A good high chair provides support, allows your child to sit comfortably, and is easy to clean! Portable chairs come in handy when eating elsewhere.
- *Steamer basket:* Inserting a steamer basket into a pot is key for cooking vegetables and some fruits.
- *Fork or potato masher:* Sometimes all you need to do is mash the item yourself with the most basic equipment.
- *Blender or the like:* A blender, food processor, or other specialty item (for example, the Magic Bullet blender) is needed to mash, chop, or puree food to the desired consistency, especially for big batches.
- *Ice cube trays:* BPA-free ice cube trays are needed to store food in the freezer. Each cube equals about two tablespoons of food.
- *Freezer bags:* Transfer frozen items to a freezer bag and use a marker to label and date it.

Optional
- *Slow cooker:* We love using the slow cooker, as it makes food soft and flavorful with minimal effort.
- *Food grinder or mill:* This is a manually powered grinder that is typically used for soups, mashed potatoes, and sauces. It's portable and good for small batches, and it allows you to puree food while traveling.
- *Toddler plates and utensils:* Easy-to-grab utensils and plates that stick to the high chair tray can be helpful, especially when children self-feed.
- *Sieve:* The woven (mesh or net) screen smoothes food even more, which may be helpful at the very beginning of feeding.
- *Mesh feeders:* These gadgets allow baby to nosh on whole foods that are hard to chew or frozen (great when baby is teething) and that are typically choking hazards when given without the mesh feeder. You can use apples, chunks of melon, and frozen fruits like grapes. Remember to clean them right after use.

Safety and Storage Guidelines

- *Keep it clean:* Make sure your hands, cutting boards, and cooking items are thoroughly cleaned and washed before you use them, and that you separate cutting boards for animal foods (such as meat and poultry) from cutting boards for plant foods. Avoid using cutting boards with crevices or cuts.
- *Wash produce and store items safely:* Wash produce before use and store meat, poultry, and fish safely, keeping them away from—and below—other foods like fruits and vegetables. Cook ground meat (beef, pork, veal, or lamb) to an internal temperature of 160°F; steaks, roasts, and chops (beef, veal, pork, or lamb) to 145°F; and poultry products to 165°F.
- *Check expiration dates:* Always check expiration dates and avoid using food from rusted, dented, bulging, or leaking cans or jars, or food from cans or jars with missing labels and dates.
- *Follow smart storage guidelines:* After preparing items, store them in the fridge or freezer promptly. To freeze, put them in ice cube trays or as one- to two-tablespoon portions on a clean cookie sheet covered with plastic wrap or tinfoil. When the food is frozen, transfer it to freezer bags, and label and date them. When the time comes, follow the reheating instructions in Table 2.9.[58] Use a small bowl when feeding baby, and throw out what you don't use.

Foods to Make "On the Spot"

- *Banana:* Simply mash the banana to the desired consistency using a fork, and mix it with breast milk or formula. Bananas can also be mixed with cereal or served alone.
- *Sweet potato:* Punch both sides of the potato multiple times with a fork, wrap it loosely in a paper towel, and put it in the microwave for about two to four minutes on each side (cooking time depends on size). After letting it cool, cut the potato in half and spoon out the flesh, mixing it with breast milk or formula until it reaches the desired consistency.
- *Avocado:* Mash a ripe avocado with a fork and mix it with breast milk or formula, or mix it with cereal or yogurt for a thicker consistency.
- *Egg yolks:* To boil eggs, put the desired number of eggs in a pan with water and place it on medium-high heat. When the water boils, turn to low heat for

Table 2.9	Baby Food Storage Guidelines			
Food Item	**Use After Prep**	**Refrigerator Storage**	**Freezer Storage**	**Reheating**
Meat, poultry, pork, eggs, dairy, fish	Serve items immediately, and throw them out if they have been left unrefrigerated for more than two hours.	Twenty-four hours	Freeze items for up to one month. Do not refreeze them after use.	Remove cubes or other pieces from the freezer bag and defrost them in the refrigerator or under cold running water—or simply reheat from frozen (do not leave the items out at room temperature). Thoroughly reheat refrigerated or frozen home-prepared baby foods to 165°F.
Fruit, vegetables, grains		Two days		

Source: Adapted from U.S. Department of Agriculture, Food and Nutrition Service. (2002, July). Feeding infants: A guide for use in the child nutrition programs; Chapter 12. Making baby food. Retrieved from http://teamnutrition.usda.gov/Resources/feeding_infants.html.

twelve additional minutes. Remove the eggs promptly and place them in cooled water to stop the cooking process. Remove the yolks and add water, breast milk, or formula to reach the desired consistency. Egg yolks are great mixed in cereal or yogurt.

• *Raw mild fruit:* Unlike with hard fruits, such as apples and pears, you don't need to cook soft fruits. Babies can consume ripe, mild (and skinless) fruits, such as cantaloupe and mango. If the fruit is super-ripe, you can mash it with a fork; otherwise throw it in the blender.

Stepping Up the Purees

In addition to preparing food on the spot, you can cook, puree, and store vegetables, beans and legumes, meat, and grains very easily. The instructions here are followed by some sample recipes. Once baby accepts a plain pureed food, feel free to add herbs and spices, onions, and healthy fats when cooking, while keeping the sugar and salt low.

Vegetables (and Fruit)

Check out the feeding chart in Table 2.4 for suggested first veggies. Although spinach, beets, turnips, carrots, and collard greens contain higher amounts of nitrates, which in rare cases can cause a certain type of anemia called methemoglobinemia, the AAP says this is only a concern for babies under three months of age.

- *Cook:* Place veggies in a steamer basket in a pot with a little water and cover. Or microwave frozen veggies, following the directions on the package.
- *Boost the flavor:* Try sautéing the cooked veggies with olive oil and garlic; prepare them Asian-style with oil, a touch of soy sauce, and ginger; or roast them to bring out their natural sweetness. See Appendix D for more vegetable preparation ideas.
- *Puree:* After cooking and flavoring, puree or mash food to the desired consistency in a blender or food processor, using liquid from the steaming or low-sodium or homemade broth. To save time, puree or mash the same veggies you are eating for dinner.

Meat, Poultry, and Fish

Before cooking meat, poultry, and fish, remove visible fat, skin, and bones. Don't feed babies raw or partially cooked meat, poultry, or fish, as this can cause food poisoning.

- *Cook:* There are many different ways to cook meat. We like the slow cooker, but you can also boil, poach, or roast. Fish can also be baked or grilled. If you're having some for dinner, make extra to puree and store.
- *Boost the flavor:* Cook meat in low-sodium broth with onions, garlic, and other seasonings. Use darker meat for babies, as it's not only softer but also higher in iron.

- *Puree:* Cut the meat, poultry, or fish into small pieces and add water, broth, or the juice from cooking, and puree until the desired texture is reached. Chicken, turkey, lamb, and fish tend to work best, and warmer meat is easier to puree than cold.

Dried Beans

- *Cook:* Follow the directions on the package for cooking dried beans on the stove top, or soak the beans overnight and cook them in your slow cooker for eight-plus hours until they are soft enough to puree or mash. To save time you can use canned beans, but be sure to rinse them well to decrease sodium.
- *Boost the flavor:* Cook beans in low-sodium broth with onions; garlic; and seasonings like cumin, chili powder, onion powder, and garlic powder.
- *Puree:* Add water or broth and puree to the desired consistency.

Grain Products

- *Cook:* Boil pasta, such as macaroni or spaghetti, until soft. Rice, oats, barley, and other grains can be cooked by following the directions on the package.
- *Boost the flavor:* Cook grains in low-sodium broth instead of water, and boost the flavor with sautéed onions, garlic, mushrooms, and other veggies.
- *Puree:* Add water or broth and puree to the desired consistency.

Five Easy Baby Food Recipes

Slow Cooker Chicken Puree

Ingredients

¹⁄₃ onion, cut into rings

3 garlic cloves, halved

½ pound skinless, boneless chicken thighs

1 cup homemade or low-sodium chicken broth

Directions

Place the sliced onions on the bottom of the slow cooker, followed by the chicken. Top with garlic cloves and broth. Cook the chicken on high for 3 to 4 hours, or on low for 5 to 6 hours (check temperatures and doneness, as cook times vary with different slow cookers). Take the chicken out and place it on a dish until it has cooled a bit. Puree the chicken with the leftover broth.

Makes: About seven 2-tablespoon servings

Key nutrients per serving (baby percent nutritional requirements [%NR]): Iron (2), zinc (7), magnesium (4), niacin (22)

Garlicky Green Puree

Ingredients

1 head broccoli, washed and cut, or 12-ounce bag (about 6 cups raw)

2 teaspoons oil

1 or 2 cloves garlic, minced

Directions

Steam the broccoli until it is tender (test with a fork). When the broccoli is done, place it in a strainer and put the oil in a pan with garlic. Once the garlic sizzles, add the broccoli and sauté for a couple of minutes. Puree with leftover steamed water to the desired consistency.

Makes: About fifteen 2-tablespoon servings

Key nutrients per serving (baby %NR): Iron (3), zinc (8), magnesium (14), potassium (22), vitamin A (8), and vitamin C (67)

Homemade Apple Sauce

Ingredients

4 apples (red delicious, gala, or McIntosh), peeled and cut into 1-inch pieces

¾ cup water

¼ teaspoon cinnamon

1 teaspoon lemon juice

Directions

Put all the ingredients in a large pot and mix. Bring the mixture to a boil, then lower the heat and simmer (covered) for 15 to 20 minutes or until softened. Use a slotted spoon to scoop out the apples (leaving some water in the pan), and mash on the spot (for a thick texture). For a smoother texture, blend with more water from cooking.

Variations: Try this same recipe with pears, but use ground ginger instead of cinnamon.

Makes: About ten 2-tablespoon servings

Key nutrients per serving (baby %NR): Potassium (4)

Baby Pinto Beans

Ingredients

1 cup dried pinto beans

1½ cups water

1½ cups low-sodium chicken or vegetable broth

¼ onion (chunk)

¼ teaspoon cumin

¼ teaspoon garlic powder

Directions

Rinse and drain the beans. Then add all of the ingredients to the slow cooker. Cook on high for about 8 hours, or until the beans soften. Check during cooking to see if more water is needed. Puree to the desired consistency.

Quick Tip: Serve with avocado.

Makes: About thirteen 2-tablespoon servings

Key nutrients per serving (baby %NR): Iron (8), magnesium (26), manganese (30), zinc (13), potassium (25), folate (85)

Baby Banana and Mango Oats

This recipe is courtesy of Estela Schnelle, registered dietitian and blogger at Weekly Bite.

Ingredients

¼ cup quick-cooking oats

½ cup water (or breast milk or formula)

½ banana

¼ cup chopped mango

Directions

Combine oats and water in a small pot, and cook over medium heat for about 5 to 8 minutes (or until the oats are fully cooked). Set the oats aside to cool. Add the banana and mango to a food processor or blender and blend until smooth. Once the oats have cooled, pour the banana and mango mixture over the oats. Use a spoon to mix the fruit and oats together.

Makes: Two servings (or one serving for a big eater)

Key nutrients per serving (baby %NR): Iron (5), zinc (13), vitamin C (20), potassium (25), folate (22)

Mix and Match

Once baby accepts most single food items, you can start to mix and match, putting together balanced meals, as shown in Table 2.10.

Fab Finger Foods

Parents are often thrown off by the short-lived baby food stage, asking *What do I feed now?* Baby can eat much of what you are eating as long as the food is soft and cut into small pieces. Table 2.11 gives you some ideas for finger foods. Then it's on to Chapter Three for information about and recipes for older toddlers and preschoolers.

Table 2.10	Mixing and Matching Baby Food	
Try This . . .	**With This . . .**	**Tip**
Whole milk yogurt	Fruit, veggie, avocado, salmon	Yogurt makes a great base food. Serve it daily to provide beneficial bacteria.
Whole grain cereal	Mashed egg yolk, fruit and veggie purees	Because of the iron-absorbing vitamin C they provide, cantaloupe, mango, peaches, kiwi, strawberries, and jarred organic fruits (with added vitamin C) make the perfect addition to iron-fortified cereals.
Meat, poultry, fish	Potatoes, fruit, veggies, whole grains	You can add extra ingredients during cooking—just throw everything in a slow cooker or pot!
Beans	Veggies and tomatoes (canned tomatoes; tomato paste; or cut, whole tomatoes)	Vitamin C–rich tomatoes make a good and tasty complement to beans. You can also serve beans with meat, poultry, and fish.
Tofu, other soy products	Green and red peppers, broccoli, cauliflower, kale	Choose vitamin C–rich veggies alongside vegetarian protein sources.

Table 2.11 Finger Food Ideas		
Food Group	**Food Items**	**Tips!**
Protein	Chopped soft meat and fish, scrambled eggs, chopped boiled eggs, cooked tofu, soft beans	Tough meat is a choking hazard. Try low-mercury sources of fish (see Appendix G). Serve beans and tofu with vitamin C–rich fruits or veggies.
Veggies	Chopped sweet or white potatoes, chopped steamed veggies, soft tomatoes, thinly sliced blanched veggies for dipping, frozen peas (heated or thawed)	Boil, bake, or microwave sweet or white potatoes. Steam veggies (roast them with olive oil for a flavor booster). Always have some ready to go in the fridge.
Fruit	Chopped, soft fruit	Peel and grate harder fruits, such as apples.
Whole grains	Pasta, iron-rich cereals (Cheerios), pieces of bread, other whole grain dishes	Get baby using the spoon with brown rice and quinoa dishes.
Dairy	Grated natural cheeses	Let baby practice eating yogurt with a spoon.
Healthy fats	Thinly spread nut butters on toast, avocado, oils for cooking	Spoonfuls of nut butters are a choking hazard.
All-in-one meals	Salmon cakes, veggie or bean burgers, frittatas, meatloaf, turkey burgers, lasagna, fruit-filled pancakes, sandwiches (grilled or cold)	Prepare these meals ahead of time and freeze them, chopped up, for quick meals later on. When possible, add in extra veggies.

CHAPTER 3

Fearless Feeding for Your Toddler and Preschooler (Two to Five Years)

The toddler and preschool years are a time when many parents start down a fearful feeding path. There's the worry of providing the right nutrition and dealing with erratic appetites and the struggles for independence that show up at the table. We help you skip the food battles by giving you a deeper understanding of nutritional needs, growth, and cognitive development at this stage, showcasing why positive feeding strategies really do work. You can do this!

Nutrition in Practice: Fitting It All In

When Celia's son, Henry, was close to two years old, he became more picky and eventually became suspicious of every vegetable. He even gave up corn on the cob, one of his most beloved foods. "I cannot for the life of me get my two-and-a-half-year-old son to eat vegetables, at all, in any form," she says. "He is very wary of any new foods, especially with textures that are uncomfortable for him. This frustrates me to no end."

In this developmental stage of eating, ages two to five, the honeymoon phase of feeding ends. It's usually a gradual change, but by age two many kids take a turn in the eating department. They go from eating everything to being much more selective. Their appetite seems to disappear, but will return on random days when they can't put enough food away.

If you're worried about nutrition during this phase, you're not alone. We've received countless messages from parents concerned that their toddlers and preschoolers have stopped drinking milk, never touch vegetables, or only want bread. Although these concerns are understandable, they can almost always be quelled with the right information. As you will learn shortly, your child is once again changing, which explains the WHY behind her eating habits.

The first step to becoming a Fearless Feeder of your toddler and preschooler is getting your arms around the nutritional issues—and feeling confident that you can meet your child's needs with foods and supplements, if necessary. This section primarily focuses on the WHAT of feeding, including information about nutrition and age-appropriate food choices, with the goal of simplification.

What to Expect

Although growth slows after a child's first birthday, it declines even more after age two and remains relatively stable until the next major growth spurt—puberty.

> ### Fearless Fact
>
> Slowed growth means slowed appetite. Around age two, growth slows and stabilizes, with average gains of 4.5 to 6.5 pounds and 2.5 to 3.5 inches per year. Consistent growth, not appetite, is how pediatricians track nutritional status and progress.

Your independent-minded child is active and coordinated enough to run fast, jump, and move quickly. During this period, fat stores decrease (as does the "potbelly" described in Chapter Two), limbs and trunk lengthen, and a leaner body emerges as toddlers turn into preschoolers. This slowed growth shows up in appetite, which often plummets.

By five to six years of age, body fat declines to its lowest point in childhood before it starts increasing again, a phenomenon called the "adiposity rebound." Yet there is a concern about growth acceleration in this age group, as obesity rates in two- to five-year-olds have more than doubled over the past three decades.[1] Experts believe this is a critical period: children with early adiposity rebound, who gain extra weight before age five or six (instead of thinning out), may be at increased risk of obesity throughout childhood and the adult years.[2]

We don't like harping on obesity statistics, but we do want to make you aware of growth norms, so you can detect when something isn't quite right. Tracking growth is important for children: you can use growth charts, and after your child reaches age two, you can use his body mass index (BMI) as a weight and health guide (www.cdc.gov/growthcharts /clinical_charts.htm#Set1). The BMI takes into account your child's weight in relation to stature, with desired percentiles between the 5th and 85th.

> **Fearless Fact**
>
> If your child falls outside of the desired growth percentiles, it doesn't always indicate a problem. Some children are programmed to be bigger or have more muscle mass, whereas some are genetically small. You mainly want to see your child's growth be relatively stable, with no drastic jumps in either direction. For troubleshooting weight concerns, see Chapter Seven.

After a child turns two, yearly checks at the pediatrician are the norm. If you are concerned about your child's growth at any time, make an appointment with your pediatrician without alarming your child.

Nutritional Changes

After age two, children come out of the "critical nutrition" period, and growth reaches a new, stable level. Iron needs, and the risk of iron deficiency, decrease somewhat, and docosahexaenoic acid (DHA) stops being deposited into the brain and retina at a high rate.[3] Even though the major brain growth spurt is over, the brain continues to grow and develop, reaching 90 percent of adult brain size by age five.[4] Although research concerning DHA is limited after the age of two, it's still an important part of the diet.

By the time children reach their fourth birthday, their calcium needs expand to that of most adults, as young children experience increased bone growth and skeletal formation.[5] Children also need adequate vitamin D to absorb calcium. After the age of two, fat needs decrease, but fat nevertheless remains important for adequate growth and development. Fat is also needed to absorb the fat-soluble vitamins A, D, E, and K. Some parents make the mistake of limiting fat to less than 25 percent of calories, which can negatively affect growth and increase appetite.[6]

Your child is becoming a master at feeding himself during this period—using his hands and utensils, and drinking from open cups. Even though self-feeding can still be messy, children benefit developmentally from it, and they will continue to get better at it as their fine motor skills improve. It is not uncommon for children with speech delays also to have feeding issues, as the same muscles used for eating and drinking are used for speech.[7] If your child appears to be behind in self-feeding, in accepting different textures, and in drinking from a cup, visit Chapter Seven to see if your child will benefit from additional help. Remember that chewing and swallowing functions are not fully developed until age eight, and children aren't able to use a grinding motion until age four, so cutting up foods and supervision at meals are paramount.

> **Fearless Fact**
>
> The preference for sweet foods in childhood is biologically driven and universal.[8] Researchers hypothesize that this is a protective function that has evolved because sweetness signals "energy-richness" (needed for growth), and bitter and sour foods signal potential toxins. Kids can learn to like a variety of foods with time, patience, and exposure.

With budding language, children are able to ask for what they want—and aren't always requesting the healthy foods they ate before. In fact, young children are drawn to energy-rich, high-carbohydrate foods over lower-calorie, more bitter-tasting vegetables. This preference for sweet and energy-dense foods, such as fruit, desserts, and juices, may be annoying to parents, but it is normal and to be expected. Continue to offer rejected items, as repeated exposure and tastes (even spitting food out!) all work toward the goal of food acceptance.

Food Preferences

Children's preferences at this stage are constantly changing, and it will seem as if what they like today, they dislike tomorrow. It's also common for toddlers to go through "food jags," when they want to eat the same food for days in a row. Remember, food and eating are novel to young children—and they will favor certain foods the same way they do toys.

"My son is in the stage of liking something one minute, but not the next," says Amy, mom of three-year-old Theodore. "Sometimes he will only eat fruit all day. Some days he barely seems to eat at all. If it were up to him, he'd eat fruit snacks, Mini-Wheats, and mandarin oranges for every meal."

Despite the challenges that go along with this period, parental influence is strongest in early childhood, when food preferences are being formed. You get to role-model, and you determine the food environment and the types of foods your child is exposed to. Yes, children may prefer to eat Fun Foods, which we never recommend denying, but you get to decide how often they're available compared to nutritious items.

> ### Fearless Fact
>
> According to research, roughly half of children's food preferences come from their experience with food and what is familiar.[9] The other half of their preferences are related to biologically determined factors, such as preferences for sweet tastes. Bottom line: early and rich experiences with a variety of nutritious foods increase the quality of a child's diet now and in the future.

To summarize, this slow period of growth translates to decreased appetite and interest in food. This may not occur in every child—some will continue to have a strong appetite and eat a good amount at mealtimes. Most toddlers and preschoolers will have erratic food intake along with ever-changing food preferences. Parents help shape these preferences by providing a variety of nutritious foods. Although getting the needed nutrition into little ones can be tricky, it's not as difficult as parents think.

Food for Thought

Before digging into the Fearless Food Guide, there are some important things you need to know about, including nutrition pitfalls, nutrition myths, and important transitions during this stage.

Nutrition Pitfalls

As demonstrated in Table 3.1, this developmental stage is a vulnerable period in which not-so-good eating habits can take root. For example, children tend to eat

Table 3.1 Top Nutrition Pitfalls for Toddlers and Preschoolers		
Nutrition Pitfall	**Reality**	**Health Consequences**
Getting away from fruits and vegetables	Twenty-five percent of toddlers do not eat fruits and vegetables on any given day.[10]	Children have inadequate intake of potassium and fiber. Healthy foods become less preferred and less familiar.
Eating processed and dessert-type snacks frequently	Almost 90 percent of preschoolers consume one or more energy-dense snack food or beverage every day.[10]	Children have higher-than-recommended intakes of saturated fat and sugar. They acquire a taste for energy-dense food.
Consuming too many calorie-containing beverages	Fruit juice consumption is double what is recommended by the American Academy of Pediatrics (AAP). Fruit punch, the leading sugar-sweetened beverage among two- to five-year-olds, has been on the rise for two decades.[11]	Too many calorie-containing liquids can displace other nutritious foods, and can increase the risk of over- and underfeeding and nutrient deficiencies, such as iron deficiency.[12,13]
Overusing sippy cups	Sucking on sippy cups filled with milk, juice, or juice drinks allows sugar (even natural sources) to stay in the mouth longer.	Almost one-third of two- to five-year-olds have an increased risk of tooth decay from overusing sippy cups.[14]

fewer fruits and vegetables, consume an excessive amount of juice, and get plenty of Fun Foods. This has implications not just for health but also for the formation of taste preferences.

Learning about development can help put your child's eating in perspective. Once Janice, mom of four-year-old Grace, understood that slowed growth and appetite were common during this stage, she could see that constant snacking wasn't needed to make up for her daughter's low meal intake. She also felt relieved that her child's desire for carb-rich snacks was normal—and not a sign of hopeless eating habits. She was especially surprised to discover that her girl was filling up on liquids, decreasing her appetite significantly at mealtimes. And finally, she realized that Grace's finicky taste buds were getting used to—and preferring—the energy-dense and nutrient-poor snacks that had become a large part of her diet.

Nutrition Myths

Although nutrition pitfalls are common, so are nutrition myths! When a child's eating gets erratic, parents often react out of fear that their child isn't getting enough of certain nutrients. One common myth is that children have to eat vegetables to meet their nutritional needs. Another is that vitamins are needed, when in fact some kids may be getting too much of certain nutrients due to the plethora of fortified foods on the market. In Table 3.2, we give you some food for thought on common nutrition myths and corresponding truths.

> **Fearless Tip**
>
> Redefine what the word "snack" means in your home from popular desserts, sweetened beverages, and salty packaged items to mostly real food (cheese, whole grains, yogurt, fruits, and vegetables). From 1977 to 2006, two- to six-year-olds had the largest increase in snacking calories from unhealthy snacks (182 calories more) and had increased eating occasions (two to three additional times per day).[15]

Important Transitions

Although children do well with feeding and a variety of textures, they still need to be supervised at mealtime and have food cut up for them, as choking remains a risk. Children are developmentally ready to give up sippy cups by two to three years of age, moving to the occasional use of straw cups to prevent spills. We also recommend that you gradually switch your child to low-fat dairy products during this stage. And if you're not doing so already, include your child at family meals and continue to watch out for food allergies, which can still develop (most occur before a child's sixth birthday).

Somewhere during this period, if not sooner, your child will resist the high chair, and you will need to find an alternative option to make mealtime safe. For

Table 3.2   Nutrition Myths for Toddlers and Preschoolers

Nutrition Myth	Nutrition Truth	What You Can Do
Kids have to eat vegetables and meat to meet their nutrient needs.	Vegetables and meat are not necessary for a nutritionally adequate diet.	A varied fruit intake (including sources of vitamin A and vitamin C) can cover low veggie intake, and nonmeat protein sources can substitute for meat.
Most kids need to take multivitamins.	Studies show that most young children don't need multivitamins—and may even get too much of certain nutrients when they do take them.[16,17]	Check fortified sources of nutrients and food group frequency before deciding on a multivitamin.
Kids benefit from a low-fat diet.	Diets too low in fat can negatively affect growth and development in children.[18]	Ensure that toddlers and preschoolers have enough fat for growth by including healthy fat sources at meals.

some meals, you can have him eat at a smaller table and chair, where he can touch his feet on the ground and not fall over. For family meals, try a modified high chair that can be strapped right on the adult chair so you can push him up to the table. Last can be a booster seat until he is ready for a regular chair.

After the age of two, your child will go to the doctor for wellness checks less often, typically yearly. If problems arise, such as concerns about growth, bowel changes, or potential food allergies, don't hesitate to make an appointment. If early heart disease or high cholesterol runs in your family, talk to your child's pediatrician about cholesterol screening. See your doctor if constipation lasts more than two weeks, as this tends to occur during toilet training transitions (holding it too long!), and the doctor can help you decide if stool softeners are needed to break the cycle.

Two- to Five-Year-Old Transition Checklist

✓ Prevent choking hazards by cutting up grapes, hot dogs, chunks of cheese, and nuts, and don't allow hard, round candies, chunks of raw veggies, gum, big spoonfuls of peanut butter, or popcorn.

✓ Find safe alternatives, such as strap-in chairs or booster seats, when your child resists the high chair.

✓ Lessen your child's dependence on sippy cups—use mostly open cups and straw cups.

✓ Have your child eat with the family and avoid short-order cooking.

✓ Switch to lower-fat dairy products unless otherwise directed by your doctor or dietitian.

✓ Continue to check for allergic reactions and signs of intolerance to food, such as vomiting, a rash or hives, a swollen tongue, itching, breathing problems, and changes in bowel movements.

✓ Talk to your pediatrician about cholesterol screening for your child sometime between the ages of two and eight, if you or your partner have high cholesterol or early heart disease runs in your family, as recommended by the National Heart, Lung, and Blood Institute.[19]

✓ Notify your pediatrician of any lasting changes in bowel movements, such as constipation, if changes to your child's diet don't seem to be working.

Now that you have been primed with just the right amount of information, let's get into the nuts and bolts of WHAT to offer your child with help from the Fearless Food Guide.

Fearless Food Guide

Having a plan when it comes to offering food to little ones is invaluable—and that's exactly what the Fearless Food Guide provides for you. Here, we discuss how to balance offerings, including sweets, and how to put it all together using the Real Deal Meal Plan.

The Fearless Food Guide in Appendix A categorizes foods based on the role they play in the diet: Nourishing Foods, Half-and-Half Foods, and Fun Foods. The key is to balance all three food types with the appropriate frequency to maximize nutrition and food enjoyment. Here, we take the guide and make it specific to the toddler and preschooler's needs.

After Janice learned about which food groups to offer, she felt more confident planning meals for Grace. She still included such refined grains as pretzels and crackers (Half-and-Half Foods), but did so less often. She increased her offerings of Nourishing Foods, such as fruits and vegetables, and kept Fun Foods, such as cookies and chips, to three times a week, as Grace also ate those foods outside the home. She stopped giving in to Grace's frequent requests for juice or milk; she served juice daily at lunch (four to six ounces), and served milk twice a day during breakfast and dinner. She made water the beverage of choice between meals. See Table 3.3 for the details.

Having a plan for Fun Foods is an often overlooked detail, but it can help prevent them from getting out of control or from being regulated too tightly. Obviously, these items provide no nutritional benefits, but there is room for such foods in a balanced diet. Some children are satisfied with eating only one or two Fun Foods each week, whereas others are constantly begging for them. The goal is to find the routine food offerings that work best for your family, and to make changes as needed.

"My five-year-old was picky for the first three years but now is pretty good with a range of food," says Jenna. "I tried to keep sweets to the weekend, but she was always asking if we could buy gummies, bake cupcakes, or stop for a donut." Jenna realized it was time to include sweets more often in response to her daughter's requests.

Real Deal Meals and Snacks

The goal of the Fearless Food Guide isn't to get your child to eat exactly what is listed, but to give a better sense of what to offer, and how often. The starter portion size is a reminder that children need smaller portion sizes than adults do,

Table 3.3	Fearless Food Guide for Toddlers and Preschoolers				
Food Groups	**Two- to Three-Year-Old Daily Servings**	**Starter Portion Sizes**	**Four- to Five-Year-Old Daily Servings**	**Starter Portion Sizes**	**Comments**
Meats and nonmeat protein sources:	**2 ounces**	1 to 2 ounces	**3 ounces**	1 to 2 ounces	Include beans and fish twice weekly. If desired, include higher-fat meat protein sources less frequently.
Chicken, pork, fish and shellfish	1 ounce				
Egg	1 egg				
Nuts and seeds	½ ounce				
Nut butters	1 tablespoon				
Beans, tofu	¼ cup				
Dairy and nondairy sources:	**2 cups**	½ cup	**2½ cups**	½ to ¾ cup	Include low-fat dairy choices, allowing higher-fat options less often.
Milk, yogurt	1 cup				
Cheese	1½ ounces				
Nondairy alternatives	1 cup				
Fruits:	**1 cup**	½ to 1 small 3 to 4 ounces juice	**1 cup**	½ to 1 small 4 ounces juice	Keep juice to four to six ounces daily. Include sources rich in vitamin C each day.[a] Fruit and vegetables are interchangeable.
Fresh, frozen, or canned fruit	1 medium or 1 cup				
Dried fruit	½ cup				
100 percent fruit juice	1 cup				

Table 3.3 *(continued)*

Food Groups	Two- to Three-Year-Old Daily Servings	Starter Portion Sizes	Four- to Five-Year-Old Daily Servings	Starter Portion Sizes	Comments
Vegetables:	*1 cup*	2 to 3 tablespoons cooked A few pieces raw	*1½ cups*	3 tablespoons to ¼ cup cooked Several pieces raw	Include sources rich in vitamin A daily.[b] Fruit and vegetables are interchangeable.
Cooked vegetables, raw vegetables	1 cup				
Leafy salad greens	2 cups				
Grains:	*3 ounces*	½ to 1 slice bread ¼ to ½ cup cooked cereal ½ to 1 cup dry cereal	*4 ounces*	1 slice bread ½ cup cooked cereal 1 cup dry cereal	Make at least half of the grains whole grains.
Wheat, rye, barley, oats, quinoa, rice	½ cup				
Bread	1 slice				
Pasta, rice, cooked cereal	½ cup				
Dry cereal	1 cup				
Bagel, English muffin	½ item				
Fats:	*3 teaspoons*	1 teaspoon	*4 teaspoons*	1 to 1½ teaspoons	Include fat from plant sources most often, and offer or cook with animal fats, such as butter, less frequently. (Fats are inherent in many foods, such as nuts, seeds, dairy products, and meats. Amounts here represent fat added to foods.)
Vegetable oils (olive, canola, flax), butter or soft margarine	1 teaspoon				
Mayonnaise, salad dressing	1 tablespoon				
Avocado	⅛ medium				
Fun Foods: Cookies, pastries, ice cream, fried foods, candy	*0 to 1 serving*	Small amount to start	*0 to 1 serving*	Small amount to start	Start with small portions, but allow children to enjoy more as long as they stay at the table.

[a]   Vitamin C can be found in orange juice, peaches, oranges, kiwi, strawberries, broccoli, pineapple, cantaloupe, sweet potato, sweet red and green peppers, kale, and fortified juices.

[b]   Vitamin A can be found in carrots, sweet potato, cantaloupe, pumpkin, squash, spinach, kale, and romaine lettuce.

and that smaller eaters can get overwhelmed with big portions. There will be times when your child wants to eat more, or less, and that is fine (and completely normal at this age!). In fact, these are minimums, and some kids (for example, active and larger children) will need more, so following your child's lead is important.

In Table 3.4, we've put together a sample day differentiating between what is offered and what is eaten, showing that needs are met despite eating that appears erratic. Children between two and five years of age need to eat every three hours or so, with younger children needing to eat more frequently than older children (every two to three hours versus every three to four hours, respectively). Young toddlers may still have milk before bed or a small snack if dinner is early.

One of the reasons parents perceive their young children as barely eating is that these kids only need about half the food adults do. For example, the minimal amount of lean protein children need, two to three ounces a day, is less than what most adults eat at a meal (an ounce is the size of your thumb). Take out your measuring cup and look at what a quarter of a cup and a half of a cup look like—about half your fist—and those are child-sized portions of fruit and grains, respectively. Do the same for vegetables, two to three tablespoons and a quarter of a cup—which are reasonable portions to start, depending on age. Another practical guideline to follow is offering a tablespoon per year of age for each food group.

A Word on Snacks

Snacks help fill in the nutritional gaps that occur at mealtimes. Does your child skip fruit in the morning? Offer some again at the midmorning snack. Maybe your child didn't eat her turkey at lunch. Serve another protein source like peanut butter with apple slices for her afternoon snack. Although it's smart to keep sugar intake as low as you can, sweetened, nutrient-dense foods, such as cereals and flavored yogurts and milk, can improve a child's overall nutrition.[20] If your child already accepts plain yogurt and milk, keep serving it to her, and boost nutrition with a side of fruit. If she doesn't like it, try adding your own sweetener, like honey, or look for products that offer the least amount of sugar for the most taste.

Table 3.4 Real Deal Meal Plan for Toddlers and Preschoolers

Time	Meal or Snack	Food Groups	What's Offered	What's Eaten	Nutrition Stats
7:00 a.m.	Breakfast	• Meat or nonmeat • Fruit • Grain • Dairy or nondairy	• 1 boiled egg • ¼ cup chopped cantaloupe[a] • ½ cup fortified cereal • 4 ounces low-fat milk	The child eats half of the egg, and asks for more fruit (1 cup). He eats 1 cup of cereal, and half of the milk from the cereal.	The added nutrition from cereal includes almost 100 percent the iron needed daily (8 milligrams), 50 percent of B vitamins, 100 percent of folic acid, and 75 percent of zinc. The child has exceeded his vitamin A needs with cantaloupe.
10:00 a.m.	Snack	• Dairy or nondairy • Fruit	• Cheese stick • ¼ cup mandarin oranges	The child eats half of the cheese stick. He wants more oranges (½ cup).	The child meets his vitamin C needs.
12:30 p.m.	Lunch	• Meat or nonmeat • Grain • Vegetable • Fat • Fruit • Dairy or nondairy	• 1 ounce tuna salad • 1 slice whole wheat bread • Carrot sticks[b] • 1 tablespoon hummus • ½ small apple • ½ cup low-fat milk	The child asks for more tuna (eating 2 ounces total), and skips the accompanying bread. He eats half of the carrot sticks and half of the hummus. He doesn't eat any apple. He asks for more milk (drinking 6 ounces total).	By this point, the two- to three-year-old child has met his protein serving needs by eating the tuna.

3:00–3:30 p.m.	Snack	• Fun Food • Dairy or nondairy	• Homemade cookies • ½ cup low-fat milk	The child eats a cookie and a half, and drinks 1 cup of milk.	Whether he is a toddler or a preschooler, the child meets his dairy needs.
6:00 p.m.	Dinner	• Meat or nonmeat • Vegetable • Fruit • Grain • Fat	• 1 ounce soft pork tenderloin • ¼ cup sautéed broccoli • ¼ cup strawberries • ¼ cup rice pilaf • Olive oil (for sautéing broccoli) • Water	The child eats half an ounce of meat, and has a few bites of broccoli.[a] He eats half of the strawberries[a] and all of the rice.	Those few bites of meat get the four- to five- year- old to his 3 ounces.

[a] This indicates a Vitamin C–rich food.
[b] This indicates a Vitamin A–rich food.

Beverages and Fat Matter

Following simple guidelines for beverages can make a big difference in appetite at meals, such as keeping water as the beverage between meals, limiting 100 percent fruit juice servings to four to six ounces daily, and offering milk with meals. This helps prevent your child from filling up on milk and juice between meals. If your child fills up on beverages during the meal, hold off on the drink until the end of the meal so it doesn't interfere with eating. Finally, limit such sugar-sweetened beverages as juice drinks, lemonade, and soda to parties and special events.

Joanna, mom of two-year-old Gavin, wrote us saying her son was hungry every hour. After seeing what he was eating, we pointed out that he was getting very little fat, something she never even considered. Be sure to provide fat sources at meals, as children need more than adults do and burn it at a faster rate.[21] It's always good to avoid the extremes, such as a diet high in fat or a diet too low in fat.

What About the Big Eater?

If your child has a big appetite, you may be feeling concerned that your child is out of the norm. Some kids simply have bigger appetites! Rather than limiting intake, provide rhythmic meals and nutritious and filling foods (protein and healthy fat sources). Allow your child to eat until satisfied, and avoid feeding in response to emotional distress. Not allowing big eaters to become satisfied may increase the likelihood that they will obsess over food and become poor regulators, meaning they will be more likely to eat when not hungry.

Next, we help you fill in the nutritional gaps when children consistently fall short on certain food groups. Getting acquainted with the Fearless Five Nutrients for toddlers and preschoolers is just what you need!

The Fearless Five Nutrients

We recommend that instead of giving multivitamins to compensate for imperfect eating habits, you implement a "food first" strategy—tweaking the food in your child's diet and then adding supplements if needed. The Fearless Five Nutrients listed in Table 3.5—calcium, vitamin D, iron, vitamin E, and potassium—are important nutrients at this stage of your child's development *and* the ones kids this age are most likely to fall short on. We show you how to use the Fearless Five Nutrients chart with the examples in the paragraphs that follow. You can find more foods and their specific nutrient values in Appendix B.

Table 3.5   Fearless Five Nutrients for Toddlers and Preschoolers

Nutrient	Function	Recommended Daily Allowance (RDA)	Sources	Comments
Calcium	Calcium is a key nutrient needed for bone formation. It contributes to muscle and nerve functioning.	*One to three years:* 700 milligrams *Four to eight years:* 1,000 milligrams	Calcium-fortified orange juice (500 milligrams); calcium-fortified soy beverages (80 to 500 milligrams); yogurt (338 to 452 milligrams); low-fat milk (305 milligrams); cheese (307–452 milligrams)	Most one- to three-year-olds meet their needs for calcium. After age four, the RDA for calcium increases, making the task of meeting calcium needs more challenging.[5]

Table 3.5 *(continued)*				
Nutrient	**Function**	**Recommended Daily Allowance (RDA)**	**Sources**	**Comments**
Vitamin D	Vitamin D aids in the absorption of calcium and phosphorus for bone mineralization. It plays a role in the prevention of chronic disease.	600 international units (IU)	Sockeye salmon (792 IU), canned light tuna in water (152 IU), vitamin D–fortified orange juice (136 IU), low-fat milk (116 IU), soymilk (108 IU), egg (28 IU)	Average vitamin D intake for this age group is roughly half of the RDA.[5] Sunlight is not a reliable source of vitamin D because it is limited by sunscreen use, excessive time indoors, higher altitudes, winter months, dark-colored skin, and excess weight.
Vitamin E	Vitamin E functions as an antioxidant, protecting cells from free radical damage, which may decrease the risk of heart disease and cancers. It is involved in immune function.	*One to three years:* 6 milligrams *Four to eight years:* 7 milligrams	Fortified ready-to-eat cereals (3.2 to 13.5 milligrams), sunflower seeds (7.4 milligrams), almonds (6.8 milligrams), sunflower oil (5.6 milligrams), mixed nuts (3.1 milligrams), peanut butter (2.9 milligrams), canola oil (2.4 milligrams), olive oil (1.9 milligrams), spinach (1.9 milligrams), avocado (1.5 milligrams)	Sixty-three percent of toddlers and 37 percent of preschoolers have levels of vitamin E that are lower than recommended.[16]

Table 3.5	(continued)			
Nutrient	**Function**	**Recommended Daily Allowance (RDA)**	**Sources**	**Comments**
Iron	Iron carries oxygen and stores it in cells, a process that is accelerated in times of rapid growth. It is an important component of enzymes and protein.	*One to three years:* 7 milligrams *Four to eight years:* 10 milligrams	*Heme:* Beef (3.1 milligrams), dark meat turkey (2 milligrams), dark meat chicken (1.1 milligrams) *Nonheme:* Iron-fortified cereal (varies), soybeans (8.8 milligrams), black or pinto beans (3.6 milligrams), raisins (1.6 milligrams)	Four percent of three- to five-year-olds are iron-deficient.[22] Animal sources (heme) are more readily absorbed than plant-based sources (nonheme). Increase absorption of the latter by adding vitamin C sources to meals.
Potassium	Potassium is an essential mineral that plays a role in the transmission of nerve impulses. It is also called an electrolyte.	*One to three years:* 3,000 milligrams *Four to eight years:* 3,800 milligrams	Potato (1,081 milligrams), white beans (595 milligrams), yogurt (556 milligrams), fresh orange juice (496 milligrams), soybeans (485 milligrams), banana (422 milligrams), beans (300 to 400 milligrams)	High potassium intake protects against high blood pressure and the effects of excessive sodium. The estimated intake for most two- to five-year-olds is about 2,000 milligrams.[23]

Dairy Dilemma

Growing bones need calcium and vitamin D, and with recommendations even higher since 2010, these nutrients take center stage. Most kids this age get adequate calcium from such items as milk, cheese, and yogurt, but developing the habit of consuming dairy now helps later when needs shoot up. Check Table 3.5 and the more detailed list of sources of calcium in Appendix B to see if your child is getting enough (seven hundred milligrams for one- to three-year-olds versus one thousand milligrams for four- to eight-year-olds) and add sources as needed. Also be sure to track how much calcium your child gets from fortified food products and supplements. The daily value (DV) for calcium is one thousand milligrams, so if a food product contains 30 percent DV, that's three hundred milligrams. Most multivitamins contain little calcium.

Vitamin E and Healthy Fats

Survey data show that children do not meet recommended amounts of vitamin E, found in vegetable oils and nuts and seeds (which are also sources of healthy fats).[16,17] Check the Fearless Five Nutrients chart and add sources of vitamin E to your child's diet. Young children who don't eat nuts (choking hazard), can get vitamin E from vegetable oils used in cooking, nut butters, avocados, wheat germ in baked goods and smoothies, and fortified cereals. Preschoolers can have chopped nuts as part of snacks and as a yogurt topping.

Meat Is Gross!

It's common for young children to avoid meat and other protein sources due to the texture. Iron, not protein, is typically the concern, as 4 percent of children between three and five are deficient, which can adversely affect the developing brain. Use the Fearless Five Nutrients chart to ensure that children are getting enough iron—seven or ten milligrams daily depending on age. Kids who don't eat a lot of meat can eat beans; French toast; raisins; and low-sugar, iron-fortified cereals (served with vitamin C sources).

Produce and Potassium

The Fearless Five Nutrients chart lists potassium-rich foods, as does Appendix B. Consuming fruits and vegetables increases potassium and fiber, which tend to be low in this group. There are a lot of things you can do to increase your child's intake of produce, such as putting a tray of veggies out before dinner, serving salad as the first course, and making fruit and veggies a part of most meals and snacks. See the Real Life Challenges section later in this chapter for other examples.

Supplement Checklist

If your child is slow to get adequate nutrients from foods, supplementation may be needed. Before giving supplements, always check sources of extra vitamins and minerals from fortified foods because it is possible to get too much of certain nutrients, such as vitamin A and folic acid. Table 3.6 summarizes the circumstances in which supplements—multivitamins or single nutrients—may be needed for children of all ages.

Table 3.6 Supplements and Children	
Supplement	**When It's Needed**
Multivitamins with or without iron	If your child consumes few fortified products, skips such food groups as fruits and vegetables, and is at a low weight or on a restricted diet, a multivitamin is needed. If your child eats foods that are low in iron, choose one with iron. Do not give iron supplements unless they are prescribed by your doctor.
Vitamin D	The AAP recommends supplementation when the child is unable to get vitamin D from diet alone.[24] Some food products are fortified with vitamin D (juices, yogurts, and milk), so check labels (DV used for labels is 400 IU). If your child is taking a multivitamin, check the label for vitamin D (RDA is 600 IU for kids over two).
DHA	Kids who don't eat fish may benefit from supplementation (see Appendix B for food sources and Appendix G for recommended amounts by age).
Probiotics	Probiotics are generally not needed for healthy kids. Consult with your pediatrician if you are considering supplements to help with gastrointestinal conditions.

Feeding with Confidence: The Self-Control Struggle

Jody spent her days trying to get her three-year-old to eat balanced meals. Breakfast was the best meal, followed by a hit-or-miss lunch and ending with a terrible dinner. She couldn't believe it when she started bribing her daughter with something sweet and saying things like "No more bread until you eat some meat and vegetables." Although she didn't feel good about the tension at the table, she didn't know what else to do. She felt stuck.

Jody is certainly not alone. Parents always ask us how they can get their children to eat "this" or "that." In fact, one study revealed that 80 percent of parents feel like they have no control over their child's picky eating habits. And more than 75 percent give in to their picky eater rather than struggling.[25]

What does this tell us? Parents are focusing their energy on trying to change picky eating—*getting* their children to eat. This is one of the biggest misconceptions about feeding during toddlerhood: it's not a parent's job to control a child's food intake. The parent's job is to provide balanced meals, make the eating environment positive, and respond to children appropriately (that's enough, thank you!). Attempting to control food intake is a recipe for eating problems, now or later. What parents initially view as picky eating is actually a normal developmental stage. But the more we try to change it, or cater to our children, the longer it lasts—*and the worse eating gets.*

If you've been reading *Fearless Feeding* since your child was an infant, you are prepared for the picky eating phase that is likely to come or that is already here. But if you are just getting started, welcome to one of the most challenging stages of feeding.

What to Expect

Your child's personality is blossoming. By age two, children start to separate from their parents, developing a sense of self. According to German psychoanalyst Erik Erikson, children between one and three years are gaining mastery over new skills.[26] These include fine motor skills, such as using utensils, drinking from cups, and holding crayons to color, and gross motor skills, such as leaping, climbing, and running. Children gain more control over their body as they learn to potty train (or not!), put on shoes, and attempt to dress themselves. Language and communication abilities also bloom, and a child wants more of a say in everything he does. What is viewed as the "terrible twos" is really a struggle of wills and a child's way of exerting newfound independence, which is why the word "no" and the phrase "I do it" can be heard almost daily.

Erikson calls this period Autonomy Versus Shame and Doubt because children who successfully navigate this stage, with support and guidance from caregivers, confidently learn new skills and develop a healthy sense of autonomy and positive self-concept. Children who aren't given the opportunity to learn skills, or are controlled and criticized during the process, color their ability with doubt and shame. For example, when Michelle's two-year-old son, Evan, took a long time to feed himself, she took over feeding. Evan not only relied on her to eat also but lacked confidence performing this important skill.

From ages three through five, children move from mastering basic skills to taking initiative with activities, a transition that is most apparent in how they play. Pretend and imaginary play, such as playing house, helps build skills in various developmental areas and increases learning. Pretend play also helps children build more complex language and problem-solving abilities—and is a preschooler's way of practicing adult situations in a safe setting. Instead of constantly saying "no" like toddlers, preschoolers start asking "why" as they try to make sense of the world around them.

Erikson calls this period Initiative Versus Guilt because children who successfully navigate this stage develop a sense of purpose and feel confident taking initiative. But children whose initiative is squelched begin to develop a sense of guilt around their actions, leading to less confidence and leadership. For example, if a parent insists that her child eat a certain amount, pre-plates his food, and allows for little choice at mealtime, the child can lose confidence in eating. Some children may give up and just do as they are told, whereas others show defiance, resulting in struggle and strife at the meal table or, worse, a strained feeding dynamic between parent and child. Table 3.7 summarizes these stages of development as they relate to feeding.

How Your Toddler and Preschooler Thinks

Child psychologist Jean Piaget defined four stages of cognitive development during childhood.[27] The stage that your child is in now (two to six years) is called the preoperational stage because the developing mind still isn't able to organize ideas and make logical conclusions. Preoperational thinking not only lacks logic

Psychosocial Task (One to Three Years)	Daily Actions
Table 3.7 Psychosocial Development for Toddlers and Preschoolers	
Autonomy	
Child: "I can do it." *Parent:* "I know you can—and I'm here to help if you need it."	• The child feeds herself, with help cutting food into small pieces. • The child is able to eat with her hands and get messy. • The child chooses how much and what to eat from what is offered. • The parent responds to the child's hunger and fullness cues.
Shame and Doubt	
Child: "I can't do it." *Parent:* "You're not ready to learn these skills."	• The child is fed or assisted or prompted more than necessary. • The child has controlled food choices in regard to what is offered and how much to eat. • The child isn't allowed to get messy and explore food while eating.
Psychosocial Task (Three to Five Years)	**Daily Actions**
Initiative	
Child: "Eating is fun—I'm good at it." *Parent:* "You can make good decisions."	• The child helps with meals, setting the table and cleaning up. • The child serves herself at mealtime and decides what and how much to eat. She is encouraged to honor feelings of fullness and hunger. • The child says "yes" or "no thank you" when offered food outside the home. • The child is able to voice likes and dislikes about food and feels that her food preferences are honored but not catered to.
Guilt	
Child: "Eating is not fun—I seem to mess up all the time." *Parent:* "You can't do this by yourself, you need my help."	• The parent discourages the child from making or serving food—food is plated. • The child is not allowed to turn down food or voice food preferences. • The child is pressured to finish meals, to eat more or less, or to perform a certain way during meals. • The child is required to taste everything at mealtime.

Table 3.8 Cognitive Development for Toddlers and Preschoolers

Age	Stage	Cognitive Readiness	Feeding Implications
Two to six years	Preoperational stage (characterized by the inability to organize ideas and make logical conclusions)	• Doesn't consider cause and effect • Is able to repeat words without understanding meaning • Has limited ability to understand change • Has trouble reversing an experience	• Has difficulty understanding even basic nutrition topics • For example, knows vegetables are good for children but is not sure why • Is unable to grasp long-term effects of eating choices

and is "magical" but also is naturally egocentric and self-centered. As far as young children are concerned, everything revolves around them, and other points of view don't exist, which limits understanding.

For example, young children tend to be adamant about how the food is arranged on their plate or freak out if they see pieces of something new (like veggies) in a familiar dish. They simply don't have the ability to understand that something that has been done can be reversed, as highlighted in Table 3.8. The good news is that this compulsive need for things to be just right declines around age six—as your child's thinking becomes more complex.

Food Neophobia

As kids approach two, their push for independence, rapid changes in cognition, and slowed growth (and appetite) explain why most become more selective with food choices. Parents are often disappointed to find that their previously broccoli-and-pea-loving kid now rejects anything green. Children also show signs of food neophobia, a reluctance to try new or unfamiliar foods. Food jags are common—whereby children request the same food for days in a row. There's not a parent alive who loves this stage, but just so you know, it's all pretty normal.

Food neophobia peaks between the ages of two and six, when kids become increasingly mobile, and it (thankfully) decreases throughout the course of childhood.[28] Experts believe it's an adaptive trait that protects children from ingesting poisonous or toxic food components. Although this trait might have been lifesaving during hunter-gatherer times, it is not so helpful today. When presented with a novel food, children make a judgment as to whether or not that food is "safe" based on its visual appearance. If a food looks bitter (think green veggies) or like what preschoolers think of as "gross," they may refuse to try it.

"We have gone from having an eater who would eat whatever (mostly) we put in front of her at mealtimes to one who is super-selective and whose default refrain is that she *doesn't like* this or that, or that it's *yucky*," says Amy, mom of three-year-old Maddy. "I'm struggling with keeping my patience through what I know is a phase while not caving in to just fixing macaroni and cheese every day for months."

Picky Eating

The rejection of food after tasting it—picky eating—is also common among toddlers. Researchers believe the level of picky eating a child experiences has to do with individual experiences of *taste, sensory integration*, and *appetite*. Children have more taste buds than adults do, making them sensitive to even low concentrations of bitter compounds found in vegetables, including 6-n-propylthiouracil (PROP). About 70 percent of preschoolers are tasters of these bitter compounds, and nontasters have been shown to eat more vegetables compared to tasters.[30]

Kay Toomey, pediatric psychologist and developer of the family-centered Sequential Oral Sensory (SOS) approach to feeding, explains that how food feels in the mouth, or its *sensation*, differs from child to child. Children may gag, spit up, or even vomit food when certain textures are placed in their mouth. "Some kids have a sensory system that is far more sensitive," she says. "If pushed beyond their comfort level, these kids learn that eating hurts and will avoid eating situations." Although many sensory-sensitive kids eventually learn to eat a variety of foods, some may need help—especially those with poor weight gain, those who continue to choke and gag, those who eat few foods, and those who avoid foods with a specific texture. If this is an issue for your child, see Chapter Seven for more on problem feeders.

Another factor affecting picky eating is your child's appetite. As discussed earlier in this chapter, growth slows and kids generally have a reduced desire to eat compared to during infancy. Children's appetites will increase during growth spurts, but some will continue to have a big appetite throughout this stage, which can override picky eating tendencies. Most parents don't realize that children naturally adjust their intake based on previously eaten foods, and they may push children to eat.[33] For example, a child may eat a big dinner, and then eat less than she normally does at breakfast; or she may have a big lunch or afternoon snack and not much at dinner. In addition, parents are more likely to control food intake if their child is smaller or larger than average. Even subtle cues, like saying "Just eat," or seemingly harmless restrictions, like slyly taking food away, interfere with children's food regulation.

> **Fearless Fact**
>
> Around the age of three, children's food intake is no longer "deprivation driven," whereby they seek food, eat, and stop until hunger returns. Rather, toddlers become increasingly vulnerable to environmental factors, including parental and caregiver cues for food intake.[34]

To sum up, knowing what to expect helps you approach feeding like you do other aspects of your child's learning, such as reading and writing. It takes time, patience, and a lot of practice for kids to get good at eating and accept a variety of tastes and textures. We believe a nonthreatening—and even fun—kitchen table at which the family eats together is the best antidote. And just as kids learn at different rates in school, the same goes for eating.

Feeding That Works

Because of all the changes you just read about, this is a crucial time in feeding when many bad habits can develop. Your goals are to preserve food regulation, expose your child to a variety of foods, and keep mealtime positive. These five must-have feeding practices not only help you achieve these goals but also make life easier now and in the years to come.

Structured Eating Versus Grazing

Let's peek into two different houses and the meal structure each one has (or hasn't). In the Grazing House, there is no structure or plan—the kids are able to go to the kitchen cabinet and grab crackers or goldfish whenever they want. They snack in the car, while watching TV, and in the grocery store. The main meals happen, but the kids eat too little or too much because they are either not hungry or starving. In the Structured House, there is a rhythm to meals and snacks—and between meals the kitchen is closed. These kids understand when meals happen, request food less often, only eat in the car or in front of the tube occasionally, and gather at the kitchen table for most meals. The parents make sure that eating times are not too close together, or adjust the size and type of each snack so the kids have a good appetite for meals.

These are the years to establish the habit of structured eating with your child. You want your child, similar to kids in the Structured House, to learn that meals are reliable and that hunger is the reason to eat. It's important to be flexible, not rigid. For instance, if there's less time than usual between meals, then single snack items like fruit or a cheese stick might be fine. If there is greater time between meals than usual, go for the hearty snack of cheese, whole grain crackers, and fruit.

Having structure doesn't just help children manage hunger and build an appetite for meals—it helps *you* prioritize food requests. You can let your child know that the food she wants *now* will be coming at a future meal or snack. You will be amazed at how much better this works than saying "no"!

"One of my biggest issues with my little guy is that he would literally get up from the kitchen table and exclaim, 'I'm still hungry, can I have a snack?'" says Jennifer. "The first time I explained to him that I had a snack planned for him later, he said 'okay' and walked out of the kitchen. It was literally that easy."

Feeding that works: Structure meals and snacks at regular intervals and eat most of these meals at the table or at a specific point in time. For example, your child might take a break from playing to have a snack and refuel.

Feeding that doesn't work: Constant grazing is problematic. So is eating during activities (such as watching TV), in the car, or when bored, or eating too close to mealtime.

Trust Versus Control

Now, more than ever, you need Ellyn Satter's Division of Responsibility (DOR), whereby parents decide the *what, when,* and *where* of feeding, and children are responsible for the *whether* and *how much* of eating.[35] This works because children this age don't know how to choose balanced meals or where and when these meals

> **Fearless Tips**
>
> - Feed kids regular meals and snacks approximately every three hours, an average of five to six times per day, in a designated area. Allow them to eat until full.
> - Be flexible, not rigid—move eating sooner or later, and change snacks, depending on hunger situations and the timing of meals. Consider adding a nighttime snack if dinner is more than two hours before bed.
> - Discourage eating in front of the TV, when bored (see the fruit and veggie test in Chapter Four), in the car, or while doing any activity, except for occasionally.
> - Allow for grazing at parties and outings when kids are busy exploring (or ignoring) food and enjoying themselves.

should occur, but they do know when they've had enough to eat and how food tastes and feels in their mouth. We just got through helping you with your job: the *what,* and the *when* and *where* in terms of structure, but we warn you that one of the hardest parts of feeding little ones is allowing them to do their job.

One of the benefits of allowing children choice in what and how much to eat is that it melts away the food battles so common at this stage. Your child doesn't like the mealtime choice? That's okay, she doesn't *have* to eat it. It's amazing how this changes the dynamic at the table and around food. "I think one of the biggest things for me was recognizing that my daughter's voiced 'opinions' at mealtime were just another way for her to assert her independence," says Amy.

"As my husband and I got better at remaining disinterested in her reaction, she more often would make the decision to give things a try because we weren't so invested in the outcome."

Problems with self-regulation are more likely to occur when a parent takes over the child's job (pressuring or restricting), and when a child takes over the parent's job (demanding when and what he eats).[36] Controlling feeding practices can be subtle, like saying "Good job" for eating a good portion or "You're really going to have more food?" after the child takes another serving. If you can let go of the fear of "too much" or "too little" and focus on your job of feeding, your child will learn to trust himself, which will translate to better self-regulation.

Feeding that works: Allow children to decide how much and what to eat of what you serve. Such flexibility builds on a child's eating ability, trust around food, emerging autonomy, and hunger and fullness recognition.

Feeding that doesn't work: Trying to control a child's eating or allowing her to dictate what and when to eat can decrease self-regulation, increase picky eating, and make healthy eating a chore.

> ## Fearless Tips
>
> - Instead of reacting to a child's complaint about meals ("What do you mean you don't like tacos? You ate them last week!"), say, "You don't have to eat, but you do have to join us at the table."
> - Instead of trying to get a child to eat more ("You can leave when you finish most of your dinner"), remind her when her next meal is: "The next meal isn't until breakfast tomorrow, so be sure you got enough to eat."
> - Instead of giving in to a child's request for lunch ("Mom, I wanted peanut butter and jelly instead of turkey"), tell him he'll have it another time soon: "Not today, sweetie, but let's plan on having it soon."

Sweet Enjoyment Versus Obsession

Marie remembers a childhood in which sweet foods were rarely allowed. When she was at friends' houses she'd binge on whatever junk food they had. Other parents allow too many sweets, which can overcrowd a child's diet and get him used to the taste as a main fuel source. And other families use sweets to reward good behavior (or they withhold sweets as punishment); to help a child deal with difficult emotions; or even to tempt a child to eat more "healthy" items. All of these practices can make sweets even more desirable to children, something that sticks with them into adulthood.[37,38]

"I remember even my überhealthy mom indulging in mint Milano cookies after dinner sometimes, and we were allowed to eat our Halloween candy," says Bettina, blogger at *The Lunch Tray.* "Sweets were definitely not demonized and were just a normal part of life. That said, I also don't remember having a lot of sweets around all the time."

This is exactly what you want for your child—to grow up enjoying sweets without overconsuming them, feeling like he isn't getting enough, or feeling guilty or bad about eating them. Striking this balance will help your child as he gets older, just like it did with Bettina, who is now an adult with a healthy outlook on sweets in her diet.

Feeding that works: Provide sweets on a regular and predictable

Fearless Tips

- Instead of just saying "no," explain to children why it's no and when they will get the sweet food again: "We already had something sweet, so no cake today, but we'll have some at Timmy's birthday party this weekend."
- Instead of allowing children to see the food they can't have, keep it out of sight and bring it out only when it is to be eaten.
- Instead of making dessert contingent on what they eat for dinner, try a "no strings attached" approach and rotate wholesome desserts with more indulgent types and nights without dessert (keep them guessing!), or offer sweets during snack time rather than with meals.
- Instead of overcontrolling how much children eat ("You can have one cookie"), allow them to enjoy sweets in a focused way until they are satisfied: "Let's sit at the table and enjoy the cookies."
- Instead of using sweets to control behavior ("If you are good at the store you can have the cookie"), make them an enjoyable part of eating not tied to any behavior.

basis, less often than Nourishing Foods and Half-and-Half Foods, and be neutral when discussing them with children.

Feeding that doesn't work: Restricting access to palatable foods; allowing children these foods whenever they want; or giving sweets attention through rewarding, bribing, and punishing are all inadvisable.

Inside Operation Versus Operation Eat

Parents resort to all sorts of tricks to get children to eat healthy—bribing them with dessert, praising them, hiding veggies in meals, or withholding other foods they are enjoying (pasta) until they eat "healthy" items first. Although these practices work over the short term, they can make children leery of healthy fare and *less likely* to make eating such foods a lifelong habit.[39,40,41] The Fearless Feeding Strategy is not about using rewards or praising children to get them to eat in a certain way—it's about building your child's *internal* motivation to eat well. We believe that eating a balanced diet speaks for itself and needs no reward or pushing. Instead, *expect* that your child will eat well instead of using incentives or nagging, and she will be more likely to take the initiative.

Although a variety of factors can help increase children's liking for healthy foods, three stand out—exposure, availability, and role modeling. Remember, children at this stage are skeptical of new foods, and seeing a food over and over helps make the food familiar and more likely to be accepted. We also know that the more parents make healthy foods available—and highly accessible—the more

Fearless Tips

- Keep offering a variety of foods weekly without repeating the same meal two days in a row. When children want to go on a food jag, tell them: "We eat different things every day."
- Make healthy foods accessible by placing a fruit bowl on the kitchen table, having sliced veggies ready to go in the fridge, and letting children choose between two items (pear or apple?).
- Instead of lecturing, do what you want your kid to do: eat healthy foods, eat with structure, be adventurous, and above all enjoy yourself.

frequently children eat them. And what magnifies the benefits of both exposure and accessibility is watching other people eat the food—especially parents, as young children learn by observing.

Feeding that works: It's best to create a positive eating environment that builds on your child's internal motivation to eat well. Make healthy food and eating together the norm your child experiences on a daily basis. Encourage your child without pressuring.

Feeding that doesn't work: Using food to reward or punish, nagging, forcing, or overselling food make children ultimately leery of healthy eating. "If they want me to do it so badly, it must not be good!"

- Use accepted foods as a vehicle for new ingredients, such as by putting veggies on pizza or chicken in a quesadilla, or pairing a liked dip with a new food (be up-front, no sneaking). Provide very small portions of new foods.
- Give children one task to help with meals, like washing produce or measuring ingredients. Do as many "make your own" meals (for example, sandwiches and pizzas) as possible.
- Have salad or veggies and dip be the first dinner course. Dips like ranch have been shown to increase children's vegetable consumption.[30]

Family Meals Versus Lone Ranger

The family table is where critical food learning takes place. Even when kids choose not to eat, it's never a loss, because they get food exposure, watch you eat, spend time with the family, and learn manners! This is the time to put your "long-term view" hat on by realizing that building the ritual of family meals *will* pay off. Sally, mom and blogger at *Real Mom Nutrition,* sums up the challenge— and importance—of this practice quite nicely: "The universal truth is that family dinners can be challenging—and many nights, not much fun—when you have small kids. Our cozy 8:00 p.m. dinner for two has turned into 5:30 mayhem for four. We've slogged through some tough evenings together around the table. But we're consistent because we know it matters. And there are glimmers of hope. There are nights when the boys share stories about school, use good manners, and are so hungry that they quietly devour their meals with no complaint."

Fearless Tips

- Make sure that meals contain one or two items your child is likely to eat, and don't make an alternative meal if he doesn't like it.
- Consider your child's ability to chew and swallow, and avoid tough meats or food that is hard to eat. Extremely spicy foods may not be realistic either.
- Make your child's favorite dinner meals at least once weekly. Remind him that you made what he likes, and that tomorrow will be Mommy's (or Daddy's or a sibling's) favorite because "we all get a turn."
- Serve meals family-style and allow your child to serve himself, helping him if he is under five years old. Serving items separately instead of mixing foods can help.
- Talk about what happened during your day—and have fun.
- Take nights off for date night or quiet dinners as breaks from the chaos!

A misconception about family meals is that parents have to choose between serving all adult food or all kid-preferred food, when the answer lies somewhere in the middle. Here we summarize tips for making meals successful at this stage, including serving family-style meals (for more, see Chapter Four) and providing foods children like alongside new foods.

Feeding that works: Eat together as a family as often as possible, serving the food family-style.

Feeding that doesn't work: Preparing separate meals for children, short-order cooking for kids who don't want to partake in meals, or providing only food adults like can all create problems.

We hope this advice on feeding that works will empower you to feed your toddler and preschooler with ease and confidence. Visit this section often, especially when troubles arise and you need some helpful reminders. Next, in Understanding Nutrition, we tackle nutrition education for this stage so you can lay the foundation for healthy eating for years to come.

Understanding Nutrition

Kids at this stage may be limited in their ability to understand complex nutrition topics, but there is so much food learning going on—all with a positive spin. In fact, a 2007 study found that four- to five-year-olds had a more positive impression of healthy eating when compared to older kids.[42] Here, we help you keep nutrition education positive and effective by reminding you of the daily teachable moments, basic messages that help educate little minds, and hands-on learning that make nutrition and food fun for little ones.

Teachable Moments—and the Power of the Tummy

A majority of the learning that takes place during the toddler and preschool years is happening daily without any direct nutrition instruction going on. These teachable moments include drawing from the sample dialogue we outlined in Feeding That Works, discussing what types of food are served and when and where, allowing children to rely on internal cues to stop eating, and having children watch you and other family members eat. Parents may underestimate the power these daily interactions have, instead focusing too heavily on telling their children which foods are healthy and which are not.

Children are learning which foods are eaten often (Nourishing Foods) and which are eaten less frequently (Fun Foods) by what you choose to serve, and how you respond to food requests. They are also observing what you eat and learning that eating mostly occurs for hunger, and that it is not a cure for boredom or associated with some activity. With help from you, they learn to respond to internal cues for hunger and fullness versus the environmental cues to which they are now more sensitive. According to one study, preschoolers who don't regulate well can learn! At the end of a six-week training on internal cues, the children who under- or overate had made great improvements in their regulation of food intake.[43]

Fearless Tip

Educate kids about their own hunger and fullness cues by reminding them to tune in to their tummy, describing symptoms of hunger, fullness, and overfullness. Make it fun by asking them, "What does your tummy say?" when they want more or want to leave the table. Best of all, parents can practice reading their own cues as well, with help from Chapter Six.

Table 3.9 Age-Appropriate Nutrition Messages for Two- to Five-Year Olds

Cognitive Development and Perceptions	Message That Is Hard to Understand or Not Compelling	Say This Instead . . .
Children can state which foods are healthy, but they don't understand why. They are more motivated by texture and appearance.	"Eat this because it's healthy or good for you."	*"Look at this colorful food we have today. We eat a rainbow of colors."*
Children have trouble putting food in categories, such as fruits, vegetables, and meats.	"You haven't eaten enough vegetables today, so let's have some for snack."	*"Eating many different foods helps your body grow. What haven't we eaten today?"*
Children can only understand one message at a time.	"Make sure you eat real food that comes from the ground."	*"These apples came from our garden."*
Children are unable to understand change that occurs over time.	"If you eat too much, you will gain weight."	*"We listen to our tummy and stop when it's happy or full."*

Super-Basic Nutrition Messages

During family meals, encourage kids to take a little bit of everything, and discuss what the food is, especially if it's new. As children reach preschool age, you can start basic nutrition education, but we caution against going overboard. As discussed earlier, kids at this age are in the preoperational stage—they don't understand complex topics and lack the ability to think logically. Table 3.9 summarizes young children's cognitive limitations and nutrition messages that are effective.

Hands-On Learning

Age three or four is a good time to have kids help in the kitchen, as they learn about food by touching it, seeing it, and helping prepare it. Start by helping them pick out the food at the farmers' market, at the grocery store, and from your own garden as available. "Education should focus on sensory experiences with food and the importance of hand washing, and should include regular food preparation activities," says Connie Evers, author of *How to Teach Nutrition to Kids*. "Preschoolers can participate in tasks such as stirring, simple measuring, rinsing and tearing lettuce leaves, squeezing lemons, and slicing bananas."

If your child is resistant to helping in the kitchen, don't force it. She may be more willing to help with items she likes best (and that are easy), such as homemade pizza, cookies, and other simple meals. Yet at this young age, most children like to be little helpers, so keep it simple and make helping part of your child's daily routine.

Nutrition education for young children is a daily occurrence that is not about formal instruction. Keep food and eating positive for your child, and he will remain receptive to nutrition and healthy eating for years to come.

Real Life Challenges for Toddlers and Preschoolers

No one ever said feeding toddlers and preschoolers was easy—even when you have the tools in this chapter. In this section, we showcase real examples of common challenges at this age. Whether it's the toddler who won't sit for dinner, the preschooler who won't try anything, or the carb-crazed kid, we show you how to initiate positive change.

The Toddler Who Won't Sit for Dinner

Challenge: Two-and-half-year-old Eli was having trouble cooperating at dinner. According to his mom, Michelle, he wouldn't sit for long, barely ate anything, and wanted to play instead. She even allowed toys at the table, but that didn't work. Michelle and her husband, Jeff, didn't always have everything on the table when they all sat, so they were constantly getting up, and Eli was still having milk before bed. "It's simply not working well now with Eli," Michelle admitted. "I feel like we need a better plan and structure for how we *do dinner*."

Diagnosis: Eli had a short attention span (WHY) and decreased hunger (HOW), and was often tired by the time dinner rolled around. Changing HOW they handled dinner was key.

Intervention: Eli's parents needed to check the timing of his afternoon snack to make sure it was offered before 3:30 p.m., allowing for an appetite for dinner by 6 p.m. They were told not to allow toys or other distractions at the table so Eli could focus on eating, and to let him know the expectations, such as sitting for at least five minutes. They needed to make sure all the food was on the table before starting dinner, and that dinner included something Eli liked to eat. Eli was also ready to transition to having milk with dinner instead of before bed.

Outcome: In no time, things were back on track. "I just wanted you to know that so far so good," says Michelle. "He's been staying at the table, and the transition to no milk at bedtime was seamless."

Myth: Toddlers are being difficult during meals on purpose.

Busted! It can be hard for toddlers to sit for long, as they have short attention spans—especially by the end of the day when they are tired. Giving too much attention to negative behaviors only makes those behaviors worse.

> **Fearless Tip**
>
> Acceptable behavior is eating with hands; turning down food politely ("no thank you"); and sitting for five to ten minutes (toddler) or ten to fifteen minutes (preschooler). Unacceptable behavior is throwing food, bringing toys to the table, making negative comments about food, and coming back to eat after leaving.

The Carb Eater

Challenge: Jake's mom, Alisa, tried to let her son, Jake, eat freely, but she had a hard time watching him eat only the pasta at dinner and bread at lunch. When he asked for more starchy foods, she insisted he have at least a few bites of protein and veggies first. Jake complained; often ate poorly; and usually asked for something to eat an hour or so after dinner, a request to which Alisa generally gave in.

Diagnosis: Alisa was right: Jake's starchy carb intake was high, and his diet was low in lean meats, fruits, and vegetables (WHAT). This preference for carbs is common in children between the ages of two and five (WHY). But what was making matters worse was HOW she was feeding him, as there were too many starchy carbs being offered, the micromanagement at dinner wasn't working, and it was too easy for Jake to skimp on dinner with the snack he was allowed to have.

Intervention: Alisa learned about food groups and developed a plan of offering different items. Jake actually liked fruit, but often chose starchy foods first. So she offered fruit—especially cantaloupe—and the one veggie he liked—carrots, which contain vitamin A—to make up for his lack of green veggies, along with cheese, for snacks (no starch). Alisa didn't always have pasta or bread at dinner, and on the nights she did, she left the choice up to Jake to have more—but reminded him of the other items available. She enforced a "kitchen is closed" rule after dinner, which meant no after-dinner snacks.

Outcome: The first few meals were tough, as Jake ate quite a bit of his favorites and begged for food after dinner. But over time he began to try different foods, eventually ate more of a variety, and no longer panhandled for food after dinner.

Myth: It's horrible to allow a child to be hungry before bed.

Busted! Children who know they will get their preferred foods right after dinner will have less of an incentive to eat or try new things. When you avoid hunger at all costs, you send the message that hunger is "bad" instead of a natural physiological response.

> ### Fearless Tip
>
> Try responding to after-dinner requests with something like this: "It looks like you didn't fill your tummy at dinner. I hope tomorrow night you get enough to eat, because we don't eat again until breakfast." For the young toddler, or when dinner is early, you can add a bedtime snack, such as cheese and fruit, or simply milk before bed.

The Obsessed-with-Sweets Preschooler

Challenge: Holly's five-year-old daughter, Emmy, was becoming increasingly focused on treat foods. Ice cream was sold at Emmy's preschool, and Emmy asked for it daily. Holly made up a story about how the teachers only wanted the kids to eat ice cream once a week because it was so unhealthy—so ice cream was only allowed on Fridays. This made things worse, as Emmy kept asking *all week* if it was Friday yet. Emmy was also a bigger-than-average child, making her requests even more worrisome.

Diagnosis: Emmy's desire for sweets was normal—young children are drawn to energy-rich foods and ask for them as language and awareness develop (WHY). Holly's reaction to limit sweets (and make up a story) created more desire from Emmy (HOW). Holly's worry about her daughter's size affected the way she handled the situation, which added to the complexity.

Intervention: Holly stopped saying how "bad" sweets were and making up stories that brought more attention to Fun Foods. Instead, she stayed calm and let Emmy know that although these foods are enjoyable, they are eaten less often. Instead of limiting ice cream to once a week, Holly provided it at home. She discussed this with Emmy to find a resolution: "I know you love ice cream, but we are not going to buy it every day at school. Would you like to have some at home for snack on Monday or for dessert during the week?" When Emmy did ask for sweets, Holly reassured her she'd get them again. "It's not snack time, so let's skip it. We'll have it again soon."

Outcome: Once Emmy understood that she was getting the treat foods she loved on a regular basis, and was reminded of that, she calmed down and was more willing to accept when she couldn't have them.

Myth: WHAT a child eats is most important for her weight.

Busted! Although WHAT a child eats matters, so does HOW you feed her. Research consistently shows that parental restriction is closely tied to increased eating and weight gain—eating more when the desired food finally becomes available.[44]

> **Fearless Fact**
>
> According to one study, kids with poor food regulation at three to five years of age gained weight fastest and had the highest BMIs over a nine-year period.[45] Supporting your child's food regulation is important at this stage.

The Won't-Try-Anything Kid

Challenge: Maria was prepared for the picky eating stage. Once her daughter, Lilly, turned three, it was like a switch went off: Lilly's unwillingness to try new foods and her tendency to reject previously liked items were at an all-time high.

Maria had been following Ellyn Satter's DOR, allowing Lilly to choose from what she offered, but when Lilly turned four, and things didn't get better, she was ready to try something else—*anything*!

Diagnosis: In addition to taking normal development into account, we discovered that Maria was also reluctant to try new foods when she was a kid, meaning that there might be an underlying genetic tendency (WHY). With more digging, we found that even though Maria didn't think she was pushing food (HOW), Lilly perceived it that way based on her temperament (WHY). In addition, the variety (WHAT) Maria was providing had decreased over time, and she was in a food rut.

Intervention: First, Maria was happy to discover that her daughter was meeting her nutritional needs; she ate food from most food groups, and her varied fruit intake covered her low veggie intake. This helped Maria drop the agenda and put her desire to get Lilly to eat aside, making the whole process more fun. Maria worked to increase variety with a meal rotation that included a new food at main meals, alongside accepted items, and she used snack time to fill in nutritional gaps. Maria invited Lilly to help with meals and switched to family-style dinners, putting food into bowls and allowing Lilly to serve herself. Maria encouraged her daughter to take everything, and when Lilly didn't, Maria made a separate "learning plate" that she used to talk about the food, encouraging Lilly to touch, smell, or even lick each item. Once Lilly learned enough about a new food, Maria encouraged tasting.

Outcome: A year later, Lilly had expanded her food repertoire in a slow and steady fashion. Now Maria accepts her daughter's cautious nature as part of her personality, and is confident that she will continue to add new foods through the years.

Fearless Tip

For sensory-sensitive kids, encourage playing with, smelling, touching, and even licking the food to get them comfortable before taking bites. Researchers often encourage small tastings of food, with the option of spitting it out. You can also encourage your child with "a bite to be polite," which takes the focus off of food and places it on manners. But if any type of tasting rule causes stress or unpleasantness, give it up!

Myth: Incorporating a one-bite rule is a great way to get kids to try new foods.

Busted! Although this may work for some kids, making a child take a bite can backfire, especially in those with stubborn temperaments and those who are sensory-sensitive (gagging or throwing up with forced bites).

The Separate Meal Eater

Challenge: Sharla and Jack's two kids, ages four and five, had been on separate meals since they were babies. Although most of what they ate was relatively healthy, they were used to the same old reliable food. Sharla began to notice that her kids did not do well at eating events outside the home, as they whined for their usual fare. Even when they all sat down together at meals, her kids ate different foods than she and her husband did. She wanted to start family meals but felt overwhelmed and wasn't sure how to go about it.

Diagnosis: Sharla and Jack's kids were used to the same old food due to the way they were fed, which didn't incentivize them to branch out (HOW). Sharla feared her kids wouldn't eat, so nutrition (WHAT) did play a role. She didn't realize how much easier it would be to take a unified approach.

Intervention: The couple sat their kids down and let them know that they were going to start eating together as a family, which meant fewer separate meals with preferred foods. They asked them for weekly input and told them to expect to see their favorites on a regular basis, determined by them. Sharla and Jack made a weekly meal plan and carefully picked sides the kids liked on nights the entrée was new or different, and had different sides on the nights the kids liked the entrée. They stood their ground that there would be one meal and that additional items were not to be made.

> **Fearless Tip**
>
> When children say they don't want to eat dinner, remind them that meals are also about family time and not just about food and eating.

Outcome: There was a lot of complaining the first couple of weeks, but after the kids understood there was no going back, family meals became more fun and the kids started to expand their food choices.

Myth: If I don't keep my child on separate meals, or short-order cook, he won't eat.

Busted! Over time, this strategy fails because kids get more particular about food and don't expand their food repertoire.

The Grazer

Challenge: Four-year-old Jerry was an underweight, active boy who liked to play and stay on the move. His mom, Laurie, was so desperate to get him to eat that she would strap him in the baby bouncer. She left food out all over the house in the event that he would graze, and she often resorted to spoon-feeding him. He refused most of the stuff she offered, and mealtime was long and stressful.

Diagnosis: Laurie had a hard time accepting her son's small appetite (WHY) and his inability to sit for long periods. The more she pushed, the more Jerry pushed back (HOW). As far as we could see, there were no underlying problems, as he accepted a decent variety but just ate very little. Feeding was strained, and both mother and son were out of sync.

Intervention: Laurie tried to accept her child for what he was capable of in the eating department. She stuck to a regular routine of food offerings, no longer left food around the house, and had Jerry sit at the table for meals without interfering with his eating (the hardest part!). Laurie made sure she provided balanced meals (small portions designed not to overwhelm him) with all the food groups, but she also kept her child on full-fat dairy and provided adequate fat sources (butter on bread, sliced avocados, nut butters, meats, dips with veggies), as he needed a diet high in energy *and* nutrition. We recommended a multivitamin with iron until his eating came around.

Outcome: At first Jerry did not eat much, which was a challenge for Laurie. But after a few weeks he picked up the pace and began to eat, and his weight, although still below average, stabilized and seemed to be right for his body type.

Myth: If I don't push my child to eat, he will wither away.

Busted! Research shows that pressuring kids to eat backfires, creating a negative food environment. One study showed that a group of children pressured to eat soup not only ate less but also made a total of 157 negative comments during the meal, compared to 30 negative comments in the group of children who weren't pressured.[46]

> **Fearless Tip**
>
> When first left alone, children may not eat much, but once they realize the pressure is off, they will come around. If growth is an issue, or if there are any of the red flags listed in Chapter Seven indicating an underlying problem, get help.

When challenges arise, parents often look just to food (WHAT) as the solution. We hope you will consider all of the Fearless Feeding Fundamentals so you can find solutions that address the problem at its root. To help you along, we provide recipes in the next section that will help you maximize nutrition and food enjoyment at this stage.

Real, Easy Recipes for Toddlers and Preschoolers

Nearly every mom of a toddler has been enticed with a "kid-friendly" recipe, only to look at it and think: *There's no way my kid is eating that!* We know that our readers are coming to this chapter at different stages. Some of you will have been dealing with a picky eater for months, whereas others may have toddlers who will eat almost anything (and many more of you will be somewhere in between!). This is why we give you variations for every meal and tips on how kids can help in the kitchen. We provide key nutrients for each recipe here, with full nutrient lists available on request through the contact page of our website, www.fearlessfeeding.com. Let's get started with breakfast and end with some nutrient-packed snacks.

Pack a Punch at Breakfast

Toddlers and preschoolers tend to be hungriest at breakfast—so we maximize nutrition with classic favorites. Be honest with your child when you are adding a fruit or veggie to a meal or a food they accept, and have them help you. Never try to sneak it in, as that sends the message that the healthy ingredient is so bad you have to hide it. The homemade granola bars listed in the snack ideas can also be used for a quick breakfast.

Yogurt and Flax Waffles

This recipe is courtesy of Sally Kuzemchak, registered dietitian and blogger at Real Mom Nutrition.

Ingredients

2 tablespoons butter

1 cup milk

1 cup plain low-fat yogurt

4 eggs

1 tablespoon vanilla

6 tablespoons ground flaxseed

1 cup white flour (or whole wheat pastry flour)

1 cup whole wheat flour

2¾ teaspoons baking soda

¾ teaspoon salt

Cooking spray

Directions

Preheat the waffle iron and spray it with cooking spray. Melt the butter in a medium bowl; add the milk, yogurt, eggs, vanilla, and flaxseed; and stir. Combine the dry ingredients in a separate bowl, and then combine them with the wet ingredients. Pour the batter into the waffle iron in batches and cook until golden brown.

Variations: For children transitioning off of store-bought waffles, consider using all white flour initially and slowly transition to whole grain flour. Whole wheat pastry flour, which can be found in most stores, has a soft texture and is great in baked products.

Little Helpers: Allow kids to measure dry ingredients and place them in the bowl.

Daily Dialogue: "What is flaxseed, Mom?" "Flax is a seed that comes from a tall, thin plant. It has a nutty taste, but you probably won't taste it with the amounts we are using. It helps your brain and body be healthy and grow."

Makes: Eight to ten waffles

Key nutrients (percent daily value [%DV]): Calcium (13), iron (11), manganese (43), selenium (35), thiamin (21), riboflavin (20)

Pumpkin French Toast

Ingredients

2 eggs

¼ cup milk

¼ cup pumpkin

½ teaspoon cinnamon

¼ teaspoon vanilla

4 pieces whole wheat bread (or bread of choice)

Cooking spray or butter

Directions

Beat 2 eggs in a bowl. Add the milk, pumpkin, cinnamon, and vanilla, and mix well. Dip the bread in the mixture, and then place the bread on a grill greased with butter or cooking spray.

Variations: For kids who are selective, start with basic French toast using soft bread, and once that is accepted try whole wheat bread and eventually pumpkin.

Little Helpers: Let them crack eggs and measure ingredients.

Daily Dialogue: "Why are you adding pumpkin, Dad?" "It's fun to try new foods when you cook. Pumpkin has a sweet taste, so it goes well with French toast."

Makes: Four servings

Key nutrients (%DV): Iron (8), vitamin A (39), selenium (28), manganese (34)

Quickie Lunches

Getting lunch into kids before nap time can be challenging. These quick and healthy lunches are great options for breaking the lunch rut and keeping a variety of wholesome foods coming. Other ideas include quesadillas, make-your-own sandwiches, and baked potatoes (zap them in the microwave!) with a toppings bar so kids can add their own.

Easy Bean and Cheese Burrito

This recipe is courtesy of Estela Schnelle, registered dietitian and blogger at Weekly Bite.

Ingredients

1 whole wheat tortilla

3 tablespoons low-fat refried beans

1 to 2 tablespoons shredded cheddar cheese

Olive oil

Directions

Preheat the oven to 400°F. Spread beans over the entire tortilla and sprinkle cheese over the beans. Roll the tortilla up tightly. Place the burrito (seam side down) on an oven-safe dish. Brush the burrito with a little olive oil and sprinkle a bit of cheese on top (if desired). Bake for 7 to 10 minutes, or until the tortilla is lightly browned and crispy. Slice the burrito in half to make two toddler servings.

Variations: Serve with a side of salsa and guacamole and add chicken.

Little Helpers: Have them spread beans on the tortillas and sprinkle cheese.

Makes: One or two servings (one burrito)

Key nutrients (%DV): Calcium (12), phosphorus (19), selenium (29), iron (11)

Rainbow Pasta (Hot or Cold)

Ingredients

2 cups whole grain rotini or tricolored pasta

2 teaspoons olive oil

2 teaspoons lemon juice (about ½ lemon squeezed)

¼ cup Parmesan cheese

¼ teaspoon garlic powder

¼ teaspoon salt

1 cup cooked peas and carrots (or other vegetable of choice)

Directions

Cook the pasta according to the directions on the package. In a large bowl, mix all the ingredients, including the cooked pasta.

Variations: For more selective children, try plain pasta first. Then add vegetables, and even try protein, such as beans, tofu, or canned salmon or tuna.

Little Helpers: Serve the added goodies separately, and allow children to add various ingredients on their own.

Daily Dialogue: "Let's see how much more color we can add to the pasta."

Makes: Ten ½-cup servings

Key nutrients (%DV): Selenium (21), phosphorus (8), vitamin K (6)

Kid-Friendly Dinners

Parents of toddlers and preschoolers often tell us their kids aren't interested in dinner. So having a couple of items children love as options, and rotating them in the mix (as sides or main dishes), can help immensely. Asking your little one for input as you plan your weekly meals can make a difference too.

Homemade Chicken Nuggets

Ingredients

1 cup bread crumbs (try panko for more crunch)

½ cup Parmesan cheese

1 teaspoon salt

½ teaspoon paprika

½ teaspoon garlic powder

½ teaspoon mustard seed

½ teaspoon pepper

1 egg, beaten

1 pound chicken breasts or tenders

Cooking spray

Directions

Preheat the oven to 400°F. In a medium bowl combine and mix the first seven ingredients. In a small bowl, beat the egg. Cut the chicken into 1- to 1.5-inch pieces, dip the chicken in the egg, and then dredge through the bread crumb mixture. (For children used to store-bought nuggets, you can pulse chicken in a food processor or used ground chicken.) Place the chicken on a cookie sheet lined with foil (sprayed with cooking spray) or parchment paper. Bake the chicken for about 20 to 22 minutes, or until the chicken is cooked through. Freeze what you don't use for quick meals.

Variations: Try this recipe with fish—1 pound salmon cut into 1- to 1.5-inch fingers, cooked at 400°F for 8 to 10 minutes or until cooked through. Zucchini fries also work (cutting zucchini in strips, putting them in the egg, and dipping them in bread crumbs), but cook these at a higher temperature (450°F) for about 25 minutes, turning once during cooking. For a nutrition boost, add flax meal or wheat germ, and for a richer nugget, use melted butter instead of egg for dipping.

Makes: About six four-nugget servings, depending on the size of the nuggets

Key nutrients (%DV): Iron (8), manganese (10), phosphorus (10), niacin (20), selenium (18), vitamin B6 (9)

Fearless Tip

Get your little one excited about salads by buying her a special salad bowl and trying the following:

- *Baby bok choy:* Inspired by one of our blog readers, Jenny, this mix of bok choy, apple, and yogurt is perfect for kids. Thinly slice 3 baby bok choy. Add 1 small red apple cut into small pieces, ¼ cup thinly sliced scallions (green onions, white and green parts; optional), ¼ cup plain low-fat yogurt, 1 tablespoon lemon juice, and salt and pepper to taste. Mix all the ingredients and enjoy.
- *Greens, fruit, and nuts:* Mix greens of choice; fruit (grapes, strawberries, apples, and dried fruit); and nuts, such as sliced, dried almonds. Toss with a mild or sweet vinaigrette dressing of choice.
- *Make-your-own salad:* Ask your child to choose at least 3 ingredients (making one a mandatory green) to put in his salad with a dressing of choice. Allow dipping goodies in the dressing or have the salad tossed.

Black Bean Sliders

Ingredients

1 (14-ounce) can black beans, drained and rinsed

2 teaspoons olive oil, and more for brushing

1 teaspoon cumin

½ teaspoon garlic powder

½ teaspoon chili powder

1 egg

⅓ cup bread crumbs

1 medium sweet potato (or two small), cooked and mashed (without skin)

½ cup Mexican blend cheese

Cooking spray

Directions

Preheat the oven to 350°F. Drain and rinse the beans. Add oil and seasonings to the beans and pulse them in a food processor until chunky (do not puree). Combine the bean mixture with the egg, bread crumbs, mashed sweet potato. and cheese. Form the mixture into small patties (about ten) and place them on a large cookie sheet sprayed with cooking spray. Brush the patties with olive oil, and bake at 350°F for 15 minutes (flip after 10 minutes and cook an additional 5).

Variations: Serve the patties with bread or a tortilla, or simply top them with avocado or salsa. To round out the meal, serve with a side of fruit.

Little Helpers: Have them help rinse the beans and form the patties.

Daily Dialogue: "We are going to make burgers with black beans to experiment. I can't wait to see how it tastes!"

Makes: Ten sliders

Key nutrients (%DV): Iron (7), magnesium (7), phosphorus (9), manganese (11), vitamin A (50)

Maximizing Snack Time

This is a time when snacking on processed foods can get out of control. Here we entice little ones with homemade versions of appealing snack foods. See Appendix C for more healthy snack ideas.

Homemade Granola Bars

Ingredients

2½ cups rolled oats (not quick cooking)

½ cup flour (whole wheat pastry flour works well)

½ cup wheat germ

½ teaspoon salt

2 teaspoons cinnamon

¼ cup canola oil

1 egg

⅓ cup honey

¼ cup brown sugar

2 teaspoons vanilla

¼ cup applesauce (plus more if needed)

Cooking spray

Up to 1½ cups additions (chocolate chips, chopped nuts, dried fruit)

Directions

Preheat the oven to 350°F. In a large bowl, mix together the first five ingredients (including the oats). In another bowl, mix together the rest of the ingredients, minus the cooking spray. Combine the wet and dry ingredients and any additions you have. The mixture should be moist but not too wet. If it seems too dry or crumbly, add applesauce by the spoonful. Spray an 8- by 8-inch square pan with cooking spray or use parchment paper, and press the mixture into the pan. Cook for about 30 minutes, but check for browning earlier. Let the cooked mixture cool for 5 minutes, and then cut into squares (if you wait too long to cut the mixture, it can harden). Allow the squares to cool more. Refrigerate or freeze leftovers.

Variations: If your child is used to store-bought granola bars, start with ¾ cup chocolate chips and slowly add nuts and dried fruit. Play around with this recipe to find what you like. You can substitute wheat germ for flax or do half and half. Using more flour and less oats makes it chewy. The possibilities are endless.

Makes: About twenty-one small bars

Key nutrients (%DV): Iron (6), manganese (23), phosphorus (8), magnesium (8)

Fruit and Veggie Smoothie

Ingredients

1 cup greens (spinach and kale work well)

1 cup frozen or fresh fruit (strawberries or mixed berries)

1 banana

½ cup orange juice

½ cup plain low-fat yogurt

2 tablespoons wheat germ or flax

Handful of ice (if using fresh fruit instead of frozen)

Directions

Blend all the ingredients in a blender. Serve with a straw in ½-cup servings to start.

Variations: For the child used to sweet tastes, try using vanilla yogurt and skip the greens and wheat germ. Once accepted, add these ingredients and switch to plain yogurt as a last step.

Little Helpers: Kids can measure ingredients and toss them in the blender. Be sure to have them help or watch when adding new ingredients, including the greens.

Daily Dialogue: "Let's make smoothies today. I want to try and add some spinach—let's see if it changes the taste and color."

Makes: Just over four ½-cup servings

Key nutrients (%DV): Vitamin C (72), vitamin K (47), riboflavin (9), potassium (11), calcium (8), folate (13), vitamin B6 (10)

CHAPTER 4

Fearless Feeding for Your School-Age Child (Six to Twelve Years)

Good nutrition and feeding remain center stage during the school-age years, as eating habits and food preferences are being molded for a lifetime. Physical growth is steady early on, but many children may start puberty. The world gets bigger. School, friends, and media influence your child's thoughts and eating habits. We help you navigate nutrition and feeding, teach nutrition, and handle the outside influences so you can continue on the journey of raising a healthy eater. We're confident you can!

Nutrition in Practice: Navigating the Outside World

Rachel is worried, and it's a dull, nagging worry that she can't get off her mind. Her nine-year-old daughter, Audrey, comes home telling stories of trading lunchbox items with her friends, a classmate's birthday party with "the best cupcakes ever!" and her (thinner) best friend's take on "bad" chicken nuggets at school. To top it off, "Audrey asked me last night if I thought she was fat." According to Rachel, "Life was easier when Audrey wasn't in school."

Many parents like Rachel initially view the school-age years as "easy," until they're in the thick of it. Parents face several dilemmas during these years. They want their child to be independent, but that often leads to poor food choices.

They relish the ability their child has to make her own snack or breakfast, but they quickly realize that the health quality of the food choices over the course of a day may suffer. They enjoy allowing more food freedom, but the influence of friends and school may creep in and turn their child into an "unhealthy eater." It's enough to make parents nervous and on the hunt for ways to retrieve the innocence of the toddler years—and the control they once had.

Welcome to the new demands, pressures, and conundrums of the school-age years. In this chapter, we will build on the Fearless Feeding Strategy and what you learned in the previous chapter. We know you want your child to eat healthy foods so that she can grow to her full potential, and that's exactly the focus of this chapter.

What to Expect

The elementary years, ages six to ten, are known as the *latent period* of growth before the pubertal growth spurt. During this time, weight and height gains occur in "spurts," or bursts of growth, followed by periods of little to no growth. As you have learned from previous chapters, appetite reflects growth, with growth spurts triggering surges in food consumption and slowed growth translating to lags in appetite, both of which are typical for this stage.

Children morph in appearance from mostly trunk with short arms and legs to dangly and gangly as puberty hits. Each child truly is different, and children's growth reflects their genetic potential and the environment in which they live. Although you *should* count on the school-age years to be a time of steady growth, you need to be aware of upward or downward trends in weight, which may indicate excess weight gain or loss. Awareness of these deviations can head off troublesome challenges, such as excess weight or poor growth or undernutrition.

> **Fearless Fact**
>
> The average seven-year-old child gains about 4.5 pounds per year and 2 to 2.5 inches in height, whereas the average ten-year-old gains almost 9 pounds per year. By ten years, the average girl is taller and heavier than the average boy, as girls outpace boys during this stage, creating a "growth gap." During puberty, girls add more fat mass than boys, and boys add more lean mass than girls.

You can watch what's going on with your child's growth by looking at his growth chart, which you are likely to review with your pediatrician at checkups, noting growth and the body mass index (BMI) trend. A "healthy weight" is a BMI that falls between the 5th and 85th percentiles for age (www.cdc.gov/growthcharts /clinical_charts.htm#Set1). As with the infant and toddler years, the overall growth pattern is the best indicator of your child's health and nutritional status.

Onset of Puberty

On average, girls begin puberty between ages ten and eleven (well before the teen years), whereas boys begin about two years later, between eleven and twelve years of age. Despite starting later, boys grow for two additional years after girls stop, and they grow more during their growth spurt than girls do. Many changes occur during puberty, which we'll discuss in the next chapter. Here, we'll focus on girls, as many physical transitions are under way before age thirteen.

School-age girls experience extra weight gain around the middle, curvy hips, breast development, and thicker extremities, all of which are normal signs of maturation. These changes can throw parents off and heighten concern about weight, especially the emerging "belly," which is normal. If you note overall weight gain, confer with your pediatrician. Parents can also become concerned their son isn't beefing up and gaining muscle. This, too, is all about the timing of puberty.

"Why is my ten-year-old starting her period *now*?" asked Karen, who didn't start her own menses until she was almost fourteen years old. "She's not old enough!"

Although this seems young, it's not uncommon. We know that when breasts begin to "bud" and pubic hair begins to sprout, the first period is just around the corner. Although the median age of menarche (the first period) is twelve and a half years for U.S. girls, varying slightly with race and ethnicity, it's clear that this age norm is declining.[1]

> **Fearless Fact**
>
> Menarche may be more correlated with weight status, specifically higher BMI scores, than with age.[1] For some kids, early development occurs even before hitting double digits, due to what experts call precocious puberty (pubertal onset before eight years in girls and nine years in boys).

Activity

Most children's activity centers around play, and if children are getting outside to play, they are probably meeting the recommended activity guideline of one hour per day.[2] All physical activity counts, including recess, gym, outdoor play, and structured sports. If your child begins structured activity (sports), you may notice an increase in appetite. Staying the course with regular meals and snacks and offering adequate hydration are most important.

Changing Nutritional Needs

All growing school-age kids have specific nutrient needs for normal growth, including calories, protein, vitamins, minerals, fiber, and fluids. For example, protein is required for the formation of new muscle, organ, and bone tissue, which is exactly what growth is all about. Most children ages six to twelve require approximately 0.4 to 0.5 grams of protein per pound of body weight.[3] Fat still remains important, but the types of fat in your child's diet deserve attention, as many kids are getting too much of the wrong kinds of fat: saturated fat (from animal fat sources) and trans fat (from products made with hydrogenated oils). Vitamins and minerals (micronutrients) are necessary for the normal metabolic activities related to your child's growth.

One nutrient that is especially important is calcium. At age nine, the recommendations for this nutrient increase to 1,300 milligrams, much higher than for younger children.[3] Bone growth is rapid during these years and in adolescence, making this time to "invest" in your child's bone health. Fiber and potassium are at rock bottom in children's diets these days, crowded out by poor snack choices; picky eating; and low exposure to whole grains, fruits, and vegetables.[2] Finally, calorie needs vary from child to child, as outlined in Table 4.1, and they increase tremendously during this time, exceeding the calories needed by most adults!

Appreciation for Hunger

Hunger is a real biological force and your child's barometer for knowing when to eat. Typically, school-age children get hungry every three to four hours. Hunger pangs are influenced by how much your child eats (quantity); what she eats

Table 4.1	Energy Needs of the School-Age Child					
Age	Sedentary (Calories)		Moderately Active (Calories)		Active (Calories)	
	Males	Females	Males	Females	Males	Females
Six to eight years	1,200–1,400	1,200–1,400	1,400–1,600	1,400–1,600	1,600–2,000	1,400–1,800
Nine to twelve years	1,600–2,000	1,400–1,600	1,800–2,200	1,600–2,000	2,000–2,600	1,800–2,200

Source: Adapted from U.S. Department of Agriculture & U.S. Department of Health and Human Services. (2010). *Dietary guidelines for Americans, 2010* (7th ed.). Washington DC: U.S. Government Printing Office.

(composition); when she eats; and, as we just discussed, growth and activity level (energy expenditure).

It's important to remember that as your child marches toward puberty, hunger and appetite will climb to new heights. This is normal. We know that hunger can be managed with meals and snacks, spaced at intervals that avoid prolonged periods without food, and planned with attention to their makeup. We have seen countless families restructure their "feeding plan" to promote satisfaction and meet nutritional needs while avoiding the common pitfalls: overeating and choosing less-than-healthy options.

Understanding your child's growth, puberty onset, activity, and hunger can quell your worries. But that's not all there is to know—keep reading for more information on how to handle outside influences.

Food for Thought

Now that you know what to expect with growth and nutrient needs, feeding your child should be easy, right? As you launch your kindergartner-turned-grade-schooler into the world, you are starting the fight—the war against the world of food influences—and preserving your own influence over your child's eating patterns, choices, and behaviors. In the paragraphs that follow, you'll learn about the influences on your child's food choices: peers, school, and media.

Friendly Perspective

Through friendship, your child will be exposed to different foods, attitudes, and values, influencing his eating.[4] Even if you feed your child the healthiest of meals, in the outside world it is likely that your child will notice the foods around him, try them, trade, and maybe even come home with new requests that you've never heard before! Friends influence your child, and you may become acutely aware that these little people have pull, and not always in the right direction.

A family nutrition mantra can help keep your child on course as he grows. Messages as simple as "We eat real food," to more complex ideas outlining your beliefs about food balance, daily activity, and food exploration, help your child identify your family's beliefs about nutrition. A nutrition mantra is a guiding light, so to speak, helping your child navigate the nutrition world without you.

Fearless Tip

On the home front, Dayle Hayes, registered dietitian and president of Nutrition for the Future, suggests parents help their children through what she calls "grounding and guidance." "Grounding," she explains, "comprises the family values about nutrition: the basic sense of what to eat, when to eat, and when to stop. Family mealtime is the centerpiece for this solid foundation. Guidance is the advice parents give their children for exploration of the food world, which ultimately evolves into a personal eating style."

Getting Schooled

If your child buys a school lunch, it can provide approximately one-third of his nutritional needs (about 25 percent comes from the School Breakfast Program), with a balanced representation of all food groups.[5] School lunch is improving, thanks to attention directed at food quality, nutrient balance, and kid appeal, but it can still be hard to manage when it comes to healthy eating.

Packed lunches can be a good alternative, yet these may fall short on nutrients, especially calcium, vitamin D, fiber, and potassium, and may lean on the high side of fat and sugar due to the inclusion of chips and sweets.[6] A la carte items, the food that kids buy to supplement their sack or school lunch, may also add extra fat and calories, and are known to contribute to lower fruit and vegetable consumption.[7]

If your child gets "extras"—classroom parties, snacks, food rewards, and concessions—these may add too many calories and too much sugar and fat. In fact, kids can receive more than half of their nutritional requirements for the day from school.[6] This can be frustrating for many parents who are trying to manage healthy eating.

"My eight-year-old is offered a birthday treat, a morning snack, and a packaged after-school snack almost every day," said Meg. "How am I supposed to keep healthy eating at the forefront when my child is offered these foods routinely?"

Helping children decide whether or not to partake in these "extras" is part of a positive approach, but there is more you can do. You can get involved like Meg did. Initially, she started sending a morning snack for her son each day and suggested a list of "acceptable snacks" for the whole class, and eventually the school. When Meg was assigned "treat for the week," she made sure to provide healthy options like fresh fruit and cheese sticks or yogurt with graham crackers for the entire class. She also suggested a once-a-month birthday party for all kids celebrating their birthdays instead of every individual birthday being another opportunity for cakes and other treats. The list that follows shows ways that you can get involved in school nutrition and make a difference.

Ten Ways to Influence What Your Child Eats at School

1. Develop an open, positive, and communicative relationship with your child's teacher.
2. Send a snack to school with your child.
3. If you can, provide healthy snacks for the whole class.
4. Get involved through an organization like the PTA! Individually, you can do something; as a group, you can do a lot.
5. Join the wellness movement (or start one) in your school.
6. Be creative and stay realistic. Small steps work better than radical makeovers.

(continued)

7. Get kids involved in setting parameters around classroom party foods, concessions, and vending machine contents—they are the best agents of change.
8. Maximize peer-to-peer opportunities, such as school gardens or farm clubs like 4H or Future Farmers of America.
9. Align nutrition changes with school mascots, the school mantra, or school goals, personalizing health and wellness to the school.
10. Help revamp vending machines to hold truly healthy food items (fresh fruit, vegetables, yogurt, string cheese), not "faux health foods" (baked chips, organic soda).

Media: Need We Say (See) More?

The influence of media is powerful and can be overwhelming, but we know you can manage it. We'd love to tell you that turning off the TV will solve your problems, but TV is just the tip of the iceberg. Magazines, computers, portable games, phones (and their apps), and social media sites like Facebook that have surged in popularity prove to be the sneaky influences that are more difficult to quantify, and control.

Studies indicate that food advertising to children consists almost entirely of messages in favor of nutrient-poor, high-calorie foods, such as sugary cereals and beverages and salty, fatty snacks. As a result, children learn to request these products by name. Children exposed to food ads request these foods at a higher rate, and healthier foods (fruits and vegetables) at a lower rate.[8,9,10]

Talking with your child about the rationale and goals behind advertising and setting rules about watching TV, such as time limits or acceptable days for viewing, may be the best things you can do to prevent negative eating patterns. One study found that restricting advertising was only effective in children under eight years old. After that, the combination of setting limits on TV and media consumption while helping children understand the goals and intentions of advertising was more effective in curbing food ads' negative influence.[11]

In Table 4.2, we've summarized the top three influencers for the school-age child and outlined effective action steps you can take to manage their sway.

Table 4.2 Top Three Nutrition Influencers		
Influencer	**Impact on Kids**	**You Are the Antidote!**
Peers	• Kids eat more sweets and nutrient-poor foods when eating with friends and consume fewer fruits and vegetables.	• Talk about and set a family nutrition mantra. • Plan for moderate amounts of sweets throughout the week. • Pack extra fruits and vegetables for sharing.
School	• Kids consume extra empty calories from à la carte items, parties, and snacks. • Having more than one meal and snacks at school may mean excess calories. • Competitive foods from vending machines, parties, or concessions encourage less-than-healthy choices.	• Bolster the health quality of foods offered at home. • Scale back on sweets, soda, and fried foods in sack lunches. • Provide healthy snacks for parties and events. • Effect healthy changes in school policies concerning extra foods from outside.
Media	• The influence of media molds kids' preferences for less-than-healthy foods. • Kids request advertised food products by name. • Media messages capitalize on kids' desire to fit in.	• Set media viewing rules. For example, limit TV viewing to less than two hours per day, implement a "no media" rule during the school week, or a try a combination of these. • Educate children at home about the methods and intentions of advertising, and encourage the provision of such education in school.

Fearless Food Guide

If children are to grow normally, they need just the right amount of calories, macronutrients, and micronutrients—not too much and not too little. Paying attention to nutrition during this time can optimize your child's learning in school, prevent nutrient deficiencies, and normalize growth (avoiding underweight and overweight).

The Reality of Eating

As just alluded to, the quality and adequacy of your child's diet have an impact on academic performance, from your child's ability to pay attention in class to her performance on tests. One study surveying over five thousand socioeconomically diverse fifth graders and their parents found that students who ate a limited variety of food and insufficient amounts were more likely to fail a standardized test than students with an optimal diet (higher fruit and vegetable consumption and lower fat intake).[12] Eating breakfast has also been shown to improve attention, focus, and concentration, and has positive effects on weight status, eating patterns, and appetite regulation.[13]

School-age kids today are living on the edge of excess and deficiency when it comes to nutrition. They are consuming too many calories; too much saturated fat, total fat, sugar, and salt; and not enough calcium, Vitamin D, potassium, and fiber. Sugar-sweetened beverages, convenience snack foods, and meals consumed away from home provide most of the extra calories kids are eating.

Given this information, our goal is to help you choose foods that will capitalize on health and minimize these nutrition threats. See Chapter One for more descriptions of each food category (Nourishing Foods, Half-and-Half Foods, and Fun Foods), and see Appendix A for details on each food group.

> **Fearless Fact**
>
> More than 23 percent of calories eaten by U.S. kids comes from snacks. According to a 2010 study out of the University of North Carolina, snacking is associated with greater consumption of protein, fat, carbohydrates, folate, Vitamin C, magnesium, iron, potassium, and fiber, but it also increases kids' intake of sugar and saturated fats.[14]

What's the Right Portion?

We recognize that your child lives in a world of larger-than-life portions. Many researchers have associated bigger portion sizes with the growing child obesity trend in the United States. As mentioned in Chapter One, we prefer the term *portion awareness* rather than *portion control*. Portion awareness embodies knowledge rather than restriction, and feeds into a child's ability to make food decisions independently.

Serving bigger portions usually means eating more than the body needs. We believe you should model portion awareness when planning and serving meals, so children get a more realistic view of portion sizes.

Table 4.3 outlines the age-specific serving sizes for each food group, and the daily amounts needed to meet nutritional requirements. We recommend you use this chart for a "check and balance" approach to daily feeding—it's not meant to place maximums or minimums on your child's eating, but rather to guide you to create balanced meals and correct imbalances that may occur. For more food group details, see Appendix A.

Real Deal Meals and Snacks

Children need three meals and one or two snacks each day. Most school-age children already have a routine and timing that allow for eating every three to four hours. Your meal plan should provide a steady supply of nutrients to your child's brain and body, but sometimes this can get off track. For example, if your child has a late lunch at school, send in a morning snack. If your child has an early lunch and there will be a long stretch until dismissal, consider adding an afternoon snack. Of course, this will be dependent on your child's school schedule and hunger level. When packing snacks, pay attention to food group balance and include age-appropriate portions when possible.

Table 4.4 shows how this can work with a sample meal plan for an eight-year-old. Males have slightly higher calorie requirements than females, which translates to additional food items or larger portions. For the older school-age

Fearless Fact

Kids eat more when they are served more—up to 33 percent more when entrées are doubled, resulting in more calories eaten from the meal (13 to 39 percent more) and for the day (about 12 percent more).[15]

Fearless Tip

Model normal portion sizes and keep an eye on oversize ones. When dining out, watch out for words like "value meal," "combo," "ultimate," "tub," "supreme," "biggie," "deluxe," and "supersize." Split large meals and take half home with you for later, order the standard or "original" version, or share entrées with another person.

Table 4.3 Fearless Food Guide for School-Age Children

Food Group	Serving Sizes	Six- to Nine-Year-Old Total Daily Servings	Ten- to Twelve-Year-Old Total Daily Servings	Comments
Meats and nonmeat protein sources:		4 to 5	5	Include beans and fish twice weekly. Serve high-fat meats less often (up to twice weekly).
Chicken, pork, fish and shellfish	1 ounce			
Eggs	1 egg			
Nuts and seeds	½ ounce			
Nut butters	1 tablespoon			
Beans, tofu	¼ cup			
Dairy and nondairy sources:		2½ to 3 cups	3 cups	Include low-fat or nonfat dairy foods; minimize high-fat options.
Milk, yogurt	¾ to 1 cup			
Cheese	1½ ounces			
Nondairy alternatives	¾ to 1 cup			
Fruits:		1½	1½	Keep juice to 8 to 12 ounces daily or less. Include a vitamin C source daily. Fruits and vegetables can be interchanged to total 5 servings per day. Ideally, you want a blend of both fruits and vegetables each day.
Fresh, frozen, or canned fruit	1 medium or 1 cup			
Dried fruit	½ cup			
100 percent fruit juice	1 cup			

	Serving			
Vegetables:			2	Include vitamin A sources daily. Vegetables and fruit are interchangeable; aim for 5 servings daily. Ideally, you want a blend of both fruits and vegetables each day.
Cooked vegetables	½ to 1 cup			
Raw vegetables	1 cup			
Leafy salad greens	2 cups			
Grains: Wheat, rye, barley, oats, quinoa, rice	½ cup	5	6	Choose whole grains at least half of the time.
Bread	1 slice			
Pasta, rice, cooked cereal	½ cup			
Dry cereal	1 cup			
Bagel, English muffin	½			
Fats:		4	5	Cook and stock the kitchen with healthy fats. Offer and cook with saturated and trans fat less often. (Fats are inherent in many foods, such as nuts, seeds, dairy products, and meats. Amounts here represent fat added to foods.)
Vegetable oils (olive, canola, flaxseed), soft butter	1 teaspoon			
Mayonnaise, salad dressing	1 tablespoon			
Avocado	⅛ medium			
Fun Foods: Cookies, cakes, pies, candy, sugar-sweetened drinks, pastries, fried foods	1 serving	1 (10 percent of daily intake, or up to 150 calories per day)	1 to 2 (10 percent of daily intake, or up to 250 calories per day)	Limit sugar-sweetened beverages to 12-ounce portions. We suggest keeping soda out of the home and reserving it for special occasions. Pay attention to serving sizes. Eat Fun Foods as part of a meal or healthy snack.

Table 4.4 Real Deal Meal Plan for an Eight-Year-Old

Time	Meal or Snack	Food Groups	Female	Male
6:30 a.m.	Breakfast	• Meat or nonmeat • Vegetable • Fruit • Grain • Fat • Dairy or nondairy	• 1 scrambled egg • ½ cup spinach • ½ apple, sliced • 1 slice whole grain toast • 1 tablespoon olive oil spread • 8 ounces low-fat milk, fortified with vitamin D	• 1 scrambled egg • ½ cup spinach • ½ apple, sliced • 1 slice whole grain toast • 1 tablespoon olive oil spread • 8 ounces low-fat milk, fortified with vitamin D
10:00 a.m.	Snack	• Fruit	• ½ cup mandarin oranges	• ½ cup mandarin oranges
12:30 p.m.	Lunch	• Meat or nonmeat • Vegetable • Grain • Fat • Dairy or nondairy	• 2 ounces turkey breast; 1 tablespoon hummus • 1 lettuce leaf; ½ cup sugar snap peas • 2 slices whole wheat bread • 1 teaspoon mayonnaise • ½ cup low-fat fruit yogurt • Water	• 2 ounces turkey breast; 2 tablespoons hummus • 1 lettuce leaf; 1 cup sugar snap peas • 2 slices whole wheat bread • 1 teaspoon mayonnaise • 1 cup low-fat fruit yogurt • Water
3:30 p.m.	Snack	• Grain • Dairy or nondairy	• 1 cup ready-to-eat cereal • 8 ounces low-fat milk, fortified with vitamin D	• 1 cup ready-to-eat cereal • 8 ounces low fat milk, fortified with vitamin D
6:30 p.m.	Dinner	• Meat or nonmeat • Vegetable • Fruit • Grain • Fat • Fun Food	• 3 ounces salmon • 1 cup sautéed broccoli • 1 cup strawberries • ½ cup rice pilaf • 1 teaspoon olive oil (for sautéing broccoli) • 1 small brownie • Water	• 3 ounces salmon • 1 cup sautéed broccoli • 1 cup strawberries • ½ cup rice pilaf • 1 teaspoon olive oil (for sautéing broccoli) • 1 small brownie • Water

child (ten to twelve years), you can follow the same meal plan but with slightly larger portion sizes.

Planning to incorporate food groups into each meal or snack allows you to maximize Nourishing and Half-and-Half Foods, substitute different foods based on your family's preferences, and start with appropriate serving sizes. You'll note that meals are balanced with nearly all the food groups, and they are heftier than snacks. Although snacks are necessary, their role is to provide a steady source of fuel and keep hunger in check during the active part of the day, as well as to contribute to the nutritional content of your child's diet.

The Fun Foods in the meal plan are there to give you a sense of how they can fit in a day. We encourage you to strategize about how often you offer them. For example, if your child is getting high exposure to Fun Foods at school, you may consider scaling back on them at home. We do, however, believe it is okay to have Fun Foods present in the home—beneficial, even, as this neutralizes them for everyone and gives kids the chance to learn how to eat them in a healthy and balanced way.

Provide fruits and vegetables frequently throughout the day. In fact, in our sample meal plan, they make an appearance at nearly every meal and snack. With this approach, you not only improve (and maybe correct) the potassium deficit mentioned earlier but also hit the mark with fiber. For good sources of potassium and fiber, see Appendix B.

Because the need for calcium and vitamin D is great in children, we've planned a fortified dairy or nondairy source at key points throughout the day. Some families employ a "milk with meals" policy, ensuring three servings of calcium and vitamin D daily. Others use snacks to offer protein, calcium, and vitamin D and to increase satisfaction.

Finally, you'll see that a source of protein, either meat or nonmeat, dairy or nondairy, is infused into the meal plan at all the major meals and some (if not all) of the snack opportunities. Not only do meat or nonmeat items supply protein, which helps with fullness and satisfaction, but also these items can provide a source of iron and zinc for the growing child. You can find more sources of these nutrients in Appendix B.

We don't expect every day to be perfect—that's not necessary! A week gives you more than twenty-one opportunities to get to these goals, so be flexible and realize you'll overachieve, underachieve, and even hit the mark—and all will probably balance out in the end. Most important, you'll have the nutrition knowledge to feed your child and not go crazy with fear and self-doubt.

Fearless Five Nutrients

Part of raising healthy eaters is adjusting the meal plan and filling in nutrient gaps with food, if needed. For example, if your child shies away from meats, provide more dairy, beans, nuts, and eggs to supply needed protein and iron. If your child isn't big on fruits, then you can rely on vegetables and 100 percent juices to meet his needs. If he's not keen on either, then a multivitamin can supply the needed nutrients while you work on the task of introducing and exposing your child to these foods. And if dairy is not his thing (or he's allergic), you will need to find an alternative nondairy source that can provide calcium and vitamin D, such as soymilk, rice milk or other milks made from grains (see Appendix G). All this is possible! It just requires some extra thought and effort on your part.

We help make it easier for you with the Fearless Five Nutrients in Table 4.5, which highlights the nutrients that are critical for your child's growth and development at this stage and helps you address any gaps. Calcium, vitamin D, potassium, iron, and fiber top our list, as we know these are the nutrients on which kids are most often falling behind. Iron becomes more important with the upcoming growth spurt and during menstruation, and with alternative eating patterns, such as extended picky eating, dieting, or vegetarianism. You can find more foods and their specific nutrient values in Appendix B.

When children hit the school-age years, their calcium needs increase (from 1,000 milligrams to 1,300 milligrams), and their intake plummets.[2] The requirements for potassium increase at age nine, and intake is low due to reduced fruit, vegetable, and dairy intake. Iron, as we mentioned, becomes a star player for girls due to menses. Finally, fiber intake among kids is miserable, with only 3 percent of children ages six through twelve meeting this requirement, due to low intake of whole grains, fruit, vegetables, and such fiber-rich protein sources as beans, seeds, and nuts. Use Table 4.5 to target foods that will cover your child's nutrient gaps. For serving sizes, see Appendix B.

Even with good meal planning, some children just don't get enough and will need extra supplementation. Bottom line: if it's clear that getting the right amount

Table 4.5 Fearless Five Nutrients for School-Age Children

Nutrient	Function	Recommended Daily Allowance (RDA)	Sources	Comments
Calcium	Calcium is needed for bone mineralization and normal muscle contraction.	*Four to eight years:* 1,000 milligrams *Nine to thirteen years:* 1,300 milligrams	Ready-to-eat cereals (100 to 1,000 milligrams), calcium-fortified orange juice (500 milligrams), plain nonfat yogurt (452 milligrams), low-fat fruit yogurt (338 to 384 milligrams), mozzarella (333 milligrams), low-fat milk (305 milligrams), salmon (181 milligrams), vanilla ice cream (84 milligrams), white bread (73 milligrams), chocolate pudding (55 milligrams), whole wheat bread (30 milligrams), cream cheese (14 milligrams)	Sixty-seven percent of girls and 80 percent of boys ages four to eight meet adequate intake (AI) levels.[2] Fifteen percent of girls and 22 percent of boys ages nine to thirteen meet AI levels.[2]

Table 4.5 (continued)

Nutrient	Function	Recommended Daily Allowance (RDA)	Sources	Comments
Vitamin D	Vitamin D partners with calcium for bone mineralization. It plays a role in the prevention of cancer, cardiovascular disease, autoimmune disease, and infectious disease.	*One to eighteen years:* 600 international units (IU)	Sockeye salmon (792 IU); canned light tuna in oil (228 IU); vitamin D–fortified orange juice (136 IU); nonfat, low-fat and reduced-fat milk (116 IU); soymilk (108 IU); fortified ready-to-eat cereals (36 to 100 IU); hard-boiled egg (28 IU)	About 47 percent of girls and 53 percent of boys older than nine years meet AI levels of vitamin D from food alone.[2] Sunlight is also a source of vitamin D, but this is limited with sunscreen use, excessive time indoors, higher altitudes and winter months, dark-colored skin, and excess weight.
Potassium	Potassium assists in muscle contraction, maintenance of fluid and electrolyte balance, nerve conductivity, and metabolism. High intake lowers blood pressure, blunts the effect of salt on blood pressure, and may reduce bone loss.	*Four to eight years:* 3,800 milligrams *Nine to thirteen years:* 4,500 milligrams	Small baked potato (1,081 milligrams), white beans (595 milligrams), plain yogurt (531 to 579 milligrams), tomato juice (556 milligrams), sweet potato (542 milligrams), orange juice (496 milligrams), low-fat or reduced-fat chocolate milk (422 to 425 milligrams), banana (422 milligrams), spinach (370 to 419 milligrams), tomato sauce (405 milligrams)	Less than 3 percent of four- to eight-year-olds and nine- to thirteen-year-olds meet AI levels.[2]

Iron	Iron carries and stores oxygen, a process that is accelerated during growth. Iron is an important component of enzymes and protein.	*Four to eight years*: 10 milligrams *Nine to thirteen years*: 8 milligrams	*Heme*: Beef chuck (3.1 milligrams), ground beef (2.2 milligrams), dark meat turkey (2 milligrams), canned light tuna in water (1.3 milligrams), dark meat chicken (1.1 milligrams), light meat chicken (.9 milligrams) *Nonheme*: 100 percent iron-fortified cereals (18 milligrams), instant oatmeal (11 milligrams), 25 percent iron-fortified cereals (4.5 milligrams), enriched bagel (4.4 milligrams), black beans (3.6 milligrams), fresh spinach (3.2 milligrams), raisins (1.6 milligrams)	Nine percent of twelve- to forty-nine-year-old women are iron-deficient.[2] Dieters may be at risk for deficiency. Heme sources of iron come from animal sources and are more readily absorbed than nonheme sources, which come from plant sources. Increase absorption of the latter by adding vitamin C sources to meals.
Fiber	Fiber is responsible for normal digestion and bowel movements. It plays a role in the reduction of cardiac disease, gastrointestinal problems, and cancer. It assists in weight management and blood sugar control.	*Four to eight years*: 25 grams (girls and boys)[3] *Nine to thirteen years*: 26 grams (girls) or 31 grams (boys)[3]	100 percent bran ready-to-eat cereal (9.1 grams), artichoke (7.2 grams), pear (5.5 grams), green peas (3.5 to 4.4 grams), whole wheat English muffin (4.4 grams), raspberries (4 grams), sweet potato (3.8 grams), apple with skin (3.6 grams), almonds (3.5 grams), whole wheat spaghetti (3.1 grams), banana (3.1 grams), orange (3.1 grams), baked potato (3 grams)	Less than 3 percent of children ages four to eight years and nine to thirteen years are meeting AI for dietary fiber.[2] Fiber adds a filling factor to meals and snacks. Total fiber comes from soluble and insoluble fiber sources, and most high-fiber foods contain both types.

of nutrients from foods isn't working, then a supplement should be considered. See Chapter Three, Table 3.6, for guidance on when vitamin and mineral supplements are needed. We caution you against viewing supplements as an insurance policy—the best policy for the long haul is a *food policy*. A nutritious diet is balanced with wholesome food, meals, and snacks planned strategically throughout the day, and with an added supplement, if needed. Finally, if you still have more questions, check out Appendix G, which will provide answers to those "beyond basic" nutrition questions.

Feeding with Confidence: Family Meals Matter

Eleven year-old Matt didn't take nutrition seriously enough, according to his dad, John. John felt Matt was too thin, was too picky about food, and had terrible eating habits. "I want Matt to take responsibility for his health," said John. "I want him to eat healthy—I think it would make a world of difference for him." Matt, however, just wanted to eat in peace. He felt pressure every time he sat down at the table, and couldn't bring himself to eat enough or the right foods to please his dad. Needless to say, there were unmet expectations and disappointment all around.

Here's what John didn't realize: he and Matt were communicating on two different levels. John expected his son to value food and fitness, make grown-up food choices, and understand nutrition concepts before he was ready. This struggle around food and nutrition was frustrating for both, and wasn't effective at changing Matt's eating habits or perspective on nutrition.

The child's body is growing, and so is his mind. In the previous section, we dug into the WHAT of feeding your child: nutrition, and all the food "stuff" you need to know to get nutrition right. However, this is just part of raising healthy eaters. When you have an understanding of your child's capabilities, motivations, and areas of development, you will be fearless, nurturing, and more effective when feeding your child.

What to Expect

Many things are happening with your child, from changes in thinking and understanding, to social and emotional transformations. All children learn and develop at an individual pace, even siblings! Knowing what to expect can help you prepare for and address these changes, and it can help get both you and your child through them relatively unscathed.

The Way Your Child Thinks

Psychologist and learning theorist Jean Piaget calls the school-age child's stage of cognitive development the concrete operational stage, a time when children think in concrete, or black-and-white ways.[16] Because children are limited in grasping complex ideas, such extremes as "good and bad" or "right and wrong" prevail. The child loves boundaries, and likes to live within them (despite what you may see on the home front), as they help him make sense of the world and feel safe. He lives in the present—the consequences of today's choices are difficult to conceive and aren't important. That's why John's attempts to motivate Matt with promises of a healthy body and a long life weren't working. They meant nothing—Matt wanted instant gratification (great-tasting and predictable food) when he sat down at the table.

As children's brains grow, education becomes the central focus. School-age children can understand new ideas and concepts based on generalizing them from past personal experiences. "I've hated green beans since I was a baby, I don't like them now, and probably never will," said Matt when asked about his food preferences. It's normal for kids to focus on the "here and now," but as parents, we know that eating *does* change with time. In fact, when you arm yourself with knowledge and approaches that work, your child's food preferences and eating will expand and improve.

In later childhood (ten to twelve years), the mind can grasp and understand broader, more complex ideas. Actions and consequences, innuendos and subtleties, and an understanding of the big picture emerge, but full adult cognition isn't reached until the end of adolescence. No matter how much nutrition information your child receives, he will not be able to understand and use it until he is developmentally ready. Table 4.6 summarizes your child's learning stage and how he interprets information about nutrition.

Your Child's Psychosocial Development

Psychologist Erik Erikson gives us insight into the psychosocial development of the child, outlining the important crisis the child faces as he grows socially and

Table 4.6 Cognitive Development for School-Age Children			
Age	**Stage**	**Cognitive Readiness**	**Feeding Implications**
Seven to twelve years	Concrete operational stage	• Begins to understand cause and effect, if it's concrete • Is able to reverse thinking, considering original and changed states • Can think through a chain of events • Can classify objects and concrete ideas • Lives in the present • Makes rule-based choices	• Understands that food is changed by digestion, but has a limited understanding of how this happens. • Understands that baking and cooking alter food (batter to cake), and that health and illness are not permanent ("I was healthy, then I got sick, now I am healthy again"). • Understands that food goes from farm to table. • Knows that pork and beef are in the meat group. • Is not concerned about the impact of today's food choices on future health. • Has a black-and-white idea of "good food" (food he likes) versus "bad food" (food he doesn't like).

emotionally during this time: Industry Versus Inferiority (or capable versus incapable).[17] The developmental end goal of the school-age years is to gain skills, and to experience success as a result of those skills. Skill acquisition gives your child an opportunity to build a healthy sense of self-worth. Fostering industry over inferiority is key to achieving this goal.

The task of feeding your child has a powerful impact on his psychosocial development. The mere act of participating in daily meals can promote or discourage healthy development. Table 4.7 shows everyday feeding and how it encourages the development of either industry or inferiority.

A good, hearty sense of self is years in the making, but it begins now. Skill development can help this process along and is accomplished in many ways, from

Table 4.7 Psychosocial Development for School-Age Children	
Psychosocial Task	**Daily Actions**
Industry	
Child: "I am capable." *Parent:* "You are able. I trust and support you."	• The child identifies hunger or fullness and is supported to act on these signs. • The child is allowed to make snacks or simple meals. • The child can weigh in on menu ideas for meals. • The child makes suggestions for new foods. • The child prepares food and shares it with friends or family. • The child gives input on schedules for mealtimes.
Inferiority	
Child: "I am not capable." *Parent:* "You cannot do this; I don't trust you."	• The child's food is mostly plated or pre-served. • The child is discouraged from making or serving food. • The child is pressured to finish meals, eat more, stop eating, or perform a certain way during meals. • The child is required to taste everything at mealtime.

playing a sport to succeeding in a difficult task. You may see an increased interest in food and cooking as well as in meal items, and you may hear more questions related to nutrition—these are normal signs your child is becoming more aware of the food world around him. This heightened interest presents opportunities to teach your child, cultivate a positive attitude about food, and work on skill development.

Peer Power, Food Fears, and Pickiness
Psychosocial development plays out in friendships. The desire to belong is a normal part of development, and eating what other friends eat is part of belonging. This desire is strong enough to change not only what and how much your child eats but also how she feels about herself.[18] Media images and food ads also have this power.

School-age children often become more adventurous eaters because their taste buds mature and peer pressure encourages food experimentation. Martha, mom of three, thought her kids would eat plain pasta forever. She was surprised to see that her children eventually tried different sauces, vegetables, and combination foods like lasagna. "I never gave up on expecting them to eat what we ate, so I just separated the pasta from the sauces and extras. They eventually got comfortable enough to add them in," she says. "Once one child had a good experience, then the others followed suit."

More and more, we see older children and their families plagued by picky eating. A combination of factors may be keeping your child stuck in the picky eating stage: sensitivity to taste, smell, appearance, or texture; her particular eating style or temperament; a physical problem; anxiety; a learned behavior that works; or a combination of these.[19] Regardless of cause, picky eating affecting growth, social development, or self-esteem warrants further investigation and assistance. Make sure you are responding to picky eating appropriately by reviewing Chapter Three and troubleshooting in Chapter Seven.

My Body, My Self-Esteem

Older children (ages nine to twelve) become more aware of their body, especially during puberty when they are changing dramatically. Your child may feel embarrassed or uncomfortable and show a heightened concern with her appearance. "Ew, I don't want to change," said eleven-year-old Katherine. "I want to stay like me!" The desire to grow up and the reluctance to change are at odds with each other for many pubertal children. Comparisons to friends or to unrealistic media images may occur. Boys and girls alike experience doubt and wavering body image: girls feel pressure to be thin, and boys want to be bigger or more muscular. Parents can find this part of school-age development particularly worrisome, fearing for their child's self-esteem and the repercussions of a low one.

The consequences of poor body image can go in two weight directions. Many experts link poor body image to the rise in disordered

Fearless Fact

Girls as young as six years are dieting due to body dissatisfaction.[20] According to one study, 21 percent of five-year-old girls, 37 percent of nine-year-old girls, and 50 percent of eight- to thirteen-year-old girls reported concerns about their weight.[21]

eating (chaotic or erratic eating whereby hunger or fullness may be ignored), which can trigger an eating disorder over time. And others note that overweight children also experience poor self-esteem that results in ongoing weight gain and worsening health status. If you feel your child is at risk for an eating disorder or excess weight, you can read more about this in Chapter Seven.

Your best bet for helping your child avoid low self-esteem is to provide opportunities for learning new skills; be a positive influence; acknowledge and navigate the influence of peers, media, and school; and provide developmentally appropriate nutrition information. After all, your child's body acceptance and healthy self-esteem are key to her emerging from the school-age years as a confident teen.

Now that we've covered the key points in your child's development, you have a better understanding of the important issues of this age group. You know that when children are expected to take on more responsibility for their health and eating before they are ready, eating and the parent-child relationship may suffer. Cultivating a healthy body and sense of self seems like a big task (and it is!), but it's not as hard or complicated as you may think. Your daily duties of feeding your child can go a long way in making this phase of childhood a huge success!

Feeding That Works

Good nutrition coupled with a good attitude and positive feeding practices are essential to raising healthy kids. Here, we highlight role modeling, meal and snack structure, and family meals to encourage healthy food choices. We'll also cover the pitfalls of feeding this age group, and how getting kids into the kitchen can serve as a bridge to their skill development and improved self-worth.

Parents as Role Models

Now, more than ever, your child is looking to you for guidance. You are the reference point for your child.[22,23,24] If you skip meals, so may your child. If you value exercise, it's likely your child will too. If you fly through the day without eating, your child will be noticing that as well. It can be a lot of pressure to feel a set of eyes on your back all day, and quite a responsibility to fulfill the role of healthy eater and exerciser yourself. Bottom line: your actions speak louder than your words.

A positive parent role model eats regular meals and is able to balance Nourishing and Half-and-Half Foods with Fun Foods. A good role model avoids dieting, food group elimination, and negative food talk. A healthy attitude prevails—all foods fit in a healthy diet, particular foods are not demonized, and appreciation for your body is emphasized. Activity is part of daily living, and sedentary time is moderated.

Even the best parent role models struggle! Sometimes kids are slow to adopt the health practices they see every day. Don't give up—it's worth it. You are the number one influence on your kid's eating and exercise patterns, giving you the power to steer your child toward a healthy adulthood. Table 4.8 offers suggested behaviors and language to help you be a positive role model for your child. If healthy habits are a struggle for you, see Chapter Six.

Maintaining Meal and Snack Structure

A daily breakfast has numerous benefits for your child: breaking the overnight fast and bumping up blood sugar levels, revving up the metabolism and starting

Table 4.8 What Great Role Models Do and Say

Positive Behaviors	Positive Dialogue
Eating regular meals	*"Regular meals and snacks keep my body and brain energized for the day."* *"Eating regularly provides the fuel my body needs."*
Balancing Nourishing Foods, Half-and Half-Foods, and Fun Foods	*"All foods can fit into a healthy diet."* *"I balance foods so that my body is getting important nutrients and I am satisfied too."*
Avoiding dieting, eliminating "bad" foods, or demonizing foods	*"No one food will make you healthy or not—unhealthy behaviors are what make people unhealthy."* *"Diets don't work and don't satisfy my body."*
Appreciating exercise as part of daily living	*"I move my body every day to keep it healthy."* *"Our bodies were designed to move, so I make sure I do so every day."*
Showing moderation in nutrition attitudes and actions	*"Balancing what I eat with daily movement keeps my body healthy and happy."*

the calorie burn for the day, enhancing focus and attention in school, and helping him avoid intense hunger before lunch rolls around. Not only do kids skimp on breakfast but also they may eat a light lunch, leading to out-of-control snacking after school. When meals get off track, it can turn into out-of-balance eating. Keeping the structure and timing of meals and snacks is the best way you can prevent haywire snacking, overeating, low appetite for meals, or a combination of these.

> ### Fearless Fact
>
> Depending on age, 10 to 30 percent of children skip breakfast. Breakfast eaters consume more calories but are less likely to be overweight, while demonstrating better memory, higher test scores, and fewer absences from school.[13]

Managing Outside Food Choices and Snacking

A major challenge during this stage is that children are making more food choices outside the home, and they need guidance on how to make *smart* choices. Over the summer, nine-year-old Kate was in overdrive with Fun Foods. She was choosing soda and ice cream at the pool, having sleepovers and "pigging out on junk food," and indulging on vacation. Her mom felt that things had reached a serious crossroads—Kate had put on weight over the summer, despite swim team practice every day, and seemed obsessed with sweets and other Fun Foods.

We taught Kate and her mom how to use the 90:10 Rule, whereby 90 percent of foods eaten are from Nourishing and Half-and-Half Foods and 10 percent are from Fun Foods. We asked Kate to keep Fun Foods to one or two each day. Kate was able to classify Fun Foods (no surprise, this concept fed right into her concrete thinking) and understood that *which* Fun Foods to eat was her choice. Her mom helped anticipate Fun Foods each day so Kate could think through her options. She skipped the donuts at church, opted for water instead of soda at the pool and restaurants, and had no Fun Foods until the celebration started on party days. Kate still opted for ice cream at the pool, as it was her most prized Fun Food. The 90:10 Rule allowed Kate to pick the Fun Food most important to her, and enjoy it without guilt.

When a child is constantly asking for snacks, we encourage you to step back and first look at what is going on. When and what is she eating, and is it enough? Did he have an active day? Is he in a growth spurt? Is she eating out of habit, boredom, or emotions? *Eating in the absence of hunger (EAH),* a term that describes eating due to boredom, emotions, or stress (not hunger), is a learned behavior that peaks between the ages of five and nine years.[25,26] Knowing the WHY behind snacking and food choices helps you manage the decisions you make in positive ways. We have three strategies to help you manage EAH, snacking, and hunger:

- **The fruit and veggie test:** If your child complains that he is hungry, ask him, "Would you eat an apple (or any other piece of fruit or veggie)?" If your child responds, "No, I want some chips," then he is not truly hungry (because when you're hungry, you'd eat anything, right?). If your child responds with a "yes," then go for it—he probably is hungry. We believe "fruit is always a yes." This philosophy provides assurance to children that food is available if they are truly hungry, even if it is off schedule. For the child who does not eat fruits and veggies, offer milk or yogurt.
- **Guided snacking:** Make snacks look like mini-meals, incorporating two or three food groups (including a protein or healthy fat source) in normal serving sizes. A balanced snack is more satisfying, potentially reducing excessive eating. As early as six years (and for some, even younger), children can assemble their own snacks, such as cheese, fruit, and crackers. For older children, a snack guide or template can be helpful. You can find a lunch and snack packing template in Appendix C.
- **A "kitchen is closed" policy:** Encourage children to eat when meals and snacks are served. When kids ask for a snack right after dinner, an appropriate reply is, "I'm sorry but the kitchen is closed now. It will be open in the morning for breakfast." This sets up boundaries around extra eating, encourages self-regulation, and may discourage EAH over time. Table 4.9 highlights common snacking problems and how to handle them.

Table 4.9	Snacking Problems and Solutions	
Problem	**What to Do**	**Outcome**
The child asks for food outside of meals and snacks.	• Try the fruit and veggie test. • Practice "fruit is always a yes." • Implement a "kitchen is closed" policy.	• The child learns to identify true hunger versus EAH • The availability of fruit quells true hunger and offers important nutrients. • The child is encouraged to eat at mealtime.
The child is not hungry for meals.	• Check the timing and size of snacks, and make adjustments as needed.	• The child's appetite for meals improves.
The child is "starving" before dinner.	• Optimize the satisfaction level of snacks (include sources of protein and healthy fat with snacks; take a mini-meal approach). • Practice "fruit is always a yes," or give the mealtime vegetable early.	• The child learns better hunger management. • Fruit and vegetables satisfy hunger and contribute nutrients.

Family Meals

The act of sitting together around a table positively influences healthy eating and weight, fosters the parent-child connection, and improves academic performance and social adjustment in children and teens.[27] Family meals also promote the consumption of fruits, vegetables, whole grains, and calcium-rich foods as well as the intake of protein, calcium, iron, folic acid, fiber, and vitamins A, C, E, and B6.[28] A pleasant meal environment, in which conversation and connection occur, coupled with wholesome food, can have lasting benefits for your child's overall health and well-being. Aim for three to five family meals per week to reap these benefits, but if possible, eat together daily. Remember, family meals can happen any time—breakfast, lunch, dinner, and even snack time. Make sure to sit with your child to eat, even if he eats later than everyone else, and minimize distractions, like the TV.

Eat In or Dine Out?

Families eat outside of the home an average of four to five times per week.[29] The frequency of dining out may ultimately weaken your child's willingness to try new foods at home, and may strengthen his preference for high-fat, salty, and sugary foods. The home is a place where everyone eats the same foods—and where boundaries can be created around healthy and not-so-healthy foods. We recommend you take an honest assessment of what your family's dining out habits are and *cut them in half.*

Serving Meals Family-Style

Children tend to eat better when they serve themselves and make food selections on their own. Placing food in bowls and on platters that are then passed around the table is the essence of family-style meals, an authoritative way to approach mealtime. With family-style service, the child selects which foods he will eat and how much, but you determine the menu, timing, and location. Be sure to teach and practice manners ("please" and "thank you"), too. Family-style meals not only shift the control to your child but also capitalize on skill development and success.

"I thought Isabella would only eat bread and pasta if I served our meals this way," says Sharon, mom of nine-year-old Isabella. "I was thrilled to see her choose more variety on her plate than I expected, but what surprised me most was the peace and enjoyment we had—the whole family drama stopped!"

Although plating food for your child is precise, you can also use family-style meals to get portions right. Prepare foods in the appropriate serving sizes and place them on platters or in bowls as a starting point. For example, you may cut chicken breasts into three-ounce portions; purchase small potatoes; use eight-ounce glasses for milk; and use half-cup serving spoons (or the actual measuring cup) for dishing out grains, veggies, and fruits. And it always works to teach the MyPlate approach: divide your plate in fourths and cover each section with a grain, meat or nonmeat protein, a fruit, and a vegetable, and serve a dairy or nondairy alternative food on the side. If you've got a veggie lover, let half of the plate be veggies, and the same goes for fruit: these food groups can be interchanged, as long as they make up half the plate. With both family-style meals and the MyPlate approach, you're modeling healthy, balanced eating and building portion awareness, rather than restricting or controlling food intake. Of course, let your child eat to her satisfaction, and don't be surprised if she opts for seconds, especially if she is active and growing. If you are worried about your child's eating with family-style meals, make sure your feeding style isn't getting in the way (see Chapter One).

The family meal is a place for conversation, and what you choose to discuss can have positive or negative effects on eating. We discourage you from using the meal table to discuss topics related to nutrition, eating, and food. Frankly, it can feel like too much pressure, especially if your child is picky or overweight. Instead, keep the topics light, fun, and entertaining. You want the meal table to be a place your children enjoy!

The Child as a Helper

Children can help in the kitchen, from setting the table to making a side dish. Now is the time to help your child learn to make his own snacks and pack his lunch. Younger children can make snack and lunch choices with guidance from parents (see Appendix C, Table C.2), whereas older kids can follow a snack or lunch template and assemble their own. Make sure to have plenty of Nourishing Foods on hand, so your child is able to get the nutrients he needs.

If supervising the production of lunches and snacks feels overwhelming, step back and take the long-term view. With regular practice, you eventually will have a child who is an asset in the kitchen, capable of making a balanced meal, and confident with cooking skills. How many adults do you know who have achieved that?

Now that you know HOW to feed your child in ways that nurture development, confidence, and self-esteem, we'll tackle the subject of teaching nutrition.

Understanding Nutrition

Parents frequently confess their fear of talking about nutrition with their child, concerned they will damage self-esteem or provide information that could be harmful. Sally knew her son, Brent, was making too many unhealthy choices, but she was afraid to bring it up, scared of blowing it out of proportion and hurting his self-esteem. Sally made the mistake of letting her fear take over and wishing his eating would improve on its own. But it didn't. Brent gained too much weight, adopted unhealthy eating habits, and needed outside help to get back on a healthy track.

Here, we show you how to teach your school-age child about nutrition. We'll help you with developmentally sensitive language, timing, and topics while addressing how to talk about the tough stuff: weight, body image, and long-term health. Our goal is to arm you with the know-how to help you prevent and deal with such issues before they get overwhelming.

Heavy-Duty Learning About Nutrition

Connie Evers, registered dietitian and author of *How to Teach Nutrition to Kids,* believes that the school-age years are a critical time for learning about nutrition. "Submerge older school-age children in heavy-duty learning about nutrition now, and they will have a solid foundation of nutrition knowledge that extends into adulthood," she says. "Nutrition education should come from all angles: computer learning, MyPlate guidelines, label reading, recipe use, math skills, science, gardening, and getting kids into the kitchen at home." Many parents use trial and error when it comes to educating their kids, not knowing what to expect with children's readiness to learn. Evers advises, "The biggest way to learn is through what happens at mealtimes and the activities of daily living. Parents should try to get kids involved in shopping, planning a meal, and gardening, and use fewer instructional methods and more hands-on experiences."

Knowing your child's developmental and cognitive stage helps guide your tone and manner of conversation. As already discussed, younger children think in black-and-white terms, whereas older children

> **Fearless Fact**
>
> Active learning, or hands-on participation, is necessary for intellectual development.[16] Let your child experiment with cooking, measuring, portioning, making lunch, and other hands-on skills.

can begin to wrap their head around more complex ideas. Active learning in the kitchen is a great way to teach about nutrition!

Nutrition Topics That Make Sense

When it comes to nutrition, if you provide too much information, younger kids will simplify the message and perhaps misunderstand it. Conversely, if you keep it basic for the older child, she may lose interest. Children indicate the amount of information they need when they lead the conversation with questions or observations. Keep your ears open for these opportunities to discuss nutrition or other related topics, as reviewed in Table 4.10. If you build your child's knowledge base gradually with age-sensitive information, she will understand and adopt good nutrition habits for a lifetime.

Talking About the Tough Stuff

Children may worry about and comment on their weight. If these concerns are repeated, don't put them off or ignore them. Explore and listen to how your child is feeling and try to get to the root of the problem. If you find your child just needs affirmation and reinforcement, provide it. If there is more to it, like dieting attempts, fasting, overexercising, depression, or anxiety, it's time to seek outside support. We have encountered many parents who have ignored fear and worries about nutrition, only to learn they were "spot-on" from the beginning.

Poor body image may be the underlying cause of worries about weight and nutrition. You'll always want to support healthy body image development, especially now. We've included some important messages in Table 4.11.

The school-age years are prime time for educating your child about nutrition. Make room in the kitchen for your child's helping hands, let him start to make food choices on his own, accept his help with planning meals and grocery lists, and let him ask questions. Remember, keep nutrition messages positive and avoid categorizing food as "good" or "bad." Above all, let your responses and nutrition education efforts reflect his ability to understand. Remember, you are the biggest nutrition resource in your child's life, and he'll be counting on you to help guide him.

Table 4.10 Nutrition Concepts to Teach Your School-Age Child

Nutrition Concept	Fearless Dialogue	How to Do It
Portion awareness	*"Let's compare a serving of this cereal to a serving of that cereal."* *"A serving is not a limit to your eating; you can eat more or less; eat until you're satisfied."*	• Modeling normal servings at meals and snacks • Reading the nutrition facts panel and paying attention to serving sizes • Practicing measuring everyday foods • Pointing out portion distortion (large portions)
Food balance	*"A healthy meal has a sampling of most of the food groups."* *"Nourishing and Half-and-Half Foods should be most of what you eat during a day."*	• Using a balanced plate (MyPlate), which means covering half of the plate with fruits and vegetables, a quarter with a protein source and a quarter with grains, and offering dairy or a nondairy alternative on the side • Eating Nourishing, Half-and-Half, and Fun Foods • Using the 90:10 Rule • Knowing the composition of a healthy meal and a healthy snack • Incorporating four to five food groups into meals, and two to three food groups into snacks
Simple nutrient information (older child)	*"Each nutrient has a special function and is important to your body's health."*	• Introducing basic nutrients for health, including calcium and vitamin D for bones; iron for energy and strength; vitamin C for immunity; and protein for growth and height • Understanding calories are for energy and growth • Prioritizing water for hydration
Food for health and happiness	*"Food provides nutrition and enjoyment; all foods can fit into a healthy diet, if balanced."* *"You should love food! It's an important part of everyday life, and you should be smart about it."*	• Promoting food enjoyment • Not labeling food as "good foods" and "bad foods"
Growth, development, and body weight	*"Every body is different and grows at a different pace; take care of yours so you have a healthy one for a long time."*	• Conveying realistic and healthy attitudes • Acknowledging that there is no perfect weight, size, or shape • Pointing out that bodies grow (heavier, taller, stronger) • Clarifying that weight and size discrimination is a form of bullying

Table 4.11 Important Messages for Building Healthy Body Image

Positive Message	Fearless Dialogue	Reality
Your body is yours!	"There are no replacement parts; take care of your body, you'll have it for a long time."	Fifty percent of your body weight, shape, and size are determined before you are born.
Look at what your body can do.	"Your legs allow you to travel; your hands allow you to converse; your arms can share emotions . . ."	Bodies can do a lot of different things to keep you healthy—play sports, exercise, and so on.
Change what you can, let go of the rest.	"Height and shoe size are not something you can change. How you eat, how you exercise, and how you treat others are things you can change for the better."	Some things can be changed, and some things cannot. Focusing on the things you cannot change is a waste of time and energy.
Nix the negative self-talk.	"A frown is a smile turned upside down—smile more, and look for the bright side!"	Putting yourself down allows others to do so easily.
Highlight your internal qualities.	"You are kind, funny, smart, loyal, fair, adventurous, sensitive, generous, and more!"	All individuals have a special blend of qualities that makes them unique. No two people are exactly alike, even twins!
Get healthy.	"Your body needs healthy, nourishing foods to move every day and to sleep well each night. How are you doing with that?"	Eating well, moving your body, and getting enough sleep every day are things you can do to feel strong, powerful, and good about yourself.
Limit negative influences.	"Remember, too much TV, surfing the Web, reading magazines, watching movies, or surrounding yourself with people who judge you based on appearance or status may be bringing you down. Surround yourself with people and influences that bring you up and make you feel good about yourself."	Media deliver unrealistic physical images that convey a "thin is in" ideal, and they market unhealthy food as healthy and desirable. Peers who want to be thin sway their friends to desire thinness too. Imitating others (friends or models) may lead to lower self-esteem.

Real Life Challenges for School-Age Children

School-age children have a variety of nutrition challenges, ranging from ongoing picky eating to nutrition gaps in their diet, weight changes, and body insecurities—and everything in between! Although kids have several challenges going on at once, you can get your child back on course with savvy know-how and help from the Fearless Feeding Strategy.

My Child Is Still a Picky Eater

Challenge: Ten-year-old Graham's picky eating had been a mainstay at the family dinner table since he started solids as a baby. Graham's shunning of vegetables, pasta, meats, and many fruits concerned and frustrated his parents. Graham wouldn't spend the night at friends' houses for fear there was nothing he could eat, nor would he buy school lunch. He was reluctant to try new foods and subsisted on dairy (but no cheese), bread, and other processed foods like chicken nuggets. As a result, his nutrition and social life suffered.

     Diagnosis: Graham was experiencing both pressure (HOW) and reinforcement of his limited diet (WHAT). Graham had a sensitive temperament, and problems with constipation throughout childhood, and was experiencing pressure to eat (WHY). Graham was also given alternative meals, which only made things worse.

     Intervention: Graham's parents were advised to take the pressure off Graham. Loren de-pressured the meal table, staying neutral about what and how much Graham ate, *even if it was something new,* as praise for eating can also be interpreted as pressure. They were also instructed to dial back on favorite foods. We advised that Loren make one meal for the whole family (rather than a separate one for Graham) and introduce new foods while keeping old familiar foods limited to one or two items per meal. Finally, we suggested encouraging a small taste (without pressure!). They gave Graham permission to lick food, let it rest on his tongue and politely spit it out, chew it and spit it out, or actually chew and swallow—and he could advance at his own pace. Graham selected three foods to work on after school regularly. He tried a small bite of each food while alone and in a quiet place (minimal pressure). He kept a journal of what he tried; whether he liked it (yes, no, maybe); and why.

Outcome: After a year, Graham now eats pasta (loves it!) with sauces, a variety of meats, and more fruit, and he continues to work on vegetables. Loren states, "Last night he proceeded to make himself a plate of chicken, pasta with sauce, romaine lettuce with balsamic vinegar, and some fruit. He looked at his plate, and everyone else's, and said, 'Look how good my plate looks tonight!'"

Myth: Picky eating is a choice.

Busted! Although it may appear that your child is getting a kick out of making extra work for you, he's probably not. In response to picky eating, parents often make two mistakes: either they criticize or put pressure on their child to eat, resulting in anxiety at the meal table and interference with learning about new foods, or they limit food options to the items their child will readily eat, reinforcing picky eating.

My Child Wants to Be a Vegetarian

Challenge: "I want to be a vegetarian," said twelve-year-old Sarah, sending her meat-loving parents, Sue and Joe, into a panic. Children can be perfectly healthy on a vegetarian diet. In fact, about 1.4 million youth in the United States are vegetarian, according to a survey by the Vegetarian Resource Group.[30] However, parents make two common mistakes when their child becomes a vegetarian: they take a hands-off approach and allow their child to take charge, possibly leading to nutrient deficiencies, or they don't understand their child's nutrient needs (iron, zinc, vitamin B12, calcium, and vitamin D) and fail to cover them.

Diagnosis: Sue and Joe weren't familiar with vegetarian nutrition (WHAT) or what approach to take in feeding Sarah (HOW).

Intervention: The first step was to educate the parents. An understanding of vegetarianism—which foods to eliminate and which to include—would help Sue and Joe guide Sarah. Together with Sarah, they decided the nonmeat alternatives and dairy foods as well as the vegetable and grain sources in her diet. They also needed to stay in charge and be supportive. Sarah needed support and guidance from her parents balanced with independent practice so she could learn to make good choices. Sarah's parents needed to be vigilant (not militant!). Sue and Joe had to make sure Sarah consumed adequate nutrients, watching for missing food groups. They could use the Fearless Five Nutrients chart (see Table 4.5) to fill in the gaps with food or supplements. Iron was the toughest nutrient, as Sarah didn't care for beans or most leafy greens. Her parents included a snack mix that contained iron-fortified cereal, raisins, cashews, and dried apricots. Finally, Sarah's parents needed to execute the vegetarian diet and support her choice. They did this by including a nonmeat protein source at meals, but served regular sides. Two nights each week, the whole family ate a vegetarian meal.

Outcome: Sarah decided to stay a vegetarian and eliminate meat. The whole family benefited, as they ate more plant-based meals. Sarah was able to meet her nutritional needs with the knowledge and support her parents gave her.

Myth: Vegetarian diets are healthier for children.

Busted! Some children fail to eat vegetables, whole grains, beans, and nuts, opting for diets heavy in refined grains, dairy products, and processed foods. Although it is admittedly convenient, the unhealthy practice of allowing your child to become a "starchy vegetarian"—only eating pasta, pizza, and other grain-heavy foods—is a recipe for nutrient deficits and potential weight problems and is *not healthier* for kids.

My Child Says He's "Starving"

Challenge: Eleven-year-old Benjamin was always hungry after school. He couldn't seem to satisfy himself with one snack and needed a prolonged feeding session before he was ready to move on to homework. This was squelching his appetite for dinner, and he was eating too much overall (and the wrong things).

Diagnosis: Benjamin wasn't eating much at breakfast, just a piece of toast or a small muffin (WHAT). Between talking and a time crunch at lunch, he barely ate his lunch and was choosing nutrition-poor options, lowering his satisfaction (WHY).

Intervention: Benjamin was "back-loading," eating heavier at the end of the day, which contributed to a cycle of uncontrolled appetite and eating. We wanted him to "front-load," eating more at the beginning of the day, to help with hunger later. We suggested they explore fruit-based smoothies; instant breakfast drinks; and "grab-and-go" ideas, such as homemade and commercial trail mix, nut packets, and breakfast bars. We stressed the importance of eating lunch, suggesting he eat his sandwich or main entrée first before joining in the conversation. Benjamin could follow the 90:10 Rule, which would promote Nourishing and Half-and-Half Foods and keep a cap on Fun Foods. We suggested satisfying snacks like a bowl of cereal with fruit and milk; a cheese quesadilla cooked in the microwave and served with fruit; or chopped nuts, dried fruit, and cereal mix. Instead of raiding the fridge, Benjamin spent twenty to thirty minutes of playtime right after school as part of his new routine. Benjamin could go outside, play in his room, or do his chores, which took the emphasis off food and gave him the opportunity to de-stress, have fun, or relax. His mother also incorporated a "kitchen is closed" rule between meals and snacks.

Outcome: Once breakfast and lunch were squared away, Benjamin came home hungry but not voracious, and his eating and nutrition improved.

Myth: Hunger is bad.

Busted! Hunger is the body's alarm clock, letting children know when it is time to eat, and is driven by a host of biological processes. Sometimes hunger builds due to increased growth, poor eating habits, suboptimal food choices, or bad timing. Parents make two main mistakes when dealing with hunger: either they ignore it, not realizing that appetite varies with their child's growth rate and the quantity and quality of the food eaten, or they overrespond by offering food, failing to assess true hunger.

My Child Thinks She's Fat

Challenge: Eleven-year-old McKenzie went from being a happy-go-lucky girl to being acutely aware of her body. She complained about how thin her friends were compared to her and how they could eat anything and still be skinny. One day she asked her mom, Kate, "Do you think I'm fat?"

Diagnosis: McKenzie's focus on her body in comparison to others' was a normal part of development (WHY).

Intervention: This was the first time the question had come up, so we asked Kate to reassure McKenzie that she looked great, and to stay away from using words like "big" or "small," "thin" or "heavy"—she probably just wanted reassurance she was normal. If she questioned again, then Kate needed to give it more time and attention. We suggested beginning a conversation with, "You have asked me this question a couple of times—what's this about?" Above all, McKenzie needed to hear she is accepted and loved regardless of what she looks like. We reminded Kate to use positive comments about herself in front of her children, even if she was less than satisfied. Children pick up on body insecurity and dissatisfaction from their parents, and this can foster their own insecurity about weight, shape, and size. Also, McKenzie was exposed to a lot of media—TV, magazines, the computer, and social networking sites. We asked Kate to teach McKenzie about media so she could interpret images and messages with a level head (and ask questions if she needed to).

Outcome: McKenzie's question opened a door for Kate to discuss values and ideals concerning body weight, shape, and size. They enjoyed many conversations about a host of topics as McKenzie grew up, navigating the teen years without major eating or weight issues.

Myth: Concern about body weight, shape, and size means your child is on the path to an eating disorder.

Busted! During preadolescence, children have a developmental urge to find out if they are normal, and this is done through self-comparison to others. Children compare their physical appearance and their academic, athletic, and social standing with those of others. Many parents are taken aback by self-assessment questions and make two common mistakes: either they ignore the question, not acknowledging a potential real concern, or they launch into panic mode and make a big deal of the situation.

My Child's Eating Is Out of Control, and She's Obsessed with Food!

Challenge: "Julie is obsessed with food. She goes crazy with eating at parties, at church, and at other people's houses," said Gayle and Arnie. Julie had been overweight since birth and loved food, especially bread, pasta, and chips. "We are trying very hard to have a healthy environment in our home," said Gayle. "But every time she leaves, I feel worried about how much (and what) she's eating."

Diagnosis: When Julie was a baby and toddler, she was often riding in the car and meals were unpredictable (HOW). Gayle felt guilty and let Julie have whatever sweet food she asked for, and used food to reward her (WHAT and HOW). When Julie's older siblings went off to college, she was lonely and bored, and turned to food for comfort (WHY). Because she appeared "obsessed," Arnie and Gayle cut back on her eating at home (HOW), causing more food insecurity and coping using food (WHY).

Intervention: We helped Gayle and Arnie understand why Julie was obsessed with food and overeating outside of the home, including their having pacified her with food when she was a baby, their use of food as a reward and comfort, and their restrictive feeding. Gayle and Arnie adopted an authoritative feeding style, focusing on predictable, satisfying meals and holding the line on locale. We taught them to use Ellyn Satter's Division of Responsibility (see Chapters One and Three), a "kitchen is closed" policy, and family-style meals, and showed them how to balance meals, set servings, and target nutrients for optimal nutrition and feeding.

Gayle and Arnie were unknowingly producing an environment of scarcity (because they feared more weight gain), which caused more food obsession and out-of-control eating. We felt that if Julie could observe an abundance of food variety, see ample quantities to eat for the whole family, and be allowed to eat until satisfied at home, she would be reassured and more secure around food. We suggested they incorporate family-style meals and allow Julie to serve herself. Julie needed to get better at recognizing hunger, fullness, and satisfaction. We reminded them that Julie was the best gauge of her own satisfaction, not them. They could train her with the fruit and veggie test, stay on a meal and snack schedule, and encourage alternative outlets for boredom or emotions.

Outcome: Once Gayle and Arnie shifted their feeding style, trusted Julie with decisions about food, helped her identify real hunger, and optimized the balance of nutrition, Julie relaxed about eating—and so did they. There was a two-week period during which she ate more than they liked, but after she realized she could be satisfied, she calmed down and ate reasonable amounts.

Myth: Children can't be trusted with food.

Busted! Most children are born with good self-regulation skills, but the environment, including feeding styles, feeding practices, food availability, and outside influences, may change this. Many children who appear "obsessed" with food have lost their self-regulation skills, or they have a larger appetite or higher metabolism, creating a greater demand for food. And some children really love food and enjoy eating.

When parents are worried about their child's eating, sometimes *they* become obsessed with their child's eating! The following two mistakes tend to increase the focus on food: restricting or controlling types of foods (salty, savory, or sweet), food portions, or second helpings, or failing to recognize or honor the child's appetite.

Help! I'm Making Three Meals Each Night! How Do I Feed My Family One Meal?

Challenge: Lee Anne had an overweight son and a picky daughter who was on the thin side. She found herself making three different meals—one for her daughter that included the foods she would eat; one for her son that included salads, fruit, and lean meats; and one for the adults.

Diagnosis: Lee Anne was a short-order cook (HOW), and feeding her family was not working. She needed a streamlined plan!

Intervention: Lee Anne believed that having successful family dinners meant pleasing everyone, when in reality her job was to plan and cook one well-balanced meal. Although she was afraid of her family's response (rejection), we helped her deal with that. We encouraged Lee Anne to be authoritative and set the menu, allowing input from family members. We encouraged family-style meals and asked her to keep it simple. Lee Anne could satisfy most taste buds with a gallon of low-fat milk, a bowl of fruit, and a loaf of bread or crackers as additions to the main entrée and vegetable. We asked her to nix the backup plan of cereal, a peanut butter sandwich, or yogurt that she offered the child who wasn't eating at the table, as it was sending the message that by refusing the meal, that child could still get whatever he or she wanted. If her kids decided to pass on dinner, for example, she needed to remind them that they were making the choice not to eat, and stick to the meal structure of breakfast in the morning so they could eat then. Finally, we encouraged Lee Anne to pat herself on the back for switching to one meal for the whole family—getting three balanced meals and one to two snacks on board in a structured fashion is no easy feat! When she did this, she had done her job. Now it was time to let her children do their job: eat or not.

Outcome: Lee Anne actually *saved time* by planning one family meal. Meals became more enjoyable and relaxed, and her children had fun helping her plan and prepare meals. "Now, I put out one meal at dinner, instead of running around like a crazy short-order cook," she says. "Our family enjoys mealtime so much more, and I am confident everyone is eating what, and the amount, they need."

Myth: You have to feed children separate meals to match their nutritional needs.

Busted! The more you accommodate personal preferences, the more unsuccessful mealtime becomes. Parents who cater to each family member make these two mistakes: either they become short-order cooks and gravitate to convenience foods for speed, or they give up on family meals at home and opt to eat out more frequently.

Real, Easy Recipes for School-Age Children

Your school-age child is ready to start cooking! Are you? We know you're busy, and the idea of getting your child in the kitchen may seem overwhelming. Let's make this clear: you don't have to give your child a crash course on cooking. The goal for the school-age child is to get more involved in the kitchen, while becoming more independent over time.

If time is a barrier, use it when you have it—regular and long weekends, holidays, and over the summer when schedules are looser and time is abundant. Start simple—after-school snacks, breakfast, and lunch on the weekends, eventually advancing to breakfast and dinner on school days.

Having children participate in cooking is also an opportunity to teach them about kitchen safety. See Table 4.12 for some kitchen safety essentials to remember and teach your child.

By the end of his fifth year, your child should be able to scrub vegetables; snap beans; tear lettuce; spread butter, jam, or peanut butter; peel fruit or vegetables; roll dough; mash an avocado or potato; pour liquids; and measure ingredients. If these skills aren't mastered, teach your child now and have him practice.

Around the age of six, your child will be ready to broaden his skill base, including making his own snack and lunch. Other skills your child should be working toward include cracking and separating eggs; reading recipes; warming food in the microwave; making a sandwich; stirring or flipping food on the stove (supervision advised); baking; using a blender, can opener, or other appliance; grating cheese; cutting vegetables or fruit; and slicing bread. No doubt, this is a learning process! Remember, your child will be learning and advancing these skills over the next six years, so if a skill like dicing an onion seems too advanced for your seven-year-old, save it for later or help him with this task to facilitate the process.

Here, we provide recipes *that your child can make*, with a little help from you in the beginning, and eventually on his own. These are simple recipes, on

Table 4.12 Keys to Kitchen Safety

What	How and When	Why
Washing hands	Using hot, soapy water, wash hands before touching food, and after touching raw meats or eggs.	Washing hands reduces the risk of contamination from germs and food-borne illness.
Supervising	Be in the kitchen or close by when kids are cooking; never leave a young, inexperienced cook alone in the kitchen. Never leave cooking food unattended.	Accidents happen, and your help may be needed! Unwatched pots can boil over, cause fires, or create other disasters.
Handling kitchen equipment properly	Teach children how to use utensils and equipment. Don't assume they know how to use them just because they have been around or have watched.	Many kitchen appliances are dangerous: knives, food processors, ovens, gas stoves, blenders, and so on. Teach your child that metal and microwaves do not mix!
Wearing proper attire	Wear short sleeves; avoid long necklaces and jangly bracelets; and tie hair back if it is long. Wear an apron. Use oven mitts.	Long sleeves can catch fire, and necklaces and bracelets can catch on appliances. Hair can become a sanitation issue. Aprons protect from grease, boiling water, splatters, and spills. Oven mitts protect hands from burning.
Knowing fire safety	Teach children when to call 911; where to find the fire extinguisher; and how to put out a fire (grease or other).	Practicing fire safety and having an action plan can help avert a disaster.
Avoiding cross-contamination	Teach kids that cooked and raw foods should never mix! Clean surfaces that raw meat or poultry have touched.	Bacteria can transfer between foods and cause food poisoning if ingested.
Knowing safe temperatures	Teach children minimum temperatures for safety, such as 145°F for beefsteaks, roasts, and chops; 160°F for ground beef, pork, veal, or lamb; and 165°F for poultry.	Complete cooking ensures your food (especially meats) is safe to eat.
Practicing knife skills	Teach "one hand on the food and one hand on the knife handle." Fingers should be tucked under, like a claw. You can practice knife holding with a table knife and graduate to a chef's knife and beyond, once children become skilled.	Knives are dangerous, and kids don't know instinctively how to use them. Teach them to carry a knife pointed down to the floor.
Knowing how to get basic first aid	Make sure children know how to get help to treat a burn, cut, or other injury.	Another important life skill!

purpose. We know that simplicity leads to success, and mastery builds confidence and more interest! We provide key nutrients for each recipe here, with full nutrient lists available on request through the contact page of our website, www.fearlessfeeding.com. For more family meal ideas and recipes, see Chapter Eight.

Breakfast

Breakfast sets the tone for how the day will unfold—firing up the metabolism, feeding the brain, and prepping the body for activity.

Rule of thumb: Target three food groups, include a protein source, and keep foods and variety rotating.

Egg in a Hole

Ingredients

Glass with a large mouth (4- to 5-inch diameter), or biscuit cutter

1 slice whole wheat bread (or other bread)

1 egg

Cooking spray, oil, or butter

Makes: One serving

Directions

Make a hole in the center of the bread by pressing the glass opening onto the bread, creating a circle and a "frame." Spray cooking spray (or oil or butter) onto a pan or skillet and turn the burner to medium. Butter both sides of the bread circle and place it on the hot skillet, alongside the frame. Crack the egg and place it inside the frame. Cook until the egg is set and the bread is browned; then flip the whole thing, as well as the bread circle, and cook the other sides.

Fearless food groups: Grains, protein, fat

Key nutrients per serving (percent daily value [%DV]): Selenium (37), protein (18), riboflavin (17), phosphorus (16), vitamin B12 (11), iron (10)

Lunch

Lunch keeps children fueled for the midday routine—learning in the classroom or playing outside on the weekends. A variety of foods and a healthy, balanced plate keep kids interested and satisfied.

Rule of thumb: Include at least three food groups or more, incorporate protein and fiber for satisfying fullness that lasts, and serve vegetables or fruits on the side when possible.

Homemade Pepperoni Pizza

Ingredients

1 premade pizza dough round, flatbread, or naan (whole wheat or other whole grain)

¼ cup pizza sauce

¼ to ½ cup mozzarella cheese

8 to 10 slices turkey pepperoni

Directions

Preheat the oven to 400°F. If you're using dough, use a quarter portion; sprinkle a clean surface with flour and roll out the dough into an 8- to 10-inch round. Spread tomato sauce onto the dough or pizza round, covering most of the surface, up to ½ inch from the edge. Sprinkle cheese all over the tomato sauce. Top the pizza with pepperoni slices. Bake for about 10 minutes or until the cheese is melted and the crust is browned at the edges.

Variations: Add chopped vegetables (onions, green peppers, red peppers, mushrooms, spinach, olives, artichoke hearts, and so on); have it plain with cheese only; or try different meats, such as prosciutto, Canadian bacon, ham, turkey sausage, or lean hamburger meat.

Makes: One serving

Fearless food groups: Grains, dairy, protein

Key nutrients per serving (%DV): Selenium (45), B vitamins (30–34), phosphorus (27), calcium (26), iron (26), vitamin K (24), fiber (21)

Chef's Salad

Ingredients

½ head romaine lettuce, cleaned and chopped

¾ cup shredded cheddar cheese (or other type of cheese)

1 tomato, cut in eighths

1 avocado, cut in slices

½ cucumber, sliced

¾ cup diced ham

¾ cup diced turkey

2 hard-boiled eggs, sliced in quarters

4 slices cooked turkey bacon (or regular bacon)

Directions

Layer the lettuce in the bottom of a serving bowl. Sprinkle cheese over the lettuce. Arrange the tomato, avocado, cucumber, ham, turkey, eggs, and bacon on top of the lettuce and cheese in a colorful manner. Top with your favorite salad dressing.

Variations: Alter the types of lettuce, vegetables, and meat and cheese used.

Makes: Two servings

Fearless food groups: Vegetables, protein, dairy, fat

Key nutrients per serving (%DV): Phosphorus (79), selenium (60), vitamin A (55), potassium (45), fiber (38), zinc (37), calcium (30)

Snacks

Snacks are an important delivery system for missed nutrients during the day.

Rule of thumb: Opt for wholesome food in normal serving sizes, and squeeze in at least two food groups. Some ideas are cheese, crackers, and fruit; layered yogurt and fruit in a parfait glass; cereal and milk; peanut butter and crackers; raw vegetables and low-fat dip; deli meat and cheese roll-ups; a half sandwich and fruit; and low-fat chocolate milk and graham crackers.

Gorp

Ingredients

1 box oatmeal squares cereal

2 cups lightly salted peanuts

1 bag waffle-style pretzels

2 cups raisins

2 cups M&M candies

Directions

Mix all the ingredients together. Store the mixture in an airtight container.

Variations: Vary the cereal, nuts, and dried fruits to create different flavors.

Makes: Thirty-six ½-cup servings

Fearless food groups: Grains, protein, fat, fruit, Fun Food

Key nutrients per serving (%DV): Manganese (31), folate (30), iron (25), niacin (14), zinc (12), phosphorus (12)

Homemade Pita Chips

Ingredients

3 whole wheat pita rounds

½ teaspoon kosher salt

Olive oil or cooking spray

Directions

Preheat the oven to 350°F. Split the pitas in half; you should have 6 rounds. With kitchen scissors, cut the pitas into 6 wedges each. Spray a cookie sheet with cooking spray. Place the wedges on the cookie sheet and spray them with cooking spray or drizzle the wedges with oil. Sprinkle kosher salt evenly over the wedges. Bake for 8 minutes or until golden brown.

Variations: Sprinkle the pita chips with cinnamon and sugar, cumin, paprika, rosemary, Parmesan cheese, or garlic salt. Serve them with white bean dip, hummus, guacamole, or artichoke dip.

Makes: Thirty-six pita chips (six servings)

Fearless food group: Grains

Key nutrients per serving (%DV): Manganese (28), fiber (9), selenium (20)

Desserts

Desserts are Fun Foods and are meant to be enjoyed in balance with other Nourishing and Half-and-Half Foods.

Rule of thumb: Eat desserts in recommended serving sizes; eat them slowly and savor the flavor.

Triple Chocolate One-Bowl Brownies

Ingredients

1 cup semisweet chocolate chips

2 ounces unsweetened chocolate, chopped

1 stick butter, cut into 8 pieces

3 tablespoons cocoa powder, sifted

3 large eggs

1¼ cups sugar

1 tablespoon vanilla extract

½ teaspoon salt

1 cup all-purpose flour

Cooking spray

Directions

Preheat the oven to 350°F; place the rack in the center of the oven. Spray an 8- by 8-inch square baking pan with cooking spray. Melt the chocolate chips, unsweetened chocolate, and butter in a microwave-safe dish on high for 1 minute. Remove and stir the mixture with a spatula until the chocolate is melted. Return it to the microwave for 30-second intervals to melt the chocolate completely, if needed. Add the cocoa powder and stir. Allow the melted chocolate to cool. Stir in the eggs, sugar, vanilla, and salt until combined. Add the flour and stir, mixing until combined. Pour the batter into the square pan, taking care to push the batter into the corners of the pan, and smooth with a spatula. Bake in the oven for 35 to 40 minutes. Use a toothpick to check if the brownies are done—the toothpick should be clean or have a few moist crumbs attached. Allow the pan of brownies to cool to room temperature on a wire rack. Cut the brownies into 2-inch squares.

Makes: Sixteen 2-inch brownies

Fearless food group: Fun Food

Fruit and Cream Supreme

Ingredients

1 cup sliced strawberries

1 cup blueberries

1 cup raspberries

½ cup light whipping cream

3 tablespoons sugar

½ teaspoon vanilla

4 tall parfait glasses or other clear, tall glasses

Directions

Rinse the berries and let them dry on a paper towel. Slice the strawberries. In a mixer, add the cream and beat on medium-high speed for 2 minutes (avoid splattering!). Add the sugar and vanilla. Increase the speed to as high as possible without splattering. Stop mixing when the cream is thick and has lost its shiny or glossy appearance. When you stop, peaks of whipped cream should form when you pull up the whisk. In the following order, layer strawberries, whipped cream, blueberries, whipped cream, raspberries, and whipped cream in each glass. Place the berry of your choice on top. Refrigerate the glasses until ready to serve.

Variations: Try different combinations of fruit.

Makes: 4 servings

Fearless food groups: Fruit, dairy

Key nutrients per serving (%DV): Vitamin C (57), manganese (24), fiber (15), vitamin K (14), vitamin A (10)

CHAPTER 5

Fearless Feeding for Your Teenager (Thirteen to Eighteen Years)

The teen years are a roller coaster ride, and they challenge even the best of parents. Independence is in full throttle; teens are growing like weeds; and they're hard to pin down, spending more time outside the home than in! Teens need help crossing the passage to adulthood, and *you* are the ideal candidate to help with this transition. We assist you in launching a healthy adult (and possibly a future parent) by helping you understand the physical and mental changes your teen is experiencing, how to connect and talk about nutrition, and how to handle typical challenges. We've got the support you need!

Nutrition in Practice: Hazardous Nutrition

Cindy had survived a daughter's adolescence twice, though it hadn't been pretty. She vowed with her third daughter, sixteen-year-old Lexi, she wouldn't be as involved in her day-to-day life. She would give her more freedom and meddle less, especially when it came to food. It was as if Lexi was already living the college life—independent, eating on her own, and self-sufficient. When Cindy and her husband found out Lexi was too thin, they were both surprised. The truth was that Cindy had stopped feeding Lexi in an effort to support her independence and freedom, but Lexi didn't know what or how to feed herself.

Although adolescence is the last stop of childhood, it's not a time to go on cruise control. It's a crucial time to prepare teens for adulthood. Here's the good news: you've been preparing your child for this all along, especially if you've been teaching healthy eating habits, covering nutritional needs with daily meals, and maximizing your role as a Fearless Feeder. If you're just opening this book now, we suggest you familiarize yourself with the Fearless Feeding Strategy in Chapter One, so that you have a basis for our discussion.

What to Expect

The teen years are a time of immense growth, second only to the growth experienced in infancy. During this time, your teen will magically morph from a gangly school-age child to a full-size adult. By ages sixteen to eighteen, most girls will have finished growing, and boys will be done by ages eighteen to twenty. For girls, the majority of growth occurs before menses. Boys' growth spurt happens after girls' (about two years later) but lasts longer, resulting in more overall growth and greater muscle deposition.

Fearless Fact

The maximal height growth among boys is 3.7 to 4.1 inches per year, whereas girls' maximal height growth is 3.3 to 3.5 inches per year. Teens reach their final weight status after reaching their peak height. Females gain an average of twenty-one pounds and males an average of thirty-four pounds during adolescence. Boys tend to be taller and more muscular than girls, whereas girls have more body fat than boys.

Muscle, Fat, and Skeletal Growth

Muscle, a component of lean body mass, is the largest single tissue of the body and consists mostly of water. Lean body mass is metabolically active (requiring energy to keep it going) and consists of muscles, internal organs, and bones. At birth, 25 percent of body weight is from skeletal muscle, which grows to 50 percent by adulthood. Girls gain muscle up to age sixteen, whereas boys' muscle growth starts around age thirteen and continues well into the late teens. Although your son may want to bulk up earlier, his muscle mass growth relies on increases in testosterone levels and the onset of puberty.

Body fat is where extra energy is stored. Although both genders accumulate fat in the torso area, girls add fat tissue to the breasts, buttocks, and thighs, and across the backs of the arms, accentuating what is commonly known as the "womanly figure." Body fat is important for menstruation, which begins at twelve and a half years on average. Body fat produces estrogen, a key hormone in the menstrual cycle. When girls have too little body fat, menstruation can stop or be delayed, and too much body fat can initiate menses early and interfere with fertility later on. In addition, menstruating girls are at increased risk for iron deficiency due to more blood loss.

Bones grow too! Whereas the child experiences steady bone growth, the teen experiences rapid changes in bone growth and ultimately stature (height). Adequate intake of calcium, vitamin D, magnesium, and phosphorus is important for this process and future adult bone health.[1] Teens make mineral deposits in their "bone bank," setting a future withdrawal system that will be used for the rest of their lives. If mineral needs are not met, this withdrawal system starts early, weakening your teen's bones prematurely. Research shows that teens who end their growth phase with low bone mass (low calcium stores) are more likely to develop osteopenia (weakening of the bones) or osteoporosis during adulthood.[1,2] Girls reach peak bone mass earlier than boys, between twenty and twenty-five years, making adolescence a time when calcium needs are at their highest and "banking and building" calcium stores are important tasks.[3]

Appetite

Teens are growing, and they need more calories and nutrients to support the process. If you're a parent of a teenage male, you'll be interested to know that teen males have the highest requirements for calories each day, as compared to any other adolescent group, due to increases in muscle mass. Of course, each teen has different nutritional needs, depending on activity, stage of growth, and individual body composition, as shown in Table 5.1. Because energy needs are high, increased appetite during adolescence influences food choices.

Activity

At this time when your child is, for the most part, coordinated, strong, and possibly interested in physical activity, the opportunities for regular exercise slip

Table 5.1	Energy Needs of Teens					
Age	Sedentary (Calories)		Moderately Active (Calories)		Active (Calories)	
	Males	Females	Males	Females	Males	Females
Thirteen years	1,600–2,000	1,400–1,600	1,800–2,200	1,600–2,000	2,000–2,600	1,800–2,200
Fourteen to eighteen years	2,000–2,400	1,800	2,400–2,800	2,000	2,800–3,200	2,400

Source: Adapted from U.S. Department of Agriculture & U.S. Department of Health and Human Services. (2010). *Dietary guidelines for Americans, 2010* (7th ed.). Washington DC: U.S. Government Printing Office.

Fearless Fact

Teens are spending more time on the computer for nonhomework activities (up to three or more hours a day), especially social networking, which has replaced TV viewing as the main sedentary activity.[5]

away. As high school students age, their participation in physical education classes declines by as much as 40 percent. Only 18 percent of high school students are physically active for the recommended hour each day.[4] Being less active has an impact on their ability to maintain a healthy weight, especially in the face of typical teen eating trends and habits.

Weight

In the face of reduced physical activity levels, poor eating habits, and unhealthy patterns, the possibility of overshooting daily energy needs can become more of a concern for the teen. Seventeen percent of teens are overweight or obese, with the highest rates occurring in males. Recent trends indicate a leveling off of the prevalence of obesity over the last decade, which is good news.[6] We know that teen eating habits and food choices contribute to weight gain, so you should still keep an eye on your teen's growth.

The opposite can also happen in adolescence: weight loss. Not eating enough or exercising too much can create a negative energy balance for both males and females. Weight loss of 5 percent or more is an eyebrow raiser, and means it is time to figure out what is going on. You'll want to understand if weight loss is healthy (and needed), the result of undiscovered medical issues, or an intended result of dieting. Ongoing weight loss may take on a life of its own, becoming a significant mental and physical health concern, known as an eating disorder.[7] According to the National Eating Disorders Association, ten million women and girls and one million men and boys have anorexia or bulimia.[8] In a recent review, researchers confirmed that the incidence rate of eating disorders has remained stable over the past decades, with the exception of the high-risk group of fifteen-to nineteen-year-old girls, for whom rates are increasing.[9] Up to 50 percent of high school girls may have disordered eating behaviors, a known risk factor for the development of a full-blown eating disorder.[10] If you're concerned about your teen being under- or overweight, see Chapter Seven.

With changes in growth and appetite, and fluctuations in weight and activity level, there is a lot to sort out. Knowing these norms can help you anticipate and deal with challenges, when and if they occur. These are just the basics, though—there is much more going on with teens and their eating, so read on!

Food for Thought

Adolescents are faced with many distractions in today's food landscape, including convenience foods, calorie-rich beverages, fast-food establishments, large portions, and commercials for unhealthy items. The "thin is in" message is everywhere too, pushing weight loss diets, fasting, skipping meals, and overconsumption of caffeine, all in an effort to keep a slim body. To the teen, it can appear that there are only two paths to take: the road to Nutrition Overdo It (eating too much of the wrong foods), or the road to Nutrition No-No's (avoiding foods that are perceived to be "bad"). What you want for your teen is the road to Nutrition Balance, a path on which teens are in sync with eating, matching food with nutritional needs, indulging in Fun Foods less often, and engaging in healthy amounts of exercise. But first you need to know *why* teens get off track in the first place.

Fearless Fact

Satisfaction may make a difference in how much a teen eats. According to Brian Wansink, author of *Mindless Eating*, if adults eat until they are satisfied, then overall they eat 20 percent *less* food than if they eat until they are full. Liking what you eat and getting a variety of foods increase satisfaction.

Fearless Tip

Make sure to have a variety of foods available—both familiar foods and unfamiliar ones to keep interest up and satisfaction high.

Taste, Hunger, and Satisfaction

Food needs to taste good, or teens won't eat it. That's why teens gravitate toward sweet, salty, and fatty foods—they taste delicious! Rather than fight against the foods teens love, find ways to modify them so that they remain tasty and pack more nutrients. For example, pizza can be a nutritious food with some simple adjustments. Swap out the high-fat cheese with low-fat mozzarella, use a whole grain crust, and top with lots of veggies and lean meat to create a healthier (and still tasty) pizza your teen will eat.

Your teen *will* be hungrier due to the accelerated growth we discussed earlier. This hunger may translate to more food and bigger portions. Rather than worry about extra hunger, be prepared for it with quality food on hand and regular meals that satisfy your teen.

Food Availability

Teens tend to eat what they are served most often, and prefer foods that are readily available. Fast food is easy to get and quick to eat. Many foods in the school lunchroom—hamburgers, pizza, French fries, hot dogs—are fast-food "mimics," appealing to teen palates. And if your home is full of fast snacking foods, this too will solidify your teen's preferences. Make sure your teen sees plenty of health-filled foods on a regular basis to cultivate her preferences for them.

Meal Skipping

Meal skipping can have a negative impact on weight status, nutrient intake, and diet variety. Skipping meals also makes it harder to regulate appetite and may promote overeating or undereating.[11,12,13] Some teens skip meals to help lose weight, maintain their weight, or prevent weight gain. Other teens are just short on time and fail to prioritize meals, especially breakfast. If you want your teen to be fueled for the day, make sure she is eating three meals daily.

Snacking

The flip side of skipping meals is the potential problem of too much snacking, snacking on the wrong things, or both.[14] The right amount of snacking depends on the growth, appetite, and physical activity of your teen. If your teen participates in sports, he will likely need more than one snack, or another meal, to cover nutritional needs. Conversely, sedentary teens or occasional exercisers may only need one snack. We don't advise a "no snacks" policy for growing teens, but emphasize healthy snack options.

Dining Out

Eating outside of the home is associated with consuming more calories; more fat; and fewer nutrients like vitamin A, iron, calcium, and fiber. Eating away from home may contribute more than half of the total calories eaten daily for teens.[15] As teens get older and become more independent (for example, driving), fast-food establishments, restaurants, and convenience stores become fair game. Eating out is also a way of socializing with other peers, but if it's being done too frequently it can start adding a lot of calories to your teen's diet.

Dieting

Teens who diet may be concerned with their appearance and suffer from low self-esteem. Dieting can take many forms: calorie reduction, elimination of foods, skipping meals, vegetarianism, an emphasis on high-protein foods, avoidance of carbohydrates, eating only vegetables and fruit, fasting, cleansing, and the list goes on. Don't get dieting confused with healthy eating, though. Cutting back on soda, sweets, and fatty snacks, the main culprits of extra calories, is a healthful way to manage teen eating. If dieting seems to be taking over, however, your teen may need professional help (see Chapter Seven).

Fearless Fact

Up to 50 percent of teenage girls and 25 percent of teenage boys have tried to diet, some of whom were already at a healthy weight. Statistics show that dieting before the age of fourteen leads to an eightfold increase in the risk of developing an eating disorder.[7]

Over the long run, teen dieting is linked to a higher risk for weight gain and obesity, and, as already mentioned, eating disorders.[12] What teens eat and their daily habits may take them down an unhealthy path, but there are ways you can help!

What Parents Can Do

Part of the dilemma is that parents often either take a hands-off approach with teens or nag for better habits—neither of which works. But let's discuss the good news first.

Many teens are interested in new, different foods and show openness when it comes to trying them. Sarah's sixteen-year-old daughter ordered a salad plate with hummus and pita on her own one day, and the food adventure began. "It's really amazing how she has taken the lead in wanting to eat more exotic foods, trying new foods, and appreciating the differences in flavors—and it's all her own doing!" says Sarah. Beyond having this willingness to try new foods on your side, there's much you can do to tip habits into a healthier place, as summarized in Table 5.2.

Table 5.2 How to Manage Eating Influences		
Food Influences	**Potential Problems**	**Better Solutions**
Taste	• Eating too many sweet, salty, and fatty foods	• Offering homemade versions of favorite foods, such as sub sandwiches, pizza, tacos, and nachos
Hunger	• Overeating • Large portions • Grabbing quick, convenient items	• Having good, nutritious food on hand • Serving regular, satisfying meals

Table 5.2 (*continued*)		
Food Influences	**Potential Problems**	**Better Solutions**
Food availability	• Too much fast food • The prevalence of convenience foods, which drives preferences for them	• Making sure your teen frequently sees what you want him to eat (fruit, vegetables, whole grains, low-fat dairy, lean meats, healthy fats)
Meal skipping	• Overeating or undereating • Weight gain or weight loss • Poor nutrient intake • Limited diet variety • Difficulty regulating appetite	• Preparing three meals each day • Taking care to include breakfast • Shooting for meals and snacks every three to five hours
Snacking	• Too many calories • Nutrient-poor foods • Interference with appetite for meals	• Limiting snacks to one or two per day, depending on activity • Choosing Nourishing or Half-and-Half Foods for snacks • Thinking of snacks as mini-meals
Dining out	• Excess calories • Poor sources of nutrients • Large portion sizes	• Limiting dining out to two or three times per week • Choosing healthier options • Asking for steamed veggies or a baked potato as a side dish • Sharing or splitting decadent desserts • Opting for gravies, sauces, and dressings on the side • Splitting meals or taking half home in a doggie bag

There are many challenges during the teen years, but all is not lost. As you read on, you'll find ways to navigate nutrition, help maximize good eating, and troubleshoot nutritional shortfalls along the way.

Fearless Food Guide

Your role during adolescence is to continue to be a "provider"—stocking healthy foods in your home, serving meals regularly, and offering guidance along the way. You'll rely on history—all the work you've done in the past with feeding—and a realistic attitude. Although teen eating may go off the rails, many teens (eventually) find their way back to the foundation of good nutrition you've been cultivating all along.

A Word About Protein, Fat, and Cholesterol

The basic structure of three meals and at least one snack each day, if not more, is what your teen needs to cover growth and activity needs. Protein requirements reflect an increased growth rate, as protein provides building blocks for muscle development. Most teens get plenty of protein, and pushing extra doesn't result in extra muscle or improved athletic or academic performance.[16] Most teens need about 0.4 to 0.5 grams of protein per pound of body weight and can meet this requirement with food.[17]

Fearless Fact

One in five U.S. children has abnormal cholesterol levels, with family history and weight status typically being the culprits. Cholesterol screening should occur in children between ages nine and eleven, and again between ages seventeen and twenty-one, according to the National Heart, Lung, and Blood Institute guidelines.[18]

Fat is needed in the teen diet too, although the teen diet tends to be full of the unhealthy kinds—saturated and trans fats. These are known to elevate cholesterol and contribute to high blood lipids, and are associated with the development of cardiovascular disease. Healthy fats (monounsaturated and polyunsaturated fats) are associated with its prevention. We like to see teens eating mostly healthy fats, found in nuts, olive and other plant oils, and avocado, while trimming back on unhealthy ones. All fats are created equal when it comes to calories (nine calories per gram)—but not so when it comes to health effects.

The Keys to Balanced Eating

The right balance of Nourishing, Half-and-Half, and Fun Foods creates a healthy diet for your teen. To give you a better idea of the amounts and types of foods your teen needs, we've included Table 5.3, our Fearless Food Guide for teens. You can find additional information in Appendix A. Our nutrition philosophy is a positive one: *add nutritious foods* into the diet to make it balanced and healthy rather than worrying about what to take away.

> ### Fearless Tip
>
> Add foods to your teen's diet that lower cholesterol naturally: oats; barley; beans; eggplant; okra; nuts; vegetable oils; strawberries; citrus fruits; apples; grapes; soy; fatty fish; and foods fortified with sterols and stanols, such as margarine, granola, and chocolate. Cut saturated fat and cholesterol: use skim or low-fat dairy products; olive oil and vinegar or lemon juice for salad dressings; olive oil–based spreads instead of butter; lean meats like turkey, chicken, or very lean red meats; fish; and popcorn instead of chips.

Real Deal Meals and Snacks

Now that you are familiar with balancing WHAT your teen should be eating, we put it all together for you in Table 5.4, our sample meal plan for a seventeen-year-old. Remember, missed meals, no snacks, or too many snacks make it difficult to get proper nutrition and to manage appetite and weight. We targeted age seventeen, a time of slowing growth for a female and rapid growth for a male, and you'll see that food amounts reflect this. Amounts will vary for the younger and older teen, depending on activity and the teen's growth phase, as outlined in Table 5.3.

There are some highlights in this meal plan that are important to point out. Meals and snacks are spaced in three- to five-hour intervals to help manage appetite and supply energy and a variety of nutrients. A source of protein is included at all meals and snacks to help manage blood sugar and appetite, and to provide the protein needed for growth. Fruits and vegetables make a frequent appearance throughout the day, helping to meet the "five a day" goal, cover

Table 5.3   Fearless Food Guide for Teens

Food Group	Serving Sizes	Thirteen-Year-Old Total Daily Servings	Fourteen- to Eighteen-Year-Old Total Daily Servings	Comments
Meats and nonmeat protein sources:		5 (females) 5 (males)	5 (females) 6½ (males)	Include beans and fish twice weekly. Serve high-fat meats less often (for example, twice weekly).
Chicken, pork, fish and shellfish	1 ounce			
Eggs	1 egg			
Nuts and seeds	½ ounce			
Nut butters	1 tablespoon			
Beans, tofu	¼ cup cooked			
Dairy and nondairy sources:		3	3	Include low-fat or nonfat dairy foods; provide high-fat options less often.
Milk, yogurt	1 cup			
Cheese	1½ ounces			
Nondairy alternatives	1 cup			
Fruits:		1½ (females) 1½ (males)	1½ (females) 2 (males)	Keep juice to 8 to 12 ounces daily. Include vitamin C sources every day. Fruits and vegetables can be interchanged to total 5 servings each day.
Fresh, frozen, or canned fruit	1 medium or 1 cup			
Dried fruit	½ cup			
100 percent fruit juice	1 cup			

Table 5.3 (continued)				
Food Group	**Serving Sizes**	**Thirteen-Year-Old Total Daily Servings**	**Fourteen- to Eighteen-Year-Old Total Daily Servings**	**Comments**
Vegetables:		2 (females) 2½ (males)	2½ (females) 3 (males)	Include vitamin A sources daily. Vegetables and fruit are interchangeable; aim for 5 servings daily.
Cooked vegetables	½ to 1 cup			
Raw vegetables	1 cup			
Leafy salad greens	2 cups			
Grains: wheat, rye, barley, oats, quinoa, rice		5 (females) 6 (males)	6 (females) 8 (males)	Choose whole grains at least half of the time.
Bread	1 slice			
Pasta, rice, cooked cereal	½ cup			
Dry cereal	1 cup			
Bagel, English muffin	½			
Fats:		5 (females) 5 (males)	5 (females) 6 (males)	Cook and stock the kitchen with healthy fats. Offer and cook with saturated and trans fat less often. (Fats are inherent in many foods, such as nuts, seeds, dairy products, and meats. Amounts represent fat added to foods.)
Vegetable oils (olive, canola, flaxseed), butter, soft margarine	1 teaspoon			
Salad dressing, mayonnaise	1 tablespoon			
Avocado	⅙ medium			

Table 5.3 *(continued)*				
Food Group	**Serving Sizes**	**Thirteen-Year-Old Total Daily Servings**	**Fourteen- to Eighteen-Year-Old Total Daily Servings**	**Comments**
Fun Foods: Cookies, cakes, pies, candy, sugar-sweetened drinks, pastries, fried foods	1 serving	1 to 2 (10 percent of daily intake, or up to 250 calories per day)	1 to 2 (10 percent of daily intake, or up to 300 calories per day)	Limit sugar-sweetened beverages to 12-ounce portions. We suggest keeping soda out of the home, and that it be used for special occasions only. Pay attention to serving sizes. Eat these Fun Foods as part of a meal or healthy snack.

Table 5.4 Real Deal Meal Plan for a Seventeen-Year-Old				
Time	**Meal or Snack**	**Food Groups**	**Female**	**Male**
7:30 a.m.	Breakfast	• Meat or nonmeat • Fat • Fruit • Grain • Dairy or nondairy	• 2 tablespoons peanut butter • 1 large banana • 2 slices 100 percent whole grain toast • 8 ounces skim milk	• 2 tablespoons peanut butter • 1 large banana • 2 slices 100 percent whole grain toast; 1 cup cereal • 8 ounces skim milk

Time	Meal or Snack	Food Groups	Female	Male
11:30 a.m.	Lunch	• Meat or nonmeat • Vegetable • Grain • Fat • Dairy or nondairy • Fruit • Fun Food	• 3 ounces turkey • 1 lettuce leaf; 2 slices tomato • 2 slices whole grain bread • 1 tablespoon lite mayonnaise • 1 cup low-fat yogurt • 1 cup blueberries • Water	• 3 ounces turkey • 1 lettuce leaf; 2 slices tomato • 2 slices whole grain bread • 1 tablespoon lite mayonnaise • 1 cup skim milk • 1 cup blueberries • 1 ounce potato chips
2:30 p.m.	Snack	• Vegetable • Grain • Meat or nonmeat	• 1 cup carrot sticks • 2 tablespoons hummus • Water	• 1 cup carrot sticks • 1½ cups flat pretzels • 2 tablespoons hummus • Water
6:30 p.m.	Dinner	• Meat or nonmeat • Vegetable • Fruit • Grain • Fat • Dairy or nondairy	• 4 ounces chicken • 1 cup broccoli • 1 cup tomato sauce • 1½ cups spaghetti; 1 garlic breadstick • 1 tablespoon olive oil • 8 ounces skim milk	• 4 ounces chicken • 1 cup broccoli • 1 cup tomato sauce • 2 cups spaghetti; 2 garlic breadsticks • 1 tablespoon olive oil • 12 ounces skim milk
10:00 p.m.	Snack	• Fun Food	• 1 cup frozen yogurt	• 1 cup frozen yogurt

Table 5.4 *(continued)*

vitamins A and C, and provide a regular dose of fiber. Three servings of dairy or nondairy are included to help meet calcium and vitamin D goals. Healthy sources of fat are detailed so you remember to include them, and grains round out most meals. Of course, Fun Foods are included, but they don't have to be.

The Truth About What Teens Are Eating

A change in teen eating habits has been brewing over the past forty years, resulting in lower consumption of fruits, vegetables, milk and milk products, whole grains, and, for the female teen, protein sources.[14,19,20] This is partly why calcium, vitamin D, potassium, dietary fiber, and other nutrients are lacking in the teen diet. Snacking is prevalent, with 83 percent of teens snacking on any given day, contributing an average of 526 calories (23 percent of calories) and a third of teens' total sugar intake.[14] Beverages also supply extra calories *on top of* regular food calories. Soda drinking is up 74 percent among male teens and 65 percent among females, while at the same time milk consumption has declined by 25 percent for males and 20 percent for females.[19] This may be why fourteen- to eighteen-year-olds consume the most sugar—about thirty-four teaspoons per day (549 calories' worth!).[20] And teens don't downsize their solid food intake when they drink calorie-containing beverages. Some beverages, like milk and 100 percent fruit juice, do supply critical nutrients and can be an asset to your teen's health. Table 5.5 summarizes the biggest contributors of fat and sugar (and calories) to the teen diet.

The Fearless Five Nutrients and Special Considerations

What is missing from the teen diet reflects what teens *are* eating as well as what they *aren't*. In many cases, what they *are* eating (sugary and fatty foods) fills them up with empty calories (calories from foods with negligible nutrients), leaving them full but not nourished. What they *aren't* eating (fruits, vegetables, whole grains, dairy sources) adds insult to injury—creating a host of nutrient insufficiencies. With some attention to detail, you can cover nutrient gaps and ensure a better-quality diet for your teen. We make this easy with the Fearless Five Nutrients for teens in Table 5.6, in which we target iron, magnesium,

Table 5.5	Sources of Fat and Sugar	
Food Group	**Top Sources of Fat**	**Top Sources of Added Sugar**
Grains	Cake, pie, cookies, donuts, crisps, cobblers, granola bars	Cake, cookies, pies, pastries, crackers, ready-to-eat cereals, yeast breads, snacks
Dairy	Regular-fat cheese, ice cream, cream, dairy-based desserts, whole milk	Dairy-based desserts (such as ice cream, puddings, and custards)
Fruit		Fruit-ades, sugar-sweetened fruit drinks
Vegetables	French fried potatoes	
Meats	Sausage, franks, ribs, bacon, regular ground beef, marbled meats, poultry skin	
Others	*Animal fats:* Butter, chicken fat, pork fat *Hydrogenated fats:* Shortening, stick margarine	Soda, sports drinks, energy drinks, candy, syrup, toppings, jam, jelly

Source: Adapted from Reedy, J., & Krebs-Smith, S. M. (2010). Dietary sources of energy, solid fats, and added sugars among children and adolescents in the United States. *Journal of the Academy of Nutrition and Dietetics, 110,* 1477–1484.

calcium, vitamin D, and vitamin E, all notably low or "at risk" for the teen. The truth is, teens are falling behind on several nutrients, some of which deserve special attention. If you are unable to fill the gaps, your teen may benefit from a multivitamin and mineral supplement. We remind you, however, that some nutrients in supplements (such as calcium) may be inadequate, whereas others (such as folic acid and vitamin A) may be excessive. You can read more about supplements in Chapter Three, and can find more foods and their specific nutrient values in Appendix B.

Table 5.6 Fearless Five Nutrients for Teens

Nutrient	Function	Recommended Daily Allowance (RDA)	Sources	Comments
Iron	Iron carries and stores oxygen, a process that is accelerated during growth. It is a component of enzymes and protein.	*Nine to thirteen years:* 8 milligrams *Fourteen to eighteen years:* 15 milligrams (females) or 11 milligrams (males)	*Heme:* Beef chuck (3.1 milligrams), ground beef (2.2 milligrams), dark meat turkey (2 milligrams), canned light tuna in water (1.3 milligrams), light meat chicken (.9 milligrams) *Nonheme:* 100 percent iron-fortified cereals (18 milligrams), instant oatmeal (11 milligrams), white beans (3.9 milligrams), fresh spinach (3.2 milligrams), whole wheat bread (.7 milligrams)	Nine percent of twelve- to forty-nine-year-old women have inadequate body stores of iron.[17] Fifteen to 17 percent of teen girls have intake levels below Estimated Average Requirement (EAR).[a,17] Dieters may be at risk for deficiency. Heme sources are more readily absorbed than nonheme sources. Absorption of nonheme sources is enhanced by consumption of vitamin C sources.

Magnesium	Magnesium is needed for normal muscle and nerve function. It keeps the teen's heart rhythm steady, supports the immune system, and keeps bones strong.	*Nine to thirteen years:* 240 milligrams *Fourteen to eighteen years:* 360 milligrams (females) or 410 milligrams (males)	Pumpkin or squash seeds (156 milligrams), spinach (78 to 81 milligrams), almonds (80 milligrams), cashews (74 milligrams), white beans (67 milligrams), soymilk (61 milligrams), peanut butter (49 milligrams), baked potato (48 milligrams), plain yogurt (43 milligrams), banana (32 milligrams), avocado (22 milligrams)	About 69 percent of fourteen- to eighteen-year-old males and 89 percent of fourteen- to eighteen-year-old females have inadequate intake of magnesium.[21] Half of all individuals over one year of age have inadequate intake.[21]
Calcium	Calcium is needed for bone mineralization and normal muscle contraction.	*Nine to thirteen years:* 1,300 milligrams *Fourteen to eighteen years:* 1,300 milligrams	Ready-to-eat cereals (100 to 1,000 milligrams), calcium-fortified orange juice (500 milligrams), plain nonfat yogurt (452 milligrams), mozzarella (333 milligrams), low-fat milk (305 milligrams), salmon (181 milligrams), vanilla ice cream (84 milligrams), whole wheat bread (30 milligrams)	Fifteen percent of girls and 22 percent of boys ages nine to thirteen are above adequate intake (AI) levels.[17] Only 10 percent of fourteen- to eighteen-year-old girls and 42 percent of boys in that age range are above AI levels.[17]

Table 5.6 (continued)

Nutrient	Function	Recommended Daily Allowance (RDA)	Sources	Comments
Vitamin E	Vitamin E is an antioxidant that protects body cells from damage. It is involved in immune function. It is also known as alpha-tocopherol (AT).	*Nine to thirteen years:* 11 milligrams *Fourteen to eighteen years:* 15 milligrams	1 tablespoon wheat germ oil (20.3 milligrams), fortified ready-to-eat cereals (3.2 to 13.5 milligrams), sunflower seeds (7.4 milligrams), almonds (6.8 milligrams), peanut butter (2.9 milligrams)	Ninety-three percent of Americans do not consume foods rich in Vitamin E daily. However, less than 5 percent of the U.S. population has inadequate blood levels.[17] Typical oils and nuts used (soybeans, peanuts, peanut butter) are not high–Vitamin E sources.
Vitamin D	Vitamin D partners with calcium for bone mineralization. It plays a role in the prevention of cancer, cardiovascular disease, autoimmune disease, and infectious disease.	*Nine to thirteen years:* 600 international units (IU) *Fourteen to eighteen years:* 600 IU	Sockeye salmon (792 IU); smoked salmon (580 IU); vitamin D–fortified orange juice (136 IU); nonfat, low-fat, or reduced-fat milk (116 IU), soymilk (108 IU); fortified ready-to-eat cereals (36 to 100 IU), hard-boiled egg (28 IU)	Only 50 percent of male teens and 25 percent of female teens exceed AI for Vitamin D.[17] Sunlight is also a source of vitamin D, but it is limited with sunscreen use, excessive time indoors, higher altitudes and winter months, dark-colored skin, and excess weight.

[a] EAR: the average daily nutrient intake level estimated to meet the requirement of half of the healthy individuals of a particular age and gender.

Bone Health

Calcium is the most recognized nutrient for bone health. You may be surprised to learn that a diet including three to four cups of milk or fortified nondairy milk is still short of meeting the target 1,300 milligrams each day.[22] If your teen is a vegan, the odds against hitting this target increase. Researchers have found that dairy-free diets *do not meet* calcium needs unless enhanced with calcium-fortified foods, such as citrus juice.[23] Both milk drinkers and non–milk drinkers can use the Fearless Five Nutrients to target calcium-rich sources. If all else fails, consider a calcium supplement, such as a calcium and vitamin D chew. Remember, multivitamin supplements have little calcium and generally don't improve overall calcium intake.

Vitamin D is also important for the absorption of calcium and bone health. Vitamin D needs, in particular, are difficult to meet with food alone, so supplements may be necessary.[1] Phosphorus, another bone health nutrient known to be deficient in teen diets, is often taken care of when foods rich in calcium and vitamin D are included.

How Do I Know If My Teen Is Vitamin D–Deficient?

A blood test of serum 25–hydroxyvitamin D that falls below twenty nanograms per milliliter (or fifty nanomoles per liter) is considered deficient. Your doctor may treat this deficiency with a higher dose of vitamin D (up to fifty thousand IU once weekly for six to eight weeks) to correct it. We recommend following up with your physician to evaluate the ongoing need for supplementation. It's important to note that the recommended intake of six hundred IU per day is a daily dose to "prevent deficiency" and is not enough if your teen is already deficient.[24,25]

Reproduction

Menses and potential pregnancy place teen girls at risk for iron deficiency. It's estimated that 6.5 million teen girls and women have an iron deficiency, which can cause your teen to feel tired and weak and can negatively affect academic performance, deregulate body temperature, and impair immune function.[26]

Fearless Fact

Some food components, such as calcium and phytates (in grains), interfere with iron absorption, but other foods enhance its absorption.[27]

Fearless Tip

Pair iron-containing food sources with vitamin C sources (see Appendix B); beef, fish, and poultry; or a combination of these to increase iron absorption significantly.

Eating low amounts of meat, fish, iron-fortified foods, and vitamin C–rich foods; dieting; skipping meals; or a combination of these contribute to low iron status. Teen athletes in endurance sports (swimming, cross-country running, cycling, or other) are at higher risk also. Your pediatrician can determine if your teen is anemic with a blood test. Because females are at higher risk, the Centers for Disease Control and Prevention recommends testing every five years. If your teen has been anemic or shows risk factors for anemia, screening should occur annually.[26]

Folic acid is another important nutrient for female teens of childbearing age. Experts advise four hundred micrograms of folic acid daily to prevent birth defects in babies. Good folic acid intake now means a good foundation of folic acid status (and eating habits) later on. Food sources include flour (and products made with flour, such as bread and baked goods); cereals; orange juice; beans; and such vegetables as asparagus, spinach, broccoli, corn, and baked potato.

Nutrition for the teen is important because there is a lot going on with nutritional requirements, growth, eating, and laying the foundation for adult health. Be sure to check Appendix G, where we answer some of the more common "beyond basic" nutrition questions. Last but not least, you'll find a list of ten power foods for your teen in Table 5.7. Including these *regularly* will help ramp up your teen's diet with the critical nutrients he needs at this stage.

Use the Fearless Food Guide presented earlier and in Appendix A to get started with an outline of what your teen needs to eat each day, then troubleshoot with the Fearless Five Nutrients and fill in the nutrient gaps, adding nutritious foods to improve your teen's diet. With this approach, we know you can fix any nutritional shortfalls without fear!

Table 5.7 Ten Power Foods for Your Teen		
Food	**Why?**	**How**
Seeds	Seeds are rich in healthy fats and fatty acids, vitamin E, fiber, and magnesium.	Sprinkle seeds on cereal or salads, or eat a handful.
Nuts	Nuts are rich in healthy fats and fatty acids, and are a good source of fiber, protein, magnesium, and vitamin E.	Nuts are good on yogurt and cereal, and as a snack.
Instant and ready-to-eat fortified cereals	Cereals are a good source of iron, folic acid, and vitamins A and E.	Cereal is great for breakfast or a snack, or for dinner in a pinch.
100 percent orange juice (fortified with calcium and vitamin D)	Orange juice is a good source of calcium and vitamin D when fortified, folic acid, and vitamin C.	Orange juice is great at any time. Keep it to 12 ounces per day max.
Beans	Beans are a good source of iron,[a] zinc, and magnesium.	Beans are good in ethnic dishes, on salads, and in soups. Try roasting!
Low-fat cheese	Low-fat cheese provides calcium, vitamin D, potassium, and protein.	Use low-fat cheese on sandwiches, in casseroles, alone as a snack, or atop salads.
Low-fat yogurt	Low-fat yogurt supplies calcium, vitamin D, potassium, protein, and magnesium.	Yogurt is part of a healthy breakfast, snack, or lunch. It is a good substitute for milk.
Low-fat milk or soymilk (fortified with calcium and vitamin D)	Low-fat milk or soymilk is a good source of calcium, vitamin D, protein, and potassium. Check labels on soymilk for amounts.	Milk or soymilk is great as an accompaniment to a meal or snack, or as a recovery drink after vigorous exercise.

Table 5.7 *(continued)*		
Food	**Why?**	**How**
Dark-green leafy vegetables	Dark-green leafy vegetables offer iron and calcium.	Serve these vegetables as a side dish, as the main entrée, or as part of a snack. They make a great addition to a salad. Try kale chips!
Orange fruits and vegetables	Orange fruits and vegetables are rich in vitamins C, E (mango), and A, as well as potassium.	Use 100 percent fruit juice (up to 12 ounces per day). Include these fruits and vegetables with meals and snacks.

ᵃ Lean red meats get an honorable mention for their rich iron content.

Feeding with Confidence: Get Them to the Table

"I keep trying to emphasize healthy foods, but Abby just rolls her eyes and complains that I am 'obsessed' with eating healthy . . . or she ignores me," says Melissa. "But if I say nothing at all, her eating would be way off kilter, and who knows the damage she'd be doing to her body. I struggle with being 'that mom' who nags my teen versus ignoring nutrition altogether."

In our many years of working with teens, we often hear dismay and exasperation from parents (especially moms) like Melissa when it comes to teens' eating habits. Many feel helpless in guiding their teens to better nutrition choices and struggle with how to get involved. Worse yet, some parents retire from feeding, relinquishing their role when teens need them the most. Even in the face of more independence, more influences on eating, and possible resistance, there are ways to keep your teen close to home and the meal table. With competition for her attention, it's important for you to remain a central influence in her life. Have no fear, we'll show you how!

What to Expect

Over the teen years, you will see more sophisticated reasoning, impulsivity, budding independence, and risk-taking behaviors. Although some parents dread this time, we help calm your fears by preparing you for the typical nutrition-related transformations. After all, you'll need to be on your toes for the myriad influences that can take over, something we'll get into soon.

Your Teen's Thinking

Beginning around age twelve, the soon-to-be-teen enters the formal operational stage detailed by Jean Piaget, grasping abstract concepts and understanding the potential consequences of a particular action or choice.[28] Teens are also able to use deductive reasoning by thinking through hypothetical situations. Systematic planning, or the ability to organize their approach to solving a problem, is also emerging. Believe it or not, teens do have better impulse control than children, but impulsivity remains a hallmark of this age group.

Cognitively, teens are better able to assess risk versus reward. In fact, new insight into the teen brain helps us understand why teens jump in feetfirst and will do just about anything, without fear. Teens are more motivated to take risks if they can get the reward they want—and they have a higher regard for rewards than adults do. You can see this play out in drastic dieting behaviors. Teens are enticed by the reward of rapid weight loss, despite the risks that dieting may present. Risk taking peaks at fifteen to twenty-five years, with the biggest risk takers being teens ages fourteen to seventeen.[29]

Compared to children, teens also have better memory, improved language skills, and better self-regulation of emotions (phew—no more tantrums in the grocery store!). All these cognitive changes make learning about nutrition easier for the teen, and in some cases your teen may even appreciate the impact of sodas and desserts on his future health.

The teen brain undergoes a massive reorganization, starting at age twelve and lasting through age twenty-five, resulting in a major upgrade in wiring and networking. This makes the brain much faster and more efficient with thinking. Researchers believe that the remodeling is extensive, making teens erratic in their behavior as they adapt to the new "layout."[29] If you remodel your kitchen, it takes some time before you know where everything is located—and this is true with the teen brain. Teens are open to anything new and novel, including ideas, foods, diets, and people. And they love a thrill. Obviously, there are advantages and disadvantages to this. On the one hand, experimenting with a new, drastic diet;

avoiding a food group due to a fad diet; or driving too fast may not be beneficial for your teen. On the other hand, being open to new foods can be a plus.

With all the changes in brain functionality and thinking, as outlined in Table 5.8, this is a sensitive time, and one that necessitates involvement from you. But this is where the hard part comes in—the other piece of development, social and emotional changes, which we discuss next, may push you off to the sidelines.

Table 5.8 Cognitive Development for Teens			
Age	**Stage**	**Cognitive Readiness**	**Feeding Implications**
Twelve to eighteen years	Formal operational stage	• Is able to understand complex ideas • Can see others' points of view • Is able to use deductive reasoning and weigh future outcomes • Can see outcomes of actions • Uses systematic planning to solve problems • Is impulsive • Values reward over risk • Is a sensation seeker	• Can see effects of today's eating on tomorrow's health ("A high-fat diet can contribute to heart disease"), which may or may not motivate a change in behavior. • Can link eating habits with potential health outcomes ("If I eat chips and drink soda, I may gain weight"). • Can identify with others' feelings or situations ("She gets teased because she's overweight—that must be hard"). • Can make today's food choices by predicting tomorrow's outcome ("If I eat better, maybe I'll improve in swimming, or not"). • Can relate food and exercise choices with appearance, feeling good, peers, acceptance, and desire for independence.

Your Teen's Psychosocial Development

The road to adulthood is paved with finding an identity, navigating social interactions, and dealing with moral issues. Erik Erikson, the developmental psychologist, points out that unlike any previous developmental stage, this stage is influenced by *what teens do.* Erikson calls this developmental stage Identity Versus Role Confusion, or in other words, the "Who am I?" stage of life.[30] Teens now begin to separate from their family (mostly parents) and become part of a bigger world. This separation is necessary, as it helps them define their identity (or sense of self and values) so they can become healthy adults.

Early, middle, and late adolescence represents a continuum of development, and the early stages are marked by a desire more to fit in than to be unique or independent, as shown in Table 5.9. Membership in groups at the early stage of adolescence sets the foundation for future movement throughout different groups when teens get older. This means that younger adolescents are more susceptible to peer pressure, because they want to identify with a group (usually the one imposing the pressure), and older teens are motivated to resist peer pressure for the sake of individuality.

Peer relations continue to influence food choices, attitudes, and eating behaviors in adolescence. Food may be viewed as "healthy" (associated with eating at home and family) or as "junk food" (associated with friends, having fun, gaining weight, and guilt). Making food choices is one way teens assert independence and separate from their parents.[31]

Parents may use coaching or coaxing to get teens to eat well, and teens may respond with complaining about, ignoring, or refusing the advice. It's not a losing situation, though. Making certain food choices may appear to be a negative act of defiance, but when given autonomy, teens take responsibility for their actions, reflect on their behaviors and choices, and keep in mind their parents' advice, according to one study.[32]

As teens go out in the world, it's not unusual for them to regress to a more dependent state, coming back to be cared for and nurtured. Albeit confusing for the parent, this back-and-forth is a normal part of growing up. Despite rejection, rolling eyes, and rebellion, teens do care deeply about the ideals expressed by the important adults in their lives and look to them as trusted sources of information.[32] This makes it very important to keep the lines of communication open.

Table 5.9 Teen Developmental Changes

Stage	Emotional Changes	Cognitive Abilities	Social Influences
Early adolescence (twelve to fourteen years)	• Adapts to physical changes • Develops body image	• Focuses decision making on schoolwork, such as homework, and home-related tasks, such as chores • Questions authority and society's standards • Forms personal views related to own life	• Experiences strong peer influence
Middle adolescence (fifteen to seventeen years)	• Separates from parents	• Questions and analyzes more extensively • Begins to form own code of ethics • Sees different possibilities for daily and future decisions • Develops own identity • Begins to consider future goals • Makes own plans • Thinks long term	• May practice increasingly risky health behaviors, such as dieting or fasting, driving too fast, or smoking cigarettes
Late adolescence (eighteen to young adult)	• Establishes a personal sense of self • Separates further from parents	• Understands more global concepts like justice, history, politics, and patriotism • Holds idealistic views on various topics and concerns • Thinks about career choices • Thinks about being an adult	• Has improved impulse control • Grows socially independent

In part because growth and development occur at individual rates, feelings of dissatisfaction, inferiority, and low self-esteem can occur in adolescence.[33] A male "late bloomer" may feel inadequate and try weight-gain diets, steroids, or amino acid supplements for muscle building. Conversely, females who are "early developers" may experience poor self-esteem and poor body image; dabble in dieting; and possibly develop disordered eating, a risk factor for eating disorders. Being sensitive to your teen's developmental stage and promoting a positive self-image will help reduce these behaviors and feelings, something we'll cover in Feeding That Works later in the chapter.

Media exposure puts pressure on teens, too. Seventy-eight percent of all food ads to teens (and children) target less-than-healthy foods, often promoting fast-food and other restaurants, and teens are seeing more of them (up to 16.2 ads per day).[34] It's not just food you have to worry about—the overpromise of diet products and diets "guaranteeing" fast weight loss is becoming increasingly pervasive. The good news is that as your teen ages, he can better understand the underlying messages, intent, and fantastical nature of media.

> **Fearless Fact**
>
> Children and teens spend more than seven hours each day involved with a variety of different media. Television is the predominant source, with more than 70 percent of teens having a TV in their bedroom, and one-third of teens having a computer with Internet access.[35]

The "thin is in" ideal, a belief that your health (and acceptance in the world) are tied directly to weight status, taps into teens' desire to fit in, developing body image, and emerging sense of self. A different message that targets fitness and muscularity may contribute to excessive exercising and disordered eating. Both males and females are sensitive to these societal pressures.[36]

It's no surprise, when the world is telling your teen she needs to be thin and fit to be popular, healthy, and successful, that she would dabble with a diet, cut back on eating, or become a disordered eater to achieve this ideal. The reasons for these actions are associated with the spectrum of teen development, such as the desire to fit in, the novelty of trying a new diet, the reward of fast weight loss, the pursuit of independence with eating decisions, and the appeal of standing out from the crowd (individuality). Both dieting and disordered eating are possibilities you'll want to keep an eye on and address during this stage.

Our goal is to help you be prepared with an understanding of what you and your teen are up against. Physical changes are vast, but so are emotional and cognitive transformations—information about all of which, when understood and appreciated, can help you guide your teen through this potentially rocky time. The good news is, you still rock! And we're going to show you how to max out your rock star status (and hold on to your powerful influence) next, so keep reading.

Feeding That Works

There are more challenges to feeding your teen than ever before. Here, we'll show you several effective ways to guide your teen to healthy and balanced eating, despite the natural pull away from you and your family routines. Communication, family meals, getting your teen into the kitchen, and mindful eating top our list of important topics.

Maintaining Communication

Communication is an essential piece of staying present and in tune with your teen in his day-to-day life.[32,37] Opportunities to communicate abound, from riding in the car together to sitting around the family table. Small doses of information or dialogue that include your stance on such topics as dieting and what it means to be a healthy individual give insight to your teen.

Parent-teen communication may get off track because both parents and teens are living in two different worlds—developmentally, that is. You're worried about your teen's future health, whereas your teen is worried about food taste, weight gain, and how she looks in the outfit you bought her. You fly off the handle when your teen diets, whereas she's just participating in something her friends are doing. You take it personally when your teen makes a mistake, and he's just naturally making errors.

Successful communication relies on an understanding outlook, factual information, and mutual trust.[31] Keeping a positive, personal, and engaging tone when talking to your teen can temper the push-pull nature of the parent-child relationship. Allowing choice and cooperative decision making as well as conveying a neutral attitude and approach with teens (and all children) work best. Table 5.10 highlights ways to successfully communicate with your teen.

The family table is often where communication happens. Fourteen-year-old Maddie said, "Emily's going on a diet, but she doesn't really need to lose weight." Her mom didn't let this topic lose steam, and gently inquired for more information by asking, "What do you think about that?" Maddie revealed insecurity with her own body ("If Emily needs to lose weight, then I must be huge!"); fear for her friend ("But Emily is fine, why would she do that?"); and the pressure Emily's dieting was placing on her group of friends ("Now everyone is talking about going on a diet").

How you respond to comments and tough questions about food, nutrition, and dieting can set the tone for your teen's food attitudes, eating behaviors, and lifestyle choices.[38] We ask that you have an appreciation for the impact of your opinions and responses when dealing with teens, because what you say can help or hinder your teen and his developmental progress.

A strong connection between teen and parent, whereby the teen values the parent's opinion, can help prevent dangerous and risky behaviors. One study showed a positive impact on teens' eating, namely lower soda consumption; increased regularity of breakfast consumption; and eating healthier foods (milk, fruit, and vegetables) when family cohesion was strong.[32]

Keeping Family Meals Going Strong

As we reviewed in Chapter Four, family meals result in healthier eating and better psychosocial health for school-age children, and this is true for teens as well.[39] But there are many barriers to family meals. One to contend with is the physical absence of your teen due to after-school sports, a job, or other activities. These outside commitments can sidetrack the family meal. We tend to see two different scenarios with family meals. A parent in the Everybody Eats on His or Her Own family asks the teen if he will be joining dinner; if he's not home, he is expected to find dinner on his own. Joining the family for meals happens infrequently. As a result, the teen has very little opportunity to connect with his parents during the school week, may eat a poor-quality diet, and spends a lot of money on eating out. Although he may embrace the independence this scenario affords, he may also feel lonely and burdened by the task of feeding himself.

Table 5.10 Ways to Communicate Successfully with Your Teen

Effective Communication Behaviors	Positive and Productive Comments	Unproductive Comments	Why?
Having an understanding outlook	*"It stinks those jeans don't fit anymore, I know they are your favorite pair. Why don't you try the tan corduroys? We can get new jeans soon."*	"See, this is what happens when you don't eat right—I told you!"	You may worry about the future, but all she cares about is today. Empathy today builds trust tomorrow.
Removing your emotions	*"I'm sorry you chose to eat that before practice; you'll figure out what works best for your body."*	"What do you think will happen if you eat chips and soda all the time?!" "It's not my fault you're hungry."	Your role is that of "guide." Show your teen options; ultimately she will choose based on what is important to her, and this is not a reflection on you. Have faith she will figure it all out—the learning curve is steep!
Using curiosity when questioning	*"What do you think of Sandy's dieting?" "I'm curious why you didn't eat lunch today . . ."*	"Why in the world is that skinny girl dieting?"	Loaded questions put teens on the defensive. Show confidence in your teen's ability to make good choices.
Controlling your reactions	*"I see you ate a hefty snack before dinner."*	"No wonder you're full and not eating dinner. You ate too much earlier!"	Keep a neutral reaction, even when mistakes are made. Know that mistakes are part of the learning curve, and likely do more to positively influence your teen's decision-making skills than shaming or blaming.
Staying calm	*"I understand you're unhappy with your weight and want to lose some. Let's talk about how we can do that in a healthy way."*	"This is exactly what I was afraid would happen. I'm calling a nutritionist!"	You are the adult; getting upset can lead to a fight with your teen, breaking down communication.

The Eat Dinner Together family has a plan for dinner every night, whether the teen shows up or not. If the teen is home, he is expected to join in the meal, and if he's not home, he is expected to come home and eat the meal that has been reserved for him. Structure and expectations are clear, and rhythmic meals continue regardless of who attends. This approach is authoritative in nature.[40,41,42] The teen in this family knows there is a plan for food, and this builds security, not to mention a greater likelihood that his food consumption will be healthier.

Naturally, teens are becoming more responsible for their eating, but you are still "on the job." Continue to plan and prepare meals and set the expectation that your teen will attend. On nights when he can't be there, set aside a plated meal for him. Consider opening your home to host more than just your family, including your teen's friends. This satisfies the developmental need to be with peers, gets him to the meal table, and makes healthy eating easier.

HOW you feed, as covered in Chapter One, also has an impact. An authoritative feeding style lends itself to better connection, more family meals, healthier eating, and fewer weight problems, as well as a greater ability to self-regulate mood and behavior.[40] Keep your role model status polished so that you remain a powerful and positive influence on your teen.

> ## Fearless Fact
>
> Teens who eat at least five meals a week with their family are 35 percent less likely to engage in disordered eating, such as binging and purging, taking diet pills, self-inducing vomiting, using laxatives or diuretics, fasting, skipping meals, cutting back on eating, or smoking cigarettes to lose weight. In addition, teens who eat three family meals per week are 12 percent less likely to be overweight. Family meals are also correlated with reductions in teen stress, alcohol drinking, the drive for thinness, and body dissatisfaction.[43]

Getting Teens in the Kitchen

Your kitchen is a laboratory, a place where your teen can experiment, and can learn and master the basic skills that will carry him into adulthood. Give your teen the goods (food and utensils) and see what he creates. If busy schedules get in the way of frequent cooking, assign a regular night each week or weekend on

Fearless Fact

A 2009 report showed that 33 percent of adults learned how to cook from their parents, but don't have the time or patience to get their own children involved in the kitchen. Half of youngsters never or rarely help prepare dinner.[45] This transmission breakdown—cooking skills and wisdom not getting passed on—may have negative implications for future generations.

which your teen is in charge of the family meal. Have him plan the menu, develop the shopping list, shop (if time allows), and plan and execute the preparation. If this isn't possible, use school vacations, holidays, and long weekends.

Mindful Eating

Now eating hits a new level—you will gradually hand over the reins so your teen *takes on the responsibility* for regulating himself. Mindful eating taps into natural internal signals to control what and how much food is eaten. As you learned in Chapter Two, infants are born with an innate sense of hunger and fullness and are inclined to self-regulate their food intake. Although a host of external factors can cause your growing child to lose this sense, mindful eating can preserve or rejuvenate this regulation system.

A mindful eater honors his hunger with eating, recognizes his fullness by stopping, and enjoys the pleasures associated with eating. If self-regulation has gone by the wayside, now is the time to resurrect it. Chapter Six can give you a better understanding of mindful eating that you can share with your teen.

You can see that communication, family meals, getting your teen in the kitchen, and mindful eating are important components of raising your teen to be a healthy adult. But learning about nutrition is just as important!

Understanding Nutrition

Your teen still has a lot to learn, and the good news is that he will be easier to teach: understanding nutrition is not as hard for teens as it is for school-age children. Remember to keep nutrition messages positive and the lines of communication open. Scare tactics almost never work, and cause more rebellion than resolutions to change. Let's look at how you can help your teen understand nutrition.

Using the Fearless Food Guide

We encourage you to use the Fearless Food Guide in Table 5.3 and in Appendix A as a starting point for teaching your teen WHAT to eat. These guidelines can now be used to help your teen understand the balance of food and nutrients his body needs for lifelong health. Although the calorie needs in adulthood will be less than they are now, the general concepts around balanced eating, food groups, and nutrients are the same.

Keeping Nutrition Messages Realistic

Although adolescence is a popular time for experimenting with diets and foods, it's also high time for you to convey realistic and balanced messages about food and nutrition. What you say about food and nutrition can either help your teen or muddy the waters and confuse him more. Watch the temptation to paint a gloomy picture about his future health, as he'll be more interested in eating well to have energy on the football field or clear up his skin than to prevent heart disease or diabetes. Table 5.11 helps you keep your nutrition messages on target.

Media Literacy

Let's face it, advertising works! Media literacy, or the ability to decode media messages and their intent, helps decrease your teen's vulnerability to these messages, reduces requests for commercial products, improves nutritional habits, curbs obesity, and improves body image.[35]

Help your teen understand that airbrushing or photoshopping (a computer process that wipes away all imperfections, from lines and wrinkles to bumps and bulges) is routinely used to create a "perfect" image. Point out discrepancies between the product being advertised and the person advertising it, or its value. For example, take a "value" meal that is high in calories, fat, and sodium. Yes, it has a cheap price, but in relation to your teen's health, how valuable is it actually? What do you get that is of value from this meal? Fat, calories, and sodium, minus the important nutrients teens need. Discussing these discrepancies with your teen helps her keep it real and (ideally) make better choices.

Dining Out

As we discussed earlier, eating outside of the home is associated with greater calorie and fat consumption and lower intake of calcium, iron, and vitamin C in

Table 5.11 Keeping It Real: What (and What Not) to Say

Topic	Say This . . .	Why?	Don't Say This . . .	Why?
Dieting	"If you're worried about your weight, let's talk about healthy ways to help, like balanced eating and exercise. Diets don't work for the long haul—in fact they make you gain weight."	This statement empathizes with weight concerns, discourages dieting (which can lead to more problems), and provides positive solutions.	"The xyz diet is the best! My friend Sally lost twenty pounds in three weeks on that diet!" "I need to go on a diet—I've gained so much weight over the holidays!"	These comments promote dieting and a quick fix. Preoccupation with weight can lead to poor body image.
Food	"What you choose to eat will have an impact on your weight and health, no doubt, but it's all about balancing mostly healthy foods with exercise."	Saying this promotes teen autonomy, and provides guidance without judgment.	"That is bad for you—don't eat it or you'll gain weight." "This is the best food for you—see, it says so on the package!"	These statements promote fear-based eating and food rules. They suggest a "magical" quality of food that is unrealistic.
Exercise	"Exercise makes it easy for you to stay fit and balance your eating, but like everything else, too much can be harmful. Let's talk about the right amount for you."	Saying this promotes balance while acknowledging the importance of exercise to health. It also promises guidance.	"You'd better exercise every day, or else you'll suffer the consequences!" "I exercise every day because if I didn't, I'd gain so much weight."	Such comments may lead to compulsive and unhealthy exercise. They promote a fear of weight gain, negative body image, and weight bias.

Peer choices	*"Everybody has the right to make his or her own choices, and sometimes mistakes are made. If you have questions about what your friends are doing, let's talk about it and go over what you think is best for you."*	This statement offers communication to discuss difficult topics. It is nonjudgmental, representing a calm and neutral approach.	"How can Betsy gain so much weight? It's so bad for her!" "Wow, Betsy looks great! You've got to find out what diet she was on!"	These statements are judgmental, which can put your teen on the defensive. They take a narrow view of the situation, reflect weight bias, and promote dieting.
Media	*"Don't always believe what you see and hear on TV—this commercial is trying to make you buy that product."* *"Did you know that before a picture goes into a magazine, they make it 'perfect' with a computer?"*	Saying these things balances reality with intent; provides neutral information; and offers communication and teachable moments.	"I wish I looked that good!" "I've gotta get that—they say it will help me lose weight." "Don't watch that, it'll ruin your mind!" "Don't read that, it'll hurt your self-esteem!"	These comments promote unrealistic images and an ideal physique. They feed into a quick-fix mentality and encourage dieting, and promote fear over understanding.

teens.[44] But eating out should be associated with enjoyment or celebration, not rules and limits. If your teen eats out more than three to five times each week, she'll need to pay more attention to her food choices. If it's less often than that, encourage enjoyment. Help your teen make better choices around dining out by following the tips in Table 5.12.

Must-Master Nutrition Concepts

Few teens manage their own nutrition, instead having Mom or Dad take care of their needs, mimicking what their friends are choosing, or just adopting the latest

Table 5.12 Must-Master Nutrition Concepts for Teens			
Concept	**Why?**	**Daily Practices for the Teen**	**Caution!**
Maintaining a healthy weight	A healthy weight that's right for each individual body type helps prevent dieting and long-term health problems. It encourages a healthy balance of food, eating patterns, and exercise for lifelong health.	Put together well-balanced meals and snacks using the Fearless Food Guide, exercise regularly, eat at regular intervals, and use mindful eating practices, such as listening to internal cues of hunger and fullness.	Dieting to achieve a healthy weight is a short-term fix that is dangerous to health and results in weight gain over time. It may contribute to an eating disorder.
Healthy, balanced eating	This type of eating promotes weight maintenance, helps meet nutritional needs, and optimizes future health. It regulates appetite.	Eat three meals and at least one snack per day. Eat approximately every three to five hours, and drink plenty of fluids. Use the Fearless Food Guide and keep Fun Foods reasonable.	Orthorexia, or only eating "healthy" foods, can become an obsession and a disorder. Be sure to have some Fun Foods too.

Table 5.12 (*continued*)			
Concept	**Why?**	**Daily Practices for the Teen**	**Caution!**
Interpreting food labels	Knowing how to read food labels helps teens make informed food choices, and assists them in keeping portions reasonable.	Read labels for portion size and nutrient contributions. Be aware of restaurant foods and menu labeling.	Avoid using food labels as a way to restrict eating. Eat for enjoyment and mindfully.
Portion awareness	Such an awareness provides a reference for how much to eat, and helps keep nutrition balanced.	Start with reasonable portions (see the Fearless Food Guide) and eat to satisfaction.	It's normal to overdo portions sometimes—overall balance is the key.
Exercise for life	Exercise helps keep body weight at a healthy level, helps prevent chronic disease, and builds confidence and self-esteem.	Move your body every day. Incorporate exercise and weight training regularly.	Overexercising can become an obsession and contribute to an eating disorder. Moderate exercise is best.
Intelligent dining out	Teens should learn to navigate menus, and should be able to choose what to order based on taste, preference, and nutrition quality.	Use information from menus, websites, and brochures to become aware of food options. Balance food choices with health promotion and taste preferences. Eat intuitively.	Don't view foods as "good" or "bad"; nutrition labels can be used in a negative way, as a means of placing unhealthy restrictions on eating.
Basic cooking skills	Cooking is a life skill that will help nurture an overall interest in nutrition and nutritional intake.	Practice in the home kitchen, taking responsibility for snacks and simple meals (breakfast and lunch). Plan and prepare family meals.	Food safety skills are important to keep teens safe. Make cooking flexible and fun, not a burden.

food trends. This lack of knowledge can lead to poor food choices and eating patterns that result in unwanted weight gain or loss. Make sure your teen is successful outside of the nest by helping him understand basic nutrition concepts, as outlined in Table 5.12. Also, don't miss the recipes at the end of the chapter, which allow you to teach an important life skill: cooking.

"I never learned how to cook, balance meals, or read a label, and was never encouraged to exercise when I was younger. I wish I had known these things when I was a teen!" says Lisa, mom of fifteen-year-old Sarah Grace. "I would be a lot different now, with fewer struggles, had I received this information at a younger age." As you can see, there's a lot to learn in the teen years! If your teen enters the real world without a working knowledge of nutrition, what will follow is a lot of worry, angst, and frustration—and an ongoing cycle of trial and error. By preparing your teen, you're giving a gift that's priceless.

Nutrition and Future Health

Teens often show an increased interest in and understanding of nutrition, even though eating behaviors may not reflect this immediately. Now is the time to plant the seed about the impact of food, nutrition, and eating habits on future health outcomes. Proper nutrition can deter chronic illnesses, such as heart disease, cancer, osteoporosis, and obesity, leading to a longer and healthier life.

Your teen may be conflicted about what is considered healthy eating and the reality of her everyday habits. Cognitively, teens are able to self-reflect—look at their actual eating and exercise behaviors compared to optimal ones. The discrepancy between these two presents an opportunity for change. Although you may want to jump in and offer guidance right away, your teen may not be ready to make big changes. We caution you not to go overboard with information and a gung-ho attitude. Rather, you'll want to use small steps and offer information that reflects his readiness for change, as is outlined in Table 5.13.

Some teens jump into nutrition in a negative way, becoming overly interested in food and perfecting their nutritional intake. As you have learned, dieting and disordered eating can take root during the teen years, causing a host of problems.[46] Although experimentation is a natural part of adolescence, you will need to be on the alert, watching for signs of disordered eating patterns and

Table 5.13 Recognizing Small Steps for Change		
If Your Teen Is...	**Then You Can ...**	**Sample Dialogue**
Not aware of a problem and hasn't thought about changing a nutrition behavior	Explore existing knowledge and build on that, if he is open to listening. Ask permission to share information.	*"What do you know about balanced eating?"* *"Would it be alright if I shared what I know with you?"*
Thinking about adopting a new nutrition behavior	Make suggestions and discuss small steps for change, barriers, and possible solutions.	*"We could make sure to include fruit or a veggie in your lunchbox each day."*
Ready to take action soon and taking small steps to prepare for a bigger change	Help and support your teen by collaborating to put together an action plan.	*"Let's make a chart of how we can work in five servings of fruit and veggies and have some alternatives if your schedule gets busy."*
Practicing and committed to a new nutrition behavior	Support his decision, help as needed, and reinforce his successes.	*"I've noticed how loyal you are to your plan—you're an inspiration!"* (Have plenty of fruits and veggies on hand.)
Set with a new, healthier behavior	Support him with reminders, tools, or alternatives needed to stay successful.	*"Which fruits and veggies would you like this week?"* (Shop for and stock them.)

recognizing behaviors that have crossed the line from healthy to unhealthy. For more on eating disorders, see Chapter Seven.

Too much talk about weight and diets can have an unwanted effect—more disordered eating. Always keep these conversations supportive and nonjudgmental, and remember that the most effective guidance is to lead by example and have a home food environment that supports healthy eating.[44,47]

> ### Five Messages You Don't Want to Give Your Teen About Weight
>
> 1. Your value as a human is tied to how much you weigh.
> 2. How you eat at one meal dictates your weight and health.
> 3. Losing weight is good (deserves reward), and gaining weight is bad (deserves punishment).
> 4. Weight status is an acceptable topic for name-calling or teasing.
> 5. Thinness or muscularity equals beauty or health, respectively.

Real Life Challenges for Teens

Many parents we know want to keep their teens nourished, informed, and healthy but struggle with balancing the typical teenage challenges. Meanwhile, teens are trying to balance nutrition, their health, and understanding it all. Here we take you through some of the common twists and turns of adolescence, whether it's getting your teen to show up for a meal or navigating the temptations of tasty (but less-than-healthy) foods.

Getting Dinner on the Table with Busy Teens

Challenge: Betsy had found herself making dinner on the fly, grabbing takeout, or ordering in. With two busy teens, she was never sure who would be home and what they would want to eat. She ran her kitchen like a restaurant, making something different for each teen, and at different times. Worse, she was strung out, exhausted, and resenting her family's demands.

Diagnosis: Betsy's teens were busy (WHY), and she had allowed this to control the structure around family mealtimes (HOW).

Intervention: We encouraged Betsy to check her and her family's schedules. Betsy was able to find two days during the week her family could have breakfast together. She also saw that Sunday nights were open, and started Sunday night dinner in the dining room. On Wednesdays and Fridays, they were all together for a late dinner. Betsy sat her family down and outlined her new approach to family meals: dinner at 7:00 p.m., the same meal for everyone (absentees eat a plated meal from that dinner), a twice weekly limit on dining out, and expectations around helping with food preparation and cleanup.

Outcome: Once she took the lead on family meals and put a framework in place, Betsy had more success with feeding her family. "I didn't realize how simple it would be to turn things around," she says. "Things are flowing better, and my kids are happier with this system."

Low Calcium Intake

Challenge: Jacqueline disliked milk and yogurt. She would eat foods made with milk, but her overall calcium intake was poor. Her average calcium intake was 500 milligrams per day, well below the suggested amount of 1,300 milligrams per day.

Diagnosis: Jacqueline's food preferences were interfering with adequate nutrition, specifically calcium intake (WHAT).

Intervention: Jacqueline's parents needed to help her eat other calcium-containing products. We helped Jacqueline and her mom identify and add calcium-fortified orange juice (up to twelve ounces per day); calcium-fortified breads and other grains; tofu; dairy desserts, such as pudding and ice cream; and low-fat cheeses in sandwiches, as part of snacks, and in casseroles.

Outcome: Jacqueline was able to increase her calcium intake significantly.

Drinking Too Many Caffeinated Beverages

Challenge: Eighteen-year-old Beth went to the local coffee bar for breakfast, drinking an extra-large coffee drink. For lunch, she drank a packaged smoothie drink, nursed a couple of diet sodas between classes, and drank regular soda and energy drinks (to stay awake for studying) at home. She was in a vicious cycle of staying up late, getting up early, and feeling tired all day. Worse, she couldn't understand why she was gaining weight.

Diagnosis: Beth's beverages (WHAT) were contributing to her weight gain and to her tiredness! Many of Beth's drinks were full of caffeine (and sugar in some cases), and although they camouflaged her tiredness during the day, they also interfered with a good night's sleep. Beth was also over the top in craving sweetness, training her taste buds to desire more sugar and increasing the likelihood of overeating.

Intervention: We advised that Beth scale back on lattes and cappuccinos to twice weekly and substitute with decaffeinated versions the rest of the week. Energy drinks at night were a big no-no (high amount of caffeine), and we asked her to stop drinking those entirely. We suggested she limit regular and diet sodas and smoothies to three to four (twelve-ounce) servings per week and opt for water, milk, and 100 percent fruit juice (max of twelve ounces per day). We also helped Beth schedule seven to eight hours of sleep each night and suggested she stick to a calming bedtime routine so she was energized for the next day.

Outcome: Scaling back on coffee drinks, eliminating energy drinks, and keeping a cap on weekly sodas helped Beth sleep better, feel more energized, and stop gaining weight.

The Buzz on Caffeine

Caffeine is present in regular soda, diet soda, coffee, tea, energy drinks, and some enhanced waters. Caffeine consumption should be limited to 1.25 milligrams per pound of body weight for children and teens (for example, 150 milligrams for a 120-pound teen). When teens consume too much caffeine, they can experience agitation, anxiety, poor sleep, rapid heart rate, increased blood pressure, and altered mental states. Regular caffeine intake can lead to physical dependence (addiction) and weight gain.[48]

Freedom in the Fast-Food Lane

Challenge: Mike got his driver's license at age sixteen, along with a bonus: twenty-five pounds of weight gain in six months! He used his weekly allowance to hit the drive-thru after lacrosse practice, on the way to school, and on the weekends.

Diagnosis: Mike was using food to test-drive his new independence (WHY), which is a normal part of teen development. But he needed the tools and support to make good food decisions (WHAT).

Intervention: We wanted Mike to familiarize himself with healthier fast-food items so he could make balanced decisions *most of the time* when placing his order. He tried yogurt parfaits, bagels with protein, egg and ham sandwiches, grilled sandwiches, salads, fruit cups, fruit smoothies, and hot cereals. Because Mike didn't want to take the time to make something for himself in the morning, we suggested his parents take the lead and prepare breakfast three or four days per week, using simple, nutritious items. We also asked them to keep healthy snacks on hand, such as nuts, trail mix, milk boxes, dry cereal, and dried fruit, so that Mike could pack them for lacrosse practice. Finally, Mike needed boundaries around eating out. We suggested his parents establish a spending limit, the frequency (three times per week), occasion-specific guidelines (weekends only), or a combination of these for eating out. They established a twenty-five dollar limit per week, and encouraged dining out only on the weekends with friends.

Outcome: Mike scaled way back on fast food with the help and support of his parents, and over time (and with lacrosse practices) his weight normalized.

Overdoing Exercise

Challenge: Fifteen-year-old Maria was a dancer, cross-country runner, and track athlete, and she filled her off-season time with yoga and running. She was exercising every day of the week, often doing more than one activity, for several hours a day. She became jittery and irritated if she couldn't exercise, and she was losing weight.

Diagnosis: Although adolescents need an hour of physical activity daily, multiple daily workouts may be too much, causing undue stress on the body. In addition, when exercise shifts from an enjoyable experience to one of compulsion, guilt, and anxiety, there's a problem. Maria's drive to exercise was taking over (WHY). Backing off and improving her eating (WHAT and HOW) would allow her body to restore itself to a healthy weight.

Intervention: We asked Maria to limit exercise to one hour per day, take one day off per week, and make sure she was fueling her body with good nutrition. It's a lofty goal to get a compulsive exerciser to slow down, but we wanted to give her an idea of what was healthy. Maria needed extra help for her exercise compulsion, body image issues, and stress management. We advised her to talk with a counselor who could address her specific concerns. We also suspected an eating disorder was brewing and wanted her to have more support. Maria's parents were very encouraging of her athletic endeavors, but they were pushing her to perform and excel. When we pointed out that their support was enabling the compulsion, they backed off and enforced healthy limits. We reminded Maria's very active parents to keep the weight and exercise messages positive, and to be moderate in *their own* exercise.

Outcome: Maria had a hard time backing off on exercise. She proceeded to get extra professional help.

Red Flags for Compulsive Exercise

- Won't skip a workout, even if tired, sick, or injured
- Feels obligated to exercise
- Seems anxious or guilty when unable to work out
- Misses one workout and doubles exercise to make up the difference
- Constantly thinks about weight and exercise routine
- Doesn't sit still or relax; is worried that not enough calories are being burned
- Loses weight
- Exercises more after eating more
- Is too busy with exercise to see friends, participate in activities
- Attributes self-worth to frequency and number of workouts completed and training effort
- Never is satisfied with physical achievements

Dabbling with Diets

Challenge: Seventeen-year-old Jessica was not happy with her weight (even though she was at a healthy place), and wanted to lose five to ten pounds. She dieted by eating a low-calorie breakfast, salad for lunch, and a normal dinner with the family. This worked great until she went crazy with candy or other sweets at night.

Diagnosis: Jessica was using deprivation, elimination, and avoidance techniques (WHAT and HOW) to induce weight loss—approaches we know backfire. And yet, she was at a healthy weight, and didn't need to lose. Through dieting, Jessica was also developing an unhealthy relationship with food, setting herself up for issues in the years to come.

Intervention: We helped Jessica identify easy, nutritious breakfasts to include, such as Greek yogurt, fruit, and nuts; oatmeal and fruit; and nut butter on toast with milk. Reliable meals would help her regulate her appetite and maintain a healthy weight. We encouraged a mindful eating approach (mostly eating for hunger), as it would help her eat for the right reasons, instead of diets, which were causing her to lose touch with internal cues. Jessica's Fun Food consumption was out of hand due to deprivation, hunger, and cravings. We advised that she allow herself one Fun Food each day, after dinner.

We reminded Jessica that exercise is one of the best weight-balancing behaviors to adopt. She started exercising most days of the week, for an hour, opting for walking, running, and an occasional Zumba class with her friend. Finally, we reminded Jessica that real success comes from healthy behaviors, including food choices and exercise, day in and day out—not from the quick fix of a diet.

Outcome: Jessica is still working on accepting her body weight, but eating right and exercise have broken the cycle of eating sweets and gaining weight she was once in.

The Underfueled Athlete

Challenge: Amos was a seventeen-year-old elite tennis player who paid little attention to his diet. He ate erratically—skipping meals and eating late at night—and chose loads of convenience foods. As a result, Amos wasn't meeting his energy and nutrient needs, hadn't gained weight or grown in over two years, and was increasingly fatigued. Amos needed more nutrition to cover his energy demands.

> **Fearless Fact**
>
> Although dieting seems like a quick and easy solution, the impact is short term. Teens who diet tend to be dieting a decade later; experience significant weight gain over time; and demonstrate more body dissatisfaction, depression, and nutrient deficiencies.[10,11]

Diagnosis: Unlike the recreational athlete who is sporadic with exercise or only competes for a season, the elite athlete works out several hours a day, most days a week, for the majority of the year to his sport of choice (WHY). Amos's tennis game had stagnated, and he was exhausted earlier and more frequently after practices and matches. We needed to help him with nutrition (WHAT) and structure (HOW), while appreciating his desire to be a normal teen (WHY).

Intervention: We helped Amos maximize nutrition at meals and snacks with a structured meal and snack plan of three meals and three snacks spaced out every three to four hours so he could keep his body fueled for maximal performance. He used an electronic app to keep track of his eating. We recommended more quality carbohydrate sources (whole grains, fruits, vegetables, and low-fat dairy) and protein sources (lean meats, low-fat dairy, beans, nuts, and nut butters), and fewer fatty convenience items. Amos included a preworkout snack of low-fat foods with carbohydrates and protein (for example, peanut butter on whole grain bread, a banana, and a cheese stick) to ensure his body was ready for exercise. He consumed a snack containing carbohydrates and protein (low-fat chocolate milk) within thirty to forty-five minutes postexercise to aid in muscle recovery. Amos also dropped fast food during the week, having it on Sundays after matches, when he had time to spend with friends.

Outcome: Amos felt more energized on his new meal plan and noticed he wasn't as tired after practices and matches. It was hard for him to "eat on a schedule," as he had to think about it more often, but he was committed to taking his tennis game to the next level, and slowly began to gain weight.

Real, Easy Recipes for Teens

We bet you're feeling the heat! Somehow, some way, the teen years sneak up on you, and panic sets in when you realize your little one is now verging on adulthood and will be out in the world . . . to handle nutrition alone.

Transforming the teen into a competent cook is an important nutritional goal of the teen years. We've heard many families tell us they want their teen to be able to cook and make a meal before leaving the family nest. Somehow, when this is accomplished, the job of raising a healthy eater feels complete.

Beth Hirsch, owner of the Cooking Coach 101 in Los Angeles, shares two important tips for the budding teen chef: read the recipe through to the end and assemble all the ingredients before starting. These simple measures can make the process of cooking run smoothly and help avoid recipe failures. We've outlined some common cooking terms to keep recipe reading successful:

Common Cooking Terms

- *Knead:* Work the dough with hands. Fold the dough and press forward with hands, turn the dough, and repeat.
- *Mince:* Cut food into very tiny pieces, usually with a knife.
- *Puree:* Grind or mash food until it forms a smooth, thick mixture.
- *Julienne:* Cut food into strips or "matchsticks."
- *Steam:* Cook food using moist heat and a food basket, suspending food above a small amount of simmering water.
- *Sear:* Cook food over high heat to brown it quickly and seal in juices.
- *Sauté:* Quickly cook food over high heat in a small amount of oil.
- *Simmer:* Cook food in liquid below the boiling point, with bubbles forming but not breaking the surface.
- *Fold:* Mix gently, bringing a spatula or spoon down through the mixture, across the bottom, and back over the top, until blended.
- *Stir-fry:* Cook small pieces of food over high heat, stirring constantly.

Teens are more likely to make the foods they *want* to eat, so we've included homemade versions of teen favorites. Your teen will be able to entertain friends and gain some "go-to" recipes to fall back on in his independent future. We provide key nutrients for each recipe here, with full nutrient lists available on request through the contact page of our website, www.fearlessfeeding.com.

Appetizers

Guacamole

Ingredients

2 ripe Haas avocados

1 lime

½ plum tomato, seeded and chopped

2 tablespoons Vidalia sweet onion, diced

¼ teaspoon Tabasco sauce

1 teaspoon kosher salt

Directions

Cut each avocado in half and remove the pit. Quarter the avocados and peel off the skin. Place them in a bowl and mash with a fork. Squeeze the juice of the lime onto the avocados. Add the chopped tomato, diced onion, Tabasco, and salt, and mix thoroughly. Serve immediately.

Serving tip! Serve guacamole with tortilla chips, atop chicken or fish, or as a spread on sandwiches.

Makes: Four servings

Key nutrients per serving (percent daily value [%DV]): Fiber (19), vitamin K (19), vitamin C (17), folate (16), potassium (11), vitamin B6 (11)

White Bean Dip

Ingredients

30 ounces canned white beans, such as cannellini or small white beans, drained and rinsed

1 lemon, juice only

3 tablespoons olive oil

1 teaspoon dried rosemary (or 2 teaspoons fresh rosemary, chopped)

1 small clove garlic, minced

1 teaspoon kosher salt

¼ teaspoon pepper

Directions

Place the rinsed beans in a blender or food processor. Add the juice of 1 lemon, olive oil, rosemary, garlic, salt, and pepper. Blend until the ingredients are fully mixed.

Serving tip! Serve this dip with vegetables or homemade pita chips (see Real, Easy Recipes in Chapter Four).

Makes: Sixteen 2-ounce servings

Key nutrients per serving (%DV): Manganese (13), fiber (10), folate (8)

Dinner

Mexican Lasagna

Ingredients

2 teaspoons extra virgin olive oil

1 pound ground chicken

2 teaspoons cumin

2 teaspoons chili powder

½ red onion, chopped fine

15 ounces canned black beans, drained

1 cup salsa

1 cup frozen corn

Salt and pepper to taste

8 flour tortillas

2 cups shredded Mexican blend cheese

3 green onions, white and green parts, sliced

Cooking spray

Directions

Preheat the oven to 350°F. Heat the oil over medium-high heat in a large skillet, and brown the ground chicken for about 5 to 7 minutes. Add the cumin, chili powder, and red onion. Once the chicken is cooked thoroughly, add the black beans, salsa, and corn. Add salt and pepper to taste. Simmer. Coat the bottom of a 9- by 13-inch casserole pan with cooking spray. Cut the tortillas in half, and layer 8 halves on the bottom of the pan, covering completely. Add half of the filling on top of the tortillas. Top with half of the shredded cheese (1 cup). Layer the remaining 8 tortilla halves. Top with the remaining filling. Cover with the remaining shredded cheese and sprinkle the sliced green onions on top. Bake for 25 to 30 minutes, or until the lasagna is heated through and the cheese is melted.

Make a meal! Add a side of fruit, a salad, or both.

Makes: Twelve servings

Key nutrients per serving (%DV): Phosphorus (23), calcium (18), B vitamins (15–17), fiber (16), folate (13), iron (12)

Asian Turkey Sliders

Ingredients

1 pound ground turkey

¼ cup panko (bread crumbs)

2 tablespoons soy sauce

1 tablespoon ginger paste

2 tablespoons sesame oil

2 scallions (green onions), white and green parts, thinly sliced

12 bakery-style dinner rolls

Directions

If using an oven, preheat to 400°F. Mix the ground turkey, panko, soy sauce, ginger paste, sesame oil, and scallions together in a large mixing bowl. Roll the mixture into 10 to 12 small balls and press each into a 2-inch circle. Bake the sliders on a cookie sheet for 15 minutes, or grill until done. Serve the patties on dinner rolls.

Make a meal! Pair the sliders with homemade French fries or sweet potato fries and Greek chopped salad.

Makes: Ten to twelve sliders

Key nutrients per slider (%DV): Selenium (25), manganese (22), niacin (14), thiamin (11), iron (10), phosphorus (10)

Chicken Stir-Fry with Soba Noodles

Ingredients

1 pound soba noodles, or thin spaghetti

2 tablespoons canola oil

2 6-ounce chicken breasts, thinly sliced

1 large white onion, chopped

2 red bell peppers, thinly sliced

1 tablespoon ginger paste

2 cloves garlic, minced

4 tablespoons soy sauce

3 tablespoons sesame oil

2 scallions (green onions), white and green parts, thinly sliced

Directions

Heat a large pot of water to boiling and cook the soba noodles or spaghetti according to package directions. Meanwhile, heat the oil in a wok or large skillet over medium-high heat. Add the chicken to the wok and stir-fry until the chicken is cooked through, about 3 to 4 minutes. Add the onion, red bell pepper, ginger, and garlic, and stir-fry for 5 minutes. Stir in the soy sauce and sesame oil and simmer for 2 minutes. Drain the soba noodles, add them to the mixture, and toss. Garnish with scallions.

Make a meal! End with yogurt and fruit for dessert.

Makes: Eight servings

Key nutrients per serving (%DV): Vitamin C (69), niacin (43), manganese (41), vitamin B6 (30), phosphorus (26), vitamin A (19)

Side Dishes

Homemade Sweet Potato Fries

Ingredients

1 large sweet potato

1 tablespoon extra virgin olive oil

Kosher salt and pepper to taste

Cooking spray

Directions

Preheat the oven to 450°F. Peel the potato (or leave the skin on); if you keep the skin, make sure to wash and dry it completely before adding other ingredients. Cut the sweet potato in half. Take one half and cut ¾-inch slices; then do this for the other half. Cut the slices into ½-inch fries. In a Ziploc bag, add the potatoes, the olive oil, salt, and pepper. Zip the bag closed and shake the ingredients to coat the potatoes. Spray a cookie sheet with cooking spray and place the fries on the sheet—you want them evenly spaced and not touching. Bake for 15 minutes, turn the potatoes over, and bake for another 10 minutes.

Make a meal! Use these fries as a side to pork chops, chicken, fish, or beef; add cooked vegetables, salad, or fruit and milk.

Makes: Two servings

Key nutrient per serving (%DV): Vitamin A (184), vitamin C (37)

Salads

Greek Chopped Salad

This recipe is courtesy of Aviva Goldfarb and the Six O'Clock Scramble.

Ingredients

1 head romaine lettuce, washed and chopped into bite-size pieces

1 red onion or red bell pepper, diced

1 cucumber, peeled, halved, seeded, and chopped

1 cup Kalamata olives, pitted

15 ounces canned cannellini beans, drained and rinsed

6½ ounces canned light tuna in water, drained

⅓ cup feta cheese, cubed

1 medium tomato, chopped

2 tablespoons fresh dill, chopped, or 2 teaspoons dried

1 to 2 lemons, juice only (about ¼ cup)

¼ cup extra virgin olive oil

1 teaspoon dried oregano

¼ teaspoon black pepper

1 teaspoon garlic (about 2 cloves), minced

Directions

In a large, wide, and shallow bowl, layer the lettuce, onion or bell pepper, cucumber, olives, beans, tuna, cheese, tomato, and dill. In a large measuring cup or a jar, combine the lemon juice, oil, oregano, black pepper, and garlic. Whisk the dressing together until it is emulsified (thickened). When you are ready to serve the salad, toss it with the dressing or drizzle the dressing over individual servings at the table.

Make a meal! This can be a stand-alone meal. Add a piece of fruit, yogurt, or both if desired.

Makes: Six to eight servings

Key nutrients per serving (%DV): Vitamin K (114), vitamin A (106), vitamin C (77), folate (39), selenium (28)

Caesar Salad

Ingredients

1 head romaine lettuce, washed and cut into bite-size pieces

½ cup Parmesan cheese, grated

Homemade croutons (after this recipe)

Caesar salad dressing (after this recipe)

Makes: Six to eight servings

Directions

Place lettuce, Parmesan cheese, and croutons together in a large salad bowl. Add the Caesar salad dressing and toss. Serve immediately.

Key nutrients per serving (%DV): Vitamin K (114), vitamin A (92), folate (51), selenium (29), calcium (20), iron (19)

Homemade Croutons

Ingredients

2 tablespoons olive oil

4 cups leftover bread (French, Italian, or sourdough), cut into 1-inch cubes

1 teaspoon kosher salt

Directions

Heat the oil in a skillet over medium heat. Add the bread cubes to the pan, sprinkle them with salt, and toss. Brown the croutons over medium heat until they are crunchy (about 10 minutes).

Caesar Salad Dressing

Ingredients

¾ cup mayonnaise

1 tablespoon lemon juice

1 teaspoon Worcestershire sauce

1 clove garlic, minced

¼ teaspoon salt

⅛ teaspoon pepper

½ cup Parmesan cheese

2 tablespoons milk (plus more if needed)

Directions

Add all the ingredients to a food processor (or whisk by hand) and blend thoroughly. Add more milk to thin the dressing if necessary.

Make a meal! Add grilled fish or chicken atop the salad for a protein source. Complete the meal with fruit.

CHAPTER 6

The Parent Trap

How to Break Free from Your Food History and Attitudes

Like a lot of moms, Cindy was conflicted about feeding her seven-year-old son. On the one hand, she was constantly saying "no" to his requests for sweets, but on the other hand, she used them as a reward for eating dinner and good behavior. She also struggled with her own weight and self-control issues, complicating the picture. Then one day, it hit her: *My mom did the same thing, and look where it got me.* Come to think of it, her brother was doing the same with his kids! She knew she wanted to break free of this cycle, but how?

We hope that every one of you was fearlessly fed as a kid, and that all of you are Fearless Eaters, but we know that's wishful thinking. We also wish that our society weren't obsessed with thinness, fast food, dieting, and "good" and "bad" foods. It's important for you to take some time to think about your own eating—and what's behind it. In fact, we believe *it's imperative to your effectiveness as a feeder.*

We hope that the process of learning the WHAT, HOW, and WHY of feeding has sparked you to think about your own upbringing in regard to food and eating. You know you are your child's biggest role model when it comes to eating and health—but knowing that isn't enough. In fact, that type of pressure can leave parents feeling like they have to be perfect. But here's what no one is telling you: children are our most important teachers in matters of food and health. You just need to add a new type of awareness to the mix, and the life-changing lessons will come rolling in.

We are going to start with the most common feeding traps: mindless, reactive, and projective feeding. We will help you determine what's behind your eating habits and food attitudes by exploring potential contributing factors. We end with tips on how you can become a Fearless Eater who puts your own health and well-being at the top of the priority list.

Common Feeding Traps

There are many factors that contribute to your feeding approach, including how you were fed as a kid, you're attitudes toward food, and your child's eating personality. Although many parents unconsciously feed like their parents did, others go in the opposite direction due to unpleasant memories. We know that parents' (especially mothers') relationship with food and their own body can rub off on the type of feeding style they use.[1] For example, moms who worry about their own weight may restrict or control food in an effort to prevent their child from gaining weight. When you understand the motivations behind your feeding beliefs and actions, it gives you a clearer picture of whether or not you want to change them.

Mindless Feeding

We inherit a lot—good and bad—from our parents, including their feeding style. For example, pleasant memories of gaining cooking skills and eating family meals improve our attitudes about feeding. Other memories—of being pressured to eat, constant exposure to unhealthy foods, and being restricted from Fun Foods— aren't so pleasant. Because people are not taught to think about HOW they were fed, most don't give it much thought.

This is what Sandy was doing. She had two kids and made just enough food for everyone, never more, because that is how it was when she grew up. But her son often complained he wasn't getting enough, which eventually turned into a problem. With more digging, we found that her grandparents grew up during the Great Depression and the "waste is not tolerated" message was ingrained in her own parents, and passed down to her. Minimizing waste, rather than satisfying her child's hunger, was the priority at mealtime.

Many feeding strategies handed down from previous generations are based on times when food was scarce—when children needed to eat when the food was there, and often finish it, because the next meal wasn't so certain. But today, even though this no longer applies to most families, many parents continue this legacy. We find that being controlling with feeding (authoritarian style) has particularly strong ties to the past, and requires a conscious effort to change. This can be especially difficult if you have picky or overweight children.

"I understand where the 'clean your plate' mentality came from, having grandparents who were children at the end of the Great Depression," says Melissa. "But it's funny that our parents suffered through that rule and then subjected us to it in turn. It's amazing seeing how much a simple rule can imprint your personal food philosophy." Melissa broke the cycle by taking the good of her upbringing and leaving out the not-so-helpful aspects: "I hope to pass along to my daughter much of what my mother gave to me . . . but I'm leaving out the 'clean your plate' part."

> **Fearless Tip**
>
> Keep the good aspects of your upbringing, including traditions, family meals, and positive food experiences; let go of what was unproductive; and create what you didn't get, whether it's cooking skills, regular meals, or a supportive environment.

Reactive Feeding

Other parents take a completely different approach and go to the opposite extreme of their parents. Sue was very picky as a child and was made to sit at the table for hours after everyone else had moved on. If she still hadn't finished her dinner by bedtime, it became breakfast. Because Sue was made to eat, she adopted an opposite approach with her now thirteen-year-old daughter. "I wish she'd eat more things than she does and feel horrible for not at least asking her to try more foods," she says. "I realize it's not too late, but I struggle with asking her to do something I hated being forced to do at her age."

We have found that reactive feeding often stems from painful memories of food and eating, especially being forced to eat. The problem with going to the opposite extreme is it brings on a whole new set of problems, whether it's catering to a child because you were forced to eat or being too lenient because you had too many limits around food.

"I never liked to eat fruit as a kid—and my mom says I am the only two-year-old she ever saw turn her nose up at a banana!" says LeAnne. "My father was relentless about forcing me to try and eat foods like fruit, and needless to say, I still hate fruit as an adult." Luckily, LeAnne learned about Ellyn Satter's Division of Responsibility (described in Chapters One and Three) when her twins were born, and not only has she been able to avoid exerting the same pressure she got as a kid but also she has allowed her kids to be exposed to a variety of food without going to the other extreme of becoming a short-order cook.

Projective Feeding

It can be difficult to separate your feelings about food and eating from your child's. Parents' own insecurities or nutritional beliefs color their feeding in ways that can be beneficial or not, and it's even trickier for parents who struggle with food, weight, and healthy eating.

Joanna's daughter, Jamie, had a big appetite and frame, making both Joanna and her husband worried, as they too struggled with weight. Joanna wanted to spare Jamie the same hardships, so she cut Jamie's eating off when she thought she'd had enough. But the real issue was Joanna's own eating, as she often dieted, eating superhealthy, followed by a period of out-of-control eating (what researchers call disinhibition). Joanna's disinhibition may have contributed to her daughter's eating in the absence of hunger and increased weight.[2] When Joanna realized that her lack of trust around Jamie's eating had more to do with her not trusting herself, she was able to stop restricting and adequately support her daughter.

Unhealthy habits are not the only problem. Jake and Reida were healthy and active, and they wanted their son, little Jake, to grow up to be a healthy eater too. Everything went beautifully until he was around three and became more selective and overly focused on Fun Foods (like many kids that age!). Watching little Jake's food obsession grow, they soon realized that they couldn't expect their son to skip food experimentation and not be allowed to enjoy the same sweets they had loved as children. After all, it took them years to come to a healthy place with eating, and they needed to give their child some wiggle room without sabotaging his diet.

Another issue parents face is having two different feeding styles. One parent may be too lax, while the other is trying to stay authoritative—and the child ends up with mixed messages. In addition, outside caregivers may feed your child differently, complicating things further. Be sure to share this book with your spouse or partner, family members, and other caregivers to get them on board with the Fearless Feeding Strategy.

Once you understand the reasons behind your feeding style, the real healing can begin. But just like you learned with your kid, you need to understand more about WHY you eat the way you do.

Understanding Your WHY

We believe that all feeding stages are connected, including adulthood, which is why the Fearless Feeding Fundamentals—the WHAT, HOW, and WHY—apply to you too. Although a variety of factors affect WHY you eat the way you do, your upbringing has great influence, as childhood is a time of intense learning about food and eating. Yet many people, like Sue, underestimate this connection: "I've struggled with being overweight, but I attribute that to other issues. I've been 'out of the house' for years now, and could certainly do something about my weight if I really tried."

This is not about pointing fingers or blame. Parents do the best job with the information they have at the time. Instead, the goal is to look at your eating habits in a whole new light. So instead of assuming you eat too much because you lack willpower, we want you to see other reasons, opening your world and self-understanding.

Memories of Food and Feeding

There are a handful of studies that show a link between adult eating behaviors and memories of food and feeding as children.[3,4,5,6,7] One study with college students revealed that what students learned in childhood stayed with them into adulthood: those allowed to stop eating when full did the same as adults, but those asked to clean their plate ate more food as adults.[3] Another study with young adults revealed that most of those who were forced to eat in childhood still didn't eat the forced food (70 percent) and were pickier overall.[5] Other research found that those adults who were obese reported significantly more food rules as children, including "clean your plate," than those at a normal weight and those considered successful dieters.[4] Although these studies merely demonstrate potential links, they should make you think.

"I feel a little sad realizing that most of us lost the ability to follow our bodies' cues when we were kids," says Pat. "But I am glad to have had the opportunity to let my kids dictate to me when they're done eating—or want more."

And for those of you who grew up overweight, had dieting mothers, or experienced restricting and a weight-focused household, you may have learned that thin equals acceptance. For example, Jackie looked back on pictures of herself in high school when she thought she was fat and realized that wasn't the case. Why did she place so much importance on her body shape and being super-thin? Her mom had something to do with it—she was constantly dieting and commenting on other people's weight. No one was there as a healthy role model or to tell Jackie that her body was perfect and to focus on her other strengths. Jackie's body loathing turned into years of dieting and weight gain, and more dieting and weight gain. Now, as an adult, she struggles with weight and health issues.

Take some time to mull over your experiences with food growing up and your current eating habits. Did you have family meals? Was eating stressful or enjoyable? Were signs of hunger or fullness identified, and were you encouraged to listen to them? Were you pressured to eat more or less than you wanted? What kinds of food were you exposed to? Were healthy foods presented in a negative light? No doubt, the things you were taught have influenced your belief system about food. Table 6.1 summarizes the limiting beliefs about food that can develop from past feeding experiences—and their potential consequences in adulthood.

Food Culture

Food culture has an impact on food beliefs, too. We live in a thin-obsessed world in which weight loss is promoted as "quick and easy" with fad diets and

Table 6.1 Feeding Influences on Food Beliefs and Attitudes		
Feeding Practice	**Limiting Belief**	**Implication**
You were forced to eat healthy foods, such as veggies, or had low exposure to them.	I don't like vegetables or healthy food.	Healthy eating seems like drudgery. You now have poor eating habits.
You were prompted to eat more or clean the plate.	I never get full.	You don't regulate food well, and experience weight gain or weight fluctuations.
Your food intake was restricted as a child, and you were encouraged to diet. You made many attempts to diet as you got older.	I can't trust myself around food.	You frequently diet, with periods of out-of-control eating. You also have poor body image.
There was no or very little cooking in your house growing up, and there were high amounts of processed food or lots of eating out.	I don't have time to cook— it's too complicated.	You see any food preparation as overwhelming.
Treats were used as a reward or taken away as punishment.	It's Friday, vacation, Flag Day—let's eat!	You binge on palatable foods, diet, stress eat, and so on.
You had no or very few regular meals. You were able to eat in front of the TV and out of boredom.	I graze all day, can't help myself.	You eat in the absence of hunger due to habit, food associations, or both.

unrealistic promises. Food is seen as black or white, with media and diet books bombarding people with messages of the latest "good" and "bad" foods. We've seen the rise and fall of calorie counting, low-fat diets, and carbohydrate restriction. Now wheat, processed foods, and sugar are all on trial for being the cause of America's health and weight problems.

Right next to the diet books and products are the indulgent cookbooks and packaged food. We are a nation obsessed with weight and health, yet many of the foods surrounding us are energy-dense, nutrition-poor items we *aren't supposed to have.* With almost 77 percent of people trying to lose or maintain weight, this can make it very hard—temptation is everywhere![8]

Although not the original cause of weight gain, restricting food intake, in the form of giving up favorite foods or following strict diets, does not pan out—and makes forbidden foods (the ones that are everywhere) even more desirable. If you have dieted since a young age, you know what food deprivation feels like, but you may not realize that this feeling sticks with you. Ironically, research defines a link between dieting and weight gain over time. For example, a 2012 twin study found that each dieting attempt between the ages of sixteen and twenty-five increased the risk of overweight, and that effect was independent of genetic factors.[9]

> ### Fearless Fact
>
> Unlike with restrained eating, emerging research shows that an intuitive eating style (focusing on hunger and satiety cues to guide eating) is inversely associated with BMI in men and women.[12,13] In one study, young adult males and females who reported trusting their body in regard to how much to eat experienced fewer disordered eating patterns than those who did not, and the females who intuitively ate were less likely to experience binge eating and chronic dieting.[14] Dietitians Evelyn Tribole and Elyse Resch describe *Intuitive Eating* in their book of the same name listed in Appendix E.

We get some insight into why restrictive eating doesn't work by looking at what researchers call "restrained eaters," defined as people who consciously limit and control food intake as a means to control their weight. A 2008 review pooled hundreds of studies on restrained eating, and revealed that this practice is associated with weight gain and weight cycling in female adults over time (children and adolescents too!). It's also associated with negative emotions, body dissatisfaction, preoccupation with body weight, and eating disorders.[10,11] It is believed that restrained eating can create both biological and psychological feelings of deprivation, making people more sensitive to food cues in their environment—resulting in poor food regulation.

When you throw twenty-first-century lifestyle factors into the equation, such as increased stress, more families in which both parents are working, more convenience foods, and fewer ways to be naturally active, the challenge of trying to be and stay healthy multiplies. But if you can appreciate and understand the potential WHYS behind eating—and change your approach and beliefs—fearless eating is easier than you think!

Becoming a Fearless Eater

The love parents have for their children is all-consuming and protective, and can move mountains. You may not realize it, but this love—and your child—are your stepping stones to becoming a Fearless Eater. One of the biggest parent traps of all is focusing on your child's health at the expense of your own. "I find it pretty easy to create well-balanced, nutritious meals for my daughter, but I don't find that same kind of time for myself," says Stacy. "If we are in a hurry in the morning, I make sure my daughter eats her breakfast, but many times I leave the house without eating mine or even taking a drink of water."

We have found that parents often look at children as a clean slate and view themselves as more of a hopeless cause. But we are going to be frank with you— it's much harder to be a Fearless Feeder when you have lingering food issues. If you can't control your intake of sweets, it'll be hard to watch your kid dig in. Even if you hide the fact that you hate your body, your child will still catch on. If you truly don't like veggies, your kid may not either. By freeing yourself of negative food attitudes, poor body image, and habits that don't enhance your life, you free your child. And throwing some of that fearless love you have for your child to yourself won't hurt either.

Questioning Beliefs

Most every parent has some area of struggle when it comes to food, physical activity, and health. But we are all different, so generalizing challenges isn't easy. For some of you, insecurities about cooking and food preparation may keep you feeling stuck. Some moms are dealing with weight and body dissatisfaction, whereas others are challenged with maintaining a healthy lifestyle amid the long list of "to-do's." Some of you may be heavily focused on perfecting your diet and exercising, which take a lot of energy. We hope that by this point in the chapter you have a better understanding of the WHY behind some of your eating habits and what has shaped them. It's not just your current actions that matter, but the beliefs and thoughts that precede them.

Kaylee's mother punished herself for what she ate and pinpointed what she hated about her body. When Kaylee reached adulthood and got married, she did the same thing. After she found out she was expecting her first baby, a girl, her husband asked her to stop. "That was the best advice he could've given me," she says. "I didn't just stop saying bad things about my looks, I stopped hating how I looked."

For Kaylee, understanding WHY she did what she did wasn't enough. She started questioning her beliefs. Why not love her body? After all, we are more likely to take care of something we care about. Many people wonder how they can intellectually understand what they need to do but still be stuck in bad habits. The real key is changing the daily beliefs and thoughts that actually cause the behavior, because those don't go away so easily.

Kate was overweight as a child and remembers dieting as early as kindergarten. Vegetables and fruit became punishment for being fat, so as an adult she never embraced these foods (unless she was dieting). She decided to work on changing this "healthy food is punishment" belief, and stopped dieting. "I'm now trying to teach myself that fruit and vegetables are not punishment for being fat, but yummy, wonderful foods," she says. "It's been a very hard lesson to learn, but I won't quit trying."

The key issue with limiting beliefs is that they are not true. If we question them, they begin to lose their power—and you can replace them with more empowering thoughts, making the desired behavior easier to achieve. Table 6.2 shows examples of common limiting beliefs and how to conquer them.

Sustainable Motivation

Michelle Segar, motivation expert and behavioral goal researcher at the University of Michigan, explores what motivates women to participate in healthy behaviors. She has found in her research that the typical reasons society gives women for getting healthy (improving weight, health, and appearance) aren't particularly motivating, at least not over time.

According to one study conducted by Segar, women who exercised for daily improvements in quality of life (feeling good!) participated in significantly more physical activity than those who did it to improve their appearance, age gracefully, improve their current health, or a combination of these reasons.[15] The truth is, we

Table 6.2 Changing Food Beliefs		
Limiting Belief	**Questioning Process**	**New Belief**
Dieting and restriction are the only way I can lose weight.	Yes, restricting and diets result in short-term weight loss, but they increase eating and weight over the long haul. How has this really worked for me? Maybe it's time for a change.	*Instead of focusing solely on weight, I will work on building a healthy lifestyle that is sustainable and enjoyable—and improves weight and health over the long haul.*
I don't have time to eat healthfully and exercise.	How much time does it take to eat a balanced diet and move more? Maybe the real problem is not wanting to give up my lifestyle. But who says I have to?	*I will take small steps, include the foods I love, and make eating healthfully and movement part of my daily life, building gradually.*
I don't like to cook, so we eat out a lot.	Is it that I don't like to cook, or that I never learned? Maybe my expectations are too high. Cooking might be more enjoyable if I choose to make items that match my skill level.	*I will start slow and find a way to prepare meals that works for me.*

don't participate in behaviors without a payoff—and external benefits that come and go (weight loss) or are too far down the road (healthy aging) aren't something we can see and feel on a daily basis. But improved quality of life, having more patience with children, and keeping hunger at bay by eating satisfying food are tangible benefits we can see *today.*

"We have all repeatedly tried to make lifestyle changes to take better care of ourselves," says Segar. "Yet when life takes an unexpected turn or our kids get sick, most of us don't maintain self-care behaviors." Segar helps women see that by making healthy behaviors a priority, the daily payoffs outweigh the benefits from checking off one more item on the to-do list. "It's also simple to do," she adds. "Make sure the purpose of your lifestyle change reflects enhancing the quality of your life in very real, noticeable ways."

Fearless Tip

Instead of focusing on desired weight loss or other external reasons for practicing healthy behaviors, focus on daily benefits, such as more energy, improved mood, better sleep, happiness, better parenting, and productivity. These are the factors that will make these behaviors sustainable and, in turn, improve your weight and health.

The HOW of Eating

Now that we've gone over the WHY of adult eating and the benefits of a positive approach, it's time to go further into the details of fearless eating. The HOW of eating is similar to that discussed in the age-specific Chapters Two through Five, but unlike (or like) your kid, you may have some undesirable habits that have developed through the years. That's why, when it comes to HOW you eat, you can actually learn a thing or two from your child.

Young children are important teachers because they have what you had when you were little: the ability to self-regulate food intake. As babies, they cry when hungry and stop when satisfied. Food is a positive, satisfying experience unless they learn otherwise. You, too, were born with this ability, and by preserving this tendency in your child, you can reconnect to that wisdom of your own body. It can be hard because so many messages tell you not to trust yourself and that your love of food is the enemy—but it's not!

Many adults feel torn when it comes to eating and enjoyment. On the one hand, nutrition information has exploded over the past forty years, telling people what they should and shouldn't eat. On the other hand, people desire satisfying and enjoyable eating experiences. This can produce an internal conflict that brings up the whole issue of self-control: "I know I shouldn't eat it, but I want it," or "I don't really want the healthy food, but I know I should eat it!"

When you take judgments out of the equation and become more accepting and mindful, the struggle melts away.

Michelle May, MD, author of *Eat What You Love, Love What You Eat*, was an overweight child, dieted young, and struggled with food and eating into adulthood. She watched in amazement as her husband and two kids were able to regulate their intake with ease and not obsess about food. This inspired her to drop the dieting and trust herself with eating (what she calls getting back to "instinctive eating"). This approach was so freeing and effective that she dedicated her career to helping others do the same. "A lot of parents struggle with overeating and end up restricting their own children's eating," she says. "They don't realize that not only can they trust their children but also they can trust themselves."

May teaches people how to eat mindfully, which entails learning how to connect to the body's inner wisdom while disconnecting from all the external messages about food and eating. When people can turn off the noise in their head and tune in to their body, they can actually find out what their body needs by asking such questions as *How hungry am I? How much food do I need? How much enjoyment am I getting?* "The beauty of mindful eating is it allows people to recognize the present moment instead of reacting to a situation without thinking of what's best for them," May adds. "But the old ways of eating take time to undo."

Many fear their eating will become out of control when they allow themselves food freedom, but research shows otherwise. There is emerging evidence that a mindful eating approach has a positive impact on eating habits and well-being.[16,17] For example, one study showed that individuals with troubled eating had significant reductions in food cravings, body dissatisfaction, and emotional and stress-related eating after eight weeks in a mindfulness training program.[17]

> **Fearless Fact**
>
> Mindful eating starts with awareness. May says that when people feel like eating, they need to ask, *Am I hungry?* and differentiate between true physical hunger and "head hunger." She explains that it's still okay to eat even if you aren't hungry (no judgment here), but you'll begin to understand what you really need to take care of yourself. Sometimes it's food and sometimes it's not—and it's okay to make mistakes, because that is part of the learning process.

When you master the HOW of eating, you'll find this focus is key to enhancing self-regulation and subsequently weight. In addition, taking care of yourself by getting enough sleep and handling stress effectively is essential, as not attending to these factors can increase feelings of hunger and sabotage your efforts. Table 6.3 provides tips on how to eat to maximize eating enjoyment, health, and well-being for you and your family!

Table 6.3	Tips for Maximizing Eating Enjoyment	
Tip	**What to Do**	**Result**
Be mindful.	Be aware of what drives eating (hunger cues versus food cues). Notice the taste and texture of food, your pace of eating, and how enjoyable the experience is.	Being mindful helps you observe patterns without judgment and make better food decisions to reach your goals.
Notice hunger and satiety.	Use your internal cues of hunger and fullness as a guide for when to start or stop eating.	Paying attention to hunger and satiety leads to better food regulation and satisfaction during meals, which can improve your weight over time.[18]
Put enjoyment first.	Make eating a truly satisfying experience.	Prioritizing enjoyment makes eating rewarding, resulting in a preference for quality over quantity.
Let go of food judgments.	Avoid labeling foods as "good" or "bad." Honor your food preferences while considering nutrition.	Avoiding judgments helps maintain consistent food intake instead of over- or undereating.
Drop the three D's for the three B's.[19]	Instead of a **D**rive for thinness, value and **B**e realistic about your body as is. Instead of **D**ieting, **B**e healthy with a variety of food. Instead of body **D**issatisfaction, promote **B**ody satisfaction.	Body satisfaction improves food regulation,[20] and dieting is ineffective over the long term.[21]
Allow yourself reliable meals and snacks.	Eat on a regular routine that is similar to your child's, and eat according to your appetite.	Skipping meals can increase hunger and lead to overeating.
Focus on food.	As often as you can, eat without distraction, preferably at the table or some designated area.	Eat for hunger and enjoyment most of the time (we all eat when not hungry from time to time).

WHAT to Eat

Nutrition matters for good health—and it can be used more effectively when it's no longer about strict rules that cause rebellion. We believe in a total diet approach to eating, looking at your diet over time instead of at single foods, or what is eaten in one day. And similar to our approach with children, pairing the HOW and the WHY of eating with nutrition (WHAT) can have a significant impact on your overall health, outlook, and relationship with food. But that is not the only benefit you'll get—this approach can help you be a Fearless Feeder—of your children and yourself!

The nutrition-only message hasn't worked because nutrition is not the only reason we eat, and no one food or combination hits the nail on the head for everyone's health. Striking the balance with food that satisfies both health needs and personal preferences is key. Choosing food is also about how it makes you feel. How satisfied do certain meals make you? How long until hunger returns? What meals and foods cause an afternoon slump, making you want to take a nap? You may love the taste of cookies, for example, but eating a whole plate of them for lunch certainly isn't going to help you stay productive all afternoon. A nice meal finished off with a cookie might be better to give you the energy you need *and* the sweet taste you like. The Fearless Food Guide in Appendix A can help you make food decisions while considering the roles different items play in your diet.

> **Fearless Tip**
>
> When making food choices, consult the powerful three! When food choice is a careful decision that takes into account *nutrition, taste,* and *how food makes you feel,* eating is a very satisfying experience.

Juggling food choices is challenging. It's not about being perfect, but about striving for that satisfying balance. You may decide over time that sugar or sweet doesn't do it for you, or not to eat meat (or you may add meat back in!). Your diet may become mostly Nourishing Foods, or a healthy balance between them all. The difference is *you* are making the decision that is right for your situation instead of starting with a more extreme approach that may not fit your preferences. We know this can seem like a big step for some of you, but if you have been taking an approach to eating that hasn't worked over the long term, what have you got to lose? And this healthy approach to food is not only good for you but also good for your child.

We could fill up this whole book up with the subject of adults and eating for adults, but we only have room to cover the basics. We recommend books that can help you in Appendix E. But if you are dealing with eating issues that affect your quality of life and health, you should seek help from a registered dietitian or other qualified health professional.

Focusing on your own WHY, HOW, and WHAT is the key to developing balanced eating, regular physical activity, and a healthy relationship with food. You can become that intuitive eater you were born to be with a little practice and a lot less judgment, and by learning from your child. After all, becoming a Fearless Eater is often the missing ingredient that makes becoming a Fearless Feeder possible!

CHAPTER 7

Childhood Nutrition Problems

A Fearless Approach to Common Issues

I n a perfect world, you would have read this book when your baby was very young, raised him with the Fearless Feeding Strategy, and prevented many of the common nutrition problems afflicting kids today (if they were preventable). Some of you may be dealing with nutrition problems *now,* and that's why we wrote this chapter. Here we highlight the most common food-related issues kids are experiencing today: food allergies, weight problems, eating disorders, extreme picky eating, and behavioral conditions. We give you an overview of how to handle these using the Fearless Feeding Strategy to help you navigate them and take positive action. We also help you know when your child needs professional help.

If you are opening this book and starting here, we suggest you check the age-specific section for your child and read that first. It will provide you with the basis for what we discuss in this chapter. We know childhood nutrition problems are becoming more common—leaving parents gripped with fear, but with the right information and guidance you can be fearless and empowered!

Food Allergies

Food allergies are on the rise, with about 4 percent of children reporting or being treated for a food allergy (an 18 percent increase over a decade).[1] A food allergy is an immune response that occurs when the body encounters the *protein component* of certain foods. Eight foods cause 90 percent of allergies: milk, eggs, soy, peanuts, tree nuts, fish, shellfish, and wheat.[2,3] When a food allergic child is exposed to an allergen, a variety of responses can occur, from vomiting, diarrhea, and hives to anaphylaxis, a reaction that involves more than one body system. An allergic reaction can occur within minutes to hours of eating a food, but in the rare case of anaphylaxis, this response can reoccur or be a single, ongoing reaction for hours to days. The most effective way to avoid an allergic reaction is to eliminate potential allergens from your child's diet. Table 7.1 outlines the common food reactions in children.

Table 7.1	Food Reactions in Children			
Reaction	**Food Component**	**Symptoms**	**Avoid . . .**	**Comments**
Food allergy	Varies; top eight allergens: milk, soy, eggs, fish, shellfish, tree nuts, peanuts, and wheat	*Skin:* Hives, swelling around mouth, eyes, or both *Respiratory system:* Coughing, itchy throat, difficulty breathing *Gastrointestinal system:* Vomiting, diarrhea, stomachache	Identified food allergen	Eighty percent of children outgrow a milk allergy,[4] and 70 percent outgrow an egg allergy[5] by age sixteen. Less than 20 percent of children outgrow a milk allergy by age four.[4] About 20 percent will outgrow a peanut allergy; and 9 percent will outgrow a tree nut allergy.[6]
Celiac disease	Gluten	Gas, bloating, diarrhea, constipation, itchy skin rash, headache, poor growth	Wheat, contaminated oats, rye, barley, and products made with these ingredients	Lifelong avoidance of gluten is required to prevent damage to the intestine and malnutrition. Gluten can also be found in medicines, vitamins, and lip balms.

Table 7.1 (continued)				
Reaction	**Food Component**	**Symptoms**	**Avoid . . .**	**Comments**
Lactose intolerance	Lactose (carbohydrate found in milk)	Gas, bloating, diarrhea	Dairy products, including milk, cheese, yogurt, and ice cream	Lactose intolerance is uncommon in children. Tolerance to milk products is highly variable, and symptoms occur shortly after ingestion. Avoidance, consuming lower levels of lactose, or using lactase enzymes can relieve symptoms.
Oral allergy syndrome	Raw fruits and vegetables, commonly apples, carrots, peaches, plums, cherries, pears, tomato, melons, zucchini, cucumber, kiwi, banana	Itchy mouth, throat, and occasionally ears; lip swelling	Identified fruits and vegetables	Symptoms are limited to the mouth. Crossover contamination from pollen to food triggers the allergic response. This phenomenon is also known as pollen-food syndrome. Cooked fruits and vegetables are generally tolerated.
Eosinophilic esophagitis	Varies	*Infants:* Feeding difficulties, irritability, poor weight gain *Older kids:* Vomiting, regurgitation, heartburn; food "getting stuck" when swallowed	Identified food allergens	White blood cells (eosinophils) congregate in the throat lining. Avoidance of food allergens is necessary.

We take the whole child approach to managing food allergies, considering the WHAT, HOW, and WHY. Obviously, the focus is on food and nutrition when dealing with food allergies, but the HOW and WHY of feeding matter too. Let's dissect this with the Fearless Feeding Strategy!

WHAT

Avoiding food allergens, reading the ingredients on food labels, and watching out for cross-contamination (transferring food allergens in the process of food preparation) are the keys to keeping children safe when they are food allergic. Obvious foods your child needs to avoid are easy to spot, but the hidden allergens can be tough to identify. Food labels reveal allergens hidden in products. Such phrases as "This product may contain trace amounts of allergens," or "Made in a facility where allergen-containing products are made" are code for *don't eat this food.* The U.S. Food Allergen Labeling and Consumer Protection Act of 2004 requires that milk, soy, eggs, peanuts, tree nuts, wheat, fish, and shellfish be identified on the label, making it easier for you to avoid these ingredients. Food manufacturers *do* change their ingredient components, so be aware that a "safe" food can become "unsafe" unexpectedly. Always read labels and contact food manufacturers to ensure food is allergen-free, and if you're unsure, use the "when in doubt, keep it out" philosophy.

Finding substitutes for food allergens is also important. For example, if your child is allergic to milk, you'll need to find an alternative that contains a good source of calcium, vitamin D, and protein, such as fortified soymilk. Rice and nut milks may contain the calcium and vitamin D you're looking for, but they aren't a good source of protein. If you use these, you'll want to make sure your child gets adequate protein from other foods. When eliminating protein sources (milk, eggs, soy) from the diet, other sources of protein, such as meat, beans, or nuts and nut butters, need to be eaten. If fish and shellfish are out, look for other sources of docosahexaenoic acid (DHA) and fatty acids, such as DHA-rich eggs or other fortified products. Finally, if wheat is eliminated, experiment with alternative flours and choose sources fortified with folic acid and B vitamins.

If you have a child with multiple food allergies, life gets even trickier. In addition to avoiding many foods, food fatigue can occur (tired of the usual fare), magnifying potential nutrient deficits. Keeping food variety high, introducing new allergen-free foods, and watching for missing nutrients can be the antidote to boredom and inadequate nutrition.

HOW

Children with food allergies have naturally imposed limits on their diet, so you'll want to create choice when you can. A family-style approach to meals, whereby meal components are separated, allows your child to select the foods that are safe for him and can create a sense of control and independence. Obviously, for life-threatening allergies, avoid having those foods in your home completely. Bottom line: use a feeding approach that keeps your child safe, promotes choice, and can be consistently implemented.

> **Fearless Tip**
>
> If your child is allergic to two or more major food allergens, we recommend regular involvement with a health care team (allergist, pediatric dietitian, pediatrician) to ensure adequate nutrition and normal growth.

Educating your food allergic child to be independent (and safe) in the world is a priority. When your child is young and not in school, you are in control of his diet, and should be teaching him about his food allergy on a basic level: recognition of the foods he is allergic to and where those foods are found. Point out foods that "don't work" for your child's body. Gail made simple labels (smiley face and frowny face) and attached them to household foods and the foods she sent in to daycare for her toddler. She taught her daughter that a smiley face meant it was "okay to eat," and a frowny face meant it "hurt her body." Remember—keep messages simple and easy to understand.

By the time your child starts school, he needs to know the basics of food allergy management: recognition of the food allergy (or allergies) and symptoms, confidence to speak up, and comfort with substitutions. Suggest phrases like "That's not safe for my body" or "(Food) and I don't get along"—these can equip your child with confidence and a stay-safe strategy. Also, make sure your child knows the "when in doubt, keep it out" philosophy for making decisions about eating food on his own. Appendix E provides more resources on managing food allergies outside of the home.

If your child has minimal or no food reactions, is growing well, is socially thriving, and is "okay" with his food allergy, you're doing a good job managing it.

Check in annually with your allergist to evaluate and verify ongoing allergies, review growth with your pediatrician, and troubleshoot nutrition with your dietitian.

WHY

A family history of allergies—food or other—is associated with an increased risk of developing a food allergy.[2,3] The incidence of food allergy is rising (up 18 percent from 1997 to 2007) due to a number of factors, including our Western diet; the "hygiene hypothesis," a theory that sanitation measures and vaccines have altered immunity; and late exposure to food allergens.[1,3]

There is no known, effective strategy to prevent food allergies from developing. In high-risk children (those with parents or other close family members with an allergy), some protective factors include exclusive breastfeeding for at least four months or a specialized (low-allergen) infant formula if bottle-feeding.[2] Be sure to consult your allergist or pediatrician, especially if you are having a first child, or having more children.

> **Fearless Tip**
>
> Most children will outgrow milk, egg, soy, and wheat allergies, according to the National Institute of Allergy and Infectious Diseases. Children with tree nut and peanut allergies and those with high initial levels of immunoglobulin E (IgE) are less likely to outgrow their food allergy. Checking IgE levels annually can help determine whether your child is likely to outgrow his allergy or not.

Finally, make sure a food allergy diagnosis is based on a *combination of factors,* such as a skin prick test, a blood test, an actual reaction, food elimination, and an oral challenge, assessed and managed by a board-certified pediatric allergist. The last thing you want is for your child to be misdiagnosed and consume a narrow diet unnecessarily.

Weight Problems

Many parents are worried their child is too heavy or the opposite, underweight. You've heard the statistics—one in three children is classified as overweight or obese, increasing the risk of sleep, respiratory, intestinal, cardiac, and psychiatric problems.[7] At the other end of the spectrum, children become underweight for a variety of medical reasons, and poor eating increases the risk of poor immune function, poor growth, and learning difficulties. We know that not every big child is unhealthy, nor is every child who is thin the picture of health—you will need to look deeper to discover what is

> **Fearless Tip**
>
> Steady growth at higher or lower weight percentiles for age is better than dramatic jumps or dips, which can signal a problem. Review your child's growth chart annually with your pediatrician. If you notice extra weight gain or weight loss between appointments, it's worth an extra visit.

going on. We do know, however, that worries about weight can change how you feed your child and how well she eats.[8]

If your child is overweight, she may outgrow it, particularly if lifestyle habits are healthy and growth is steady. Case in point: Jackie's twelve-year-old Bella had a body mass index classifying her as "overweight." When we evaluated her weight and growth, it was clear that she had been growing along the 90th percentile her whole life! This was Bella's natural genetic blueprint, and trying to change it would be futile (and could potentially cause a host of other problems). Staying the course with balanced nutrition, adequate sleep, and exercise was the key to long-term health for Bella.

Many children today are on a healthy habit and lifestyle *decline* and will not outgrow excess weight unless significant lifestyle changes or outside intervention occur.[7] Diets aimed at rapid weight loss are not advised for children, as they interrupt normal growth and development. Rather, halting a weight gain trend or slow, gradual weight loss is the best approach. If your child is overweight or obese, seek professional help to manage it. Because the first two years of life are a critical time for nutrition, it's imperative to seek guidance from a health professional for this age group as well.

Food choices, activity level, feeding interactions, and eating habits form the basis for a child's weight problem.[9] In any intervention, the whole family approach is the *best approach,* as singling out an overweight or underweight child

Table 7.2	Common Reasons for Weight Problems in Children		
Problem	**WHAT (Nutrition)**	**HOW (Feeding Interactions)**	**WHY (Potential Medical Issues)**
Underweight	Too much juice; a low-fat diet; excess grains, fruits, or vegetables; a vegan diet that is too restrictive; or intake of inadequate calories and nutrients can all contribute to underweight.	A feeding style that is too controlling may result in food strikes or low intake. Excessive prompting can turn off appetite. Restricting food amounts or access to food can also be problematic, as can a neglectful feeding style.	Various medical problems, such as food allergies, gastrointestinal problems, or heart conditions, can contribute to low weight, as can medications that alter taste or appetite, or result in malabsorption of nutrients.
Overweight	Overweight results when calorie intake exceeds calories burned. This may be due, in part, to consumption of sugar-sweetened beverages and excess energy-rich foods, or to increased hunger resulting from consumption of insufficient fat or satisfying foods.	Restrictive feeding or being too controlling with food; permissive feeding or a lack of feeding structure; and demanding the completion of a meal (pressure) can all influence weight status. Neglectful feeding may cause insecurity and food-seeking behaviors. Using food to reward or taking it away as punishment can also cause problems.	Prader-Willi syndrome, Cushing's syndrome, hypothyroidism, Down syndrome, binge eating disorder, and depression are all possible contributors. Steroids and psychiatric medications also may alter appetite or metabolism and influence weight status.

adds undue pressure and stigma, potentially causing emotional disturbances. Here we take the Fearless Feeding Strategy to show you how to prevent (and even treat) weight problems, optimizing lifestyle choices to benefit your child's weight and overall health. When it comes to weight, most parents start with the WHAT, but we want you first to consider the HOW and WHY. Table 7.2 outlines the most common reasons for weight problems in kids.

Overweight and Obesity

Fourteen-year-old Shannon was pudgy, and her mom, Liz, tried hard to control her eating. But Shannon was hungry all the time and munched on food after school and late at night when her mom wasn't watching. The bigger Shannon got, the more Liz controlled her food . . . and the more Shannon sought food from other areas.

Using the Fearless Feeding Strategy, we highlight some of the common issues pertaining to overweight and obesity in children:

HOW

If you're feeding a larger child, your feeding style and practices can make or break how successful you are with managing his weight.[10,11] When parents restrict or control food intake to prevent more weight gain, it may backfire, leading to eating in the absence of hunger, sneaking, hiding, out-of-control eating, and ultimately more weight gain.[12,13] The best way to manage your child's weight is with an authoritative feeding style along with steady structure, family-style service, and at least three to five family meals per week.[14] You can also help your child tune in to hunger and fullness, and eat mindfully.[15] Often, when children have well-rounded meals, wholesome snacks, and occasional sweets, their satisfaction level increases and counterproductive eating behaviors taper off.

Stigmatizing your child for his eating or weight, and focusing too much on "healthy eating" and nutrition, aren't effective either—they just translate to more pressure. Rather, "walk the talk"—keep a healthy food environment and role-model a healthy lifestyle.

> ## Five Tips for Interacting with a Bigger Kid
>
> 1. Avoid singling your child out for his weight or as eating differently.
> 2. Allow your child to have fun and eat more Fun Foods at parties.
> 3. Focus on healthy habits, not weight.
> 4. Avoid ultimatums about losing weight.
> 5. Make sure your child understands he is loved for who he is.

WHY

Children become overweight for a variety of reasons: medical conditions, medications, feeding interactions, developmental transitions, poor eating, and lifestyle habits. Often there are many factors in play at once, making it necessary to address each one to manage weight successfully. The WHY behind your child's weight is powerful—don't assume it is merely about food and activity, or you will be frustrated that your efforts aren't having the impact you desire.

WHAT

For many children, eating is out of balance—favoring Fun Foods, convenience items, dining out, and larger portions—or it can be too controlled, leading to overeating (discussed as part of the HOW earlier). Make sure the balance (types of food and amounts) favors mostly Nourishing and Half-and-Half Foods, and offer (or model with family-style meals) recommended serving sizes, as discussed in Chapter Four. Allow Fun Foods in moderation, as avoiding them may lead to their increased desirability and overindulgence. For example, if your child eats several Fun Foods each day, scale back to one a day. Or if you've forbidden them, add them back in and allow one daily. Allowing moderate amounts eases the feeling of restriction, and in the long run results in a happier child, rather than one who is eating Fun Foods on the sly and feeling deprived. Find the balance that's right for your child and remember to be flexible.

Make nutrition swaps: substitute high-fat dairy with low-fat or nonfat sources, make sure protein sources are of the lean variety most of the time, target healthy fats and avoid fried foods as much as possible; and weave in whole grains more often. Try to offer fruits and vegetables daily (five servings, if possible).

Dine out less, but if you do, share entrées and desserts, order fruits or veggies as side items, and limit or eliminate sugar-sweetened drinks.

Promote daily exercise—not a "forced march." Exercise should be enjoyable and fun. Watch out for too much screen time (TV, computer, cell phone), setting a limit of two hours per day. Finally, make sure your child has a good sleep routine, as children who don't get enough sleep may have higher body weights than children who do.[16] Table 7.3 provides more tools for managing weight.

Table 7.3 Tools for Balancing Healthy Weight in Children	
Factor to Consider	**Tools to Try**
Food	• Find balance using the Fearless Food Guide (in the age-specific chapters and Appendix A). • Implement the 90:10 Rule (with an average of one Fun Food per day). • Promote portion awareness. • Offer five servings fruits and vegetables daily. • Practice healthy dining out (reduce frequency and make smart choices). • Have breakfast daily. • Reduce sugar-sweetened drinks. • Eat family meals.
Physical activity	• Allow plenty of opportunity for activity: sixty minutes each day.
Screen time	• Limit screen time to two hours each day. • Allow no screen time for children under two years.
Sleep	• Establish a regular bedtime hour. • Optimize the sleep environment without distractions. • Adopt a bedtime routine (wash up, read a book, and so on).
Feeding style	• Adopt an authoritative feeding style. • Avoid restricting or overly controlling food intake, rewarding with sweets or other foods, or pushing the idea of healthy eating too hard. • Stay on a meal and snack schedule.

Underweight

Young Liam was underweight, and his parents nagged him to eat, pressured him with spoonfuls of food, and squeezed his cheeks open to receive nourishment. As his weight dropped, their games and tactics intensified, from following him around the house to constantly offering bites of food and sips of milk. These efforts were fruitless (no pun intended!). The more they tried to get Liam to eat, the less he ate.

HOW

Although getting the underweight child to eat *in any way, shape, or form* seems like the right thing to do, we know pressuring, coercing, and forcing (negative feeding practices) do little to improve eating.[17] In fact, it may make eating worse! Using a positive approach—with an authoritative feeding style and optimized feeding structure—is the key to weathering the storm. Stay on schedule and maintain Ellyn Satter's Division of Responsibility in feeding, as described in Chapters One and Three, as it builds appetite and helps improve eating.

WHY

Eating style, temperament, constitution, and developmental stage—and feeding practices—contribute to why children eat the way they do. Too much attention on eating performance can backfire, reducing appetite and eating. Work with your child's developmental stage, rather than against it. For example, the toddler will be independent (the teen, too!), and you'll want to support that with a positive attitude and food environment. Let your child be in control by allowing reasonable choice, participation in family-style meals, and involvement in the kitchen. Finally, trust your child to eat enough, especially if structured opportunities and nutritious foods are in place.

WHAT

When children are underweight, more effort needs to go into the foods they eat. Remember, every bite counts, so make sure that foods are nutrient- *and* calorie-dense. Add healthy fats to foods like pasta, sandwiches, hot cereal, and vegetables. Don't "healthify" all foods, such as only offering steamed veggies, plain starches, and grains with very high fiber content (without added fats like butter or oil).

Foods prepared this way are less palatable and may be too filling, contributing to the problem. Kids need fats, which provide energy density and flavor. Watch out for too many fruits and vegetables crowding out other nutritious, calorie-dense foods. If this is a problem, stage the meal to offer protein, dairy, and grains first, followed by fruits and vegetables.

Water can be an issue too. In the underweight child, water can perpetuate the problem and shouldn't take center stage. Offer nutritious beverages, such as milk (even flavored), 100 percent fruit juice, yogurt smoothies, or breakfast drinks. Watch out for filling up on drinks, as this may reduce solid food intake. Reserve beverages for the end of the meal in this case.

While getting back on track with eating and gaining weight, a multivitamin and pre-bedtime snack rich in nutrients (peanut butter and crackers, full-fat yogurt, or an instant breakfast drink) should be considered.

Our experience has been that *all* weight problems are multifactorial, involving the WHAT, HOW, and WHY of feeding. One thing we know for sure—the interaction around food and eating is vitally important to your child's weight status.

Eating Disorders

Eating disorders are among the most *fearful* nutrition conditions for parents! About 2.7 percent of adolescents (thirteen to seventeen years) suffer from an eating disorder, with girls more than two times as likely to have an eating disorder than boys, according to the National Institute of Mental Health.[18] Sadly, eating disorders are on the rise in children under age twelve and in boys.[19] Early identification and intervention constitute the best chance for full recovery from an eating disorder, yet many parents live in suspicion without taking action.

Fourteen-year-old McKenzie was skipping meals (lunch), avoiding her after-school snack, making her own breakfast, skimping on dinner, and losing weight. "I noticed that my daughter looked thinner, ate less, and wasn't as involved with her friends, but there were so many other things that *were* going well," said her mom. "I just didn't put two and two together."

Eating disorders are characterized by extreme disturbances in eating behavior, such as eating very little or far too much; body image characterized by extreme distress over body weight or shape; or a combination of factors. For more resources on eating disorder characteristics, see Appendix E.

Anorexia is the leading cause of death from mental illness in the United States, and the typical ages for onset are thirteen to fourteen years and seventeen to eighteen years. About 3 percent of college women have bulimia (overeating large amounts of food, followed by purging) and are underweight, normal weight, or overweight. Dieting is the biggest risk factor for the development of eating disorders, with about two-thirds of cases in girls occurring among those who have dieted.[20]

The typical warning signs, as outlined in Table 7.4, include a change in weight or eating habits, concern with body weight and shape, and loss of menses.[19] If you see these signs and are concerned, schedule a visit with your pediatrician. You may miss the signs, as layering clothing to hide weight loss or gain, or to compensate for low body temperature, is common, for example.

The one take-away message we want you to get from this section is this: the outcome of an eating disorder can be dramatically different when signs are addressed early on, rather than later. Many medical complications will be resolved when a healthy weight is restored or other adverse behaviors, such as vomiting, stop. There is no doubt that if your child is demonstrating significant signs of disordered eating, treatment from qualified professionals, including a medical doctor, psychosocial therapist, and dietitian, is necessary.

Here, we give you more tools to use at home, using the Fearless Feeding Strategy:

WHAT

We often see children assume the job of feeding themselves (or others), determining the meal or making separate foods. Excluding foods or food groups is also common. As much as is possible, you want to stay in charge of WHAT will be on the menu and avoid letting your teen assume leadership in this area, as it may foster poor eating in this situation. Keep all foods in the mix and start a multivitamin, a calcium supplement, or both to cover nutrient gaps.

HOW

Offer family meals, maintaining your job of determining the timing and location of mealtime, and expect your child to attend meals and help with setup and

Table 7.4 Warning Signs of an Eating Disorder and What You Can Do		
Signs	**Do . . .**	**Don't . . .**
Weight loss or gain: Rapid weight loss or gain, significant and unnecessary weight loss of 10 percent of body weight, lack of growth, denial of hunger	• Provide regular meals and snacks • Share your concern with a health care provider	• Praise or encourage weight loss • Compliment your child on appearance • Join efforts in weight loss
Changes in eating behaviors: Eating smaller portions; skipping meals; eliminating foods or food groups; avoidance of meals with family and friends; dieting when not overweight; preoccupation with food, calories, nutrition, or cooking; episodes of binging or out-of-control eating; leaving for the bathroom after meals; peculiar food rituals	• Have family meals • Offer a variety of foods • Promote conversation and involvement at meals • Share your concerns with your child • Start multivitamin and mineral supplementation	• Support your child's preparing her own meals or skipping meals frequently • Allow eating alone frequently • Encourage dieting
Overconcern with body: Frequent weighing, standing in front of the mirror, "body checking," complaining of feeling fat when not a reality	• Remove scales from the home • Favor healthy behaviors and minimize talk about body weight, shape, and size • Highlight internal qualities and attributes	• Fall into negative discussions about weight, shape, or size • Agree with concerns about weight, body size, or shape

Table 7.4 (*continued*)		
Signs	**Do . . .**	**Don't . . .**
Loss of menstrual period: Missing more than three periods in a row, failure to start period	• Consult your pediatrician	• Overreact or ignore
Mood swings: Quickness to anger, sadness, being "high on life," giddiness, signs of obsessive-compulsive behavior, secretive behaviors, depression or anxiety, feelings of guilt	• Stay neutral and calm • Inform your pediatrician and counselor of changes	• Get overinvolved in moodiness or drama, which may lead to arguments and communication problems
Interrupted sleep patterns: Difficulty falling asleep, difficulty staying asleep	• Construct an environment for good sleep (no TV in the bedroom, minimized use of laptops, and so on)	• Allow stimulant products to help your child stay awake (excessive coffee, caffeine, energy drinks, and so on)
Hair changes: Loss or thinning of hair, extra hair growth on extremities	• Consult your pediatrician • Check for adequate protein intake	• Ignore hair loss, which can be a sign of protein malnutrition
Focus or concentration problems: Difficulty concentrating, paying attention, remembering details, or carrying on a conversation; slowness with thinking; losing train of thought	• Encourage adequate nutrition and sleep • Inform your pediatrician	• Allow abuse of caffeine or other stimulant products
Overexercise: Drive to exercise even when ill or in bad weather, vigorous and frequent exercise	• Set limits on healthy amounts of exercise • Model balance and healthy exercise	• Overprogram your child with too many sports or other activities

cleanup. Keep the mealtime atmosphere pleasant. Address concerns about eating and other behaviors in positive ways, such as "I notice that you aren't eating much at dinner, and that concerns me"; "I see that you are cold, and I'd like to help with that"; or "I can tell you're wiped out at the end of the day, what can I do to help you?" It may take several attempts to connect with your child, but keep trying. Your supportive and caring tone can help a lot.

WHY

Children and teens develop eating disorders for multiple reasons. From genetics and environment to your child's temperament and personality, many underlying factors and life experiences can contribute to an eating disorder's development.[21] The development of an eating disorder is very complex, and more research is needed to determine *which* risk factors influence *whom*, and result in *what* eating disorder.

Recovery is possible with early intervention. Longitudinal studies indicate that recovery for children and teens is better than for adults, with many resuming a normal weight, menstrual cycle, and eating pattern. But these results reflect a long period of treatment, sometimes several years. If you are concerned about or suspicious of your child's weight or eating behaviors, act! Most important—parents don't cause eating disorders, kids don't wish them on themselves, and the negative behaviors don't go away on their own. Waiting, worrying, and wishing it will disappear allow an eating disorder to gain a foothold.

> **Fearless Fact**
>
> Parents often feel responsible for an eating disorder, but it's not that simple. Although parents play a role, they are only one piece of the puzzle.

> **Fearless Tip**
>
> Be a good role model, feed your child and yourself positively, and don't focus on your child's body weight and shape. Also, help your child learn to regulate her emotions, have her eat a daily breakfast, and share family meals— these practices are protective against the development of an eating disorder.

Problem Feeders and Ongoing Picky Eating

Picky eating is a normal stage of toddlerhood (see Chapter Three), but the prevalence in older children is increasing. About one in twenty children between the ages of zero and ten is a problem feeder, refusing to eat or eating a very limited number of selected foods.[22] Children who are problem feeders may have sensory, mechanical, or medical conditions, whereas others may have behavioral challenges.

Here we take you through the Fearless Feeding Strategy so you can get a handle on how to integrate good nutrition and a healthy approach and better understand your child's preferences and sensitivities.

> ## Fearless Fact
>
> Some children are at higher risk for becoming problem feeders, including those born prematurely or with low birth weight, and those with oral-motor problems, certain behavioral conditions, food allergies, or sensory processing disorder (disorganized sensory signals to the brain causing difficulty interpreting and responding to sensation).

WHY

All children learn *how* to eat through feeding. But a child who is a problem feeder may have learned that eating hurts, which was the case with thirteen-month-old Amelia. She had reflux as a baby and learned that eating was painful, and her nutritional intake and weight suffered. Zach had frequent colds, ear infections, and environmental allergies, leaving him congested and struggling to breathe normally. Eating just made things more difficult, so he ate less. Nine-year-old Isaac had eosinophilic esophagitis and ate less due to problems swallowing and pain. Once his food allergens were figured out, he ate better, but he still had a negative association with food. Seven-year-old Samantha was a sensitive child and picky as a young toddler. She experienced yelling and punishment for not eating enough, and this left a lasting impression. She didn't eat well or enjoy eating. As you can see, there can be a variety of underlying reasons for problem feeding.

A problem feeder may have sensory processing disorder, behavioral conditions, or other associated neurological challenges; an overactive gag reflex; defensiveness to touch; or a dislike for the way food feels in the mouth. Sensory-based problem feeders may have heightened taste receptors on the tongue and more taste buds, making them acutely aware of texture. Sensitivities to food characteristics, including sounds, tastes, smells, textures, and visual appearance, can exist.[23] If problem feeding is left undiagnosed and untreated, a problem feeder may have lifelong difficulties with food, nutrient deficits, and poor growth, not to mention negative repercussions to his self-esteem.

Table 7.5 outlines common signs of a problem, categorized by age. These don't necessarily mean your child will be a problem feeder, but they indicate that there may be more to the story.

Table 7.5 Identifying a Problem Feeder by Age		
Stage	**Signs of a Problem**	**Potential Reasons**
Infancy	Difficulty latching onto the breast, gagging or choking on lumpy foods, refusing new foods or textures, lack of interest in eating, eating poorly	Oral-motor issues, gastroesophageal reflux (GER), prematurity, low birth weight, sensory challenges, other medical problems, neurological challenges
Toddlerhood	Refusing new foods, staying with similar textures or colors of food, refusing major food groups, eating fewer than twenty different foods, dropping liked foods and not regaining them, crying or breaking down with new foods, going days without eating, unpleasant and stressful mealtimes	Food allergies, oral-motor problems, frequent respiratory infections and congestion, attention deficit hyperactivity disorder, autism, too much pressure at mealtime, punishment for not eating, lack of variety in diet
School age and the teenage years	Limited diet and few accepted foods, eating different foods than the rest of the family, high awareness of food imperfections, "white" food diet, anxiety or fear of new foods, difficulty in social eating situations, overweight or underweight (depending on diet makeup)	Any of the factors already listed; learned behavior

If you suspect you've got more than a picky eater, dig deeper. Start with the pediatrician first, and if you feel you need more help, seek an evaluation with an occupational therapist or a speech therapist specializing in feeding therapy. Optimize nutrition and texture transitions with a registered dietitian. The feeding dynamic at home often complicates things further, so you may need help in this area too.

WHAT

Start a positive and systematic approach at home, focused on improving nutrition and accumulating new foods. Offer meals with a variety of foods, even foods that are challenging. There should be no mandates, rewards, tricks, or punishments for eating or not—merely bring the normal family meal to the table and include the foods your child will eat too. Family-style service is effective, as it exposes your child to the whole meal, but allows him to select foods he's comfortable eating.

Consider starting a multivitamin supplement to cover nutrient gaps until your child's food repertoire expands. For example, if your child isn't eating fruits and vegetables, or much meat, we advise a multivitamin and mineral supplement that includes zinc and iron. Target foods with key nutrients and textures that are well tolerated.

HOW

The number one goal for helping problem feeders is to create an environment in which there is positive reinforcement of normal, healthy eating patterns.[23] This is a challenging area, as problem feeders often have experienced negative feedback from the sensory components of food, *and* they've been pressured to eat.

The key to accepting a new food is repeated exposure and tasting it. Playing with food helps too, and is often a first step with young children. We remind you that there is a delicate balance to strike—you want to have your child taste new foods, but you don't want to overwhelm him, pressure him, or turn him off. Introduce *small* amounts (a lick or bite, or simply present on the table) of new foods alongside accepted foods. Watch out for your child's negative reactions—if they are strong, hold off on offering that food until a later time, as keeping the experience positive is key. Table 7.6 provides more things you can do at home; seek the help of a professional if you need help with these approaches.

Table 7.6 What You Can Do at Home with the Problem Feeder

Approach	What Is It?	Examples
Prechaining	For infants who are unable to eat or are having difficulty eating during the first year of life, this approach introduces new foods and textures in an attempt to keep children on track with the developmental norms of feeding.	Introduce very small amounts of food on a daily basis. Dip utensils into pureed foods so that infants can maintain tolerance to tastes and textures of foods until their swallowing or eating skills improve.
Food chaining	This method identifies the current and accepted foods in your child's diet and their characteristics (crunchy, smooth, spicy, sweet, bland, and so on). It creates a bridge or link (chaining) to new foods. The base of the diet is tolerated foods, and new foods with similar characteristics are gradually offered. This allows the child to be exposed to one or two foods at a time. Any new food that is even moderately accepted becomes part of what is offered routinely.	If your child eats apples, then she might like pears; if she loves pasta or noodles, then try different shapes, like rotini and macaroni; if saltines are a comfort food, expand into different flavors and shapes, like butter-style crackers or cheesy crackers. If she gravitates toward colorless foods or white foods, start bringing other similar options into the diet, such as potato, pasta, rice, bread, corn, and so on. Match properties of the foods she likes to new foods with similar characteristics.
Setting up expectations	Use dialogue or actions with each new food to prepare your child for taste, texture, temperature, and so on.	Describe the characteristics of food, such as sour, bitter, spicy, crunchy, lumpy, or tough. Relate how new foods feel in the mouth to the feel of familiar foods in your child's repertoire. Bang a hard food on the table to demonstrate that teeth will need to bite hard to break the food apart.
Pairing the old with the new	This approach builds security, as children can see familiar foods.	Add one new food to an otherwise familiar meal and offer it in small portions.
Role modeling	The child observes other people eating.	Overemphasize chewing and swallowing; be positive about food; and comment on flavor. Avoid negative comments or making faces when eating.

Nutrition and Behavior

Behavioral conditions such as attention deficit hyperactivity disorder (ADHD) are diagnosed more than ever before. With 8 to 12 percent of children affected worldwide, many experts are investigating the role of nutrition in modifying behavior, improving learning and attention, and reducing hyperactivity.[24] Although the hallmark of ADHD management is medication and behavioral therapy, improving nutrition is a complementary approach that can enhance your child's well-being.

The brain uses glucose (from foods that are eaten and digested) for normal functioning, but it doesn't have much storage space. This means the brain needs regular exposure to food and nutrients (for example, reliable meals and snacks). Research also identifies specific nutrients that may have a role in hyperactivity, concentration, and attention difficulties associated with ADHD, as outlined in Table 7.7. Not all children's symptoms will improve through addressing these nutrients, but some will, particularly for those whose diet is low in nutrients like iron, polyunsaturated fatty acids, and zinc.[25,26] You can find food sources of these nutrients in Appendices B and G.

Table 7.7 The Role of Nutrients in ADHD

Nutrient	What It Does	Findings in ADHD	Supplementation	Dose
Zinc	Zinc is required for brain development. It is involved in protein and enzyme activity in the brain, and is key in neurotransmission.	Lower zinc levels are associated with inattention in children with ADHD, but not with impulsivity or hyperactivity.	Improvement of symptoms may occur with supplementation in zinc-deficient children with ADHD.	Doses vary. Check with your health care provider.

Table 7.7 *(continued)*

Nutrient	What It Does	Findings in ADHD	Supplementation	Dose
Iron	Iron contributes to the structure and function of the central nervous system and to neurotransmission. It protects against lead exposure.	Poor cognitive development is associated with iron deficiency. Iron deficiency is also associated with restless leg syndrome.	Iron supplementation may not be effective in children with ADHD who are not iron-deficient. Iron supplementation in children with low iron levels may improve restless leg syndrome. More research is needed.	Recommended doses vary based on the research study. Consult your physician or health care professional.
Magnesium	Magnesium is needed for energy metabolism, blood flow, and synaptic nerve cell signaling. It helps regulate nerve and muscular excitability.	Low levels of magnesium may be seen in children with ADHD.	Supplementation may improve distractibility and reduce hyperactivity. More studies are needed.	Studies used 100 to 200 milligrams of supplemental magnesium per day.[26] Consult with your physician before attempting supplementation.
Omega-3 fatty acids (fish oil with eicosapentaenoic acid [EPA], DHA)	DHA is critical for nerve cell myelination and neural transmission. EPA is involved in brain circulation.	Low levels of omega-3 polyunsaturated fatty acids (PUFAs) are seen in children with ADHD. EPA is more effective than DHA in augmenting treatment of ADHD, although more studies are needed.[27]	Fatty acid deficiency is linked to problematic behavior in ADHD. PUFA supplementation is modestly effective in improving attention, hyperactivity, impulsivity, and literacy. Research suggests efficacy with higher EPA doses (500 to 600 milligrams).[27] Side effects of supplementation with PUFAs are negligible.[25]	*Omega-3:* 300 to 600 milligrams per day for two to three months are recommended.[25] Consult with your physician. *Omega-6:* 30 to 60 milligrams per day for two to three months are recommended.[25] Consult your physician.

Food additives and preservatives, colors and dyes, salicylates, and sugar may make behavior worse in children with ADHD who are *sensitive* to these food components.[25] These kids do best with avoidance. Remember, not all children with ADHD are sensitive, and narrowing the diet may do more harm than good. Check with your health care provider before eliminating foods from, or otherwise altering, your child's diet.

Historically, several diet approaches have been used to treat ADHD, including elimination or hypoallergenic diets (avoiding such foods as dairy, wheat, nuts, eggs, and citrus for two to three weeks, with gradual reintroduction of possible trigger foods) and the Feingold diet (avoidance of food additives and dyes). These may be helpful for some children with ADHD, but experts conclude that there is insufficient evidence to support the use of these diets for *all* children with ADHD.[24]

Children with ADHD often have a poor diet and rigid food preferences, and they may be problem feeders. They may have low appetite from medications and not gain weight well or grow adequately, and they may have nutrient deficiencies. Because of these, we find that many children with ADHD need a nutrition overhaul. According to Judy Converse, registered dietitian and author of *Special-Needs Kids Eat Right,* "Nutrition always matters, for any child. There is no one best set of recommendations for ADHD other than to be curious about whether your child is missing nutrients critical for learning. The usual suspects here are minerals, enough total calories during school and at breakfast, and proteins that are not inflammatory or allergenic."

Using the Fearless Feeding Strategy, here's how you can help your child at home:

WHAT

If your child favors processed fare or sweets, you'll want to tip the balance toward more natural, wholesome foods and weed out artificial food dyes and food additives. Emerging research on nutrition and ADHD favors a wholesome approach, including an "ADHD-free healthy diet" (see Table 7.8).[25] Correcting deficiencies in nutrients, such as iron, magnesium, and zinc, and attempting omega-3 fatty acid supplementation are also recommended.[24,26,27] Consider a

Table 7.8 Healthy Diet for Children with ADHD

Food Component	What to Do	Examples
Fiber	Offer more whole grains, fruits, vegetables, nuts, seeds, and beans in the daily diet.	Include whole grain cereals, breads, and crackers; fresh or frozen fruit or vegetables; dried fruit; nuts or seeds; and beans.
Folate	Offer more folate-containing foods in the daily diet.	Include fortified breads, bagels, muffins, cereals, and other products; orange juice; and beans, egg noodles, rice, and other sources of folate (see Appendix B).
PUFAs	Include more sources of plant-based fats and fish to optimize the flow of omega-3 fatty acids to the brain. Consider omega-3 and omega-6 fatty acid supplements.	Include vegetable, safflower, sunflower, and canola oils; nuts and nut butters; avocado; and fish.
Micronutrients	More food sources rich in iron, zinc, and magnesium should be included. If deficiency exists, supplement with iron, zinc, and magnesium.	See Appendix B for food sources. Check for dietary deficiency first. Use supplements under the guidance of a professional.
Processed foods	Limit these in the diet.	Choose natural, wholesome foods that have undergone minimal processing. Some children may be sensitive to *additives:* aspartame, monosodium glutamate, nitrates and nitrites, and sodium benzoate; *artificial food colors and dyes:* Allura Red (Red #40), Tartrazine (Yellow #5), and Sunset Yellow (Yellow #6); *natural salicylates:* almonds, oranges, strawberries, raspberries, apples, cherries, grapes, peaches, cucumbers, plums, and tomatoes; and *refined sugar.*

Source: Adapted from Millichap, J. G., & Yee, M. M. (2012). The diet factor in attention-deficit/hyperactivity disorder. *Pediatrics, 129,* 330–337.

nighttime smoothie, snack, or shake to improve calorie intake, if your child is underweight.

HOW

We emphasize nutrition that is optimal for the brain, but this doesn't mean eating around the clock! Keep a structured routine of meals and snacks, offered in a timely manner, as discussed in the age-specific chapters. As usual, an authoritative feeding style and some of the strategies outlined in the section on problem feeders work with children who are leery of new foods and have a limited diet. Approach diet changes slowly, picking one aspect of the diet to improve and allowing your child to get used to it. For example, if your child is keen on sugar-sweetened cereals, introduce less sugary cereals with fewer additives and colorings. Move on to tackling other foods next. Get the whole family involved in healthier eating, as it's easier for your child to make changes if everyone is doing it. Don't be lured by diet fads and claims. Every child is different—her nutritional needs, her growth phase, and her food sensitivities. If your child is struggling with nutrition, get help from a professional, so that nutrition interventions can be tailored to the specific needs of your child.

Whether you have a childhood nutrition problem in your household or not, the Fearless Feeding Strategy is a comprehensive way to address challenges and ultimately promote better nutrition and growth. There's a lot you can do at home to navigate nutrition challenges, but sometimes professional help is needed. Be sure to access health care professionals early on, especially if you are faced with an eating disorder, a problem feeder, weight issues, food allergies, or behavioral conditions that interfere with nutrition and growth. We believe in being proactive and heading off bigger problems before they get out of hand. That's what Fearless Feeders do!

CHAPTER 8

Getting Meals on the Table

Meal Planning and Shopping Strategies

I n every family there is someone who takes the lead with meal planning, grocery shopping, and cooking. Research conducted by Brian Wansink shows that this individual—whom he calls the nutritional gatekeeper—determines about 72 percent of food the family eats.[1] Nutritional gatekeepers also have an impact on the food children eat outside the home by packing lunches and giving money for food purchases. Yet it's all too easy for parents to feel like they have lost control, when this couldn't be further from the truth.

The problem is that few parents have modern-day role models for what nutritional gatekeeping should look like. Although your grandmother probably spent much of her time shopping for food and making items from scratch, most busy parents simply can't afford this luxury. Adding to the dilemma is the complexity of the food supply, confusing nutrition information, and cooking skills not always having been handed down from parents.

"I've been really feeling lately that my generation did not have adequate training for organizing shopping lists, running households, and so on," says Mandi. "All that home economics stuff went out of style. And now, with a bigger push for greener and more sustainable living, it's greatly needed again."

The goal for this chapter is to provide twenty-first-century strategies for making meals convenient, without sacrificing health or taste. We know there is a way of planning, shopping, and cooking that is perfect for you, and we want to help you get there. We start by providing guidance on what makes a healthy meal and how to ensure variety. Next, we highlight real-life examples so you can discover the meal planning system (or combination) that works for you. We then offer a fearless grocery store tour and tackle the tough questions about the food you buy. We end with some ideas to get you cooking.

Fearless Nutrition Must-Haves

When it comes to planning healthy meals, we aren't going to ask you to count carbohydrates, proteins, or fat grams or memorize the colors of the rainbow. The key to picking meals for your family is based on good old-fashioned food groups—the same ones we outline in the Fearless Food Guide (see Appendix A). Like everything in this book, these aren't strict rules, but goals to work toward. Of course, you'll want to consider your family's food preferences, but without goals it will be much more difficult to plan meals.

For main meals, shoot for four to five food groups, and target two to three at snacks. Table 8.1 shows you how to maximize food groups at main meals, and Appendix C can help you choose snacks.

Once you get the hang of using food groups, you'll want to expand the variety. For example, the veggie group has five subgroups: dark-green vegetables, red and orange vegetables, beans and peas, starchy vegetables, and other vegetables. There are many different protein sources to choose from, including meat, poultry, eggs, nuts, seeds, soy products, beans, and peas. Rotating different items within the groups enhances variety (and exposure for kiddos) along with nutritional intake. To make it simple for you, we provide some easy-to-remember "rules of thumb" here:[2]

Vegetables: *Weekly rule of three, four, and fives.* Offer three servings per week of dark-green vegetables (broccoli, spinach); four of other vegetables (zucchini, asparagus); five of starchy vegetables (potatoes, corn); and five of red and orange vegetables (carrots, red peppers).

Fruit: *Daily rule of C.* Provide at least one vitamin C–rich source daily (oranges, strawberries).

Grains: *Daily rule of half.* Make at least half of your grains whole.

Protein: *Weekly rule of two, two, four.* Provide two servings a week of seafood, two of beans and legumes, and four of nuts and nut butters. Choose meat, poultry, and eggs on other days. For vegetarian families, rotate plant sources of protein, such as nuts and seeds, soy products, and beans and peas, to increase variety.

Dairy and nondairy: *Offer it daily.* Serve dairy or a nondairy alternative daily with meals, referring to the Fearless Food Guide in the age-specific chapters for more information.

Table 8.1	Balanced Meals
Example	**Dinner (Four to Five Food Groups)**
Example 1	Traditional Meal
Start with . . .	Lean protein, such as chicken, lean beef, pork, or fish
Round it out with . . .	Grain (brown rice) Veggies (roasted broccoli) Fruit (grapes and apple slices) Dairy (milk)
Example 2	Vegetarian Meal
Start with . . .	Protein sources, such as beans, soy products, or nuts and seeds
Round it out with . . .	Grain (quinoa) Veggies (sautéed carrots and peas) Fruit (pear slices) Nondairy alternative (soymilk)
Example 3	Soups and Stews
Start with . . .	Protein sources, such as lean ground beef, beans, and tofu in lasagna, casseroles, or soups or stews
Round it out with . . .	Side salad, fruit, or veggie; dairy; or other food groups missing in the dish

Now that you have some guidelines, you'll want to start planning meals. We've got some ideas for you!

Planning Meals

"I am so aware of the tips and tricks of preorganizing meals and different hints, I don't think I can read another article about it," says Jennifer. "The challenge is to actually put the plans in motion and find a suggestion that fits our lifestyle." We certainly don't want to rehash information that is unrealistic or doesn't fit you or your life. Instead, we want to inspire you with examples of moms who have found a system that works with their lifestyle. Let's take a look.

Fearless Tips

- Do as much prepreparation as you can so the meal runs smoothly (chop the night before, roast veggies during the day).
- Always carry ingredients for a few default meals (spaghetti, quesadillas, premade frozen items, and so on) so you have alternatives if making the planned meal doesn't work out.
- Make up theme nights (Mexican, Italian, or stir-fry night) with familiar sides to make meal planning easier.
- Keep coupons and items on sale in mind when planning your weekly menu. Look at Appendix E for money-saving resources.

Weekly Planner

Planning meals a week ahead of time is the most recommended strategy— and one that Cecily, mom of two, has been using since becoming a parent. "I cannot imagine *not* planning meals," she says. "But it also fits my personality—if it's not in the schedule it doesn't get done."

Cecily starts with evening meals, Monday through Friday, looking at what is going on each day, whether her husband is home, and what the schedule entails. She looks to maximize variety with different protein sources (white meat, red meat, fish) and meat-free meals, and varies the sides, such as pasta, rice, and potato. She chooses the vegetables to help round out the color of the meal. She'll jot down lunch ideas to guide her grocery purchases. Finally, breakfast is most flexible, and she has a rotation of what she serves. She shops for all the food on Monday.

Freezer Mama

Making meals ahead of time and freezing them has become a popular strategy with busy parents. When Marisa was pregnant with her third child, she knew something had to change or dinner wasn't going to happen. "I was afraid I wouldn't be able to get dinner together every night with two small children and a newborn running me ragged," she says. "Even though I had a full-size freezer in my garage with all the basics on hand, I still didn't have a plan for what to cook for dinner every night."

Marisa started freezing easy meals like lasagna, quiche, and shepherd's pie. She found it much easier to put together a huge grocery list, prepare everything, and freeze the meals so that she wouldn't be running to the store throughout the week with three kids in tow. She divides all the meals into appropriate portions for her family size so they rarely have leftovers and waste. "In a typical week we use three to four frozen meals, and the rest we make fresh," she says. "The sides to the entrées are almost always fresh because we make a few vegetables, like bell peppers, carrots, and broccoli—items that hold up well in the fridge for a week at a time." Whenever her freezer starts to look understocked, she gets to work looking through her cookbooks.

Local Foodie

Liz Weiss and Janice Newell Bissex, authors of the family cookbook *No Whine with Dinner: 150 Healthy, Kid-Tested Recipes from the Meal Makeover Moms* and founders of the website Meal

Fearless Tips

- When making a meal, double or triple it, and freeze (especially family favorites).
- Find resources on freezing meals, such as www.onceamonthmom.com and the book *Don't Panic—Dinner's in the Freezer* (see Appendix E).
- You can freeze almost anything except canned food or eggs in shells. Other foods that don't freeze well include mayonnaise, fried food, uncooked potatoes, cream sauce, and lettuce.[3]

Makeover Moms, have worked local produce into their meals by joining a local Community Supported Agriculture (CSA). Each week they each receive a basket of the season's freshest fruits, vegetables, and herbs. They come up with recipes that use those ingredients—sometimes on the fly, and other times with the help of food blogs and Google. "The CSA produce is fresh and flavorful, and it supports local farmers," says Weiss. "The weekly deliveries often prompt me to try new ingredients or come up with clever ways to enjoy the same ingredient week after week."

Being an experienced cook is helpful. "With a CSA membership, it's not always possible to plan your week's meals," says Newell Bissex. "You have to be willing to cook last-minute, tossed-together meals!" Their biggest dilemmas are what to do when they are away on vacation and dealing with the items that no one wants to touch. A lot of effort goes into giving away the radishes that always seem to arrive in the early summer delivery! But they both think it's worthwhile, and the benefits far outweigh even the slightest inconveniences.

Fearless Tips

- To find a CSA, go to www .localharvest.org/csa/. Try it for one month and see how it goes—it might work better than you think!
- Start with ordering half a box, as the family-size box may be too big for some.
- Keep the fridge and pantry stocked with basics to make meals at a moment's notice.
- If subscribing to a CSA isn't for you, consider visiting farmers' markets or local stores for seasonal produce.

What's most important is finding a system that works with your cooking skills, financial situation, food preferences, and stage of parenting. Now that you've planned the meals, it's time to get the food!

Getting the Food

If only there were one place that had everything you needed! Although the sheer volume of grocery stores can be overwhelming, it's nice to have choice and flexibility.

Shopping Choices

Some families turn to wholesale clubs for bulk shopping. These warehouses are a good fit for big families with adequate storage space. It's a good idea for stocking up on staples, such as frozen meats and fish, canned items, and even produce (if your family can eat it in time). Although there is an annual fee to become a member, many families feel bulk purchasing is worth it. Make sure to compare prices, as items sold in bulk aren't always a better deal.

Traditional grocery stores offer well-known brands, off-label products, and other conveniences. More and more, traditional stores are carrying organic, specialty items; private labels; family packs; and bulk bin items. Many of these stores will have coupons and discounts for those who shop frequently.

There is also a wide variety of health food stores. Some of these stores focus on organic food and natural products but may be pricey. Others are more economical, but don't have the other conveniences traditional stores have (items like storage bags, straws, medicines, and so on). Farmers' markets and CSAs provide organic and local food. You will still need to supplement these purchases with items at other stores.

We suggest surveying all the options near you, writing down attractive products, prices, and other considerations important to you to help you decide where to shop. For example, Joyce stocks up monthly at wholesale clubs and her favorite health food store for nonperishable items (see Table 8.2), leaving her weekly shopping to farmers' markets and the traditional grocery store near her. Generate a list of items you use regularly so weekly trips can be short and sweet, used for picking up mostly perishable items like dairy products, meats, and fresh fruits and vegetables.

Fearless Grocery Store Tour

Let's take you through each area of the grocery store so you can become a fearless shopper. To keep from bogging you down with all the nutrition details here, we've included our list of claims (per food group) in Appendix F.

Produce

When you stroll through the produce aisle, you want to consider where fruits and vegetables come from, what's in season, and how it was farmed (organic versus

Table 8.2	Items to Keep on Hand	
Food Items	**What to Buy in Bulk**	**Tip**
Canned and jarred items	Canned tomatoes; tomato sauce; tomato paste; beans; green chili; soups; broths; pasta sauces (red and white); tuna; chicken	Note what canned items you use often and stock up. Pasta sauces are great for last-minute meals!
Grains, beans	Couscous; rice (brown, white, jasmine, and wild); barley; quinoa; dried pasta (whole grain, regular, and in a variety of shapes); dried beans; cereals; oats; nuts	On weekends, make beans in the Crock-Pot or a tasty side of grains, and refrigerate or freeze what you cook to use on busy weekdays.
Frozen foods	Meats, shrimp, and fish; fruits and veggies	Use frozen fruit for smoothies and frozen veggies at the end of the week when fresh produce runs out.
Condiments, oils, spices	Ketchup; mustard (Dijon and yellow); soy sauce; commonly used oils; vinegar; salt and pepper; pepper sauce; dry spices; honey; molasses; syrup; yeast for baking; herb and spice pastes (garlic, ginger, basil, cilantro, and so on); lemon juice (or fresh lemons); garlic; shallots; onions	Make a homemade salad dressing each week for salads. Make a marinade for lean meats using vinegar, oil, garlic, and spices.
Baking goods	Flour; sugar (white, brown, and powdered); butter; canola oil; chocolate chips; chopped nuts; oats (old fashioned and quick cooking); baking powder; baking soda; salt; vanilla extract; wheat germ and flax meal; spices; dried fruit	Flax meal and wheat germ give regular baked goods, like pancakes and waffles, a nutritional boost.

conventional). In Chapter Two, we point out fruits and veggies that contain higher levels of pesticide residues (with thinner skins, like peaches) and those with lower residues (with thick skins, like bananas), so you can streamline organic purchases. "An easy way to identify organic produce is to look for the number 9 preface on the Universal Product Code," says Leah McGrath, registered dietitian for Ingles Markets (based in Black Mountain, North Carolina). Our fruit and veggie list in Appendix D gives you the lowdown on seasonality, nutrition, storage, and ideas for preparation.

> **Fearless Tip**
>
> Choose seasonal items as often as possible, which are less expensive and are nutrient-rich, supplementing with frozen and canned items that are off season (look for "U.S. Grade A" or "U.S. Fancy" on packages to find the best-quality product). Plan meals so you use the fresh produce early in the week, and leave frozen and canned items for the end of the week.

Dairy

When we walk people through the dairy aisle, one of the first questions we get is about organic milk. According to the National Dairy Council, milk is among the agricultural products with the lowest detectable pesticide residues, and is tested for antibiotics and thrown out if any levels are found.[4] With "USDA Organic" milk, you can be assured the cows are not given added hormones or antibiotics, and are fed organic feed and given "access to pasture." All cows have the natural protein hormone bovine somatotropin (bST), which helps them produce milk. In some cases, dairy farmers supplement cows with man-made recombinant bST, or rbST, to increase conventional milk production. The U.S. Food and Drug Administration (FDA) says there isn't a significant difference between cows given rbST and not, but other experts say that the slightly higher levels of insulin-like growth factor and the higher risk of infections (mastitis) in hormone-treated cows are of concern, even though the evidence is inconclusive.[5,6]

Another consideration is the fat content of dairy products. Although some researchers question whether saturated fat from dairy has the same negative effects

Fearless Tip

All pasteurized milk is safe to drink—the choice for your child is yours. We suggest choosing lower-fat cheeses (Parmesan, part-skim ricotta, mozzarella, low-fat cottage cheese) more often than higher-fat items (cheddar, provolone, Swiss). Choose yogurt with live active cultures and not items that have been "heat treated," which decreases their beneficial bacteria.

Fearless Fact

Cage-free eggs come from hens living in barns or warehouses with more space, but they usually don't have outdoor access. *Free-range* or *free-roaming* hens live cage-free and are given outdoor access without specific requirements for how much time is spent outdoors. *USDA Organic* eggs come from hens not living in cages that are given organic (vegetarian) feed and have access to the outdoors. The first two claims (cage-free and free range) are not certified by a third party, and may not add much value. Check out the full list of claims in Appendix F.

as other sources on cardiovascular health, there isn't compelling evidence for recommending full-fat dairy products.[7] In addition, an ongoing clinical trial following children from seven months to nineteen years showed that families counseled on foods low in saturated fat had children who not only ate less of this type of fat but also had lower low-density lipoprotein cholesterol (the bad kind) over time.[8] We recommend watching (not eliminating) fat intake from dairy products—to save room for the healthy fats from plants and fish.

Eggs

Eggs contain high-quality protein; vitamins A and D; selenium; choline; and B vitamins. According to new research from the U.S. Department of Agriculture (USDA), eggs have less cholesterol than previously thought—about 185 milligrams per egg.[9] Growth hormones are never fed to hens raised for egg laying—this was outlawed in the 1960s. Hens are rarely given antibiotics. If they are, FDA requires a withdrawal period to make sure eggs are free of antibiotics.[10] Another concern is how the hens are treated and housed.

Hens are typically fed a diet of mostly corn, soybean meal, and vitamins and minerals (organic eggs get organic vegetarian feed), yet their diet can be manipulated with flax, fish meal, or algae to increase omega-3 fatty acids like docosahexaenoic acid (DHA). We believe all eggs are a good choice, and the label can help you make the best choice for your family. Make sure you choose eggs that are refrigerated; have uncracked shells; aren't out of date; and contain the USDA grade mark, meaning the eggs have been checked for quality and size.[11]

Meat, Poultry, and Pork

Safety and labeling of meat, poultry, and eggs are monitored by the Food Safety and Inspection Service, a public health agency of the USDA.[12] The first consideration when buying meat is how it was raised. We know some of you are concerned with the use of hormones, which are not allowed in poultry or hogs at all. Trace hormones, regulated by FDA, are often used in cows to enhance meat production.[13] In April 2012, FDA issued voluntary guidelines to encourage the judicious use of antibiotics, to be used solely to treat sick animals (and not for muscle growth and the prevention of illness)—but time will tell if these guidelines are effective.[14] With organic meat, livestock are never given antibiotics (or hormones, in animals allowed to get them). Effective January 2012, nutrition labeling is *required* for major cuts of single-ingredient meats and ground meat, poultry included.[15] We recommend lean meats.

> ### Fearless Fact
>
> *Natural* only tells you meat is free of artificial ingredients and added colors, but not how it was raised. A product may not be *USDA Organic,* but other claims like *certified naturally grown* are similar to organic standards. *No antibiotics* means the animal wasn't given antimicrobials.[16] Finances, health, and personal beliefs as well as frequency of meat consumption will affect your purchasing decisions.

A Word on "Grass-Fed" or "Pastured" Animal Products

Sometime during the middle of the twentieth century, ruminant animals (cattle, bison, goats, and sheep) began eating a corn-based diet instead of fresh grass, which meant they put on weight faster.[17] Research shows grass-fed cows produce meat, milk, cheese, and yogurt that contain more favorable fats (less saturated fat), more beneficial conjugated linoleic acid and omega-3 fatty acids, and higher levels of antioxidants.[17,18] Nonruminant animals (pigs and poultry) need to be fed some grain but can benefit from partial grass feeding. True grass-fed products are more expensive and aren't always sold at traditional grocery stores. To find out more, visit the American Grassfed Association (www.americangrassfed.org/).

Seafood

When choosing fish, parents are often conflicted about the health benefits versus the potential toxins, such as polychlorinated biphenyls (PCBs) and mercury. Organizations like KidSafe Seafood (www.kidsafeseafood.org/) help parents figure out which fish are the safest and healthiest to serve kids. Items to watch out for include farmed salmon, shark, swordfish, and king mackerel, as they contain higher levels of PCBs, mercury, or both. The following "best" choices from KidSafe Seafood have low contaminants, are sustainably caught, and have high amounts of omega-3 fatty acids, DHA, and eicosapentaenoic acid (EPA). Other smart choices include canned light tuna and shrimp.

- **Wild Alaskan salmon (chum, coho, sockeye):** Fresh salmon and frozen salmon are good choices, as is canned pink salmon.
- **Farmed rainbow trout:** This type of trout has a mild and nutty flavor. It is also available as boneless fillets, which are easy to prepare.
- **Farmed arctic char:** An alternative to farmed salmon, farmed arctic char is available year-round and can be found fresh, frozen, smoked, and canned.
- **Anchovies:** Anchovies are sold packaged (typically packed in oil) or whole.

- **Wild Atlantic mackerel:** This type of mackerel is available year-round as a fresh, frozen, smoked, pickled, salted, or filleted item.
- **Wild sardines:** Canned sardines are typically available smoked, with mustard flavor, or packed in tomato sauce.

Breads and Grains

Be on the lookout for whole grains, which contain all parts of the naturally occurring grain, including the endosperm, nutrient-rich germ, and fiber-rich bran. A serving of whole grains is sixteen grams—and the Whole Grains Council yellow stamp signifies products with at least half a serving of whole grains (eight grams), letting you know how many grams are in products.[19] Table 8.3 specifies the two different types of stamps used on packages. Refined grains have a majority of the bran and germ removed, resulting in losses of fiber, B vitamins, vitamin E, trace minerals, and many of the phytochemicals. This is why refined grains are enriched with B vitamins and iron (and also fortified with folic acid), thereby adding back important nutrients to a child's diet.[20] In Table 8.3, we provide guidance on what to look for when it comes to grains.

Fats and Oils

All fat sources have the same amount of calories—nine calories per gram. We recommend oils low in saturated fat and high in health-promoting unsaturated fats (monounsaturated and polyunsaturated). But here is where it gets tricky: the American diet has become inundated with omega-6 fats due to the substantial increase of certain oils in the food supply (soybean, sunflower, cottonseed, and corn oils).[21] Some experts believe that this, along with diets too low in omega-3 fats, may contribute to inflammation in the body, increasing the risk for chronic disease.[22] You have the same considerations for spreads like butter and margarine. Butter is high in saturated fat, and traditional margarines contain hydrogenated vegetable oils (hydrogenation being a process that makes vegetable oils "solid" at room temperature), so they contain trans fat—the fat you want to keep to 1 percent of calories or less (two grams or less for a two-thousand-calorie diet).[23]

Research reveals that not all saturated fats are created equal. The types most linked to heart disease are palmitic and myristic acids, which you can find in

Table 8.3	Grain Guidance	
Product	**Helpful Guidelines**	**Comments**
Cereal	• Whole grain as the first ingredient • 3 grams of fiber or more (good source) • Less than 10 grams of sugar (preferably less than 5 grams) • Less than 200 milligrams of sodium	*Look for . . .* • "The 100 Percent Stamp," indicating that all the grains are whole and that the product contains at least 16 grams of whole grains, and "The Basic Stamp," indicating that the product contains at least 8 grams—half a serving—along with some refined grains
Bread	• Whole grain as the first ingredient • 2 grams of fiber or more per slice • Less than 3 grams of sugar • Less than 150 milligrams of sodium	• 100 percent whole grain • FDA-approved whole grain heart disease claim *Watch out for . . .* • "Multigrain," which doesn't always mean whole grain • "Made with whole grains," which can have as little as 10 percent of a whole grain serving
Others	• Whole wheat, whole oats, whole barley, or brown rice as the first ingredient	

Fearless Tip

Two oils with the lowest levels of saturated fats and omega-6 fatty acids are olive oil and canola oil. For frequent use, we recommend olive oil (for sautéing and salad dressings), canola oil (for pan frying and baking), and heart-healthy spreads made with a mixture of vegetable oils. Use butter and other oils less frequently.

butter, cream, meat, and processed food. Some evidence shows that lauric acid (in coconut oil) may not be associated with heart disease, and it is well accepted that stearic acid (in dark chocolate) is not.[2,24]

All the Rest

Convenience items, including canned items, such as vegetables, soups, and broths, as well as jarred goods, such as pasta sauce, peanut butter, salsa, condiments, and salad dressing, take up the remainder of the grocery store. There are deli meats, hot dogs, and cheese and meat combos, and the frozen food aisle is filled with precooked items, desserts, fish, fruits, and veggies. In a perfect world, many of these convenience items would be made from scratch. Although that may be a goal to work toward, at least some of the time it's a good idea to have convenience items on hand that you can feel good about.

Convenience foods often have added sugar, sodium, and fats that need a second look. Some sugar is fine, and can increase palatability (and intake) of nutrient-dense foods like milk, yogurt, and cereals.[25] "Splitting the suggested calories from added solid fats and sugar evenly (5 to 15 percent for *both* solid fats and sugars), older children could have as many as eight teaspoons of added sugar, whereas younger children could have four teaspoons' worth from added sugar," says Elizabeth Ward, registered dietitian and author of *MyPlate for Moms*. "A twelve-ounce can of regular soda provides about twelve teaspoons of added sugar; four crème-filled sandwich cookies, about four teaspoons; and eight ounces of low-fat fruit yogurt, two teaspoons or more." Although no one is asking you to count teaspoons of sugar, watching added sugar in your family's diet is important. Remember, added sugar has many names besides those ending in "-ose," like maltose or dextrose, and include brown rice syrup, high-fructose corn syrup, malt syrup, molasses, cane sugar, corn sweetener, raw sugar, syrup, honey, evaporated cane juice, and fruit juice concentrate.

Sodium is added to convenience items to increase flavor and color, and to inhibit the growth of bacteria. Although sodium is essential in the diet, 90 percent of people get more sodium than they need, with most sources coming from processed foods.[26] "I tell my clients to use the Rule of Five," says Lisa Raum, registered dietitian. "Look at the percent daily value (DV) on the nutrition facts panel: 5 percent or less is low; 10 percent is moderate; 15 percent is significant; 20 percent is high." You'll want to consider the frequency of use, as all foods can fit—even high-sodium ones.

In Table 8.4, we list various convenience foods and what to look for in terms of the sugar, sodium, and fat content, along with best bets.

Although ingredients like sugar and salt have been added to food to keep it fresh for centuries, many believe modern-day additives have gone too far, with over three thousand ingredients in FDA's database! We believe the food supply is

Table 8.4 Navigating Convenience Items

	Sugar	Sodium	Fat	Best Bets!
Beverages	Watch out for "juice drink," "juice cocktail," or "juice blend," which signify little juice and added sugar. Keep other sugar-sweetened beverages, like soda, to special occasions.	Sodium is usually not an issue, except in vegetable juices.	Watch fat sources in coffee drinks and smoothies.	Water, milk, and 100 percent fruit juice are good choices. Try antioxidant-rich juices, such as grape and pomegranate.
Jarred Foods	Tomato-based products naturally have about 5 grams of sugar per serving. Check the ingredients on the label for sources of sugar.	Check claims and consider the percent DV and frequency of use.	Watch out for partially hydrogenated oil in peanut butters, even when these are trans fat–free.	"All-natural" peanut and other nut butters are safe bets, as are pasta sauces made with healthy fats.
Yogurt	Yogurt and other milk products have naturally occurring lactose sugar (12 grams per 6 ounces). Compare plain versions to flavored ones to find added sugar.	Sodium is not usually too high—check the label.	Choose low-fat options.	Plain yogurt with added fruit and nuts is a fine option. Vanilla yogurt tends to have the least amount of added sugar.
Canned Foods	Check the ingredients for unnecessary sources of added sugar.	Products vary widely. Rinse beans and vegetables to reduce the sodium content.	Fat is usually not an issue, but check sources.	Choose reduced- and low-sodium options for frequent use.

Table 8.4	(*continued*)			
	Sugar	**Sodium**	**Fat**	**Best Bets!**
Frozen Foods	The amount of sugar depends on the food item: check for added sugar.	Watch for high sodium content in dinners, entrées, and side dishes.	Watch for cream or butter sauces on vegetables.	Opt for frozen fruit and veggies.
Salad Dressings	Amounts of added sugar in salad dressing vary widely.	Check labels for amounts. Parmesan cheese–based dressings may be higher in sodium.	Watch for high levels of omega-6 fats, as in soybean oil.	Choose salad dressings that use olive or canola oil and have less than 5 grams of sugar per serving.
Snack Foods	Cookies, candy, ice cream, and other dessert-type snacks are high in sugar, which is okay when they are used as Fun Foods.	Chips, crackers, nuts, and other savory snacks may be high in sodium.	Dairy- and grain-based desserts are high in fat, which can be saturated, unsaturated, or trans, so check the ingredients on the label.	Whole grain crackers, popcorn, and nuts and seeds are great choices.

Table 8.5	Super-Easy Meal Ideas	
Protein Power	**Simple Ingredients**	**Directions**
Baked chicken	4 bone-in chicken breasts, 1 tablespoon olive oil, 1 teaspoon kosher salt, ½ teaspoon pepper	Rub the chicken with oil and season with salt and pepper. Bake the chicken in a 425°F oven for 40 minutes. Remove the skin before serving.
Crock-Pot beef	3 to 4 pounds lean beef, cut into 4 or 5 pieces; 1 onion, quartered; ¾ cup water; 1 teaspoon kosher salt; pepper	Place all the ingredients in a Crock-Pot (in this order: onions, beef, water, seasonings) and cook on low for 6 to 8 hours. Shred beef with two forks.
Poached fish	1 to 1½ pounds fresh salmon fillets; ½ cup dry white wine; ½ cup water; 1 shallot, thinly sliced; 3 fresh dill sprigs; 1 fresh parsley sprig; ½ lemon, juice only	Place all the ingredients (except the salmon) in a sauté pan and bring them to a simmer over medium heat. Place the salmon fillets skin-side down, cover, and turn the heat down to low for 5 to 8 minutes.
Tofu	2 tablespoons canola oil; 5 cups chopped veggies (red and yellow peppers, onions, squash, broccoli, bok choy, snow peas); 8 ounces firm tofu, cubed; 1 clove garlic, minced; ½ cup teriyaki sauce; 2 tablespoons sesame oil	Heat the canola oil over high heat in a wok. Add the peppers and onions first. Then add the squash, broccoli, tofu, garlic, and teriyaki sauce (cook for 3 to 4 minutes). Finally, put in any greens, like bok choy (cook for 2 minutes). Stir in the snow peas and sesame oil, and remove from the heat.
Bean soup	1 tablespoon olive oil; 1 onion, diced; 3 garlic cloves, minced; 2 cups dried black beans (soaked overnight); 32 ounces chicken broth or vegetable stock; 2 teaspoons chili powder; 1 teaspoon cumin; 1 teaspoon garlic powder; 1 teaspoon kosher salt	Sauté the onion with oil until soft, and then add the garlic and cook for 1 minute. Pour the onion mixture into the Crock-Pot along with the rest of the ingredients. Cook on low for 8 to 10 hours.

Table 8.5 (*continued*)		
Grain Dishes	**Flavor Booster**	**Directions**
Spanish rice	1 cup rice; 3 tablespoons olive oil; ½ cup chopped onion; 2 garlic cloves, minced; 2 cups chicken broth; 1½ tablespoons tomato paste; ½ teaspoon salt	Sauté the rice in oil until lightly browned; add the onion (cook for 4 minutes); add the garlic (cook for 1 minute). Add the rest of the ingredients and bring everything to boil, then turn down the heat and cover. Cook for 25 minutes, or until the rice absorbs the liquid.
Greek-style couscous	1 cup couscous; ½ cup tomatoes, chopped; ½ cup cucumber, chopped; ¼ cup red onion, chopped; ½ cup Kalamata olives, chopped; ½ cup feta cheese, diced	Cook the couscous according to the package directions. Add the veggies and cheese and toss with lemon vinaigrette (included later in this table).
Earthy quinoa and mushrooms	1 teaspoon olive oil; 1 teaspoon butter; ½ cup onion, diced; ½ cup mushrooms, chopped; 1 cup quinoa; 2 cups beef broth	Melt the butter and oil together; sauté the onion and mushrooms until soft. Add the quinoa and broth, and bring the mixture to a boil. Reduce the heat and cook for 15 to 20 minutes.
Make Your Own Salad		**Mix!**
Choose a combination of lettuce, veggies, nuts, onions, fruit, and any other items your family likes with your favorite dressing (examples of homemade options appear in this row).	*Balsamic:* 3 to 4 parts olive oil to 1 part balsamic vinegar; 1 pinch of brown sugar; 1 garlic clove, crushed *Lemon vinaigrette:* 4 tablespoons lemon juice; 4 tablespoons olive oil; 1 small garlic clove, minced; ½ teaspoon kosher salt; ¼ teaspoon pepper	Blend or whisk together all the ingredients. Consider serving the vegetables separately for kids (or have them make their own combo), allowing them to dip goodies in the dressing.

safe, but we also recommend keeping things simple by choosing items with cleaner lists of ingredients and fewer additives. For those who want to delve deeper, the Center for Science in the Public Interest has a report called *Chemical Cuisine*, which can be accessed online: www.cspinet.org/reports/chemcuisine.htm.

Get Cooking!

Now that you've done your meal planning and shopping, you're ready to start cooking. We know our readers come from various cooking backgrounds. Some of you learned to cook when you were growing up, whereas others are newbies. For those noncooks out there, check out Chapter Five's Real, Easy Recipes section for some of the basics. The good news is that anyone can build rewarding family meals, but it takes time, trial and error, and forethought. Cooking failures not only are bound to happen but also are a necessary part of the process.

For breakfast, consider a regular rotation to keep up the variety, whether it's egg in a hole and waffles for leisurely weekends, or smoothies or cereal for busy days. If you are packing lunches, check out our guide in Appendix C for ideas. For weekends, freeze some items for quick lunches, such as homemade chicken nuggets, bean and cheese burritos, or black bean sliders. Make sure to have salads prepared in the morning, to serve alongside lunch.

When it comes to family dinners, it's smart to gather your recipes and put them in one place, whether it be online, in a word document, or printed in a file folder, so you have access during meal planning, picking old standbys or searching for needed recipes. We find it works well to have a few recipes for each type of protein source—meat, poultry, fish, beans, and soy. It also helps to have a few one-dish meals, like lasagna, casseroles, and favorite slow cooker meals, along with healthy sides. See Table 8.5 for ideas, our resources for cookbooks in Appendix E, and our fruit and veggie lists in Appendix D—and don't forget to search online. Happy cooking!

Fearless Food Guide

Table A.1 Fearless Food Guide[a]

Nourishing Foods[b] are best equipped to provide a majority of the nutrients your child needs on a daily basis. Choose these items more often than Half-and-Half Foods; more whole grains than refined grains; more fresh fruits and vegetables than juices; lean cuts of meat; lower-fat dairy products; and plant and fish sources of unsaturated fat. *Aim to have most of your child's food consumption come from Nourishing Foods.*

Fruits	Vegetables	Grains
Strawberries, oranges, peaches, cantaloupe,[c] honeydew, kiwi, clementines, nectarines, grapefruit, mango,[c] apples, pears, bananas, blueberries, raspberries, watermelon, grapes, prunes, plums, dried fruit	Broccoli,[c] green and red peppers,[c] carrots, kale,[c] spinach,[c] bok choy, salad greens, sweet potatoes,[c] cauliflower, brussels sprouts, turnips, cucumber, zucchini, squash, mushrooms, tomatoes, green beans, sugar snap peas, celery *Starchy vegetables:* peas, corn, potatoes	Whole grain breads; rolls; bagels; whole grain cereals (oatmeal, bran, and shredded wheat); whole wheat waffles and pancakes; brown rice; quinoa; barley amaranth; buckwheat; bulgur (cracked wheat); millet; oatmeal; whole wheat pasta, popcorn; whole grain crackers

Half-and-Half Foods contribute nutrients, but either have been processed or contain more animal fat or sugar. These items add flavor and taste appeal to meals. Choose these items less often than Nourishing Foods, and pay attention to serving size. *Combined with Nourishing Foods, these foods should make up about 90 percent of your child's daily diet.*

Fruits	Vegetables	Grains
100 percent fruit juice Fruit roll-ups made mostly with real fruit Vegetable juice Veggie chips and straws		White bread, white rice, saltine crackers, pretzels, pasta, pancakes, waffles, whole grain chips, pita chips, sweetened cereals (more than 10 grams of sugar per serving), cereal bars, muffins

Meat and Nonmeat	Dairy and Nondairy	Fats
Fish and shellfish	Fat-free or low-fat milk	Olive oil, canola oil, safflower and vegetable oil
Poultry—chicken or turkey with white meat; Cornish hen (no skin)	Reduced-fat cheeses, such as cheddar	Salad dressings made with the oils just listed
Lean meats—lean beef trimmed of fat, more than 90 percent lean ground beef, lean pork	Naturally low-fat cheeses (Parmesan, mozzarella, and provolone)	Avocado and dips
Lean deli meats	Low-fat yogurt	Olives
Peanut butter and other nut butters	Reduced-fat cottage cheese	*Fats with protein:*
Eggs		Hummus, peanut butter or other nut butters, nuts and seeds
Soy		
Beans, other legumes, hummus		

Meat and Nonmeat	Dairy and Nondairy	Fats
Ground beef (90 percent lean or lower)	Whole milk	Salad dressings made with cream, other full-fat dairy sources, or soybean oil
Lean sausage and bacon	Hard cheeses (cheddar and Swiss)	Mayonnaise
Steak, lamb	American cheese	Cream cheese
Beef or pork ribs	Full-fat yogurt	Sour cream
Chicken wings	Chocolate milk	Butter
Turkey legs	Pudding	Margarine
Beef or turkey jerky		Half-and-half

Table A.1	*(continued)*	
Fun Foods tend to be high in sugar and fat with little nutrition, so eat them less frequently and for enjoyment. *Aim for Fun Foods to make up roughly 10 percent of your child's diet, which comes to about one to two Fun Foods per day, depending on age.*		
Fruits	**Vegetables**	**Grains**
Fruit chews, fruit roll-ups made with less than 10 percent real fruit, fruit-flavored drinks, canned fruit in heavy syrup *Other sugary sources:* Sugary candy, sodas, lemonade, sweet tea, sports drinks, Italian ice Fried veggies, such as French fries and vegetable tempura Potato chips		Cake, donuts, candy bars, brownies, pastries, cookies Tortilla chips and others, movie popcorn, candy-coated granola bars

[a] *This guide is for people two years and older (see Chapter Two for the Infant and Young Toddler Feeding Guide).*

[b] *To learn what constitutes a serving for each food group, see the age-specific chapters or visit www.choosemyplate .gov/.*

[c] *This item contains both vitamin A and vitamin C.*

Source: Adapted from the U.S. Department of Agriculture's ChooseMyPlate.gov website (www.choosemyplate .gov/); U.S. Department of Agriculture & U.S. Department of Health and Human Services. (2010). *Dietary guidelines for Americans, 2010* (7th ed.). Washington DC: U.S. Government Printing Office.

Meat and Nonmeat	**Dairy and Nondairy**	**Fats**
Bacon; hot dogs; sausages; spare ribs; salami; deep-fried meats, fish, or tofu	Ice cream and other frozen treats; whipped cream	Shortening, hydrogenated oils, lard

Food Sources
of Nutrients

Table B.1 Food Sources of Calcium

Food	Portion Size	Calcium (Milligrams)
Ready-to-eat cereal, calcium fortified	½ cup	100–1,000
Orange juice, calcium fortified	1 cup	500
Soy beverage, calcium fortified	½ cup	80–500
Yogurt, plain, nonfat	1 cup	452
Cheese, Romano	1½ ounces	452
Yogurt, fruit, low fat	1 cup	338–384
Buttermilk	1 cup	282–350
Cheese, ricotta, part skim	½ cup	337
Cheese, mozzarella, part skim	1½ ounces	333
Sardines, canned in oil, with bones	3 ounces	325
Cheese, cheddar	1½ ounces	307
Milk, low fat (1 percent)	1 cup	305
Milk, nonfat	1 cup	299
Milk, reduced fat (2 percent)	1 cup	293
Chocolate milk, low fat (1 percent)	1 cup	290
Milk, whole (3.25 percent)	1 cup	276
Chocolate milk, reduced fat (2 percent)	1 cup	272
Tofu, firm, made with calcium sulfate[a]	½ cup	253
Instant breakfast drink, various flavors and brands, powder-prepared with water	1 cup	105–250
Salmon, pink, canned, with bones	3 ounces	181
Cottage cheese, low fat (1 percent milk fat)	1 cup	138
Tofu, soft, made with calcium sulfate[a]	½ cup	138
Frozen yogurt, vanilla, soft-serve	½ cup	103

Table B.1 (continued)		
Food	**Portion Size**	**Calcium (Milligrams)**
Turnip greens, fresh, boiled	½ cup	99
Kale, fresh, cooked	½ cup	94
Kale, raw, chopped	1 cup	90
Ice cream, vanilla	1 cup	84
Bok choy, raw, shredded	1 cup	74
Bread, white	1 slice	73
Pudding, chocolate, ready to eat, refrigerated	½ cup	55
Tortilla, corn, ready to bake or fry	1 tortilla (6-inch diameter)	46
Tortilla, flour, ready to bake or fry	1 tortilla (6-inch diameter)	32
Sour cream, reduced fat, cultured	2 tablespoons	31
Bread, whole wheat	1 slice	30
Broccoli, raw	½ cup	21
Cream cheese, regular	1 tablespoon	14

[a] *Calcium content is for tofu processed with a calcium salt. Tofu processed with other salts does not provide significant amounts of calcium.*

Source: Adapted from U.S. Department of Agriculture, Agricultural Research Service. (2012). USDA National Nutrient Database for Standard Reference, release 25. Retrieved from www.ars.usda.gov/ba/bhnrc/ndl.

Table B.2 Food Sources of Docosahexaenoic Acid (DHA) and Alpha-Linolenic Acid (ALA)

Food	Portion Size	DHA (Milligrams)	ALA (Milligrams)
Salmon, Atlantic farmed, baked	3 ounces	1,238	
Salmon, Atlantic wild, baked	3 ounces	1,215	
Tuna, white, packed in water	3 ounces	535	
Sardines, packed in oil, with bones	3 ounces	433	
Tuna, light, packed in water	3 ounces	190	
Eggs, fortified with DHA	1 egg	50–300	
Tuna, light, packed in oil	3 ounces	86	
Milk, DHA fortified	1 cup	32	
Soymilk, fortified	1 cup	30–32	
Yogurt, fortified	½ cup	50–96	
Orange juice, fortified	1 cup	20	
Baby foods, fortified	3 ounces pureed, ¼ cup baby cereal	18	
Flax cereal	¾ cup		1,000
Walnuts	¼ cup		627

Source: Adapted from International Omega-3 Learning and Education Consortium for Health and Medicine, University of Connecticut. (2012). Omega-3 fatty acid content of food products (natural and enriched). Retrieved from www.omega3learning.uconn.edu.

Table B.3 Food Sources of Fiber		
Food	**Portion Size**	**Fiber (Grams)**
Beans (navy, pinto, black, kidney, white, great northern, or lima), cooked	½ cup	6.2–9.6
100 percent bran ready-to-eat cereal	⅓ cup (about 1 ounce)	9.1
Split peas, lentils, chickpeas, or cowpeas, cooked	½ cup	5.6–8.1
Artichoke, cooked	½ cup hearts	7.2
Pear	1 medium	5.5
Soybeans, mature, cooked	½ cup	5.2
Rye wafer crackers, plain	2 wafers	5.0
Bran ready-to-eat cereals (various)	⅓ to ¾ cup (about 1 ounce)	2.6–5.0
Asian pear	1 small	4.4
English muffin, whole wheat	1 muffin	4.4
Peas, green, cooked	½ cup	3.5–4.4
Bulgur, cooked	½ cup	4.1
Mixed vegetables, cooked	½ cup	4.0
Raspberries	½ cup	4.0
Sweet potato, baked in skin	1 medium	3.8
Blackberries	½ cup	3.8
Soybeans, green, cooked	½ cup	3.8
Prunes, stewed	½ cup	3.8
Shredded wheat ready-to-eat cereal	½ cup (about 1 ounce)	2.7–3.8
Figs, dried	¼ cup	3.7

Table B.3 *(continued)*		
Food	**Portion Size**	**Fiber (Grams)**
Apple, with skin	1 small	3.6
Pumpkin, canned	½ cup	3.6
Almonds	1 ounce	3.5
Greens (spinach, collard greens, or turnip greens), cooked	½ cup	2.5–3.5
Sauerkraut, canned	½ cup	3.4
Spaghetti, whole wheat, cooked	½ cup	3.1
Banana	1 medium	3.1
Orange	1 medium	3.1
Guava	1 guava	3.0
Potato, baked in skin	1 small	3.0
Oat bran muffin	1 small	3.0
Pearled barley, cooked	½ cup	3.0
Dates	¼ cup	2.9
Winter squash, cooked	½ cup	2.9
Parsnips, cooked	½ cup	2.8

Source: Adapted from U.S. Department of Agriculture, Agricultural Research Service. (2012). USDA National Nutrient Database for Standard Reference, release 25. Retrieved from www.ars.usda.gov/ba/bhnrc/ndl.

Table B.4 Food Sources of Iron		
Food	**Portion Size**	**Iron (Milligrams)**
Heme Sources		
Chicken liver, pan fried	3 ounces	11
Oysters, canned	3 ounces	5.7
Beef liver, pan fried	3 ounces	5.2
Beef, chuck, blade roast, lean only, braised	3 ounces	3.1
Beef patty, ground, 85 percent lean, broiled	3 ounces	2.2
Turkey, dark meat, roasted	3 ounces	2.0
Beef, top sirloin, steak, lean only, broiled	3 ounces	1.6
Tuna, light, canned in water	3 ounces	1.3
Turkey, light meat, roasted	3 ounces	1.1
Chicken, dark meat, roasted	3 ounces	1.1
Chicken, light meat, roasted	3 ounces	0.9
Tuna, fresh, yellowfin, cooked with dry heat	3 ounces	0.8
Crab, Alaskan king, cooked with moist heat	3 ounces	0.7
Pork, loin chop, broiled	3 ounces	0.7
Shrimp, mixed species, cooked with moist heat	4 large	0.3
Halibut, cooked with dry heat	3 ounces	0.2
Nonheme Sources		
Ready-to-eat cereal, 100 percent iron fortified	¾ cup	18
Oatmeal, instant, iron fortified, prepared with water	1 packet or ½ cup	11
Soybeans, mature, boiled	1 cup	8.8
Lentils, boiled	1 cup	6.6
Beans, kidney, mature, boiled	1 cup	5.2

Table B.4 *(continued)*		
Food	**Portion Size**	**Iron (Milligrams)**
Beans, lima, large, mature, boiled	1 cup	4.5
Ready-to-eat cereal, 25 percent iron fortified	¾ cup	4.5
Black-eyed peas (cowpeas), mature, boiled	1 cup	4.3
Beans, navy, mature, boiled	1 cup	4.3
Beans, black, mature, boiled	1 cup	3.6
Beans, pinto, mature, boiled	1 cup	3.6
Tofu, firm, raw	½ cup	3.4
Spinach, fresh, boiled, drained	½ cup	3.2
Spinach, canned, drained	½ cup	2.5
Spinach, frozen, chopped or leaf, boiled	½ cup	1.9
Raisins, seedless, packed	½ cup	1.6
Grits, white, enriched, quick, prepared with water	1 cup	1.5
Molasses	1 tablespoon	0.9
Bread, white, commercially prepared	1 slice	0.9
Bread, whole wheat, commercially prepared	1 slice	0.7

Source: Adapted from Office of Dietary Supplements, National Institutes of Health. (2007). Dietary supplement fact sheet: Iron. Retrieved from http://ods.od.nih.gov/factsheets/Iron-HealthProfessional/.

Table B.5   Food Sources of Vitamin A

Food	Portion Size	Vitamin A (International Units [IU])
Selected Animal Sources		
Beef liver, cooked	3 ounces	22,175
Milk, nonfat, fortified	1 cup	500
Milk, whole	1 cup	395
Cheese, cheddar	1 ounce	284
Egg, hard-boiled	1 large	260
Selected Plant Sources		
Sweet potato, baked in skin	1 medium	28,058
Carrot juice, canned	½ cup	22,567
Carrots, boiled	½ cup	13,286
Spinach, frozen, chopped or leaf, boiled	½ cup	11,458
Carrots, raw	½ cup	9,189
Kale, boiled	½ cup	8,854
Vegetable soup, canned, chunky, ready to serve	1 cup	5,878
Cantaloupe, cubes	1 cup	5,411
Lettuce, romaine, raw	1 cup	4,878
Spinach, raw	1 cup	2,813
Pepper, red, sweet, raw, sliced	½ cup	2,332
Apricots, canned, packed in juice	½ cup	2,063
Mango, sliced	1 cup	1,785
Peas, green, frozen, boiled	½ cup	1,680
Apricot nectar, canned	½ cup	1,652

Table B.5 *(continued)*		
Food	Portion Size	Vitamin A (International Units [IU])
Papaya, cubes	1 cup	1,330
Broccoli, boiled	½ cup	1,208
Tomato juice, canned	1 cup	1,094
Watermelon, raw	1 cup	865

Source: Adapted from U.S. Department of Agriculture, Agricultural Research Service, Nutrient Data Laboratory. (2012). USDA National Nutrient Database for Standard Reference, release 24. Retrieved from http://www.ars .usda.gov/ba/bhnrc.ndl.

Table B.6 Food Sources of Vitamin D

Food	Portion Size	Vitamin D (Micrograms)[a]
Salmon, sockeye, cooked	3 ounces	19.8
Salmon, smoked	3 ounces	14.5
Salmon, canned	3 ounces	11.6
Rockfish, cooked	3 ounces	6.5
Tuna, light, canned in oil, drained	3 ounces	5.7
Sardines, canned in oil, drained	3 ounces	4.1
Tuna, light, canned in water, drained	3 ounces	3.8
Orange juice, fortified with vitamin D	1 cup	3.4
Milk, whole (3.25 percent)	1 cup	3.2
Chocolate milk, whole (3.25 percent)	1 cup	3.2
Chocolate milk, reduced fat (2 percent)	1 cup	3.0
Milk (nonfat, low fat [1 percent], or reduced fat [2 percent])	1 cup	2.9
Chocolate milk, low fat (1 percent)	1 cup	2.8
Soymilk	1 cup	2.7
Evaporated milk, nonfat	½ cup	2.6
Flatfish (flounder or sole), cooked	3 ounces	2.5
Ready-to-eat cereals (various), fortified	¾ to 1¼ cups (about 1 ounce)	0.9–2.5
Rice drink	1 cup	2.4
Herring, pickled	3 ounces	2.4
Pork (various cuts), cooked	3 ounces	0.6–2.2
Cod, cooked	3 ounces	1.0
Beef liver, cooked	3 ounces	1.0

Table B.6 (continued)		
Food	Portion Size	Vitamin D (Micrograms)[a]
Ham, cured	3 ounces	0.6–0.8
Egg, hard-boiled	1 large	0.7
Mushrooms, shiitake	½ cup	0.6
Canadian bacon	2 slices (about 1½ ounces)	0.5

[a] *1 microgram of vitamin D is equivalent to 40 IU.*

Source: Adapted from U.S. Department of Agriculture, Agricultural Research Service. (2012). USDA National Nutrient Database for Standard Reference, release 25. Retrieved from www.ars.usda.gov/ba/bhnrc/ndl.

Table B.7 Food Sources of Vitamin E

Food	Portion Size	Vitamin E (Milligrams)
Wheat germ oil	1 tablespoon	20.3
Ready-to-eat cereals (various), fortified	¾ to 1⅓ cups (about 1 ounce)	3.2–13.5
Sunflower seeds, dry roasted	1 ounce	7.4
Almonds, dry roasted	1 ounce	6.8
Sunflower oil	1 tablespoon	5.6
Safflower oil	1 tablespoon	4.6
Hazelnuts, dry roasted	1 ounce	4.3
Mixed nuts, dry roasted	1 ounce	3.1
Peanut butter	2 tablespoons	2.9
Pine nuts	1 ounce	2.7
Canola oil	1 tablespoon	2.4
Peanuts, dry roasted	1 ounce	2.2
Corn oil	1 tablespoon	1.9
Olive oil	1 tablespoon	1.9
Spinach, boiled	½ cup	1.9
Sardines, canned in oil, drained	3 ounces	1.7
Brazil nuts	1 ounce	1.6
Orange roughy, cooked	3 ounces	1.6
Avocado	½ cup	1.5
Broccoli, chopped, boiled	½ cup	1.2
Soybean oil	1 tablespoon	1.1
Kiwi	1 medium	1.1
Mango, sliced	½ cup	0.7
Tomato, raw	1 medium	0.7
Spinach, raw	1 cup	0.6

Source: Adapted from U.S. Department of Agriculture, Agricultural Research Service. (2012). USDA National Nutrient Database for Standard Reference, release 25. Retrieved from www.ars.usda.gov/ba/bhnrc/ndl.

Table B.8   Food Sources of Vitamin C

Food	Portion Size	Vitamin C (Milligrams)
Pepper, red, sweet, raw	½ cup	95
Orange juice	¾ cup	93
Orange	1 medium	70
Grapefruit juice	¾ cup	70
Vegetable juice cocktail	1 cup	67
Kiwi	1 medium	64
Ready-to-eat cereals (various), fortified	¾ to 1⅓ cups (about 1 ounce)	26–61
Pepper, green, sweet, raw	½ cup	60
Broccoli, cooked	½ cup	51
Strawberries, fresh, sliced	½ cup	49
Brussels sprouts, cooked	½ cup	48
Papaya	½ cup	43
Grapefruit	½ medium	39
Broccoli, raw	½ cup	39
Honeydew	½ cup	39
Pineapple	½ cup	37
Tomato juice	¾ cup	33
Mango	½ cup	30
Cantaloupe, cubes	½ cup	29
Cabbage, cooked	½ cup	28
Kale, cooked from fresh	½ cup	27
Cauliflower, raw	½ cup	26
Tangerine	1 medium	22

Table B.8 (*continued*)

Food	Portion Size	Vitamin C (Milligrams)
Potato, baked	1 medium	17
Tomato, raw	1 medium	17
Peach	1 medium	10
Spinach, cooked	½ cup	9
Peas, green, frozen, cooked	½ cup	8

Source: Adapted from U.S. Department of Agriculture, Agricultural Research Service. (2012). USDA National Nutrient Database for Standard Reference, release 25. Retrieved from www.ars.usda.gov/ba/bhnrc/ndl.

Table B.9 Food Sources of Zinc

Food	Portion Size	Zinc (Milligrams)
Oysters, cooked, breaded and fried	3 ounces	74
Beans, baked, canned, plain or vegetarian	½ cup	2.9
Beef, chuck roast, braised	3 ounces	7.0
Crab, Alaskan king, cooked	3 ounces	6.5
Beef patty, ground, broiled	3 ounces	5.3
Breakfast cereal, 25 percent zinc fortified	¾ cup	3.8
Lobster, cooked	3 ounces	3.4
Pork, loin chop, cooked	3 ounces	2.9
Chicken, dark meat, cooked	3 ounces	2.4
Yogurt, fruit, low fat	1 cup	1.7
Cashews, dry roasted	1 ounce	1.6
Chickpeas, cooked	½ cup	1.3
Cheese, Swiss	1 ounce	1.2
Oatmeal, instant, plain, prepared with water	1 packet or ½ cup	1.1
Milk, low fat or nonfat	1 cup	1.0
Almonds, dry roasted	1 ounce	0.9
Beans, kidney, cooked	½ cup	0.9
Chicken breast, roasted, skin removed	½ breast	0.9
Cheese, cheddar or mozzarella	1 ounce	0.9
Peas, green, frozen, cooked	½ cup	0.5

Source: Adapted from Office of Dietary Supplements, National Institutes of Health. (2011). Dietary supplement fact sheet: Zinc. Retrieved from http://ods.od.nih.gov/factsheets/zinc-HealthProfessional/.

Table B.10   Food Sources of Potassium

Food	Portion Size	Potassium (Milligrams)
Potato, baked, flesh and skin	1 small	1,081
Prune juice, canned	1 cup	707
Carrot juice, canned	1 cup	689
Tomato paste	¼ cup	664
Beet greens, cooked	½ cup	654
Beans, white, canned	½ cup	595
Yogurt, plain, nonfat or low fat	1 cup	531–579
Tomato juice, canned	1 cup	556
Tomato puree	½ cup	549
Sweet potato, baked in skin	1 medium	542
Clams, canned	3 ounces	534
Orange juice, fresh	1 cup	496
Halibut, cooked	3 ounces	490
Soybeans, green, cooked	½ cup	485
Tuna, yellowfin, cooked	3 ounces	484
Beans, lima, cooked	½ cup	478
Soybeans, mature, cooked	½ cup	443
Rockfish, Pacific, cooked	3 ounces	442
Cod, Pacific, cooked	3 ounces	439
Evaporated milk, nonfat	½ cup	425
Chocolate milk, low fat or reduced fat	1 cup	422–425
Bananas	1 medium	422
Spinach, cooked	½ cup	370–419
Tomato sauce	½ cup	405

Table B.10 *(continued)*		
Food	**Portion Size**	**Potassium (Milligrams)**
Peaches, dried, uncooked	¼ cup	398
Prunes, stewed	½ cup	398
Milk, nonfat	1 cup	382
Rainbow trout, cooked	3 ounces	381
Apricots, dried, uncooked	¼ cup	378
Pinto beans, cooked	½ cup	373
Pork, loin chop, center rib, lean, roasted	3 ounces	371
Milk or buttermilk, low fat	1 cup	366–370
Lentils, cooked	½ cup	365
Plantains, cooked	½ cup	358
Beans, kidney	½ cup	358

Source: Adapted from U.S. Department of Agriculture, Agricultural Research Service. (2012). USDA National Nutrient Database for Standard Reference, release 24. Retrieved from www.ars.usda.gov/ba/bhnrc/ndl.

Healthy Snack Ideas

Table C.1 How to Make a Healthy Snack	
If You Have . . .	**Pair It With . . .**
Yogurt	Fruit, nuts, whole grain cereal, or a combination of these
Whole wheat crackers	Cheese, peanut butter, or cream cheese
Fresh fruit	Cubed cheese, milk, or peanut butter
Cereal	Dry fruit, milk, or soymilk
Whole wheat bread or pita	Deli meat or cheese, tuna, or peanut better and jelly
Raw veggies	Hummus, ranch dressing, guacamole, cream cheese, or any yogurt-based dip
Muffins or sweet bread	Milk, a yogurt drink, or kefir
100 percent fruit juice	Fresh fruit and yogurt, blended for a smoothie
Homemade cookies	Milk or fruit
Whole wheat English muffins or flatbread	Marinara sauce, grated cheese, and any topping (veggies, meat, and so on) for a mini-pizza
Waffles	Low-fat yogurt and sliced fruit
Peanut butter	Apple slices, graham crackers, or flat pretzels
Bananas	Yogurt for dipping, with the whole thing rolled in crushed cereal or nuts and frozen
Celery sticks	Peanut butter, with raisins for the topping
Nuts	Ready-to-eat cereal, dried fruit, and mini–chocolate chips for trail mix
Graham crackers	Frozen yogurt or peanut butter as a spread, topped with sliced banana for a "sandwich"
Baked potato	Reduced-fat cheddar cheese and salsa
Pretzel sticks	Cubes of low-fat cheese, grapes, melon balls, and strawberries, strung for a kabob
Frozen grapes	Cheese cubes, yogurt pretzels, or cheese crackers

Table C.1 (continued)	
If You Have . . .	**Pair It With . . .**
Cheese	A whole wheat tortilla or sandwich wrap, heated and served with salsa
Waffle cone	Cut-up fruit as a filling and low-fat vanilla yogurt as a topping
Granola	Vanilla yogurt and berries, layered for a parfait
Popcorn	Grated Parmesan cheese or cinnamon and sugar as a topping
Salsa (made with tomatoes, or fruit like pineapple, strawberries, or mango)	Baked wheat pita chips, whole grain tortilla chips, or veggie sticks
Cream cheese	A whole wheat tortilla or sandwich wrap, topped with turkey or ham and rolled up, and finally sliced into 1-inch pieces to make pinwheels

Table C.2 Lunch and Snack Packing Template

Lunch[a]	Snacks[b]
Main dish (sandwich, leftovers, salad with protein, and so on) *Veggies* (if vegetables are included in the entrée, you can skip) *Fruit* *Other snacks* (crackers, granola bar, and so on; add them based on appetite) Water or milk *Occasional Fun Food* (petite sweet treats or tortilla chips in small portions)	*Protein* (dairy or nondairy, meat or nonmeat—such as milk, yogurt, cheese, deli meat, a nut butter, or nuts) *Grain or produce* (fruit, vegetable, or grain source—such as grapes, sugar snap peas, whole grain crackers, cereal, or toast) *Fat* (add a fat or not, depending on appetite)

[a] *Try to get as many food groups planned for lunch as possible. Consult the age-specific Fearless Food Guide in Chapters Three through Five for serving sizes.*

[b] *Remember to keep food servings in line with age needs or serving size, and try to choose at least two food groups.*

Source: Contributed by Katie Morford, food and nutrition writer at *Mom's Kitchen Handbook* (www.moms kitchenhandbook.com).

Fruit and Veggie Lists

Table D.1 Fruits

	Peak Season[a]	Selection	Storage	Key Nutrients[b]	How to Prepare
Apples	*September through November*	Look for firm, shiny, and smooth-skinned apples with intact stems.	Refrigerate in a plastic bag away from odorous foods for up to 3 weeks.	Vitamin C	Eat whole or cut in cubes or slices; make applesauce.
Apricots	*May through August*	Look for plump, firm, and uniformly colored apricots.	Store at room temperature until ripe, then in the refrigerator in a plastic bag for 3 to 5 days.	Vitamins A, C, E, and K; niacin; potassium; copper; and manganese	Eat whole; include atop cereal, in yogurt, or in salads.
Avocados	*Year-round*	Look for firm skin and no soft spots.	Store unripe avocados in a paper bag at room temperature. Refrigerate when ripe for 2 to 3 days.	Vitamins C and K; folate; and high levels of monounsaturated fat	Substitute avocado for spreads like mayo, butter, and cream cheese; make guacamole; include avocado in salads; serve avocado raw with a drizzle of olive oil, fresh lemon juice, kosher salt, and pepper.

Table D.1 *(continued)*

	Peak Season[a]	Selection	Storage	Key Nutrients[b]	How to Prepare
Bananas	*Year-round*	Look for slight green on the stem and tip.	Store unripe bananas at room temperature. When bananas are ripe, refrigerate them for up to 2 weeks (skin may turn black).	Vitamins C and B6; magnesium; potassium; and manganese	Freeze for smoothies; bake in breads; make peanut butter and banana sandwiches.
Blackberries	*May through October*	Look for shiny blackberries that are not bruised or leaking.	Refrigerate unwashed blackberries for 3 to 6 days.	Vitamins A, C, E, and K; niacin; folate; iron; magnesium; potassium; zinc; copper; and manganese	Serve on cereals, with yogurt, and in fruit salad; bake in cobblers, muffins, and pancakes.
Blueberries	*May through September*	Look for firm, plump, dry blueberries with dusty blue color and uniform size.	Refrigerate for 10 to 14 days.	Vitamin C; potassium; and manganese	Blueberries are great on yogurt, in cereals, in muffins, in pancakes, and in fruit salad.

Fruit	Season	Selection	Storage	Nutrients	Serving
Cantaloupe	*June through September*	Look for fragrant melons with a yellow or cream undertone and a stem end that gives to gentle pressure.	Store at room temperature for up to 1 week. Refrigerate cut melons in an airtight container for up to 5 days.	Vitamins A, C, K, and B6; thiamin; niacin; folate; magnesium; and potassium	Melons can be cut into halves, quarters, wedges, or cubes; or they can be scooped into balls with a melon baller.
Cherries (Bing, Lambert, Rainier)	*June through August*	Look for firm, red cherries with stems attached.	Refrigerate for up to 10 days.	Vitamin C; potassium; and manganese	Eat whole.
Dates	*August through December*	Look for dates that are shiny, uniformly colored, and not broken.	Store at room temperature in an airtight container for several months, or refrigerate for up to a year.	Vitamins K and B6; thiamin; riboflavin; niacin; folate; pantothenic acid; calcium; iron; magnesium; phosphorous; potassium; copper; manganese; and selenium	Serve on hot cereal; bake in breads and muffins.

Table D.1 (*continued*)

	Peak Season[a]	Selection	Storage	Key Nutrients[b]	How to Prepare
Grapefruit (White, Pink)	*October through June*	Look for thin, smooth, firm skin; fruit should be heavy for its size.	Store at room temperature for 1 week, or refrigerate for 2 to 3 weeks.	*White:* Vitamins C and B6; thiamin; folate; pantothenic acid; magnesium; potassium; copper; and selenium *Pink:* Vitamins A, C, and B6; thiamin; folate; pantothenic acid; calcium; magnesium; and potassium	Eat whole; include in green and fruit salads.
Grapes	*July through December*	Look for grapes that are free from surface wrinkles and firmly attached to the stem.	Store unwashed and in plastic in the fridge for up to 1 week.	Vitamins C, K, and B6; thiamin; riboflavin; potassium; copper; and manganese	Eat grapes whole; include them chopped in salads; try frozen.

Honeydew	*May through October*	Look for honeydew with a creamy yellow color and slightly waxy skin; melons should be heavy for their size.	Store honeydew in the refrigerator for up to 2 weeks.	Vitamins C, K, and B6; folate; and potassium	Include in fruit salad.
Kiwi	*October through May*	Look for slightly firm kiwi with rough, fuzzy skin.	Store for several days at room temperature, or store unripe kiwi in plastic bags in the refrigerator for up to 6 weeks.	Vitamins C, E, and K; folate; potassium; and copper	Eat whole by scooping the flesh out with a spoon; slice; include in fruit salad.
Mandarins, Clementines, Tangerines	*November through April*	Look for unblemished fruits that are heavy for their size.	Refrigerate for up to 2 weeks.	Vitamins A and C; and potassium	Peel and eat whole; include in green salad; use zest of the rind for marinades and dressings.

Table D.1 (continued)

	Peak Season[a]	Selection	Storage	Key Nutrients[b]	How to Prepare
Mangoes	*July through October*	Look for slightly firm mangoes with a sweet aroma.	Store at room temperature for 1 to 2 days. Once mangoes are ripe, refrigerate for up to 3 days.	Vitamins A, C, E, K, and B6; and copper	Eat whole; include in fruit salad and salsas.
Nectarines	*May through September*	Look for firm nectarines with smooth skin.	Store unripe nectarines in a paper bag until ripe, then store at room temperature for use within 2 to 3 days.	Vitamins A, C, and E; niacin; potassium; and copper	Roast nectarines; eat whole.
Oranges (Also See Mandarins)	*November through April*	Look for firm, smooth skin; oranges should be heavy for their size.	Store at room temperature for 1 to 2 days. Refrigerate for 1 to 2 weeks.	Vitamins A, C, and B6; thiamin; folate; calcium; and potassium	Use zest of the rind in marinades for chicken and fish; eat whole; include in salads.

Papayas	*June through September*	Look for firm papayas that have some yellow streaks and are free of blemishes.	Keep papayas at room temperature for 2 to 3 days until they are totally yellow to orange.	Vitamins A, C, E, and K; folate; and potassium	Eat whole; include in salads.
Peaches	*May through September*	Look for firm, fuzzy skins that yield to gentle pressure when ripe.	Store unripe peaches in a paper bag. Once they are ripe, store peaches at room temperature and use them within 1 to 2 days.	Vitamins A, C, E, and K; niacin; potassium; copper; and manganese	Serve atop yogurt and cereals; include in cakes, muffins, cobblers, and pies.
Pears	*August through May*	Look for firm pears that yield to pressure near the stem.	Store unripe pears in a paper bag at room temperature until they are ripe. Refrigerate ripe pears and eat them within 3 to 5 days.	Vitamins C and K	Eat whole; include in desserts, such as tarts.

Table D.1 (*continued*)

	Peak Season[a]	Selection	Storage	Key Nutrients[b]	How to Prepare
Pineapple	*March through July*	Look for firm, large pineapples with fresh-looking green tops.	Eat as soon as possible. Refrigerate cut pineapple for 2 to 3 days.	Vitamins C and B6; thiamin; folate; magnesium; copper; and manganese	Pineapple is great in smoothies, atop pizza, and in fruit salad.
Plums	*May through October*	Look for plump plums with smooth skins and as few bruises and soft spots as possible.	Store unripe plums in a paper bag until ripe. Refrigerate ripe plums for 3 to 5 days.	Vitamins A, C, and K; and potassium	Roast plums; eat whole.
Pomegranates	*September through February*	Look for pomegranates that are plump, round, and heavy for their size.	Store in a cool, dry area for about 1 month, or for up to 2 months in the refrigerator.	Vitamins C and K; folate; potassium; copper; and manganese	Eat the arils (small, juice-filled seeds) whole; include the arils in cereals, yogurt, and fruit salad.

Raspberries	*May through November*	Look for dry, plump, and firm raspberries.	Store unwashed raspberries in the refrigerator for 1 to 2 days.	Vitamins C, E, and K; folate; iron; magnesium; potassium; copper; and manganese	Eat raspberries whole; place them on top of yogurt and cereals; in fruit salad; and in pancakes and desserts.
Strawberries	*April through August (although grown almost year-round in California)*	Look for shiny, firm strawberries with a bright red color.	Store unwashed strawberries in the refrigerator for 1 to 3 days.	Vitamin C; folate; magnesium; potassium; and manganese	Prepare as you would raspberries.
Watermelon	*May through August*	Look for symmetrical watermelons with dried stems and yellowish undersides that are heavy for their size.	Store at room temperature. Refrigerate cut watermelons in an airtight container for use within 5 days.	Vitamins A and C; and potassium	Eat watermelons fresh!

[a] This is for domestic produce. Many are imported at other times of the year.
[b] Nutrients listed constitute at least 5 percent daily value (DV).

Table D.2 Veggies

	Peak Season[a]	Selection	Storage	Key Nutrients[b]	How to Prepare
Artichokes	*April through December*	Look for artichoke heads that have tightly closed leaves and are heavy for their size.	Refrigerate artichokes in a plastic bag for up to 1 week.	Vitamins C, K, and B6; thiamin; riboflavin; niacin; folate; magnesium; iron; calcium; phosphorus; potassium; copper; and manganese	Steam, roast[c] (375°F for 40 to 50 minutes), or stuff and bake. Artichokes are great with hollandaise sauce or melted butter.
Asparagus	*January through June*	Look for odorless stalks with dry, tight tips.	Refrigerate for up to 4 days in plastic bag.	Vitamins A, C, E, and K; thiamin; riboflavin; niacin; folate; phosphorus; potassium; iron; copper; manganese; and selenium	Roast[c] (400 F° for 10 to 15 minutes); grill asparagus in tinfoil, brushed with a little olive oil and a dash of salt; for added flavor, squeeze the juice of a lemon on top.
Beets	*June through October*	Look for beets with firm, smooth skins.	Remove the leaves, leaving about an inch of the stem. Store roots in a plastic bag in the refrigerator for up to 3 weeks.	Vitamins C and B6; folate; iron; magnesium; phosphorus; potassium; copper; and manganese	Roast[c] beets at 400 F° for 35 to 60 minutes (time varies based on the size of the beets).

Bell Peppers	*June through November*	Look for firm, brightly colored peppers with tight skin that are heavy for their size.	Refrigerate bell peppers in a plastic bag for up to 5 days.	Vitamins A, C, E, K, and B6; thiamin; riboflavin; niacin; pantothenic acid; potassium; copper; and manganese	Sauté in canola oil with onions—bell peppers are great for fajitas, or atop sandwiches, burgers, and sausages; roast[c] (400 F° for 15 to 20 minutes).
Broccoli	*October through April*	Look for odorless broccoli heads with tight, bluish-green florets.	Refrigerator for 3 to 5 days.	Vitamins A, C, K, and B6; riboflavin; folate; pantothenic acid; magnesium; phosphorus; potassium; and manganese	Steam broccoli florets for 5 to 6 minutes; roast[c] (400°F for 20 minutes); stir-fry in low-sodium soy sauce; sauté in olive oil or sesame oil.
Brussels Sprouts	*June through January*	Look for firm, compact, bright-green brussels sprout heads.	Refrigerate brussels sprouts in a plastic bag for up to 1 week.	Vitamins A, C, and K; thiamin; riboflavin; folate; iron; magnesium; phosphorus; potassium; and manganese	Roast[c] (400°F for 35 to 40 minutes); steam.

Table D.2 (*continued*)

	Peak Season[a]	Selection	Storage	Key Nutrients[b]	How to Prepare
Cabbage (Green, Red, Bok Choy)	*May through October*	Look for firm bok choy stalks that are free of brown spots and have fresh leaves (not wilted). Look for green and red cabbage heads with compact leaves that are heavy for their size.	Store cabbage in a plastic bag in the refrigerator for up to 1 week.	Vitamins A, C, K, and B6; folate; potassium; and manganese	Boil; sauté; include bok choy in Asian stir-fries.
Carrots	*July through October*	Look for firm, crisp carrots with deep color and fresh, green tops.	Refrigerate carrots in a plastic bag with tops removed for up to 2 weeks.	Vitamins A, C, K, and B6; thiamin; niacin; folate; potassium; and manganese	Eat raw; steam; roast[c] (400°F for 20 minutes); sauté.

Cauliflower	*November through April*	Look for compact, creamy white curds and bright-green, firmly attached leaves.	Store in a paper or plastic bag in the refrigerator for up to 1 week.	Vitamins C, K, and B6; folate; pantothenic acid; potassium; and manganese	Steam; roast[c] (400°F for 20 to 25 minutes); eat raw with dips or plain; include in salads.
Celery	*September through April*	Look for straight, rigid stalks with fresh leaves.	Refrigerate in a plastic bag for a week or more.	Vitamins A, C, and K; folate; potassium; and manganese	Eat celery raw; top with peanut butter or cream cheese; include chopped celery in tuna and as a base in homemade soups.
Corn	*July through October*	Look for ears with green husks, fresh silks, and tight rows of kernels.	Refrigerate with husks on for use as soon as possible, or within 1 to 2 days.	Vitamin C; thiamin; riboflavin; pantothenic acid; folate; magnesium; phosphorus; potassium; zinc; and manganese	Steam; boil the ears; soak corn in the husks in water for 1 hour and grill with the husks on; include in salsa, soup, and chowder; roast in canola oil on the stove top.
Cucumbers	*May through August*	Look for firm, well-shaped cucumbers with dark-green color that are heavy for their size.	Refrigerate in a plastic bag for up to 1 week.	Vitamin K	Eat raw with dip; use in salads and in sandwiches.

Table D.2 (*continued*)

	Peak Season[a]	Selection	Storage	Key Nutrients[b]	How to Prepare
Eggplant	*July through October*	Look for an eggplant that is heavy for its size and without cracks or discoloration.	Store in the refrigerator for 5 to 7 days.	Folate; potassium; and manganese	Cube or slice the eggplant and roast[c] (400°F for 15 to 20 minutes); make baba ganoush (eggplant dip); pan fry for eggplant Parmesan.
Green Beans	*June through September*	Look for fresh, well-colored beans that snap easily when bent.	Refrigerate in a plastic bag for up to 1 week.	Vitamins A, C, and K; thiamin; riboflavin; folate; iron; magnesium; potassium; and manganese	Steam for about 5 minutes until crisp and tender; sauté in olive oil, garlic, and toasted almonds for a flavor boost; roast[c] (400°F for 20 to 25 minutes); top with Parmesan cheese; eat them raw!
Kale	*Year-round*	Look for dark-colored bunches with small to medium leaves.	Refrigerate in a plastic bag for 3 to 5 days.	Vitamins A, C, K, and B6; thiamin; riboflavin; folate; calcium; iron; magnesium; potassium; copper; and manganese	Roast[c] with olive oil and kosher salt (350°F for 10 to 15 minutes); include in salads.

Leeks	*October through May*	Look for firm, crisp stalks with as much white and light-green coloration as possible.	Refrigerate leeks unwashed in a plastic bag for up to 2 weeks.	Vitamins A, C, K, and B6; folate; calcium; iron; magnesium; potassium; copper; and manganese	Roast[c] leeks in the oven (400°F for 35 to 45 minutes); cook them on the grill; include them in soups.
Lettuce (Romaine, Leaf, Butter . . .)	*Year-round*	Look for lettuce heads with fresh, clean outer leaves and compact inner leaves.	Refrigerate lettuce in a plastic bag for use within 1 week.	*Butter:* Vitamins A and K; folate; and manganese *Leaf:* Vitamins A and K *Romaine:* Vitamins A and K	Use lettuce for salads and sandwiches; make Asian lettuce cups.
Lima Beans	*Difficult to find fresh in the United States; usually found dried, canned, or frozen*	Look for lima beans that are dry, firm, clean, uniform in color, and not shriveled.	Store dried beans at room temperature in a closed container.	Vitamins A, C, K, and B6; thiamin; riboflavin; niacin; folate; calcium; iron; magnesium; phosphorus; potassium; zinc; copper; and manganese	Slow cook lima beans; boil them; cook them on the stove top.

Table D.2 (continued)

	Peak Season[a]	Selection	Storage	Key Nutrients[b]	How to Prepare
Mushrooms	*Year-round*	Look for firm, plump mushrooms.	Refrigerate in the original container or paper bag for up to 1 week.	Riboflavin; niacin; pantothenic acid; phosphorus; potassium; copper; and selenium	Sauté; eat raw; include in stir-fries and pasta dishes; pair them with eggs.
Parsnips	*February through May*	Look for firm and dry parsnips without pits. Smaller ones may be more flavorful and tender.	Refrigerate parsnips unwashed in an unsealed bag for 3 weeks or more.	Vitamins C, E, K, and B6; thiamin; niacin; folate; pantothenic acid; calcium; magnesium; phosphorus; potassium; zinc; copper; and manganese	Roast[c] at 375°F for 45 minutes.

Peas (Green, Snow, Snap)	Green peas: *December through April* Snow peas: *November through March* Snap peas: *February through May*	Look for firm, bright-green pods. Snow peas should be shiny and flat.	Refrigerate unshelled peas in a perforated plastic bag for 3 to 5 days.	*Snow and snap peas:* Vitamins A, C, K, and B6; thiamin; riboflavin; folate; pantothenic acid; iron; magnesium; phosphorus; potassium; and manganese *Green peas:* vitamins A, C, K, and B6; thiamin; riboflavin; niacin; folate; iron; magnesium; phosphorus; potassium; zinc; copper; and manganese	Steam; eat raw; include in pasta dishes, pot roasts, and salads; incorporate into Asian dishes and stir-fries.
Potatoes (Russet, Red, White Round)	*Year-round*	Look for clean, firm potatoes that are dry and uniform in size.	Store in a cool, dark, well-ventilated place for use within 3 to 5 weeks.	*Russet:* Vitamins C and B6; thiamin; folate; pantothenic acid; iron; magnesium; phosphorus; potassium; copper; and manganese *Red and white round:* Vitamins C, K, and B6; thiamin; riboflavin; niacin; folate; pantothenic acid; iron; magnesium; phosphorus; potassium; zinc; copper; and manganese	Bake; cut in cubes and roast[c] (400°F for 25 to 30 minutes); boil; mash; include in salads.

Table D.2 (continued)

	Peak Season[a]	Selection	Storage	Key Nutrients[b]	How to Prepare
Radishes	*November through April*	Look for smooth, brightly colored, medium-size radishes.	Refrigerate in a plastic bag for use within 1 week. Remove the tops before storing.	Vitamin C; folate; and potassium	Eat raw; include in salads.
Spinach	*April through May*	Look for fresh, crisp, green bunches.	Loosely wrap spinach in damp paper towels. Refrigerate in a plastic bag for use within 3 to 5 days.	Vitamins A, C, and K; folate; iron; magnesium; potassium; and manganese	Sauté; include in salads and pastas; pair with eggs; include in sandwiches.

	Season	Selection	Storage	Nutrients	Preparation
Summer Squash	*May through July*	Look for glossy, small- to medium-size squash that are heavy for their size.	Refrigerate and use within 3 to 4 days.	Vitamins A, C, and B6; riboflavin; folate; magnesium; potassium; and manganese	Steam just until barely tender; roast[c] (400°F for 15 to 20 minutes); toss with melted butter or your favorite sauce. Sauté summer squash in olive oil, and season with herbs of your choice, salt, and pepper.
Sweet Potato	*July through November*	Look for firm sweet potatoes without cracks, bruises, or soft spots.	Store in a cool, dark place and use within 3 to 5 weeks.	Vitamins A, C, and B6; thiamin; pantothenic acid; iron; magnesium; phosphorus; potassium; copper; and manganese	Steam; mash; bake; microwave; roast[c] (400°F for 45 minutes).
Tomatoes	*June through September*	Look for bright, shiny skins and firm flesh.	Store at room temperature and use within 1 week after tomatoes are ripe. Refrigerate only to prevent spoilage.	Vitamins A, C, K, and B6; folate; potassium; and manganese	Eat raw; roast[c] (375°F for 40 minutes, then increase to 400°F for 20 minutes); include in salads, pastas, Mexican dishes, and salsas; put in sandwiches.

Table D.2 (*continued*)

	Peak Season[a]	Selection	Storage	Key Nutrients[b]	How to Prepare
Turnips	*Year-round*	Look for pearly, heavy turnips without soft spots, small to medium in size.	Store in the refrigerator in a plastic bag and use within a few days.	Vitamins C and B6; folate; potassium; copper; and manganese	Roast[c] (450°F for 45 to 50 minutes); boil; steam. The flavor intensifies during cooking, so avoid cooking for too long or the taste can be a bit overpowering.
Winter Squash (Butternut, Acorn, Spaghetti, Pumpkin…)	*September through November*	Look for squash that are firm and heavy for their size.	Store in a cool, dark place for up to a month. Once the squash are cut, refrigerate the unused portion for 1 to 2 days.	Vitamins A, C, and B6; folate; potassium; and manganese	Peel and cube the squash, and boil, mash, or roast[c] (400°F for 45 to 55 minutes). Steam slices; bake whole (cut in half lengthwise), drizzled with olive oil. Eat right out of the shell.

[a] *This is for domestic produce. Many are imported at other times of the year.*

[b] *Nutrients listed constitute at least 5 percent DV*

[c] *Toss or brush with oil, salt, pepper, and other spices.*

Resources

Table E.1 Books and Websites

	Books	Websites
General (All Ages)	*ADA's Complete Food and Nutrition Guide*, 4th ed., by Roberta Duyff; *Nutrition: What Every Parent Needs to Know*, 2nd ed., by William Dietz; *Feed Your Family Right!* by Elisa Zied and Ruth Winter; *The Best Things You Can Eat* by David Grotto	Kids Eat Right! www.KidsEatRight.org; American Academy of Pediatrics, www.AAP.org; Kids Health, www.KidsHealth.org; USDA MyPlate, www.choosemyplate.gov/; *Just the Right Byte* (Jill Castle), http://justtherightbyte.com/; *Raise Healthy Eaters* (Maryann Jacobsen), www.raisehealthyeaters.com/
Pregnancy and Infancy	*Child of Mine: Feeding with Love and Good Sense* by Ellyn Satter; *Expect the Best* by Elizabeth Ward; *First Meals* by Annabel Karmel	Wholesome Baby Food, http://wholesomebabyfood.momtastic.com/; Annabel Karmel USA, www.annabelkarmel.us/
Toddlerhood	*Love Me, Feed Me* by Katja Rowell; *Little Hands in the Kitchen* by Peggy Korody	The Feeding Doctor, www.TheFeedingDoctor.com; Wholesome Toddler Food (recipes), www.wholesometoddlerfood.com/
School Age	*Secrets of Feeding a Healthy Family* by Ellyn Satter; *How to Teach Nutrition to Kids*, 4th ed., by Connie Evers; *We Can Cook* by Jessica Levinson Fishman and Maja Pitamic; *Best Lunchbox Ever* (in press) by Katie Morford	Team Nutrition, www.teamnutrition.usda.gov; KidsHealth, www.kidshealth.org/kid

Category	Resources	References
Teenage Years	*Fueling the Teen Machine*, 2nd ed., by Ellen Shanley and Colleen Thompson; *I'm, Like, SO Fat! Helping Your Teen Make Healthy Choices About Eating and Exercise in a Weight-Obsessed World* by Dianne Neumark-Sztainer; *The Teen Eating Manifesto: The Ten Essential Steps to Losing Weight, Looking Great and Getting Healthy* by Lisa Stollman	TeensHealth, www.Teenshealth.org; Nemours, www.nemours.org
Picky Eating and Sensory Issues	*Just 2 More Bites* by Linda Piette; *Food Chaining: The Proven 6-Step Plan to Stop Picky Eating, Solve Feeding Problems, and Expand Your Child's Diet* by Cheri Fraker, Mark Fishbein, Sibyl Cox, and Laura Walbert; *Happy Mealtimes with Happy Kids: How to Teach Your Child About the Joy of Food!* by Melanie Potock	The Star Center, www.starcenter.us; Sensory Processing Disorder Foundation, www.SPDfoundation.net
Eating Disorders	*Life Without Ed: How One Woman Declared Independence from Her Eating Disorder and How You Can Too* by Jenni Schaefer and Thom Rutledge; *Goodbye Ed, Hello Me: Recover from Your Eating Disorder and Fall in Love with Life* by Jenni Schaefer; *100 Questions and Answers About Anorexia Nervosa* by Sari Shepphird	National Eating Disorders, www.nationaleatingdisorders.org; Something Fishy Website on Eating Disorders, www.something-fishy.org; Eating Disorders, www.bulimia.com

Table E.1 (continued)

	Books	Websites
Weight Management	*Your Child's Weight: Helping Without Harming* by Ellyn Satter; *Trim Kids: The Proven 12 Week Plan That Has Helped Thousands of Children Achieve a Healthier Weight* by Melinda Southern, T. Kristian von Almen, and Heidi Schumacher	Weight Control Information Network, http://win .niddk.nih.gov/publications/over_child.htm; Body Mass Index Tool, www.cdc.gov/healthyweight /assessing/bmi/; Weighty Matters, www .weightymatters.ca/; California Center for Healthy Living, www.californiachl.com/
Food Allergies	*Understanding and Managing Your Child's Food Allergies* by Scott H. Sicherer	Food Allergy and Anaphylaxis Network, www .foodallergy.org; American Academy of Allergy, Asthma and Immunology, www.aaaai.org; Allergy Nutrition, www.allergynutrition.com/
Attention Deficit Hyperactivity Disorder (ADHD) and Autism	*Special-Needs Kids Eat Right: Strategies to Help Kids on the Autism Spectrum Focus, Learn, and Thrive* by Judy Converse; *Special-Needs Kids Go Pharm-Free: Nutrition-Focused Tools to Help Minimize Meds and Maximize Health and Well-Being* by Judy Converse	Talk About Curing Autism Now, www.TACANow .org; Generation Rescue, www.GenerationRescue.org; National Resource Center on AD/HD, www .help4adhd.org; Children and Adults with Attention Deficit/Hyperactivity Disorder, www.chadd.org

Meal Planning and Cooking	*No Whine with Dinner* by Liz Weiss and Janice Bissex; *SOS! The Six O'Clock Scramble to the Rescue: Earth-Friendly, Kid-Pleasing Dinners for Busy Families* by Aviva Goldfarb; *201 Healthy Smoothies and Juices for Kids* by Amy Roskelley; *Don't Panic—Dinner's in the Freezer* by Suzie Martinez, Vanda Howell, and Bonnie Garcia; *MyPlate for Moms, How to Feed Yourself and Your Family Better: Decoding the Dietary Guidelines for Your Real Life* by Elizabeth Ward; *Cooking Light Real Family Food: Simple and Easy Recipes Your Whole Family Will Love* by Amanda Haas	*Money saving:* Food on the Table, www .foodonthetable.com/; 5 Dollar Dinners, www.5dollardinners.com/; Once A Month Mom, http://onceamonthmom.com/ *Healthy meal planning:* Six O'Clock Scramble, www .thescramble.com/ *Recipes:* Weelicious, www.weelicious.com; All Recipes, http://allrecipes.com/ *Food shopping:* Whole Grain Stamp (Whole Grains Council), www.wholegrainscouncil.org/whole-grain -stamp; Fruits and Veggies Matter, www .fruitsandveggiesmatter.gov/; LocalHarvest (CSA resources), www.localharvest.org/ *Vegetarianism:* Vegetarian Resource Group, www.vrg .org *Food additives:* Center for Science in the Public Interest, www.cspinet.org/reports/chemcuisine.htm
Adults and Eating	*Cooking Light The Food Lover's Healthy Habits Cookbook: Great Food and Expert Advice That Will Change Your Life* by Janet Helm; *Intuitive Eating*, 3rd ed., by Evelyn Tribole and Elyse Resch; *Eat What You Love, Love What You Eat: How to Break Your Eat-Repent-Repeat Cycle* by Michelle May; *Mindless Eating: Why We Eat More Than We Think* by Brian Wansink; *Women, Food and God: An Unexpected Path to Almost Everything* by Geneen Roth	The MM Method, www.mmmethodeating.com/; Health at Every Size, www.haescommunity.org/

APPENDIX F

The Claims Department

Table F.1 Egg and Meat Claims

Egg Claims[a]	What They Mean	Meat Claims	What They Mean
UEP Certified[b]	This claim signifies compliance with United Egg Producers (UEP) basic standards, including adequate space, nutritious food, clean water, proper lighting, and fresh air.	Free range (chicken, turkey, goose, duck)	This claim, regulated by the U.S. Department of Agriculture, means birds have continuous, free access to the outdoors during their production cycle.
American Humane Certified[b]	This claim, certified by the American Humane Association, means that hens can be confined in cages or can be cage-free. There are standards for breeding, for transporting, and at slaughter.	Fresh poultry	The poultry has never been below 26°F (the temperature at which poultry freezes).
Certified Humane[b]	This claim, certified by Humane Farm Animal Care, means that hens have sufficient space, and requires the producer to meet animal care standards including the provision of a nutritious diet without antibiotics or hormones, proper shelter, and available resting areas for birds while they are engaging in natural behaviors. There are standards for breeding, for transporting, and at slaughter.	Natural	The U.S. Department of Agriculture requires that meat, poultry, and eggs labeled as natural be minimally processed and contain no artificial ingredients. The claim does not include any standards concerning farm practices.
Animal Welfare Approved[b]	This is the only U.S. Department of Agriculture–approved third-party certification requiring that birds are cage-free and able to perform natural behaviors prohibiting beak cutting.	No hormones added	Documentation shows no hormones have been used in raising the animals (poultry and pork aren't allowed hormones).

Table F.1 *(continued)*

Egg Claims[a]	What They Mean	Meat Claims	What They Mean
USDA Organic[b]	This claim is regulated by the U.S. Department of Agriculture's National Organic Program. Hens are cage-free and must have an unspecified amount of outdoor access; they are fed a vegetarian, organic diet free of antibiotics and pesticides.	No antibiotics	Documentation shows that the animals were raised without antibiotics.
Cage-free	Hens live in barns or warehouses, but usually don't have outdoor access.	USDA Organic[b]	This claim is regulated by the U.S. Department of Agriculture's National Organic Program. The producer meets animal health and welfare standards; animals have been given no antibiotics or growth hormones, 100 percent organic feed, and access to the outdoors.
Free range or free roaming	Hens are cage-free, and are given outdoor access without specific requirements in regard to how much time is spent outdoors.	Grass-fed	This claim indicates a U.S. Department of Agriculture (USDA) voluntary standard, whereby animals receive a majority of their nutrients from grass throughout their life. This standard does not limit the use of hormones, antibiotics, or pesticides.

Claim	What They Mean
Raised without antibiotics	The hens were not fed antibiotics at any time, including when sick.
Pasture-fed, pastured, pasture raised	There is no formal definition, although it is likely that hens forage for vegetation and bugs at least some of the time.
Certified Naturally Grown[b]	This certified claim is a less expensive alternative to the USDA organic program. This program is tailored to small-scale farmers.
American Grassfed Certified[b]	This claim indicates compliance with the American Grassfed Association's standard of continuous access to pasture and a diet of 100 percent forage. The use of antibiotics and hormones is prohibited.
Other Claims	**What They Mean**
Organic (in food products)	*One hundred percent organic* means 100 percent organic ingredients; *organic* means at least 95 percent organic ingredients; *made with organic ingredients* means at least 70 percent organic ingredients.
Content Claims	**What They Mean**
Fat-free, trans fat–free, sodium-free	These claims signify less than .5 grams of fat, less than .5 grams of trans-saturated fat, and less than 5 milligrams of sodium, respectively.
Low fat, low in saturated fat, low sodium	These claims signify less than 3 grams of fat, less than 1 gram of saturated fat, and less than 140 milligrams of sodium, respectively.

Table F.1 (*continued*)

Content Claims	What They Mean	Other Claims	What They Mean
Good source, High in, excellent source	The product must contain 10 to 19 percent daily value (DV) of the nutrient in question. The product must contain 20 percent or more DV of the nutrient in question.	Natural	There is no formal definition, but this claim is typically allowed on products that do not contain artificial colors and flavors or other synthetic substances.
No added sugar	No sugar was added during processing.	Healthy	The product is low in total fat and saturated fat and contains at least 10 percent DV of one the following: vitamin A, vitamin C, or calcium.

[a] Most of the certified claims listed also apply to other animal products, such as meat, poultry, and pork.
[b] This claim is certified by a third party.

Source: Adapted from Animal Welfare Institute. (2012, August). A consumer's guide to food labels and animal welfare. Retrieved from http://awionline.org /sites/default/files/products/12_FoodLabelGuide080212.pdf; Certified Naturally Grown. (n.d). About CNG. Retrieved from www.naturallygrown.org /about-cng; Food and Drug Administration. (2012, November). Labeling and nutrition. Retrieved from www.fda.gov/food/labelingnutrition/default.htm.

Beyond Basic Nutrition Questions

Can I Raise My Child as a Vegetarian?

With careful planning, a vegetarian diet can meet your child's needs. Check the Fearless Five Nutrients for each age group, and see Appendix A for vegetarian sources of iron, zinc, and calcium. Consider supplementation or foods fortified with docosahexaenoic acid (DHA) and vitamin D. Because iron and zinc from plant sources are not absorbed as well, include higher-than-recommended amounts. If your child is a vegan (no animal products), he will need a supplemental source of vitamin B12, which is not contained in plant foods unless they are fortified.

Don't Forget Vitamin B12

Recommended vitamin B12 by age: Seven to twelve months: 0.5 micrograms, one to three years: 0.9 micrograms, four to eight years: 1.2 micrograms, nine to thirteen years: 1.8 micrograms, fourteen to eighteen years: 2.4 micrograms.

Daily value: The daily value (DV) given on food labels for vitamin B12 is 6 micrograms, so 20 percent DV for vitamin B12 would be 1.2 micrograms. The DV for vitamin B12 is only listed on the label when the product is fortified with this vitamin.

Vegan sources of vitamin B12: These include fortified nutritional yeast, fortified cereals, fortified soymilk, meat analogues, and other fortified foods.

How Can I Ensure Calcium Needs Are Met When My Child Doesn't Drink Milk?

For those of you with a child who doesn't drink milk, calcium equivalents for milk are listed in Table G.1. Unless fortified (check the label), these products contain little or no vitamin D—so supplementation may be needed.

Table G.1	Calcium Equivalents
1 cup milk (300 milligrams)	1 cup yogurt 1 cup calcium-fortified orange juice 1 cup calcium-fortified soy, rice, or almond milk
¾ to ⅔ cup milk	1 ounce cheddar, jack, mozzarella, Swiss, or American cheese
½ cup milk	½ cup custard or milk pudding ½ cup cooked greens (mustard, collard greens, kale)
¼ cup milk	½ cup cottage cheese ½ cup ice cream ¾ cup dried, cooked, or canned beans

Source: Adapted from Samour, P. Q., & King, K. (2010). *Pediatric nutrition* (4th ed.). Burlington, MA: Jones & Bartlett Learning.

What Types of Milk Besides Cow's Milk Can I Give My Child?

There are many alternatives to cow's milk, but in general they are lacking protein, fat, and calories needed by younger age groups. Further, some may not be fortified with important vitamins like A and D, or with calcium. Review differences in Table G.2 and check with your pediatrician for children age two and under.

Table G.2 Dairy and Nondairy Beverage Comparisons

Milk[a]	Calories	Fat (Grams)	Calcium (Percent DV)	Protein (Grams)	Vitamin D (Percent DV)	Vitamin A (Percent DV)
Whole cow's milk[1]	150	8	30	8	25	5
Soymilk[b]	90	3.5	45	6	30	10
Rice milk[c]	120	2.5	30	1	25	10
Almond milk[b]	60	2.5	45	1	25	10
Hemp milk[d]	100	6	30	2	25	10
Goat's milk[1]	168	10	33	9	30	10
Coconut milk[b]	80	5	45	1	25	10

[a] Amounts specified are per 1 cup.
[b] Amounts specified are for Silk brand (nutrition in other products may vary).
[c] Amounts specified are for Rice Dream brand (nutrition in other products may vary).
[d] Amounts specified are for Living Harvest brand (nutrition in other products may vary).

What Can I Feed My Child to Help Keep Him from Getting Sick So Often?

Good nutrition can go a long way toward helping keep a child's immune system strong. Although a well-balanced diet is key, there are certain nutrients of particular importance. Too little vitamin C can impair the body's ability to fight disease, vitamin A helps fight infections because it makes white blood cells, and vitamin E is a fat-soluble antioxidant that plays a role in immune health. Vitamin D boosts immunity, but levels tend to be low in the winter, and low zinc makes it hard for the body to fight infections. Probiotics help keep the gastrointestinal tract healthy—the first line of defense against toxins. Check Appendix B for food sources of these nutrients.

Is DHA Still Important After Age Two?

Joyce Nettleton, nutrition scientist and omega-3 fatty acid expert, explains that the rate of DHA accumulation in the brain slows at two years, but the brain continues to grow and develop. These omega-3 fats are useful throughout life. She adds that although there is less evidence for the role of eicosapentaenoic acid (EPA) in brain health, it is important. "EPA is not a structural component like DHA, but it's important for the development of a healthy immune system through life."

Some parents worry about giving younger children fish. The U.S. Food and Drug Administration recommends that high-risk groups including young children and pregnant and lactating women consume low-mercury sources of fish (salmon, trout, shrimp, tilapia, pollock, and canned light tuna) but keep it to 12 ounces or less per week (two average meals). Avoid high-mercury sources of fish, which include shark, swordfish, king mackerel, and tilefish. Provide portions for children that are smaller than for adults. Pregnant women and young children should also avoid raw fish (sushi) for safety reasons.[2] Table G.3 provides guidance on how much DHA and EPA kids of all ages need. Supplementation may be beneficial, as most children get less than half of the DHA they need.[3]

Table G.3 Combined DHA and EPA Recommendations for Children			
Daily Recommended Amounts of DHA and EPA in Children[a,4]	**Average Daily Consumption of DHA and EPA Combined**	**Food Sources of DHA**[b]	**Supplement Amounts**
Two- to four-year-olds: 100 to 150 milligrams *Four- to six-year-olds:* 150 to 200 milligrams *Six- to ten-year-olds:* 200 to 250 mg *Ten- to eighteen-year-olds:* 250 to 2,000 milligrams[c]	*Two- to eleven-year-olds:* 45 milligrams *Twelve- to nineteen-year-olds:* 40 milligrams	Salmon (1,215 milligrams), tuna (535 milligrams), sardines (433 milligrams), canned light tuna (190 milligrams), DHA-fortified eggs (50 to 300 milligrams), DHA-fortified milk[d] (32 milligrams), DHA-fortified orange juice (20 milligrams)	Check the labeled amount of DHA and EPA per serving and aim for the recommended daily amounts in the first column.

[a] There are no U.S. recommended daily allowances—this information is drawn from international recommendations.

[b] See Appendix B for serving sizes and nutrient lists.

[c] For dosages over 500 milligrams, consult your health care provider.

[d] Food products, such as milk and orange juice, are typically fortified with DHA only, and not with EPA.

What Are Probiotics, and Does My Child Need to Take Them?

Probiotics are live microorganisms that when consumed in adequate amounts provide health benefits and help keep the gastrointestinal tract healthy. Prebiotics are fuel for the good bacteria, helping increase their presence. We recommend including daily food sources of pre- and probiotics (see the box on the following page). Research in regard to probiotic supplements to treat food allergies and constipation is mixed, but such supplements may be helpful for treating antibiotic-associated diarrhea.[5] Check with your doctor before giving supplements. The USprobiotic.org site recommends choosing supplements that have research behind them.[6]

Probiotic sources: Fermented dairy products, including yogurt, specialty drinks, and cultured milk (kefir).

Prebiotic sources: Bananas, onions, garlic, Jerusalem artichokes, asparagus, chicory root (inulin), whole wheat, barley, rye, berries, raisins, tomatoes, greens, legumes, oats, buckwheat, and brown rice.

My Child Is Active in Sports—What Do I Need to Look Out For?

If your child is active in sports, you may see an increased appetite, depending on the frequency of activity, and you will need to pay attention to fluid intake. Following is a brief summary of nutrition highlights for the child athlete:

Nutritional Needs for the Active Child

For recreational sports (less than one hour of training, competition):
- Meals and snacks that contain protein, carbohydrates, and healthy fats
- Meals and snacks every three to four hours
- Water

For intense training or competition (more than one hour):
- **Pre-event:** Small snack, or regular meal (if the event is four hours away), containing carbohydrates and protein, and lower fat content (cereal and low-fat milk, crackers and hummus, or string cheese)
- **Postevent:** Carbohydrate and protein snack within thirty to forty-five minutes of the event's completion (for example, eight ounces of low-fat chocolate milk or milk substitute)
- Hydration with water
- Sports drinks only in cases of intense heat, a long training session, or extended game event time (more than one hour)
- Not too many Fun Foods!

How Do I Get My Child to Eat Breakfast?

Twelve to 34 percent of children and adolescents skip breakfast in the morning for reasons including lack of hunger, lack of time, or just the need for some extra sleep.[7] Table G.4 provides tips for getting your child to eat breakfast.

Table G.4 Tips for Getting Your Child to Eat Breakfast	
Tip	**How to Do It**
Make time.	Get your child to bed earlier so she can get up earlier.
Try grab-and-go breakfast ideas.	Serve fruit smoothies, instant breakfast drinks, trail mix, nut packets, breakfast bars, or an easy egg sandwich (see the Real, Easy Recipes in Chapters Two through Five for more ideas).
Shift your meal timing.	If your child eats later in the day, serve dinner earlier so she builds an appetite for breakfast. Bolster lunch to quell late-night snacking.
Try lunch or supper for breakfast.	Lunch items and dinner items make a suitable breakfast meal too!

Is My Child Getting Enough Protein?

Many children receive plenty of protein.[8] The average three-year-old needs at least thirteen grams per day, the average six-year-old needs nineteen grams, and the average eleven-year-old needs a minimum of thirty-four grams each day. That works out to be about two and a half cups of milk for a six-year-old and five ounces of chicken for an eleven-year-old. Most children get at least that amount in a given day, and if not, they get an average of that per day over a week. More important, getting protein from a variety of sources helps kids meet their essential nutrient needs. Table G.5 lists common protein sources and their protein content to help you troubleshoot your child's intake.

Table G.5 Common Protein Sources

Food	Serving Size	Protein (Grams)
Cottage cheese	½ cup	13–14
Tofu	½ cup	10
Low-fat yogurt	1 cup	8–10
Cow's milk	1 cup	8
Soymilk	1 cup	8
Peanut butter	2 tablespoons	8
Quinoa, cooked	1 cup	8
Beans	½ cup	7–8
Egg	1 egg	7
Lean beef, chicken, pork, or fish	1 ounce	7
Almond butter	2 tablespoons	6–7
Cheese (various)	1 ounce	4–7
Nuts	1 ounce	6
Rice milk	1 cup	1–2
Almond milk	1 cup	1–2

Source: Adapted from U.S. Department of Agriculture, Agricultural Research Service. (2012). USDA National Nutrient Database for Standard Reference, release 25. Retrieved from www.ars.usda.gov/ba/bhnrc/ndl.

What Should I Feed My Sick Kid?

When children get sick, their appetite often takes a nosedive. Allow children to play a larger role in deciding what and when to eat in times of illness. When vomiting, diarrhea, or a combination of these occurs, watch out for dehydration. The American Academy of Pediatrics recommends keeping children off of solid food for the first twenty-four hours after vomiting.[9] Ensure your child gets enough fluids by sipping water; electrolyte replacement drinks, such as Gatorade; broth; and electrolyte solutions (like Pedialyte), and sucking on popsicles.

Gradually work your child toward his regular diet, and if things don't improve, call your child's pediatrician. For mild diarrhea, keep children on their regular diet but avoid fruit juice or sweet drinks, as these can make it worse. A probiotic supplement or fermented foods may help with antibiotic-associated diarrhea.

Should I Be Cutting Back on Sodium?

All Americans should be cutting back on sodium. Many experts point out that this is difficult in our current food landscape. Sodium occurs naturally in all foods. It's abundant in many convenience foods, snack foods, and prepared meals. Dining out and eating processed convenience foods are two major sources of sodium intake. Easy ways to cut down on sodium are to use salt-free herbs and herb blends; ease back on the salt shaker; rinse canned foods with water; and eat fewer convenient, preprepared meal items and fast foods.

What Are the Needs of My High School Athlete?

High school athletes are generally in an accelerated growth phase and burning more calories through exercise than the average, nonathlete teen. Translation: higher calorie needs. *When* teens eat, or nutrient timing, is also important, as it influences how well they are prepared to perform and recover from exercise. The importance of protein, fat, and carbohydrates is magnified for the athlete, but not as much as you might think. Athletes need slightly more protein, adequate fat, and more total carbohydrates than nonathletes. Overall, athletes need a strong balance of Nourishing and Half-and-Half Foods, but they need more servings or larger portions to cover their energy burn.

The biggest trap teen athletes fall into is poor eating habits—namely eating too many fast-food or convenience items, when they require nutrient-rich and calorie-dense foods to meet their needs. They also may eat at erratic times, stretching too long between meals and skimping on food before practice or games. In the end, these habits wear on athletic performance and may cause weight loss, fatigue, poor sleeping, and reduced immunity.

Eating three balanced meals each day, supplemented with a preworkout afternoon snack and a postworkout recovery snack or drink, can help your teen manage her energy and nutrient needs. Some experts advise a "fourth meal" in the afternoon before a workout, such as a bowl of cereal with milk and fruit or a lean meat or nut butter sandwich with fruit and milk. Of course, during a workout that lasts longer than an hour, your teen should be replacing electrolytes with a sports drink or a salty snack and water to help prevent dehydration and keep blood sugar normal. After the workout is over, a protein source and carbohydrate-containing food or snack (one cup of chocolate or plain milk, fruit yogurt, or three or four crackers with peanut butter) eaten within thirty to forty-five minutes can support muscle recovery.

What Are My Child's Fluid Requirements?

Adequate fluid intake varies based on age. About five to six cups are needed for young toddlers (one to three years), about seven cups for children four to eight years, eight to ten cups for children nine to thirteen years, thirteen to fourteen cups for older teen boys, and nine to ten cups for teen girls (per day).[10] These amounts can be met with fluids from beverages and from such foods as fruits, vegetables, soups, and yogurt.

Thirst may be a practical indicator of dehydration and the need to drink fluids, but children still need to be monitored to ensure adequate fluid intake. The teen athlete needs about six milliliters of water per pound of body weight per hour to minimize sweat-related dehydration during exercise and other physical activity.[11] Exercising for more than an hour or multiple times during the day may require an electrolyte-containing beverage or food to replace sweat lost and maintain hydration. Despite popular thinking, calorie- and caffeine-containing beverages *do* hydrate, although they may be low on nutrients and high in calories.

Is It Okay for My Child to Drink Diet Soda?

Diet soda is a zero-calorie drink with taste appeal that carries the "cool factor." It's not surprising that children and teens like it and drink it. Diet soda gives an intense, sweet flavor, priming the palate for sugar and perhaps strengthening the preference for sweets. But it leaves the body confused, as the body doesn't receive any actual sugar! As a result, the artificial sugars in diet drinks may drive the body's desire for more sugar and promote the intake of more sugary foods. Studies also show that teens may feel justified in eating more food because they cut calories with a diet soda, leading to weight gain in some.[12] Then there's the issue of artificial sweeteners and the lack of nutrients supplied by diet sodas. And many diet sodas have more caffeine than regular soda! Finally, emerging research suggests a daily diet soda may increase the risk of heart attack and stroke.[13]

If your child is a regular soda drinker, diet sodas can have a temporary role in helping wean her off: substituting diet soda for regular soda can slash calories and help with weight management. Bottom line: ordering up a diet soda is something to think about, with several consequences to consider. We recommend avoiding the use of diet soda on a routine basis due to the unknown long-term effects of artificial sweeteners, lack of nutrients, presence of caffeine, and promotion of sugar preferences, all of which may have an impact on long-term health. Keep diet soda an "every now and then" beverage.

Introduction

1. Hoffman, S. D. (2009, February). The changing impact of marriage and children on women's labor force participation. *Monthly Labor Review*, pp. 1–14.

Chapter 1

1. Hetherington, M. M., Cecil, J. E., Jackson, D. M., & Schwartz, C. (2011). Feeding infants and young children: From guidelines to practice. *Appetite, 57*, 791–795.
2. *U.S. Department of Agriculture & U.S. Department of Health and Human Services. (2010). Dietary guidelines for Americans, 2010* (7th ed.). Washington DC: U.S. Government Printing Office.
3. Satter, E. (2011, January). Division of Responsibility. Retrieved from www.ellynsatter.com
4. Fox, M. K., Reidy, K., Novak, T., & Zeigler, P. (2006). Sources of energy and nutrients in the diets of infants and toddlers. *Journal of the Academy of Nutrition and Dietetics, 106*, S28–S42.
5. National Heart, Lung, and Blood Institute. (2011, January). Portion distortion and serving size. Retrieved from www.nhlbi.nih.gov/health/public/heart/obesity/wecan/eat-right/distortion.htm
6. Scaglioni, S., Salvioni, M., & Galimberti, C. (2008). Influence of parental attitudes in the development of children eating behaviour. *British Journal of Nutrition, 99*, S22–S25.
7. Eneli, I. U., Crum, P. A., & Tylka, T. L. (2008). The trust model: A different feeding paradigm for managing childhood obesity. *Obesity, 16*, 2197–2204.
8. Satter, E. (1990). The feeding relationship: Problems and interventions. *The Journal of Pediatrics, 117*, S181–S189.
9. Patrick, H., Nicklas, T. A., Hughes, S. O., & Morales, M. (2005). The benefits of authoritative feeding style: Caregiver feeding styles and children's food consumption patterns. *Appetite, 44*, 243–249.

10. Hughes, S. O., Power, T. G., Fisher, J. O., Mueller, S., & Nicklas, T. A. (2005). Revisiting a neglected construct: Parenting styles in a child-feeding context. *Appetite, 44,* 83–92.

11. Rhee, K. E., Lumeng, J. C., Appugliese D. P., Kaciroti, N., & Bradley, R. H. (2006). Parenting styles and overweight status in first grade. *Pediatrics, 117,* 2047–2054.

12. Butte, N. F. (2009). Impact of infant feeding practices on childhood obesity. *The Journal of Nutrition, 139,* 412S–416S.

13. Ventura, A. K., & Birch, L. L. (2008). Does parenting affect children's eating and weight status? *International Journal of Behavioral Nutrition and Physical Activity, 5,* 15. doi:10.1186/1479 -5868-5-15

14. Burdette, H. L., Whitaker, R. C., Hall, W. C., & Daniels, S. R. (2006). Maternal infant-feeding style and children's adiposity at 5 years of age. *Archives of Pediatrics & Adolescent Medicine, 160,* 513–520.

15. Hughes, S. O., Shewchuk, R. M., Baskin, M. L., Nicklas, T. A., & Qu, H. (2008). Indulgent feeding style and children's weight status in preschool. *Journal of Developmental and Behavioral Pediatrics, 29,* 403–410.

16. Savage, J. S., Fisher, J. O., & Birch, L. L. (2007). Parental influence on eating behavior: Conception to adolescence. *The Journal of Law, Medicine & Ethics, 35,* 22–34.

17. Slaughter, C. W., & Bryant, A. H. (2004). Hungry for love: The feeding relationship in the psychological development of young children. *The Permanente Journal, 8*(1), 23–29.

18. Webber, L., Cooke, L., Hill, C., & Wardle, J. (2010). Association between children's appetitive traits and maternal feeding practices. *Journal of the Academy of Nutrition and Dietetics, 110,* 1718–1722.

19. Orrell-Valente, J. K., Hill, L. G., Brechwald, W. A., Dodge, K. A., Pettit G. S., & Bates, J. E. (2007). "Just three more bites": An observational analysis of parents' socialization of children's eating at mealtime. *Appetite, 48,* 37–45.

20. Rees, C. (2007). Childhood attachment. *British Journal of General Practice, 57,* 920–922.

Chapter 2

1. Medline Plus. (2011, January). Potbellies and toddlers. Retrieved from www.nlm.nih.gov /medlineplus/ency/article/001989.htm

2. Centers for Disease Control and Prevention. (2010, September). WHO growth standards are recommended for use in the U.S. for infants and children 0 to 2 years of age. Retrieved from www.cdc.gov/growthcharts/who_charts.htm

3. Laraway, K. A., Birch, L. L., Shaffer, M. L., & Paul, I. M. (2010). Parent perception of healthy infant and toddler growth. *Clinical Pediatrics, 49,* 343–349.

4. Cole, S. Z., & Lanham, J. S. (2011). Failure to thrive: An update. *American Family Physician, 83,* 829–834.

5. Baird, B., Fisher, D., Lucas, P., Kleijnen, J., Roberts, H., & Law, C. (2005). Being big or growing fast: Systematic review of size and growth in infancy and later obesity. *British Medical Journal, 331,* 929–931.

6. Gungor, D. E., Paul, I. M., Birch, L. L., & Bartok, C. J. (2010). Risky vs. rapid growth in infancy. *Archives of Pediatrics & Adolescent Medicine, 164*, 1091–1097.

7. Baker, R. D., & Greer, F. R. (2010). Clinical report—diagnosis and prevention of iron deficiency and iron-deficiency anemia in infants and young children (0–3 years of age). *Pediatrics, 126*, 1040–1050.

8. Koletzko, B., Lien, E., Agostoni, C., Böhles, H., Campoy, C., Cetin, I., . . . World Association of Perinatal Medicine Dietary Guidelines Working Group. (2008). The roles of long-chain polyunsaturated fatty acids in pregnancy, lactation and infancy: Review of current knowledge and consensus recommendations. *Journal of Perinatal Medicine, 36*, 5–14.

9. Beard, J. L. Why iron deficiency is important in infant development. (2008). *The Journal of Nutrition, 138*, 2534–2536.

10. Cooke, L., & Fildes, A. (2011). The impact of flavour exposure in utero and during milk feeding on food acceptance at weaning and beyond. *Appetite, 57*, 808–811.

11. Normal nutrition, full-term infants. (2011). In *Academy of nutrition and dietetics pediatric nutrition care manual*. Available from www.peds.nutritioncaremanual.org

12. U.S. Department of Agriculture, Food and Nutrition Service. (2002, July). Feeding infants. In *Feeding infants: A guide for use in the child nutrition programs* (Chapter 2). Retrieved from http://teamnutrition.usda.gov/Resources/feeding_infants.html

13. Coulthard, H., Harris, G., & Emmett, P. (2009). Delayed introduction of lumpy foods to children during the complementary feeding period affects child's food acceptance and feeding at 7 years of age. *Maternal & Child Nutrition, 5*, 75–85.

14. Smith-Spangler, C., Brandeau, M. L., Hunter, G. E., Bavinger, J. C., Pearson, M., Eschbach, P. J., . . . Bravata, D. M. (2012). Are organic foods safer or healthier than conventional alternatives? A systematic review. *Annals of Internal Medicine, 157*, 348–366.

15. Rosas, L. G., & Eskenazi, B. (2008). Pesticides and child neurodevelopment. *Current Opinion in Pediatrics, 20*, 191–197.

16. Environmental Working Group. (2012). EWG's 2012 shopper's guide to pesticides in produce. Retrieved from www.ewg.org/foodnews/summary/

17. Growing trend: More moms making homemade baby food for health, economic benefits [Press release]. (2011, January). Retrieved from www.reuters.com/article/2011/01/26 /idUS218878+26-Jan-2011+PRN20110126

18. Grummer-Strawn, L. M., Scanlon, K. S., & Fein, S. B. (2008). Infant feeding and feeding transitions during the first year of life. *Pediatrics, 122*, S36–S42.

19. American Academy of Pediatrics Section on Breastfeeding. (2012). Policy statement: Breastfeeding and the use of human milk. *Pediatrics, 129*, e827–e841. doi:10.1542 /peds.2011-3552

20. Institute of Medicine of the National Academies. (2011, June). Early childhood obesity prevention policies: Goals, recommendations, and potential actions. Retrieved from www.iom .edu/~/media/Files/Report%20Files/2011/Early-Childhood-Obesity-Prevention-Policies /Young%20Child%20Obesity%202011%20Recommendations.pdf

21. World Health Organization. (2011, January). Exclusive breastfeeding for six months best for babies everywhere. Retrieved from www.who.int/mediacentre/news/statements/2011/breastfeeding_20110115/en/

22. Greer, F. R., Sicherer, S. H., Burks, A. W., American Academy of Pediatrics, Committee on Nutrition, & American Academy of Pediatrics Section on Allergy and Immunology. (2008). Effects of early nutritional intervention on the development of atopic disease in infants and children: The role of maternal dietary restriction, breastfeeding, timing of introduction of complementary foods and hydrolyzed formulas. *Pediatrics, 121*, 183–191.

23. Ziegler, E. E., Nelson, S. E., & Jeter, J. M. (2011). Iron supplementation of breastfed infants. *Nutrition Reviews, 69*, S71–S77.

24. Committee on Injury, Violence and Poison Prevention. (2010). Policy statement—prevention of choking among children. *Pediatrics, 125*, 601–607.

25. Wagner, C. L., Greer, F. R., & Section on Breastfeeding and Committee on Nutrition. (2008). Clinical report: Prevention of rickets and vitamin D deficiency in infants, children, and adolescents. *Pediatrics, 122*, 1142–1152.

26. Centers for Disease Control and Prevention. (2012, January 27). Anemia or iron deficiency. Retrieved from www.cdc.gov/nchs/fastats/anemia.htm

27. Butte, N. F., Fox, M. K., Briefel, R. R., Siega-Riz, A. M., Dwyer, J. T., Deming, D. M., & Reidy, K. C. (2010). Nutrient intakes of US infants, toddlers, and preschoolers meet or exceed dietary reference intakes. *Journal of the Academy of Nutrition and Dietetics, 110*, S27–S37.

28. Ziegler, E. E., Hollis, B. W., Nelson, S. E., & Jeter, J. M. (2006). Vitamin D deficiency in breastfed infants in Iowa. *Pediatrics, 118*, 603–610.

29. Joint Food and Agriculture Organization/World Health Organization (WHO) Expert Consultation on Fats and Fatty Acids in Human Nutrition. (2008, November 10–14). Interim summary of conclusions and dietary recommendations on total fat and fatty acids. WHO Headquarters, Geneva, Switzerland.

30. Dorea, J. G. (2000). Zinc in human milk. *Nutrition Research, 20*, 1645–1687.

31. Krebs, N. F., & Habidge, M. K. (2007). Complementary feeding: Clinically relevant factors affecting timing and composition. *The American Journal of Clinical Nutrition, 85*, 639S–645S.

32. Krebs, N. F., Westcott, J. E., Butler, N., Robinson, C., Bell, M., & Hambidge, K. M. (2006). Meat as a first complementary food for breastfed infants: Feasibility and impact on zinc intake and status. *Journal of Pediatric Gastroenterology and Nutrition, 42*, 207–214.

33. Holick, M. F. (2006). Resurrection of vitamin D deficiency and rickets. *The Journal of Clinical Investigation, 116*, 2062–2072.

34. Siega-Riz, A. M., Deming, D. M., Reidy, K. C., Fox, M. K., Condon, E., & Briefel, R. R. (2010). Food consumption patterns of infants and toddlers: Where are we now? *Journal of the Academy of Nutrition and Dietetics, 110*, S38–S51.

35. Satter, E. M. (1986). The feeding relationship. *Journal of the Academy of Nutrition and Dietetics, 86*, 352.

36. Martin, C. L., & Fabes, R. (2008). *Discovering child development* (2nd ed.). Independence, KY: Wadsworth.

37. Erikson, E. *Society and the child*. (1993). New York, NY: W. W. Norton.

38. Singer, L. T., Fulton, S., Davillier, M., Koshy, D., Salvator, A., & Baley, J. E. (2003). Effects of infant risk status and maternal psychological distress on maternal-infant interactions during the first year of life. *Developmental and Behavioral Pediatrics, 24,* 234–241.

39. Slaughter, C. W., & Bryant, A. H. (2004). Hungry for love: The feeding relationship in the psychological development of young children. *The Permanente Journal, 8*(1), 23–29.

40. National Center for Infants, Toddlers, and Families: Zero to 3. (n.d.). General brain development.Retrieved from http://main.zerotothree.org/site/PageServer?pagename=ter_key _brainFAQ

41. Piaget, J., & Inhelder, B. (2000). *The psychology of the child*. New York, NY: Basic Books.

42. Piette, L. (2006). *Just two more bites: Helping picky eaters say yes to food*. New York, NY: Three Rivers Press.

43. Strauss, S. (2006). Clara M. Davis and the wisdom of letting children choose their own diets. *Canadian Medical Association Journal, 175,* 1199–1201.

44. Davis, C. M. (1939). Results of self-selection of diets by young children. *Canadian Medical Association Journal, 41,* 257–261.

45. Gross, R. S., Medelsohn, A. L., Fierman, A. H., & Messito, M. J. (2011). Maternal controlling feeding styles. *Clinical Pediatrics, 50,* 1125–1133.

46. Stifter, C. A., Anxman-Frasca, S., Birch, L. L., & Voegtline, K. (2011). Parent use of food to soothe infant/toddler distress and child weight status: An exploratory study. *Appetite, 57,* 693–699.

47. Fox, M. K., Devaney, B., Reidy, K., Razafindrakoto, C., & Ziegler, P. (2006). Relationship between portion size and energy intake among infants and toddlers: Evidence of self-regulation. *Journal of the Academy of Nutrition and Dietetics, 106,* S77–S83.

48. Mennella, J. A., & Trabulsi, J. C. (2012). Complementary foods and flavor experiences: Setting the foundation. *Annals of Nutrition & Metabolism, 60,* S40–S50.

49. Shim, J. E., Kim, J., & Mathai, R. A. (2011). Associations of infant feeding practices and picky eating behaviors of preschool children. *Journal of the Academy of Nutrition and Dietetics, 111,* 1363–1368.

50. Skinner, J. D., Carruth, B. R., Bounds, W., Ziegler, P., & Reidy, K. (2002). Do food-related experiences in the first 2 years of life predict dietary variety in school-aged children? *Journal of Nutrition Education and Behavior, 24,* 310–315.

51. Black, M. M., & Aboud, F. E. (2011). Responsive feeding is embedded in a theoretical framework of responsive parenting. *The Journal of Nutrition, 141,* 490–494.

52. U.S. Department of Agriculture. (2007). Development of infant feeding skills. In *Infant feeding guide* (Chapter 2). Retrieved from http://wicworks.nal.usda.gov/infants /infant-feeding-guide

53. Hyman, P. E., Milla, P. J., Benninga, M. A., Davidson, G. P., Fleisher, D. F., & Taminiau, J. (2006). Childhood functional gastrointestinal disorders: Neonate/toddler. *Gastroenterology, 130,* 1519–1526.

54. American Academy of Pediatrics & Shelov, A. P. (2010). *Your baby's first year* (3rd ed.). New York, NY: Bantam Books.

55. Naspghan Constipation Guidelines Committee. (2006). Evaluation and treatment of constipation in infants and children: Recommendations of the North American Society for Pediatric Gastroenterology, Hepatology and Nutrition. *Journal of Pediatric Gastroenterology and Nutrition, 43,* e1–e13. Retrieved from www.naspghan.org/user-assets/documents/pdf /positionpapers/constipation.guideline.2006.pdf

56. National Digestive Diseases Information Clearinghouse. (2012, February 21). Gastroesophageal reflux in infants. Retrieved from http://digestive.niddk.nih.gov/ddiseases/pubs/gerdinfant/

57. Carruth, B. R., Ziegler, P. J., Gordon, A., & Hendricks, K. (2004). Developmental milestones and self-feeding behaviors in infants and toddlers. *Journal of the Academy of Nutrition and Dietetics, 104,* S51–S56.

58. U.S. Department of Agriculture, Food and Nutrition Service. (2002, July). Making baby food. In *Feeding infants: A guide for use in the child nutrition programs* (Chapter 12). Retrieved from http://teamnutrition.usda.gov/Resources/feeding_infants.html

Chapter 3

1. Ogden, C. L., Carroll, M. D., Kit, B. K., & Flegal, K. M. (2012). Prevalence of obesity and trends in body mass index among US children and adolescents, 1999–2010. *Journal of the American Medical Association, 307,* 483–490.

2. Taylor, R. W., Grant, A. M., Goulding, A., & Williams, S. M. (2005). Early adiposity rebound: Review of papers linking this to subsequent obesity in children and adults. *Current Opinion in Clinical Nutrition & Metabolic Care, 8,* 607–612.

3. Koletzko, B., Lien, E., Agostoni, C., Böhles, H., Campoy, C., Cetin, I., . . . World Association of Perinatal Medicine Dietary Guidelines Working Group. (2008). The roles of long-chain polyunsaturated fatty acids in pregnancy, lactation and infancy: Review of current knowledge and consensus recommendations. *Journal of Perinatal Medicine, 36,* 5–14.

4. National Center for Infants, Toddlers and Families: Zero to 3. (n.d.). General brain development. Retrieved from http://main.zerotothree.org/site/PageServer?pagename=ter_key_brainFAQ

5. Food and Nutrition Board, Institute of Medicine, National Academies. (2011). Dietary reference intakes for calcium and vitamin D. Retrieved from www.nap.edu/openbook.php?record _id=13050&page=1036

6. Lifshitz, F., & Tarim, O. (1996). Consideration about dietary fat restrictions for children. *The Journal of Nutrition, 126,* 1031S–1041S.

7. Fraker, C., Fishbein, M., Cox, S., & Walbert, L. (2007). *Food chaining: The proven 6-step plan to stop picky eating, solve feeding problems, and expand your child's diet.* Boston, MA: Da Capo Press.

8. Ventura, A. K., & Mennella, J. A. (2011). Innate and learned preferences for sweet taste during childhood. *Current Opinion in Clinical Nutrition & Metabolic Care, 14*, 379–384.

9. Cooke, L. (2007). The importance of food exposure for healthy eating in children: Review. *Journal of Human Nutrition & Dietetics, 20*, 294–301.

10. Fox, M. K., Condon, E., Briefel, R. R., Reidy, K. C., & Deming, D. M. (2010). Food consumption patterns of young preschoolers: Are they starting off on the right path? *Journal of the Academy of Nutrition and Dietetics, 110*, S52–S59.

11. Wang, Y. C., Bleich, S. N., & Gortmaker, S. L. (2008). Increasing caloric contribution from sugar-sweetened beverages and 100% fruit juices among US children and adolescents, 1988–2004. *Pediatrics, 121*, e1604–e1614. doi:10.1542/peds.2007-2834

12. Smith, M. M., & Lifshitz, F. (1994). Excessive fruit juice as a contributing factor in nonorganic failure to thrive. *Pediatrics, 93*, 438–443.

13. O'Connor, T. M., Yang, S. J., & Nicklas, T. A. (2006). Beverage intake among preschool children and its effect on weight status. *Pediatrics, 118*, e1010–e1018. doi:10.1542/peds.2005-2348

14. National Institute of Dental and Craniofacial Research. (n.d.). Dental caries (tooth decay) in children (age 2 to 11). Retrieved from www.nidcr.nih.gov/DataStatistics/FindDataByTopic /DentalCaries/DentalCariesChildren2to11

15. Piernas, C., & Popkin, B. M. (2010). Trends in snacking among US children. *Health Affairs, 23*, 398–404.

16. Butte, N. F., Fox, M. K., Briefel, R. R., Siega-Riz, A. M., Dwyer, J. T., Deming, D. M., & Reidy, K. C. (2010). Nutrient intakes of US infants, toddlers, and preschoolers meet or exceed dietary reference intakes. *Journal of the Academy of Nutrition and Dietetics, 110*, S27–S37.

17. Bailey, R. L., Fulgoni, V. L., III, Keast, D. R., Lentino, C. V., & Dwyer, J. T. (2012, June 18). Do dietary supplements improve micronutrient sufficiency in children and adolescents? *The Journal of Pediatrics, 161*, 837–842. http://dx.doi.org/10.1016/j.jpeds.2012.05.009

18. Lifshitz, F., & Moses, N. (1989). Growth failure. A complication of dietary treatment of hypercholesterolemia. *American Journal of Diseases of Children, 143*, 537–542.

19. National Heart, Lung, and Blood Institute. (2011). Integrated guidelines for cardiovascular health and risk reduction in children and adolescents. Retrieved from www.nhlbi.nih.gov /guidelines/cvd_ped/summary.htm#chap11

20. Johnson, R. K., Appel, L. J., Brands, M., Howard, B. V., Lefevre, M., Lustig, R. H., . . . Council on Epidemiology and Prevention. (2009). Dietary sugars intake and cardiovascular health: A scientific statement from the American Heart Association. *Circulation, 120*, 1011–1020.

21. Kostyak, J. C., Kris-Etherton, P., Bagshaw, D., DeLany, J. P., & Farrell, P. A. (2007). Relative fat oxidation is higher in children than adults. *Nutrition Journal, 6*, 19. doi:10.1186/1475-2891-6-19

22. Centers for Disease Control and Prevention. (2012, January 27). Anemia or iron deficiency. Retrieved from www.cdc.gov/nchs/fastats/anemia.htm

23. U.S. Department of Agriculture & U.S. Department of Health and Human Services. (2010). *Dietary guidelines for Americans, 2010* (7th ed.). Washington DC: U.S. Government Printing Office.

24. Wagner, C. L., Greer, F. R., & Section on Breastfeeding and Committee on Nutrition. (2008). Clinical report: Prevention of rickets and vitamin D deficiency in infants, children, and adolescents. *Pediatrics*, *122*, 1142–1152.

25. Abbott. (2011, August). Abbott's PediaSure brand aims to help moms with picky eaters "take back the table" by building lifelong healthy eating habits [Press release]. Retrieved from www .abbott.com/news-media/press-releases/2011-august11.htm

26. Erikson, E. (1993). *Society and the child*. New York, NY: W. W. Norton.

27. Piaget, J., & Inhelder, B. (2000). *The psychology of the child*. New York, NY: Basic Books.

28. Dovey, T. M., Staples, P. A., Gibson, E. L., & Halford, J. C. (2008). Food neophobia and "picky/ fussy" eating in children: A review. *Appetite*, *50*, 181–193.

29. Cooke, L., Haworth, C., & Wardle, J. (2007). Genetic and environmental influences on children's food neophobia. *The American Journal of Clinical Nutrition*, *86*, 428–433.

30. Fisher, J. O., Mennella, J. A., & Hughes, S. O. (2012). Offering "dip" promotes intake of a moderately-liked raw vegetable among preschoolers with genetic sensitivity to bitterness. *Journal of the Academy of Nutrition and Dietetics*, *112*, 235–245.

31. Carruth, B. R., Ziegler, P. J., Gordon, A., & Barr, S. I. (2004). Prevalence of picky eaters among infants and toddlers and their caregivers' decisions about offering a new food. *Journal of the Academy of Nutrition and Dietetics*, *104*, S57–S64.

32. Cooke, L. (2007). The importance of exposure for healthy eating in childhood: A review. *Journal of Human Nutrition & Dietetics*, *20*, 294–301.

33. Orrell-Valente, J. K., Hill, L. G., Brechwald, W. A., Dodge, K. A., Pettit, G. S., & Bates, J. E. (2007). Just three more bites: An observational analysis of parents' socialization of children's eating at mealtime. *Appetite*, *48*, 37–45.

34. Patrick, H., & Nicklas, T. A. (2005). A review of family and social determinants of children's eating patterns and diet quality. *Journal of the American College of Nutrition*, *24*, 83–92.

35. Satter, E. (2011, January). Division of Responsibility. Retrieved from www.ellynsatter.com

36. Rhee, K. (2008). Childhood overweight and the relationship between parent behaviors, parenting style, and family functioning. *The Annals of the American Academy of Political and Social Science*, *615*, 11–37.

37. Blissett, J., Haycraft, E., & Farrow, C. (2010). Inducing preschool children's emotional eating: Relations with parental feeding practices. *The American Journal of Clinical Nutrition*, *92*, 359–365.

38. Puhl, R. M., & Schwartz, M. B. (2003). If you are good you can have a cookie: How memories of childhood food rules link to adult eating behaviors. *Eating Behaviors*, *4*, 283–293.

39. Cooke, L., Chambers, L. C., Anez, E. V., & Wardle, J. (2011). Facilitating or undermining? The effect of reward on food acceptance; A narrative review. *Appetite*, *57*, 493–497.

40. Tanofsky-Kraff, M., Haynos, A. F., Kotler, L. A., Yanovski, S. Z., & Yanovski, J. A . (2007). Laboratory-based studies of eating among children and adolescents. *Current Nutrition & Food Science*, *3*, 55–74.

41. Wansink, B., Payne, C., & Werle, C. (2008). Consequences of belonging to the "clean plate club." *Archives of Pediatrics & Adolescent Medicine, 162*, 994–995.

42. Zeinstra, G. G., Koelen, M. A., Kok, F. J., & de Graaf, C. (2007). Cognitive development and children's perceptions of fruit and vegetables; a qualitative study. *International Journal of Behavioral Nutrition and Physical Activity, 4*, 30. doi:10.1186/1479-5868-4-30

43. Johnson, S. L. (2000). Improving preschoolers' self-regulation of energy intake. *Pediatrics, 106*, 1429–1435.

44. Faith, M. S., Scanlon, K. S., Birch, L. L., Francis, L. A., & Sherry, B. (2004). Parent-child feeding strategies and their relationships to child eating and weight status. *Obesity Research, 12*, 1711–1722.

45. Frances, L. A., & Susman, E. J. (2009). Self-regulation and rapid weight gain in children from age 3 to 12 years. *Archives of Pediatrics & Adolescent Medicine, 163*, 297–302.

46. Galloway, A. T., Fiorito, L. M., Francis, L. A., & Birch, L. L. (2006). "Finish your soup": Counterproductive effects of pressuring children to eat on intake and affect. *Appetite, 46*, 318–323.

Chapter 4

1. Lee, J. M., Appugliese, D., Kaciroti, N., Corwyn, R. F., Bradley, R. H., & Lumeng, J. C. (2007). Weight status in young girls and the onset of puberty. *Pediatrics, 119*, e624–e630. doi:10.1542/peds.2006-2188

2. U.S. Department of Agriculture & U.S. Department of Health and Human Services. (2010). *Dietary guidelines for Americans, 2010* (7th ed.). Washington DC: U.S. Government Printing Office.

3. Food and Nutrition Board, Institute of Medicine, National Academies. Dietary reference intakes for energy, carbohydrate, fiber, fat, fatty acids, cholesterol, protein, and amino acids (macronutrients) (2002, 2005); Dietary reference intakes for vitamin A, vitamin K, arsenic, boron, chromium, copper, iodine, iron, manganese, molybdenum, nickel, silicon, vanadium, and zinc (2001); and Dietary reference intakes for calcium and vitamin D (2011). These reports may be accessed via www.nap.edu.

4. Patrick, H., & Nicklas, T. A. (2005). A review of family and social determinants of children's eating patterns and diet quality. *Journal of the American College of Nutrition, 24*, 83–92.

5. U.S. Department of Agriculture, Food and Nutrition Service. (2012). Nutrition standards in the national school lunch and school breakfast programs. *Federal Register, 77*, 4088–4167.

6. Taylor, J. P., Hernandez, K. J., Caiger, J. M., Giberson, D., Maclellan, D., Sweeney-Nixon, M., & Veugelers, P. (2012). Nutritional quality of children's school lunches: Differences according to food source. *Public Health Nutrition, 15*, 2259–2264.

7. Briefel, R. R., Wilson, A., & Gleason, P. M. (2009). Consumption of low nutrient, energy dense foods and beverages at school, home and other locations among school lunch participants and nonparticipants. *Journal of the Academy of Nutrition and Dietetics, 109*, S79–S90.

8. Harris, J. L., Pomeranz, J. L., Lobstein, T., & Brownell, K. D. (2009). A crisis in the marketplace: How food marketing contributes to childhood obesity and what can be done. *Annual Review of Public Health, 30,* 211–225.

9. Story, M., & French, S. (2004). Food advertising and marketing directed at children and adolescents in the US. *International Journal of Behavioral Nutrition and Physical Activity, 1,* 3. doi:10.1186/1479-5868-1-3

10. Yale Rudd Center for Food Policy and Obesity. (2011, June). *Trends in television food advertising to young people: 2010 update* (Rudd Report). Retrieved from http://yaleruddcenter.org /resources/upload/docs/what/reports/RuddReport_TVFoodAdvertising_6.11.pdf

11. Buijzen, M. (2009). The effectiveness of parental communication in modifying the relation between food advertising and children's consumption behavior. *British Journal of Developmental Psychology, 27,* 105–121.

12. Florence, M. D., Asbridge, M., & Veugelers, P. J. (2008). Diet quality and academic performance. *Journal of School Health, 78,* 209–215.

13. Rampersaud, G. C., Pereira, M. A., Girard, B. L., Adams, J., & Metzi, J. D. (2005). Breakfast habits, nutritional status, body weight and academic performance in children and adolescents. *Journal of the Academy of Nutrition and Dietetics, 105,* 743–760.

14. Piernas, C., & Popkin, B. (2010). Trends in snacking among U.S. children. *Health Affairs, 29,* 398–404.

15. Fisher, J. O., & Kral, T.V.E. (2008). Super-size me: Portion size effects on young children's eating. *Physiology & Behavior, 94,* 39–47.

16. Piaget, J., & Inhelder, B. (2000). *The psychology of the child.* New York, NY: Basic Books.

17. Erikson, E. (1993). *Society and the child.* New York, NY: W. W. Norton.

18. Salvy, S. J., Romero, N., Paluch, R., & Epstein, L. H. (2007). Peer influence on pre-adolescent girls' snack intake: Effects of weight status. *Appetite, 49,* 177–182.

19. Mascola, A. J., Bryson, S. W., & Agras, W. S. (2010). Picky eating during childhood: A longitudinal study to age 11 years. *Eating Behaviors, 11,* 253–257.

20. Schur, E. A., Sanders, M., & Steiner, H. (2000). Body dissatisfaction and dieting in young children. *International Journal of Eating Disorders, 27,* 74–82.

21. Davison, K. K., Markey, C. N., & Birch, L. L. (2003). A longitudinal examination of patterns in girls' weight concerns and body dissatisfaction from ages 5 to 9 years. *International Journal of Eating Disorders, 33,* 320–332.

22. Brown, R., & Ogden, J. (2004). Children's eating attitudes and behaviours: A study of the modeling and control theories of parental influence. *Health Education Research, 19,* 261–271.

23. Golan, M., & Crow, S. (2004). Parents are key players in the prevention and treatment of weight-related problems. *Nutrition Reviews, 62,* 39–50.

24. Wang, Y., Beydoun, M. A., Li, J., Liu, Y., & Moreno, L. A. (2011). Do children and their parents eat a similar diet? Resemblance in child and parental dietary intake; Systematic review and meta-analysis. *Journal of Epidemiology and Community Health, 65,* 177–189.

25. Birch, L. L., Fisher, J. O., & Davison, K. K. (2003). Learning to overeat: Maternal use of restrictive feeding practices promotes girls' eating in the absence of hunger. *The American Journal of Clinical Nutrition, 78*, 215–220.

26. Fisher, J. O., & Birch, L. L. (2002). Eating in the absence of hunger and overweight girls from 5 to 7 y of age. *The American Journal of Clinical Nutrition, 76*, 226–231.

27. Fiese, B. H., & Schwartz, M. (2008). Reclaiming the family table: Mealtimes and child health and wellbeing. *Social Policy Report, 22*(4), 3–17.

28. Fulkerson, J. A., Story, M., Neuwmark-Sztainer, D., & Rydell, S. (2008). Family meals: Perceptions of benefits and challenges among parents of 8- to 10-year-old children. *Journal of the Academy of Nutrition and Dietetics, 108*, 706–709.

29. Americans eat out about 5 times per week. (2011, September 19). Retrieved from www.upi.com /Health_News/2011/09/19/Americans-eat-out-about-5-times-a-week/UI-54241316490172/#!/2/

30. Stahler, C. (2010). How many youth are vegetarian? Retrieved from www.vrg.org/press/youth _poll_2010.php

Chapter 5

1. Ross, A. C., Manson, J. E., Abrams, S. A., Aloia, J. F., Brannon, P. M., Clinton, S. K., . . . Shapses, S. A. (2011). The 2011 report on dietary reference intakes for calcium and vitamin D from the Institute of Medicine: What clinicians need to know. *Journal of Clinical Endocrinology & Metabolism, 96*, 53–58.

2. Abrams, S. (2011). Calcium and vitamin D requirements for optimal bone mass during adolescence. *Current Opinion in Clinical Nutrition & Metabolic Care, 14*, 605–609.

3. Nguyen, T. V., Maynard, L. M., Towne, B., Roche, A. F., Wisemandle, W., Li, J., . . . Siervogel, R. M. (2001). Sex differences in bone mass acquisition during growth: The Fels Longitudinal Study. *Journal of Clinical Densitometry, 4*, 147–157.

4. Fox, C. K., Barr-Anderson, D., Neumark-Sztainer, D., & Wall, M. (2010). Physical activity and sports team participation: Associations with academic outcomes in middle school and high school students. *Journal of School Health, 80*, 31–37.

5. Henry J. Kaiser Family Foundation. (2004, February). *The role of media in childhood obesity* [Issue brief]. Retrieved from www.kff.org/entmedia/upload/the-role-of-media-in-childhood -obesity.pdf

6. Ogden, C. L., Carroll, M. D., Kit, B. K., & Flegal, K. M. (2012). Prevalence of obesity and trends in body mass index among US children and adolescents, 1999–2010. *Journal of the American Medical Association, 307*, 483–490.

7. Rosen, D. S., & American Academy of Pediatrics Committee on Adolescence. (2010). Clinical report—identification and management of eating disorders in children and adolescents. *Pediatrics, 126*, 1240–1253.

8. National Eating Disorders Association. (n.d.). Retrieved from www.nationaleatingdisorders .org/prevalence-and-correlates-eating-disorders-adolescents

9. Smink, F. R., van Hoeken, D., & Hoek, H. W. (2012). Epidemiology of eating disorders: Incidence, prevalence and mortality rates. *Current Psychiatry Reports, 14*, 406–414.

10. Larson, N. I., Neumark-Sztainer, D., & Story, M. (2009). Weight control behaviors and dietary intake among adolescents and young adults: Longitudinal findings from Project EAT. *Journal of the Academy of Nutrition and Dietetics, 109*, 1869–1877.

11. Neumark-Sztainer, D., Hannan, P. J., Story, M., & Perry, C. L. (2004). Weight-control behaviors among adolescent girls and boys: Implications for dietary intake. *Journal of the Academy of Nutrition and Dietetics, 104*, 913–920.

12. Neumark-Sztainer, D., Wall, M., Story, M., & Standish, A. R. (2012). Dieting and unhealthy weight control behaviors during adolescence: Associations with 10-year changes in body mass index. *Journal of Adolescent Health, 50*, 80–86.

13. Savige, G., MacFarlane, A., Ball, K., Worsley, A., & Crawford, D. (2007). Snacking behaviours of adolescents and their association with skipping meals. *International Journal of Behavioral Nutrition and Physical Activity, 4*, 36. doi:10.1186/1479-5868-4-36

14. Sebastian, R. S., Goldman, J. D., & Enns, C. W. (2010, September). *Snacking patterns of US adolescents: What we eat in America, NHANES 2005–2006* (USDA Food Surveys Research Group Dietary Data Brief No. 2). Retrieved from www.ars.usda.gov/SP2UserFiles /Place/12355000/pdf/DBrief/2_adolescents_snacking_0506.pdf

15. Lachat, C., Verstraeten, R., Roberfroid, D., Van Camp, J., & Kolsteren, P. (2012). Eating out of home and its association with dietary intake: A systematic review of the evidence. *Obesity Reviews, 13*, 329–346.

16. Fulgoni, V. (2008). Current protein intake in America: Analysis of the National Health and Nutrition Examination Survey, 2003–2004. *The American Journal of Clinical Nutrition, 87*, 1554S–1557S.

17. U.S. Department of Agriculture & U.S. Department of Health and Human Services. (2010). *Dietary guidelines for Americans, 2010* (7th ed.). Washington DC: U.S. Government Printing Office.

18. De Ferranti, S., & Washington, R. L. (2012). NHLBI guidelines on cholesterol in kids: What's new and how does this change practice? *AAP News, 33*(2), 1.

19. Brener, N. D., Merlo, C., Eaton, D., & Kann, L. (2011). Beverage consumption among high school students—United States, 2010. *Morbidity and Mortality Weekly Report, 60*, 778–780.

20. Reedy, J., & Krebs-Smith, S. M. (2010). Dietary sources of energy, solid fats, and added sugars among children and adolescents in the United States. *Journal of the Academy of Nutrition and Dietetics, 110*, 1477–1484.

21. Moshfegh, A., Goldman, J., Ahuja, J., Rhodes, D., & LaComb, R. 2009. *What we eat in America, NHANES 2005–2006: Usual nutrient intakes from food and water compared to 1997 dietary reference intakes for vitamin D, calcium, phosphorus, and magnesium.* Washington DC: U.S. Department of Agriculture, Agricultural Research Service.

22. Nicklas, T. A., O'Neil, C. E., & Fulgoni, V. L. (2009). The role of dairy in meeting the recommendations for shortfall nutrients in the American diet. *Journal of the American College of Nutrition, 28,* 73S–81S.

23. Gao, X., Wilde, P. E., Lichtenstein, A. H., & Tucker, K. L. (2006). Meeting adequate intake for dietary calcium without dairy foods in adolescents aged 9 to 18 years (National Health and Nutrition Examination Survey 2001–2002). *Journal of the Academy of Nutrition and Dietetics, 106,* 1759–1765.

24. Holick, M. F., Binkley, N. C., Bischoff-Ferrari, H. A., Gordon, C. M., Hanley, D. A., Heaney, R. P., . . . Endocrine Society. (2011). Evaluation, treatment, and prevention of vitamin D deficiency: An Endocrine Society clinical practice guideline. *Journal of Clinical Endocrinology & Metabolism, 96,* 1911–1930.

25. Misra, M., Pacaud, D., Petryk, A., Collett-Solberg, P. F., Kappy, M., & Drug and Therapeutics Committee of the Lawson Wilkins Pediatric Endocrine Society. (2008). Vitamin D deficiency in children and its management: Review of current knowledge and recommendations. *Pediatrics, 122,* 398–417.

26. Deegan, H., Bates, H. M., & McCargar, L. J. (2005). Assessment of iron status in adolescents: Dietary, biochemical and lifestyle determinants. *Journal of Adolescent Health, 37,* 75.

27. Hurrell, R., & Egli, I. (2010). Iron bioavailability and dietary reference values. *The American Journal of Clinical Nutrition, 91,* 1461S–1467S.

28. Piaget, J., & Inhelder, B. (2000). *The psychology of the child.* New York, NY: Basic Books.

29. Dobbs, D. (2011, October). Beautiful teenage brains. *National Geographic,* pp. 42–59.

30. Erikson, E. (1993). *Society and the child.* New York, NY: W. W. Norton.

31. Bassett, R., Chapman, G. E., & Beagan, B. L. (2008). Autonomy and control: The co-construction of adolescent food choice. *Appetite, 50,* 325–332.

32. Ackard, D. M., Neumark-Sztainer, D., Story, M., & Perry, C. (2006). Parent-child connectedness and behavioral and emotional health among adolescents. *American Journal of Preventive Medicine, 30,* 59–66.

33. Hazen, E., Schlozman, S., & Beresin, E. (2008). Adolescent psychological development: A review. *Pediatrics in Review, 29,* 161–168.

34. Yale Rudd Center for Food Policy and Obesity. (2011, June). *Trends in television food advertising to young people: 2010 update* (Rudd Report). Retrieved from http://yaleruddcenter.org/resources/upload/docs/what/reports/RuddReport_TVFoodAdvertising_6.11.pdf

35. Strasburger, V. C., & Council on Communications and Media Executive Committee, 2009–2010. (2010). American Academy of Pediatrics policy statement: Media education. *Pediatrics, 126,* 1012–1017.

36. Berg, P., Neumark-Sztainer, D., Hannan, P. J., & Haines, J. (2007). Is dieting advice from magazines helpful or harmful? Five-year associations with weight-control behaviors and psychological outcomes in adolescents. *Pediatrics, 119,* e30–e37. doi:10.1542/peds.2006-0978

37. Franko, D. L., Thompson, D., Bauserman, R., & Striegel-Moore, R. H. (2008). What's love got to do with it? Family cohesion and healthy eating behaviors in adolescent girls. *International Journal of Eating Disorders, 41,* 360–367.

38. Frank, D. L., Thompson, D., Affinito, S. G., Barton, B. A., & Striegel-Moore, R. A. (2008). What mediates the relationship between family meals and adolescent health issues? *Health Psychology, 27,* S109–S117.

39. Hammons, A. J., & Fiese, B. H. (2011). Is frequency of shared family meals related to the nutritional health of children and adolescents? *Pediatrics, 127,* 1565–1574.

40. Berge, J. M., Wall, M., Neumark-Sztainer, D., Larson, N., & Story, M. (2010). Parenting style and family meals: Cross-sectional and 5-year longitudinal associations. *Journal of the Academy of Nutrition and Dietetics, 110,* 1036–1042.

41. Newman, K., Harrison, L., Dashiff, C., & Davies, S. (2008). Relationships between parenting styles and risk behaviors in adolescent health: An integrative literature review. *Revista Latino-Americana de Enfermagem, 16,* 142–150.

42. Rhee, K. (2008). Childhood overweight and the relationship between parent behaviors, parenting style and family functioning. *The Annals of the American Academy of Political and Social Science, 615,* 11–37.

43. Neumark-Sztainer, D., Larson, N. I., Fulkerson, J. A., Eisenberg, M. E., & Story, M. (2010). Family meals and adolescents: What have we learned from Project EAT (Eating Among Teens)? *Public Health Nutrition, 13,* 1113–1121.

44. Campbell, K. J., Crawford, D. A., Salmon, J., Carver, A., Garnett, S. P., & Baur, L. A. (2007). Associations between the home food environment and obesity-promoting behaviors in adolescence. *Obesity, 15,* 719–730.

45. Three-quarters of British children cannot boil an egg, study finds. (2009, May 20). *The Telegraph.* Retrieved from www.telegraph.co.uk/news/newstopics/howaboutthat/5352827 /Three-quarters-of-British-children-cannot-boil-an-egg-study-finds.html

46. Crow, S., Eisenberg, M. E., Story, M., & Neumark-Sztainer, D. (2006). Psychosocial and behavioral correlates of dieting among overweight and non-overweight adolescents. *Journal of Adolescent Health, 38,* 569–574.

47. Bauer, K. W., Laska, M. N., Fulkerson, J. A., & Neumark-Sztainer, D. (2011). Longitudinal and secular trends in parental encouragement for healthy eating, physical activity, and dieting throughout the adolescent years. *Journal of Adolescent Health, 49,* 306–311.

48. Berkey, C. S., Rockett, H.R.H., & Colditz, G. A. (2008). Weight gain in older adolescent females: The Internet, sleep, coffee and alcohol. *The Journal of Pediatrics, 153,* 635–639.

Chapter 6

1. Birch, L. L., & Fisher, J. O. (2000). Mothers' child-feeding practices influence daughters' eating and weight. *The American Journal of Clinical Nutrition, 71,* 1054–1061.

2. Cutting, T. M., Fisher, J. O., Grimm-Thomas, K., & Birch, L. L. (1999). Like mother, like daughter: Familial patterns of overweight are mediated by mothers' dietary disinhibition. *The American Journal of Clinical Nutrition, 69,* 608–613.

3. Branen, L., & Fletcher, J. (1999). Comparison of college students' current eating habits and recollections of their childhood practices. *Journal of Nutrition Education, 31,* 304–310.

4. Brink, P. L., Ferguson, K., & Sharma, A. (1999). Childhood memories about food: The successful dieters project. *Journal of Child and Adolescent Psychiatric Nursing, 12,* 17–25.

5. Brown, A. S., Ansfield, M. E., & Paschall, G. Y. (2002). "You will eat all of that!" A retrospective analysis of forced consumption. *Appetite, 38,* 211–219.

6. Galloway, A. T., Farrow, C. V., & Martz, D. M. (2010). Retrospective reports of child feeding practices, current eating behaviors, and BMI in college students. *Obesity, 9,* 1330–1335.

7. Puhl, R. M., & Schwartz, M. B. (2003). If you are good you can have a cookie: How memories of childhood food rules link to adult eating behaviors. *Eating Behaviors, 4,* 283–293.

8. International Food and Information Council: Food & Health Survey. (2011, September). Consumer attitudes toward food safety, nutrition and health. Retrieved from www.foodinsight .org/Resources/Detail.aspx?topic=2011_Food_Health_Survey_Consumer_Attitudes_Toward _Food_Safety_Nutrition_Health

9. Pietiläinen, K. H., Saarni, S. E., Kaprio, J., & Rissanenet, A. (2012). Does dieting make you fat? A twin study. *International Journal of Obesity, 36,* 456–464.

10. Hawks, S. R., Madanat, H. N., & Christley, H. S. (2008). Behavioral and biological associations of dietary restraint: A review of the literature. *Ecology of Food and Nutrition, 47,* 415–449.

11. Hawks, S. R., Madanat, H. N., & Christley, H. S. (2008). Psychosocial associations of dietary restraint: Implications for healthy weight promotion. *Ecology of Food and Nutrition, 47,* 450–483.

12. Madden, C. E., Leong, S. L., Gray, A., & Horwath, C. C. (2012). Eating in response to hunger and satiety signals is related to BMI in a nationwide sample of 1601 mid-age New Zealand women. *Public Health Nutrition, 15,* 2272–2279.

13. Gast, J., Madanat, H., & Nielson, A. C. (2012). Are men more intuitive when it comes to eating and physical activity? *American Journal of Men's Health, 6,* 164–171.

14. Denny, K. N., Loth, K., Eisenberg, M. E., & Neumark-Sztainer, D. N. (2013). Intuitive eating in young adults. Who is doing it, and how is it related to disordered eating behaviors? *Appetite, 60,* 13–19.

15. Segar, M. L., Eccles, J. S., & Richardson, C. R. (2011). Rebranding exercise: Closing the gap between values and behavior. *International Journal of Behavioral Nutrition and Physical Activity, 8,* 94. doi:10.1186/1479-5868-8-94

16. Adams, C. E., & Leary, M. R. (2007). Promoting self-compassionate attitudes toward eating among restrictive and guilty eaters. *Journal of Social and Clinical Psychology, 26,* 1120–1144.

17. Alberts, H. J., Thewissen, R., & Raes, L. (2012). Dealing with problematic eating behaviour: The effects of a mindfulness-based intervention on eating behaviour, food cravings, dichotomous thinking and body image concern. *Appetite, 58*, 847–851.

18. Wansink, B., Payne, C. R., & Chandon, P. (2007). Internal and external cues of meal cessation: The French paradox redux? *Obesity, 15*, 2920–2924.

19. Levine, P. (2005). Prevention guidelines and strategies for everyone: 50 ways to lose the 3 Ds; *D*ieting, *D*rive for thinness, and body *D*issatisfaction [Handout]. Retrieved from www .nationaleatingdisorders.org/uploads/file/information-resources/50-Ways-to-Lose-the-3Ds .pdf

20. Carraça, E. V., Silva, M. N., Markland, D., Vieira, P. N., Minderico, C. S., Sardinha, L. B., & Teixeira, P. J. Body image change and improved eating self-regulation in a weight management intervention in women. *International Journal of Behavioral Nutrition and Physical Activity, 8*, 75. doi:10.1186/1479-5868-8-75

21. Mann, T., Tomiyama, A. J., Westling, E., Lew, A. M., Samuels, B., & Chatman, J. (2007). Medicare's search for effective obesity treatments: Diets are not the answer. *American Psychologist, 62*, 220–233.

Chapter 7

1. Branum, A., & Lukacs, S. (2008, October). *Food allergy among U.S. children: Trends in prevalence and hospitalizations* (NCHS Data Brief No. 10). Retrieved from www.cdc.gov/nchs /data/databriefs/db10.htm

2. National Institute of Allergy and Infectious Diseases. (2011, May). *Guidelines for the diagnosis and management of food allergy in the United States: Summary for patients, families and caregivers*. Available from www.niaid.nih.gov/topics/foodallergy/clinical/Pages/default .aspx

3. Branum, A. M., & Lukacs, S. L. (2009). Food allergy among children in the United States. *Pediatrics, 124*, 1548–1556.

4. Skripak, J. M., Matsui, E. C., Mudd, K., & Wood, R. A. (2007). The natural history of IgE-mediated cow's milk allergy. *Journal of Allergy & Clinical Immunology, 120*, 1172–1177.

5. Savage, J. H., Matsui, E. C., Skripak, J. M., & Wood, R. A. (2007). The natural history of egg allergy. *Journal of Allergy & Clinical Immunology, 120*, 1413–1417.

6. American Academy of Allergy Asthma & Immunology. (n.d.). Food Allergy: Tips to remember. Retrieved from www.aaaai.org/conditions-and-treatments/library/at-a-glance /food-allergy.aspx

7. Barlow, S. E., & Expert Committee. (2007). Expert committee recommendations regarding the prevention, assessment, and treatment of child and adolescent overweight and obesity: Summary report. *Pediatrics, 120*, S164–S192.

8. Haines, J., Kleinman, K. P., Rifas-Shiman, S. L., Field, A. E., & Austin, B. (2010). Examination of shared risk and protective factors for overweight and disordered eating among adolescents. *Archives of Pediatrics & Adolescent Medicine, 164,* 336–343.

9. Anzman, S. L., Rollins, B. Y., & Birch, L. L. (2010). Parental influence on children's early eating environments and obesity risk: Implications for prevention. *International Journal of Obesity, 34,* 1116–1124.

10. Birch, L. L. (2006). Child feeding practices and the etiology of obesity. *Obesity, 14,* 343–344.

11. Faith, M. S., Scanlon, K. S., Birch, L. L., Francis, L. A., & Sherry, B. (2004). Parent-child feeding strategies and their relationships to child eating and weight status. *Obesity Research, 12,* 1711–1722.

12. Fisher, J. O., & Birch, L. L. (2002). Eating in the absence of hunger and overweight in girls from 5 to 7 y of age. *The American Journal of Clinical Nutrition, 76,* 226–231.

13. Moens, E., & Braet, C. (2007). Predictors of disinhibited eating in children with and without overweight. *Behaviour Research and Therapy, 45,* 1357–1368.

14. Patrick, H., Nicklas, T. A., Hughes, S. O., & Morales, M. (2005). The benefits of authoritative feeding style: Caregiver feeding styles and children's food consumption patterns. *Appetite, 44,* 243–249.

15. Black, M. M., & Aboud, F. E. (2011). Responsive feeding is embedded in a theoretical framework of responsive parenting. *The Journal of Nutrition, 141,* 490–494.

16. Lowry, R., Eaton, D. K., Foti, K., McKnight-Eily, L., Perry, G., & Galuska, D. A. (2012, February 12). Association of sleep duration with obesity among US high school students. *Journal of Obesity,* article ID *476914.* doi:10.1155/2012/476914

17. Webber, L., Cooke, L., Hill, C., & Wardle, J. (2010). Association between children's appetitive traits and maternal feeding practices. *Journal of the Academy of Nutrition and Dietetics, 110,* 1718–1722.

18. Eating disorders among children. (n.d.). Retrieved from www.nimh.nih.gov/statistics/1EAT_CHILD.shtml

19. Rosen, D. S., & American Academy of Pediatrics Committee on Adolescence. (2010). Clinical report—identification and management of eating disorders in children and adolescents. *Pediatrics, 126,* 1240–1253.

20. National Eating Disorders Association. Retrieved from www.nationaleatingdisorders.org/uploads/file/Statistics%20%20Updated%20Feb%2010%202008%20B.pdf

21. Mazzeo, S. E., & Bulik, C. M. (2009). Environmental and genetic risk factors for eating disorders: What the clinician needs to know. *Child and Adolescent Psychiatric Clinics of North America, 18,* 67–82.

22. Chatoor, I. (2009). *Diagnosis and treatment of feeding disorders in infants, toddlers and young children.* Washington DC: Zero to Three.

23. Toomey, K. A. (1996/2010). When children won't eat: Understanding the "why's" and how to help. Retrieved from www.spdparentzone.org/resources/When%20Children%20Wont%20Eat.pdf

24. Curtis, L. T., & Patel, K. (2008). Environmental approaches to preventing and treating attention deficit hyperactivity disorder (ADHD): A review. *Journal of Alternative and Complementary Medicine, 14,* 79–85.

25. Millichap, J. G., & Yee, M. M. (2012). The diet factor in attention-deficit/hyperactivity disorder. *Pediatrics, 129,* 330–337.

26. Sinn, N. (2008). Nutritional and dietary influences on attention deficit hyperactivity disorder. *Nutrition Reviews, 66,* 558–568.

27. Bloch, M. H., & Qawasmi, A. (2011). Omega-3 fatty acid supplementation for the treatment of children with attention-deficit/hyperactivity disorder symptomatology: Systematic review and meta-analysis. *Journal of the American Academy of Child and Adolescent Psychiatry, 50,* 991–1000.

Chapter 8

1. Wansink, B. (2006). Nutritional gatekeepers and the 72% solution. *Journal of the Academy of Nutrition and Dietetics, 106,* 1324–1327.

2. U.S. Department of Agriculture & U.S. Department of Health and Human Services. (2010). *Dietary guidelines for Americans, 2010* (7th ed.). Washington DC: U.S. Government Printing Office.

3. U.S. Department of Agriculture. (2010, June). Freezing and food safety. Retrieved from www .fsis.usda.gov/factsheets/focus_on_freezing/index.asp#18

4. National Dairy Council. (n.d.). Organic milk FAQ. Retrieved from www.nationaldairycouncil. org/SiteCollectionDocuments/footer/FAQ/dairy_nutrition/OrganicMilkFAQ.pdf

5. American Cancer Society. (2011, February). Recombinant bovine growth hormone. Retrieved from www.cancer.org/cancer/cancercauses/othercarcinogens/athome/recombinant-bovine -growth-hormone

6. U.S. Food and Drug Administration. (1994, February 10). Voluntary labeling of milk and milk products from cows that have not been treated with recombinant bovine somatotropin: Interim guidance. Retrieved from www.fda.gov/Food/GuidanceComplianceRegulatoryInformation /GuidanceDocuments/FoodLabelingNutrition/ucm059036.htm

7. German, J. B., Gibson, R. A., Krauss, R. M., Nestel, P., Lamarche, B., van Staveren, W. A., . . . Destaillats, F. (2009). A reappraisal of the impact of dairy foods and milk fat on cardiovascular disease risk. *European Journal of Nutrition, 48,* 191–203.

8. Niinikoski, H. (2012). Effect of repeated dietary counseling on serum lipoproteins from infancy to adulthood. *Pediatrics, 129,* e704–e713. doi:10.1542/peds.2011-1503

9. The American Egg Board. (n.d.). Cracking the cholesterol myth. Retrieved from www .incredibleegg.org/health-and-nutrition/cracking-the-cholesterol-myth

10. The American Egg Board. (n.d.). Other questions. Retrieved from www.incredibleegg.org /egg-facts/egg-safety/other-questions

11. Egg Safety Center. (n.d.). Egg food safety frequently asked questions. Retrieved from www .eggsafety.org/consumers/consumer-faqs

12. U.S. Department of Agriculture, Food Safety and Inspection Service. (2011, April). Meat and poultry labeling terms. Retrieved from www.fsis.usda.gov/Factsheets/Meat_&_Poultry_Labeling_Terms/index.asp

13. American Meat Institute. (2009, September). American Meat Institute fact sheet: Hormones in cattle production; Their use and safety. Retrieved from www.meatami.com/ht/a/GetDocumentAction/i/53720

14. U.S. Food and Drug Administration. (2012, April 13). Guidance for the industry: The judicious use of medically important antimicrobial drugs in food-producing animals. Retrieved from www.fda.gov/downloads/AnimalVeterinary/GuidanceComplianceEnforcement/GuidanceforIndustry/UCM216936.pdf

15. U.S. Department of Agriculture, Food Safety and Inspection Service. (2012, April 23). Nutrition labeling information. Retrieved from www.fsis.usda.gov/regulations_&_policies/Nutrition_Labeling/index.asp

16. Animal Welfare Institute. (2012, August). A consumer's guide to food labels and animal welfare. Retrieved from http://awionline.org/sites/default/files/products/12_FoodLabelGuide080212.pdf

17. Daley, C. A., Abbott, A., Doyle, P. S., Nader, G. A., & Larson, S. (2010). A review of fatty acid profiles and antioxidant content in grass-fed and grain-fed beef. *Nutrition Journal, 9,* 10. doi:10.1186/1475-2891-9-10

18. Butler, G., Nielsen, J. H., Slots, T., Seal, C., Eyre, M. D., Sanderson, R., & Leifert, C. (2008). Fatty acid and fat-soluble antioxidant concentrations in milk from high- and low-input conventional and organic systems: Seasonal variation. *Journal of the Science of Food and Agriculture, 88,* 1431–1441.

19. Whole Grains Council. (n.d.). Whole grain stamp. Retrieved from www.wholegrainscouncil.org/whole-grain-stamp

20. International Food Information Council Foundation. (2009, October 15). Whole grains fact sheet. Retrieved from www.foodinsight.org/Resources/Detail.aspx?topic=Whole_Grains_Fact_Sheet

21. Blasbalg, T. L., Hibbeln, J. R., Ramsden, C. E., Majchrzak, S. F., & Rawlings, R. R. (2011). Changes in consumption of omega-3 and omega-6 fatty acids in the United States during the 20th century. *The American Journal of Clinical Nutrition, 93,* 950–962.

22. Ramsden, C. E., Hibbeln, J. R., Majchrzak, S. F., & Davis, J. M. (2010). N-6 fatty acid-specific and mixed polyunsaturate dietary interventions have different effects on CHD risk: A meta-analysis of randomised controlled trials. *British Journal of Nutrition, 104,* 1586–1600.

23. American Heart Association. (2012, October 31). Know your fats. Retrieved from www.heart.org/HEARTORG/Conditions/Cholesterol/PreventionTreatmentofHighCholesterol/Know-Your-Fats_UCM_305628_Article.jsp

24. Lipoeto, N. I., Agus, Z., Oenzil, F., Wahlqvist, M., & Wattanapenpaiboon, N. (2004). Dietary intake and the risk of coronary heart disease among the coconut-consuming Minangkabau in West Sumatra, Indonesia. *Asia Pacific Journal of Clinical Nutrition, 13,* 377–384.

25. Johnson, R. K., Appel, L. J., Brands, M., Howard, B. V., Lefevre, M., Lustig, R. H., . . . Council on Epidemiology and Prevention. (2009). Dietary sugars intake and cardiovascular health: A scientific statement from the American Heart Association. *Circulation, 120,* 1011–1020.

26. American Heart Association. (2011, March). Sodium (salt or sodium chloride). Retrieved from www.heart.org/HEARTORG/GettingHealthy/NutritionCenter/HealthyDietGoals/Sodium-Salt -or-Sodium-Chloride_UCM_303290_Article.jsp

Appendix G

1. U.S. Department of Agriculture, Agricultural Research Service. (2012). USDA National Nutrient Database for Standard Reference, release 25. Retrieved from www.ars.usda.gov/ba/bhnrc/ndl

2. U.S. Food and Drug Administration. (2012, December 4). Fresh and frozen seafood: Selecting and serving it daily. Retrieved from www.fda.gov/food/resourcesforyou/consumers/ucm077331 .htm

3. Harika, R. K., Cosgrove, M. C., Osendarp, S. J., Verhoef, P., & Zock, P. L. (2011). Fatty acid intakes of children and adolescents are not in line with the dietary intake recommendations for future cardiovascular health: A systematic review of dietary intake data from thirty countries. *British Journal of Nutrition, 106,* 307–316.

4. Joint Food and Agriculture Organization/World Health Organization (WHO) Expert Consultation on Fats and Fatty Acids in Human Nutrition. (2008, November 10–14). Interim summary of conclusions and dietary recommendations on total fat and fatty acids. WHO Headquarters, Geneva, Switzerland.

5. Hattner, J. A. (2009). *Gut insight: Probiotics and prebiotics for digestive health and well-being.* San Francisco, CA: Hattner Nutrition.

6. U.S. Probiotics. (n.d.). Frequently asked questions and consumer information. Retrieved from http://cdrf.org/home/checkoff-investments/usprobiotics/frequently-asked-questions-consumer -information/#best

7. Koletzko, B., & Toschke, A. M. (2010). Meal patterns and frequencies: Do they affect body weight in children and adolescents? *Critical Reviews in Food Science and Nutrition, 50,* 100– 105.

8. Fulgoni, V. L. (2008). Current protein intake in America: Analysis of the National Health and Nutrition Examination Survey, 2003–2004. *The American Journal of Clinical Nutrition, 87,* 1554S–1557S.

9. American Academy of Pediatrics. (2012, October 12). Health issues: Treating vomiting. Retrieved from www.healthychildren.org/English/health-issues/conditions/abdominal/pages /Treating-Vomiting.aspx

10. National Research Council. (2011). *Dietary reference intakes for water, potassium, sodium, chloride and sulfate.* Washington DC: National Academies Press.

11. Rowland, T. (2011). Fluid replacement requirements for child athletes. *Sports Medicine, 41,* 279–288.

12. Yang, Q. (2010). Gain weight by "going diet"? Artificial sweeteners and the neurobiology of sugar. *Yale Journal of Biology and Medicine, 83*, 101–108.

13. Gardener, H., Rundek, T., Markert, M., Wright, C. B., Elkind, M. S., & Sacco, R. L. (2012). Diet soft drink consumption is associated with an increased risk of vascular events in the Northern Manhattan Study. *Journal of General Internal Medicine, 27*, 1120–1126.

American Academy of Pediatrics, Committee on Nutrition. (2001). The use and misuse of fruit juice. *Pediatrics, 107*, 1210–1213.

American Academy of Pediatrics, Section on Pediatric Dentistry. (2003). Oral health risk assessment timing and establishment of the dental home. *Pediatrics, 111*, 1113–1116.

American Academy of Pediatrics, Committee on Nutrition, & Kleiman, R. E. (2008). *Pediatric nutrition handbook* (6th ed.). Elk Grove Village, IL: American Academy of Pediatrics.

Amit, M. (2010). Vegetarian diets in children and adolescents. *Paediatrics and Child Health, 15*, 303–308.

Berger, K. S. (2006). *The developing person: Through childhood and adolescence* (7th ed.). New York, NY: Worth.

Butte, N., Cobb, K., Dwyer, J., Graney, L., Heird, W., Rickard, K . . . Gerber Products Company. (2004). The start healthy feeding guidelines for infants and toddlers. *Journal of the Academy of Nutrition and Dietetics, 104*, 442–450.

Center for Science in the Public Interest. (2007). Omega medicine? Is fish oil good for what ails you? *Nutrition Action Healthletter, 34*(8), 3–8.

Converse, J. (2009). *Special-needs kids eat right*. New York, NY: Perigee.

Craig, W. J., & Mangels, A. R. (2009). Position of the American Dietetic Association: Vegetarian diets. *Journal of the Academy of Nutrition and Dietetics, 109*, 1266–1282.

Evers, C. (2012). *How to teach nutrition to kids*. Portland, OR: 24 Carrot Press.

Greer, F. R., Shannon, M., & Committee on Environmental Health. (2005). Infant methemoglobinemia: The role of dietary nitrate in food and water. *Pediatrics, 116*, 784–786.

Healy, J. M. (2004). *Your child's growing mind* (3rd ed.). New York, NY: Broadway Books.

Hingle, M. D., O'Conner, T. M., Dave, J. M., & Baranowski, T. (2010). Parental involvement in interventions to improve child dietary intake: A systematic review. *Preventive Medicine, 51*, 103–111.

Hughes, S. O., Power, T. G., Papaioannou, M. A., Cross, M. B., Nicklas, T. A., Hall, S. K., & Shewchuk, R. M. (2011). Emotional climate, feeding practices, and feeding styles: An observational analysis of the dinner meal in Head Start families. *International Journal of Behavioral Nutrition and Physical Activity*, *8*, 60. doi:10.1186/1479–5868–8–60

Kubena, K. S., & McMurray, D. N. (1996). Nutrition and the immune system: A review of nutrient-nutrient interactions. *Journal of the Academy of Nutrition and Dietetics*, *96*, 1156–1164.

Martin, C. L., & Fabes, R. (2008). *Discovering child development* (2nd ed.). Independence, KY: Wadsworth.

May, M. (2009). *Eat what you love, love what you eat*. Austin, TX: Greenleaf Book Group Press.

National Heart, Lung, and Blood Institute. (2011). Integrated guidelines for cardiovascular health and risk reduction in children and adolescents. Retrieved from www.nhlbi.nih.gov/guidelines/cvd_ped/summary.htm#chap11

National Research Council. (2011). *Dietary reference intakes for calcium and vitamin D*. Washington DC: National Academies Press.

Otten, J. O., Hellwig, J. P., & Meyers, L. D. (2006). *Dietary reference intakes: The essential guide to nutrient requirements*. Washington DC: National Academies Press.

Pan American Health Organization. (2003). Guiding principles for complementary feeding of the breastfed child. Retrieved from http://whqlibdoc.who.int/paho/2003/a85622.pdf

Piaget, J., & Inhelder, B. (2000). *The psychology of the child*. New York, NY: Basic Books.

Saintonge, S., Bang, H., & Gerber, L. M. (2009). Implications of a new definition of vitamin D deficiency in a multiracial US adolescent population: The National Health and Nutrition Examination Survey III. *Pediatrics*, *123*, 797–804.

Samour, P. K., & King, K. (2010). *Pediatric nutrition* (4th ed.). Burlington, MA: Jones & Bartlett Learning.

Satter, E. (2000). *Child of mine: Feeding with love and good sense*. Boulder, CO: Bull.

Topham, G. L., Hubbs-Tait, L., Rutledge, J. M., Page, M. C., Kennedy, T. S., Shriver, L. H., & Harrist, A. W. (2011). Parenting styles, parental response to child emotion, and family emotional responsiveness are related to child emotional eating. *Appetite*, *56*, 261–264.

Tribole, E., & Resch, E. (2003). *Intuitive eating*. New York, NY: St. Martin's Press.

Wansink, B. (2007). *Mindless eating*. New York, NY: Bantam Books.

Watkins, B., Cooper, P. J., & Lask, B. (2011). History of eating disorder in mothers of children with early onset eating disorder or disturbance. *European Eating Disorders Review*, *20*, 121–125. doi:10.1002/erv.1125

Webber, L., Hill, C., Cooke, L., Carnell, S., & Wardle, J. (2010). Associations between child weight and maternal feeding styles are mediated by maternal perceptions and concerns. *Journal of Clinical Nutrition*, *64*, 259–265.

Moshfegh, A., Goldman, J., & Cleveland, L. (2005). *What we eat in America, NHANES 2001–2002: Usual nutrient intakes from food compared to dietary reference intakes*. Washington DC: U.S. Department of Agriculture, Agricultural Research Service.

Jill Lindeman Castle is a child nutrition expert with over twenty years' experience in the field. She started her career as a clinical pediatric dietitian in Boston, and recently owned a pediatric nutrition private practice in Nashville, Tennessee.

In addition to working with children and their families, Jill speaks to a variety of audiences, including professional groups; sports organizations; and parent, school, and community groups about a wide range of child nutrition topics.

Throughout her career, Jill has been published in peer-reviewed journals, has written scientific summary content for industry, and has provided nutrition content for consumer books and professional textbooks. She is the creator of *Just the Right Byte*, where she blogs about child nutrition, parenting, and feeding. Jill is frequently contacted as a child nutrition expert for lay magazines, such as *Parents* and *Parenting*; newspapers; and online articles, and regularly contributes to the USA Swimming website. She also shares her expertise as a child nutrition consultant for a variety of business and school organizations.

Jill received her bachelor of science degree in nutrition from Indiana University, Bloomington, and her master of science degree in nutrition (pediatric focus) from the Massachusetts General Hospital Institute of Health Professions in Boston.

She is married and lives with her husband and four children in New Canaan, Connecticut. You can find Jill on Twitter (@pediRD), on Facebook, and online (www.jillcastle.com).

Maryann Tomovich Jacobsen is a registered dietitian with fifteen years of experience in the nutrition field. Based in San Diego, California, Maryann works as a freelance writer; nutrition educator; and founding editor of *Raise Healthy Eaters*, a popular blog about family nutrition. She is an expert blogger at WebMD's *Real Life Nutrition* and the featured nutrition expert on WebMD's Answers. She has written for *Cooking Light*'s website, My Recipes, the *Los Angeles Times*, *Today's Dietitian*, and *Today's Diet and Nutrition.*

Since the creation of her blog in early 2009, Maryann has become a well-known family nutrition expert. She has been quoted in leading newspapers and magazines, including the *Chicago Tribune*, *Parents*, *American Profile*, and *Harmony*. Maryann also acts as a nutrition adviser for SchoolMenu.com and teaches classes on infant and toddler nutrition at the Parent Connection in San Diego.

Maryann received her undergraduate degree in nutrition from San Diego State University and her master's degree in nutrition from the University of New Haven in Connecticut. She is a member of the Academy of Nutrition and Dietetics and its nutrition entrepreneur and pediatric dietetic practice groups.

INDEX

Page references followed by *fig* indicate an illustrated figure; followed by *t* indicate a table.

Index